EVLIYA CHELEBI

Travels in Iran & the Caucasus in 1647 & 1655

Translated by
Hasan Javadi & Willem Floor

MAGE
PUBLISHERS

Copyright © 2010 Hasan Javadi and Willem Floor

All rights reserved.
No part of this book may be reproduced
or retransmitted in any manner whatsoever,
except in the form of a review, without the
written permission of the publisher.

Library of Congress Cataloging-in-Publication Data

    Evliya Çelebi, 1611?-1682?
     [*Seyahatname*. English. Selections]
    Travels in Iran & the Caucasus in 1647 & 1655 / by Evliya Chelebi ;
introduced, translated and annotated by Hasan Javadi & Willem Floor.
-- 1st ed.
      p. cm.
    Translated from Ottoman Turkish.
    Includes bibliographical references and index.
    ISBN 1-933823-36-4 (pbk. original : alk. paper)
    1. Iran--Description and travel. 2. Caucasus--Description and travel. I.
Javadi, Hasan. II. Floor, Willem M. III. Title. IV. Title: Travels in Iran and
the Caucasus in 1652 and 1655.
    G460.E952513 2009
    [DS255]
    915.504'3--dc22
                                      2009040982

ISBN 13: 978-1933823-36-2
ISBN 10: 1-933823-36-4
Second Printing Revisions November 2011
Printed and Manufactured in the United States

Mage books are available at bookstores,
through the internet, or directly from the publisher:
Mage Publishers, Washington, DC
202-342-1642 • as@mage.com • 800-962-0922
visit Mage Publishers online at www.mage.com

CONTENTS

TABLE OF ILLUSTRATIONS IX

INTRODUCTION XI
    Who Was Evliya Chelebi? xii
    Editions Used xiii
    Historical Background to Evliya Chelebi's Travels in Iran xv
    Evliya Chelebi's Peculiarities xvii
    Observations on the Translation xix
    Evliya Chelebi's Itinerary xx
    First Journey to Iran In 1647 xxi
    Second Journey to Iran in 1655 xxiv

THE FIRST TRAVELS
    Travel to Shushik Castle situated in Kurdistan in the province of Erzerum 1
    Description of what we saw of strange things on our journey going from the banks of the Aras River to the land of Persia and coming to Erevan, Nakhjevan and Tabriz 4
    Description of the journey to Tabriz 18
    Description of the great city, the old castle and old emporium of Tabriz, the capital of Azerbaijan in the land of Iran 23
    Describing the Visit of the Environs of Tabriz as well as of its Villages and Castles in the Company of H.E. the Khan 39
    Description of the outing we undertook with the great Khan to Sham Khazan and visiting the castles there 48
    Description of the big city, the ancient capital, and the trade emporium of Maragheh 51
    Description of the ancient capital of Iran, the city of Ardabil 54
    Journey from the province of Tabriz in Azerbaijan to the province of Erevan and the description of its villages, small towns and castles 60
    Description of the castle of Erevan of Azerbaijan in the City of Khoja Jan . . . 64

*Observations on the Journey from Erevan through the provinces of
    Shirvan, Shamakhi, Tiflis, Termenis and the castles of Arash and Baku* . . . 70

*The language and expressions of the Qeytaq, who are a section of the
    Mongol people* 75

*Description of the province of Shirvan, i.e., the castle of Shamakhi,
    may God protect it* 79

*The description of the castle of Baku on the Persian border with the
    province of Shirvan* 84

*Our Journey from Baku Castle to the province of Georgia and the
    description of the stages, villages, towns, castles and provinces.* 86

Description of the district of Shaburan in Shirvan. 89

*Description of Bandar-e Bab, i.e., the town of Bab al-Abvab,
    i.e., the wall of Alexander the Two-Horned, the castle of Demirkapu* . . . 90

Journey from Demirkapu to Georgia 97

Description of the provinces of Georgia and Shavshadistan 98

Description of the ancient castle and important capital city of Kakht . . . 99

*Description of the capital of Shavshadistan Georgia, i.e., the castle built
    by Bitlis, the strong castle of Tiflis.* 102

Concerning the genealogy of the Georgian kings 107

*Description of Sadd-e Islam and the Conquest of Selim of the province
    of Childeran, the strong castle, the mighty citadel, the great
    emporium of Ottoman Akhiskha* 109

*Description of how many **timars** and **ze'amats** there are in each **sanjaq** in
    the province of Childir.* 110

Description of the Georgian castles under the province of Childir 113

{Description of the castles near Ardahan. 114

Description of the stages that we passed going [from Akhiskha] to Erzerum . . . 114

Description of the castle of Qara Ardahan in Georgia. 114

Journey to the region of Erevan in the year one thousand fifty-seven [1647] . . . 118

*Description of the castle of Qars Dudiman, which is at the very border
    of the Ottoman Empire* 119

Description of the stages that we traveled to Erevan 125

THE SECOND TRAVELS **129**

*Description of the castle of Urmiyeh in Azerbaijan, i.e., the earthen
    fort of Ghazan* *141*

Now we will describe how we entered into the city *141*

*The question of the great Khan of the city of Urmiyeh concerning the
    reason for the killing of Ipshir Mostafa Pasha* *149*

Description of the Castle of Urmiyeh, its layout and its strength . . . *150*

Description of the Khan of Urmiyeh's troops *152*

Description of Turkestan-e Iran, i.e., the city of Urmiyeh in Azerbeijan . . . *152*

Description of the beverages and foodstuffs of greater Urmiyeh *154*

*An account of the stages, castles and large cities seen when we went with
    the letters from the Khan to the Dombuli Khan in order to obtain
    the release of our friend Morteza Pasha* *160*

*Description of our journey from Urmiyeh to Tabriz and Shah 'Abbas's Isfahan,
    which is half of the world* *167*

*Account of the stages between Tasuj and Qumlah that we traversed
    with the Shah's Agha* *173*

*Description of the province of Azerbaijan, the holy ground of the
    Ujan Mountain, the great city and ancient emporium of the pleasant
    fortified town of Tabriz, the village of Parviz* *175*

*The arrival of dreadful news from Van and Arjish {concerning a wondrous
    discussion between the Khan of Tabriz and this humble author}* . . . *178*

Concerning the beautiful city of Tabriz *181*

*Description of the castles, big cities, mountains and large rivers and all b
    uildings during our visit in the month of Dhi'l-Hijjeh in the year 1065
    [September 1655] going from Tabriz in Azerbaijan through Isfahan
    and Hamadan, the provinces of Shahrezur and Mosul until Baghdad* . . *181*

Concerning the war of the great general Ebrahim Pasha *183*

Description of the Dhu'l-Qadriyeh city, i.e., the castle of Sultaniyeh . *184*

*Description of the big and ancient city, abode of the erring people, i.e., the
    old fort of Kharzavil* *188*

*The places of pilgrimage of the martyred Ottoman viziers Beyeqli Hasan Pasha,
    Arsalan Pasha, Mostafa Pasha and Sujah Pasha* *190*

*Description of the great district of the old capital of Iran,
    the glorious province, i.e., the castle of Ardabil* *191*

Concerning the situation of the building of the town of Sahand *193*

*Description of the great town and ancient city of Nuh-e Avand, i.e.,
    castle of Nehavand* *193*

Description of the lower part of the fortification *194*

*Account of the first conquest of the castle of Nehavand in the time of
lord of the believers 'Omar b. Khattab, may God be pleased with him,
by general Sariyat al-Jabal* *196*

*Description of the royal capital, the creation of Jamshid, son of Shaddad
the faithless, i.e., the peerless city of Hamadan* *200*

General aspects of the beautiful city of Hamadan *205*

*We went from Qasr-e Shirin while hunting and traveling towards the east,
and I will describe the places that we saw* *214*

*Description of the ancient land of Abadan, on the coast of Hormuz and
Oman, i.e., the Makran-e Hazra, the castle of Basra* *241*

Concerning the places of pilgrimage of the Saints and Sufis in the city of Basra . . *249*

*Concerning the passage from the city of Basra to the region of Abadan,
to the province of Jazayer Haridat and the Sea of Hormuz; going to
the province of Hormuz and the town of Hoveyzeh in the land of the Persians* . *250*

*Description of the travels from the islands in the province of Basra to
the land of the Persians and the stages that we passed and the villages
and castles that we saw* *253*

*Description of the royal province of Hormuz at the border of the
lands of the Persian high king, the lord of Iran, Turan and
Qandahar (Bandar-e Tajdar)* *253*

*Description of the district of the Khan of Dowraq,
i.e., the prosperous city of Dowraq* *254*

GLOSSARY 256

SELECT BIBLIOGRAPHY 258

INDEX 260

ILLUSTRATION SOURCES

Brugsch, Heinrich. Reise der K.Preussischen Gesandtschaft nach Persien 1860 und 1861. 2 vols.Leipzig, 1863.
Le Bruyn, Cornelius. Travels into Muscovy, Persia and part of the East-Indies. 2 vols. London, 1737.
Chardin, Jean. Voyages du chevalier Chardin en Perse et autres lieux de l'Orient. 10 vols. ed. L. Langlès. Paris, 1811
Lewis, Bernard ed. The World of Islam. London, 1980.
Morier, James. A journey through Persia, Armenia, and Asia Minor in the years 1808 and 1809. London, 1812. And
 A Second Journey through Persia, Armenia, and Asia Minor between the years 1810 and 1816. London 1818.
Olearius, Adam. Vermehrte Newe Beschreibung Der Muscowitischen und Persischen Reyse. ed. Dieter Lohmeier.
 Tübingen, 1971.
Sazman-e mirath-e farhangi-ye melli.
Yurdaydin, Huseyin G. ed., Nasuh's-Silahi (Matrakçi). Beyan-i Menazil-i Sefer-i `Irakeyn-i Sultan Suleyman.
 Ankara 1976

TABLE OF ILLUSTRATIONS

The Ottoman Empire, 1512-1683	x
Shah 'Abbas II	xvi
Mehmet IV, Ottoman Sultan during Chelebi's travels	xxvii
The route of Evliya Chelebi's first journey through Iran in 1652	xxviii
A Persian Breakfast	3
A View of Erevan	4
A view of Uch Kalisa	7
A view of St. Stepanos, Jolfa	9
Whirling Dervishes	15
A view of the castle of Tabriz – Ark	24
An Ottoman janissary	26
Male and female dress ca. 1670	31
Illustration of Fuzuli's Bathhouse Poem	35
A woman pounding grain	36
A woman churning	37
A view of Tabriz ca. 1670	40
The Blue Dome – Maragheh	51
A view of Ardabil in 1637	56
Tomb of Sheikh Safi in Ardabil	59
An Ottoman sepahi	69
A view of Shamakhi in 1637	70
Two views of Niyazabad, south of Darband	77
A view of Tarku in 1637	86
A view of the Dagestan coast and of Darband	88
A view of Darband in 1637	91
A view of Terki in 1637	92
A royal banquet in Tiflis, ca. 1670	100
A view of Tiflis ca. 1670	102
Tomb of Sayyed Ebrahim in 1637	116
Tomb of Sayyed Ebrahim in 1702	117
The Ottoman army builds a fortress	121
Mount Ararat	123
Shaping a mill-stone	124
The route of Evliya Chelebi's second journey through Iran	128
Alkou – Lake Urmiyeh	148
Royal banquet	169
Tower of animal skulls in Isfahan	171
View of Hamadan	182
Mosque of Uljaytu – Soltaniyeh	185
View of the town of Soltaniyeh	186
The town of Miyaneh	187
The town of Dargazin	209
The town of Saveh	233
A Peasant Plowing	240

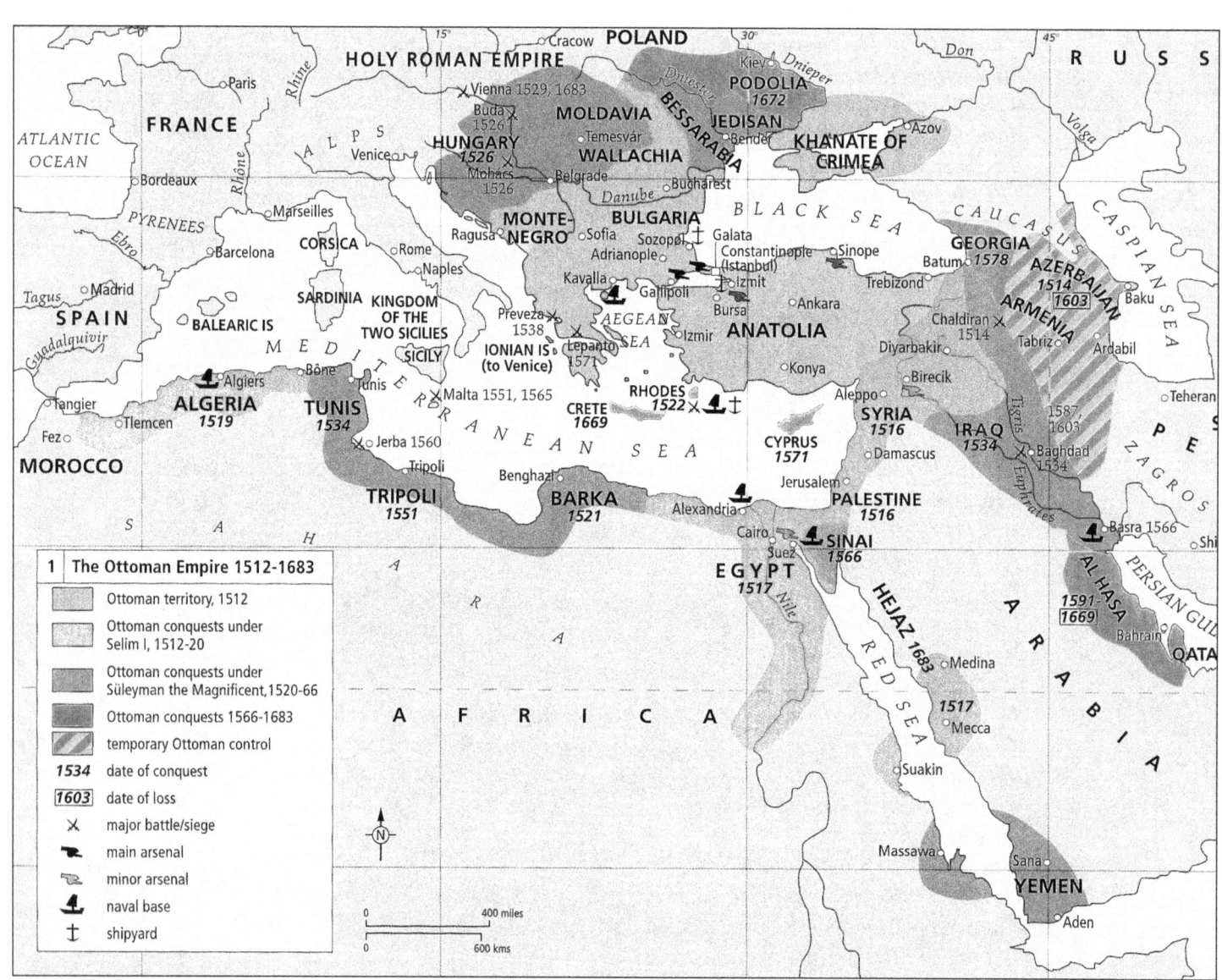

The Ottoman Empire, 1512-1683

INTRODUCTION

Although during the last two decades the study of Safavid Iran (1501-1736) has experienced an upswing, still much work needs to be done. This translation is a contribution to that field of study. We chose to translate this travelogue because scholars of Safavid Iran often complain that in Safavid studies there is too much reliance on European sources implying that more could and should be done with indigenous sources. However, despite this complaint, very little progress has been made in this area, and scholars continue to neglect published sources in Middle Eastern languages, which might somewhat correct this alleged one-sidedness in the use of sources. In particular, this holds for sources that are available in Ottoman Turkish, which are easily available but hardly ever used by scholars of Safavid Iran. Of course, this is only a reflection of the fact that the relationship of the Ottomans and Safavids still remains one of the most neglected aspects of Safavid history. One possible explanation for this neglect is the language barrier, but that cannot be the only reason, and we certainly hope that this translation will contribute to greater scholarly interest in Ottoman-Safavid historical relations.

As foreign travelers are one of the major sources of information for the study of Safavid Iran, it is surprising that so far hardly any use has been made of the travelogue (*Siyahat-nameh*) written by the Ottoman traveler Evliya Chelebi, despite the fact that it is available in printed form, even in an abridged English translation of part of the text.[1] Nevertheless, it contains much interesting information that is not to be found in either Persian or European-language sources, while it also offers a totally different view of Safavid Iran than in other sources. It is for this reason that we have undertaken to translate this important and interesting travelogue, one of the very few examples of this genre of literature in the seventeenth-century Middle East.

---

1. Available does not necessarily mean accessible. Although the Library of Congress has a copy of von Hammer's English translation of the *Siyahat-nameh* each time we asked for it the invariable reply came back that "it was not on the shelf." We finally had to borrow the copy at Berkeley. The "not on-the-shelf" syndrome from which the LoC suffers was already noted in 2003, but there has not been any improvement.

Who Was Evliya Chelebi?

The only contemporary information available about Evliya Chelebi is from his own *Siyahat-nameh*. He was the son of Darvish Mohammad Zilli, who was the chief of the goldsmiths of Istanbul. Evilya's mother was related to Abkhaz (Abaza) Malek Ahmad Pasha, which helped Evliya greatly in his career, such as it was.[2]

Evliya Chelebi was born in 1611 in Istanbul and like other youths of his background he visited the *Koran* school for a number of years and then studied Islamic sciences for seven years at the Hamid Efendi Madrasa. He later, or more likely simultaneously, studied *Koran* recitation from Mohammad Efendi at the Dar al-Qorra of Sadizadeh, allegedly for eleven years. He also apprenticed with his father from whom he learnt how to make silverwork, engraving and related craftsmanship. Because he had a beautiful voice, knew the *Koran* by heart, and had training in *Koran* recitation he was increasingly asked to perform *Koran* recitations at various occasions. The fame of his talent grew and through the influence of his mother's relative, Malek Ahmad Pasha, who was married to a daughter of Murad IV, Evliya was invited to recite the *Koran* in the Aya Sofiya. His performance must have been sufficiently pleasing to the Sultan for he was invited to complete his studies at court in the palace school. At that school, for four years, Evliya received a thorough grounding in the arts deemed necessary for a gentleman: calligraphy, poetry, and music, the latter from the famous court musician Darvish 'Omar Gulsheni. At the end of those four years he left court and was appointed to the *sepahi*s[3] and soon thereafter in 1640 he set out on the first of his many travels, which would take him throughout the entire Ottoman Empire, Iran, and much of Europe.

He traveled to Trabzon in 1640/41 in the suite of Ketenchi Othman Pasha, in 1646/47 with Defterzadeh Mohammad Pasha to Erzerum, and in 1648 with Morteza Pasha to Damascus. During all these employments he traveled much and widely within the jurisdiction of his Pasha, and, notably, made two missions to the Khans of Tabriz and Erivan in 1647. In 1650, his mother's cousin Malek Ahmad Pasha became grand vizier and from then on he remained permanently in his service. One year later Malek Ahmad Pasha fell from power and was appointed as governor of Özü (Oczakov) and later to Ilistre (Silistria) and thereafter to Sofia, where Evliya, as a member of his household, accompanied him. In 1655 Malek Ahmad Pasha was forced to accept the governorship of Van, which gave Evliya the opportunity to visit the Kurdish areas, which he described in detail. Also, during that period he was sent again on a diplomatic mission to Iran, about which more later. When Malek Ahmad Pasha died in 1662 Evliya took service with Qara Mohammad Pasha and accompanied him during the Hungarian campaign and was sent as secretary of an embassy to Vienna in 1664. One year later, when this embassy returned, Evliya received permission to travel to Europe which took him through Germany, the Netherlands, Denmark, Sweden, returning via Poland to the Crimea. Later Evliya visited Circassia and the Qalmuq steppe, and in 1669 he was part of the Ottoman army that conquered Crete. Evliya then visited the holy cities of Jerusalem, Medina and Mecca, where in 1671 he performed the hajj; he then settled down in

---

2. Robert Dankoff, *The intimate life of an Ottoman statesman: Melek Ahmed Pasha (1588-1662) as portrayed in Evliya Chelebi's Book of travels (Seyahat-name)* (Albany: State University of New York Press, 1991).

3. *Sepahi* or cavalryman. See C.E. Bosworth, "Sipahi," *Encyclopedia of Islam II*.

Cairo in 1671/72, where he remained for the rest of his life. From Cairo he made further trips along the Nile and to Ethiopia.

It was in Cairo that Evliya finally wrote his travelogue based on extensive written notes, the use of other texts, and his memory. Unfortunately, most of the time, Evliya does not distinguish between his own observations and those of other written sources. In the case of his travels in Iran it is not always clear what he had seen himself and what was hearsay. The structure of the *Siyahat-nama* suggests that Evliya intended to write more than a travelogue, viz. a geographical and socio-historical encyclopedia. He did not always stick to this pattern in the case of Iran, but he tried to collect information about the fortification and date of the foundation of each city visited, the etymology of its name, particulars concerning its socio-economic make-up such as the number of houses, bathhouses, mosques, market, local officials, shrines, buildings, language, people's dress, food and drinks, stories about prophets and saints, names of men and women, slaves and slave girls, and whatever else was of interest. When Evliya Chelebi died, in 1684 or 1685, he had written ten books that detailed all of his travels. However, the travelogue was not yet finished as he intended to add more details at a later date.

Despite having been trained for a career in the Ottoman administration and being related to a powerful Ottoman high official, Evliya never exercised any high official function. He invariably joined the household of his patrons as *Koran* reciter and reader, prayer leader, muezzin, and social companion, but he was always ready to travel and go on missions in the service of his patrons. This was perhaps because Evliya's urge to travel had come to him in a dream during his twenty-first birthday (10 *Moharram*). In this dream he saw the prophet Mohammad, surrounded by the Imams and Saints. While he wanted to ask the Prophet for his intercession (*shefa 'at*), he instead asked for travel (*siyahat*). This was granted to him and he was allowed to kiss the hands of the Prophet, Imams and the Saints. From that moment onwards his aim in life was to travel and visit the tombs of saints. He therefore also attached more meaning to his name, Evliya (meaning 'saints'), for he clearly was a *mohebb al-avliya* or a beloved of the saints, which perhaps explains why he was so fastidious in visiting and enumerating all the tombs of saints in the locations that he visited.[4]

Editions Used

There is as yet no critical text edition of the entire *Siyahat-nameh*. Richard Kreutel suggested in 1971 that the oldest available manuscript (codex Bağdat Köşkü 304-308) is in fact the autograph manuscript. Some have taken issue with this characterization pointing out the many 'mistakes' in orthography, which an educated man like Evliya Chelebi would not have made. However, other scholars have shown that these so-called 'mistakes' were part of a consistent pattern and thus were stylistic in nature. Most scholars who have studied the manuscripts in detail agree that Keutel was right in his assessment, although there are still some dissenters.

Whether this oldest manuscript is the autograph or not, there are only a few manuscripts of Evliya Chelebi's *Siyahat-nameh*, which are all copies of codex Bağdat Köşkü 304-308. It seems that some 50 years after his death the ten books of the *Siyahat-nameh* were sent from Cairo to

---

4. The short description of Evliya's life is based on R. F. Kreutel, "Neues zur Evliya Chelebi Forschung," *Der Islam* 48 (1972), pp. 269-98; P.A. MacKay, "The manuscripts of the Seyahatname of Evliya Chelebi," *Der Islam* 52 (1975), pp. 278-98; J.H. Mordtmann-H.W.Duda, "Ewliya Chelebi," *Encyclopedia of Islam II*.

Istanbul, where they landed in the library of the bibliophile Hajj Bashir Agha. The latter had a few copies made of the *Siyahat-nameh*, although it did not become popular among the educated class and remained ignored. In fact, the manuscript, which now is considered by many to be the autograph, was split up, and eight of its ten books finally found a home in the palace library. The last two books of this manuscript seem to have been permanently lost.

Europeans became aware of the travelogue when in 1814 von Hammer introduced it to the scholarly community. He followed this up with an abridged German translation in 1822 and a less abridged translation in English in 1834.[5] It was only during the *Tanzimat* period that changing world views also resulted in more and increasing appreciation for Evliya Chelebi's work among the educated class in Ottoman Turkey. Thus, in 1843, much later than in Europe, a selection of the *Siyahat-nameh* was published in Istanbul. The first printed edition of the first six books was published by Ahmet Cevdet in Istanbul between 1896 and 1901. The manuscript used was not the alleged autograph—books in the palace library were not yet available to the public—but use was made of another manuscript copy from the Pertev Pasha collection. Various scholars have rightly criticized this edition, because its editor suppressed difficult or politically sensitive passages and modernized the language, and because the manuscript also has lacunae. Despite these defects most of the later editions of the *Siyahat-nameh* were based on this edition. Hence, similar criticism also holds for the much abridged translation into modern Turkish by Zuhuri Daneshmand, which was published in 15-volumes (Istanbul, 1971). There is only a critical edition of books 7 and 8 of the *Siyahat-nameh* by Kilisli Rif`at (1928).[6] Meanwhile, the alleged autograph manuscript has finally been published in ten volumes by Seyit Ali Kahraman assisted by a number of other editors, who varied per volume. This edition, unfortunately in Latin script and without annotation, was published in Istanbul between 1996 and 2007.[7]

It is the Kahraman edition that we have used as the basis for our translation, including the markings "{}" to indicate marginal notes in the manuscript. The Kahraman et al. edition has its own problems because it is also marred by mistakes. In quite a few cases the editors read the Ottoman text differently than we did, in particular in cases of Arabic or Persian words. Therefore, we have used the Cevdet edition as an important support tool for our translation. In fact, as far as the travels in Iran are concerned, Cevdet's edition is preferable to the Kahraman one, because it almost invariably says the same thing, but fortunately in a much shorter and clearer way than Evliya Chelebi. But the main reason for using the Cevdet text is that it is in Arabic script, which is easier to read and comprehend than the editions in Latin script.

We have not translated certain paragraphs, because they did not deal with Iran, or because Chelebi sometimes waxes on and on about certain subjects, adding what we consider nonsensical stories, which do not really add anything to our knowledge. Where we have omitted or not translated text this is indicated in a footnote. Because Hammer used yet other manuscripts for his

---

5. J. von Hammer-Purgstall, "Merkwürdiger Fund einer türkischen Reisebeschreibung," *Intelligenzblatt zur Wiener Allgemeinen Literaturzeitung* 2 (1814), pp. 9-15; Ibid., *Narrative of Travels in Europe, Asia, and Africa, in the seventeenth century, by Evliya Efendi* 2 vols. in 3 (London 1834-50).

6. The above discussion is based on Martin van Bruinessen and Hendrik van Boeschoten, *Evliya Chelebi in Diayarbekr* (Leiden, 1988), pp. 5-7.

7. Seyit Ali Kahraman et al., *Evliya Chelebi Sehayatnamesi* 10 vols. (1996-2007). We have used volumes 2 and 4.

English translation and sometimes has additional information that neither the Cevdet nor the Kahraman editions offer, we have added such information, where relevant, in a footnote.

What the above shows is that there is an urgent need for a critical text edition in the original Arabic script, also because the other manuscripts often have information that is not found, or only found in a reduced form, in the alleged autograph, variants should be included as well. A case in point is the story about the cats of Divriji that were sold in Ardabil, where none of the available texts tell the same story. In fact, a manuscript not used by us has the most elaborate text on this subject.

Historical Background to Evliya Chelebi's Travels in Iran

An important aspect of Evliya's travels in Iran is his religious partisanship. He takes pride when he visits a city in relating the various occasions when it had been taken and destroyed by the successive Ottoman Sultans (Selim, Sulayman, Murad III, and Murad IV) and their generals. When the Ottomans suffered a reverse, however, it was the will of God. The Ottoman army is not just an army; it is an army of fighters of the faith (*feda'is*) or the army of Islam. Even when Evliya, for example, has something positive to say about scholars in an Iranian town he qualifies this by stating that they were Shi`ites. For that cleavage, the Sunni-Shi`a dichotomy colored not only Evliya's observations, but also the relationship between the Ottoman Empire and Safavid Iran.

In 1501, Esma`il Safavi, a grandson of Uzun Hasan Aq-Qoyunlu and nominal head of the Safavid Sufi order, triumphed in the Aq-Qoyunlu war of succession and when he conquered Tabriz he declared Shi`ism to be the religion of his state. His Sufi followers wore a red felt hat and the Ottomans therefore in derision called them Qizilbash or Red Hats, which henceforth became the standard Ottoman term to refer to the adherents of the Safavid state. This term was also used by Evliya, in addition to the more traditional term of `Ajam or Persian. Because Shah Esma`il (r.1501-1524) was the scion of a family of Sufi sheikhs and descended from the famous founder the Safavid order, Sheikh Safi al-Din, he, and later his successors, were also derisively referred to by the Ottomans as the *Sheikh-oghlu* or Sons of the Sheikh.

Given the threat that extreme forms of Shi`ism constituted in eastern Anatolia, resulting in one major revolt in 1511/12, Selim I (r. 1512-1520), who hated Esma`il I, considered it in his strategic as well as spiritual interest to neutralize, if not eliminate the Safavid threat on his eastern border, while at the same time eradicating the heresy of Shi`ism. The result of this religious conflict was 130 years of war between the two states. After Selim I defeated Esma`il I in 1514 at Chalderan and took Diyarbekr from him in 1517 there was a period of truce. The defection of Ulama Tekelu, one of Shah Tahmasp I's regents, in 1533, resulted in the loss of Baghdad in 1534, and of Alqas Mirza in 1547, the brother of Shah Tahmasp I (r. 1524-1576), led to renewed hostilities between the countries, but not to loss of land. There were 23 years of calm after the peace of Amasiya in 1555. However, war broke out again in 1578 when the situation in Iran was unsettled due to succession problems and civil war among the Qizilbash tribes. The Ottomans this time were quite successful in keeping the conquered areas, annexing most of Azerbaijan, including Tabriz, and part of western Iran. This situation lasted until 1604 when Shah `Abbas I (r. 1587-1629) gradually ousted the Ottomans from the lost Safavid territories and retook Baghdad in 1622. After Shah `Abbas I's death the Ottomans seized the opportunity to test his young and inexperienced successor and took cities in Azerbaijan, but Shah Safi I (r. 1629-1642) was able to regain these, although he had to yield Baghdad in 1638. Tired of the incessant and costly war, both countries signed an agreement in 1639 that brought peace between them for almost a century.

The new peace did not mean that there were no problems between the two countries and there were even parties that wanted to incite renewed hostilities. Also, the Ottomans were worried about the military success of Shah ʿAbbas II (r. 1642-1666) against the Moghuls, from whom he had taken Qandahar in 1649, while the Safavids were worried about military operation against the Khan of Bitlis close to their border. However, in general both sides wanted to keep the peace and took actions against those who acted against the peace treaty. It is the occurrence of such an event, which led to Evliya's first journey to Iran.

Shah ʿAbbas II

Evliya's Missions to Iran

When in 1646 Ganj ʿAli Khan, governor of Erevan, complained that the rebellious Bey of Ottoman Shushik had broken the peace treaty by pillaging districts within Erevan province, Malek Ahmad Pasha, governor of Van, mobilized his troops to take punitive action against him. Military operations in the border area were sensitive issues, because the other party immediately had suspicions about the real intentions of such doings. Evliya reported that "When the Persian Envoy saw this immense army collected, he repented of his complaint against the Bey of Shushik, because he was afraid that this army might receive orders to lay siege to Erivan." That this was no exaggeration on Evliya's part is also clear from the reaction that he received at a later occasion from the Khan of Tabriz about similar military operations against Bitlis. The operation against Shushik was successful. Malek Ahmad Pasha conquered it, but its Beg had fled. When it was learnt that he had been caught and imprisoned by the Khan of Maku, Malek Ahmad Pasha ordered three thousand men under Baqi Pasha to go and seize the Beg of Shushik. Evliya took advantage of this occasion to accompany these troops and visit Iran. We start our translation where Evliya describes his arrival at the castle of Maku. Although we have been unable to identify many of the small villages along his route, the ones that we were able to verify show that Evliya indeed made this journey and visited these places.

Evliya made his second mission to the Khans of Urmiyeh and Tabriz to reclaim forty thousand sheep that had been taken by the Khan of Urmiyeh from the Pinyanish Kurds as well as to obtain the liberation of Morteza Pasha, who had been taken and imprisoned by the Khan of Domboli. Evliya traveled to Tabriz via Urmiyeh and visited its neighboring areas. However, as is clear from Table 1., Evliya's itinerary is not in agreement with geographical reality, and therefore he either must have had incomplete notes or the information that he offers is based on unverified oral information. In fact, it is highly unlikely that Evlia visited most of the places that he mentioned after his visit to Urmiyeh and Tabriz (and the places in between) and, as van Bruinessen has already suggested, his further descriptions are but "a mixture of poorly assimilated reading or hearsay."[8] In fact, after leaving Tabriz, Evliya enumerates a number of towns and villages, sometimes suggesting that he actually traveled between them by giving the number of hours and the direction traveled, but it is impossible to determine that he actually did so. We are on firmer ground when he finally leaves Iran and travels to Baghdad, of which he gives a detailed description. He then is sent on a mission to the autonomous emirate of Basra, and the route description to that city is not entirely without historical interest. In Basra he collected information on other cities in the Persian Gulf area, but he did not travel there. Given the interest of Basra and the paucity of information from local seventeenth century sources on the Persian Gulf and Basra, we have included this part of the Travelogue, although most of his description is fanciful and invented, as he did not visit most of the places he described.

Evliya Chelebi's Peculiarities

There are a few things that are striking in the *Siyahat-nameh* on which other authors already have remarked, such as Evliya's interest in linguistics, in the etymology of names of cities, etc. As to Evliya's remarks on languages in Iran, it is our impression that he was rather uncritical in collecting

---

8. Van Bruinessen et al., *Diyarbekr*, p. 5.

and commenting on his material. The most glaring example is that of his sample of the language of the Qeytaq, a Caucasian people who speak an Ibero-Caucasian language and not Mongol at all, as he alleges. The fact that he did not collect this linguistic material himself, but copied it from Mustawfi's *Nuhzat al-Qulub* without verifying its reliability, was probably spurred by his wish to be as encyclopedic as possible in his report on the regions that he visited. The linguistic sample of the Georgian language is more reliable, as is that of the Persian language. In the latter case it is interesting that some of the words he lists are quite uncommon and not known to most speakers of that language. Moreover, as in the case of the Qeytaq language, he did not collect these words himself, but copied them uncritically from other authors. Furthermore, he reported that the people in Nakhjevan province spoke a variety of languages such as Persian, Dari, Dehqani and Pahlavi. Unfortunately Evliya did not report what these languages or dialects were, although he implies that they were not Turkish in nature. We therefore can only guess as to what these terms refer. Traditionally, Dari is used as the historical name for the Persian language, while nowadays it is used to refer to the Persian dialect spoken in Afghanistan or that spoken by the Zoroastrians of Yazd and Kerman. What dialect Evliya was referring to is not known. Similarly, the Dehqani language probably is just the vernacular Persian language spoken by peasants, which is suggested by the fact that he contrasts it with the refined language spoken by the educated class in the cities. The mention of the Pahlavi language is something that he has uncritically borrowed from Mustawfi (1340), who mentioned that it was spoken in Maragheh and Zanjan, and he extrapolated this to other neighboring parts of these towns. As such, his linguistic observations about Iran therefore cannot be considered of great importance, except that he confirms that the Turkification of Azerbaijan had yet to make major inroads.[9]

Similarly Evliya's attempts at etymology are just word plays and thus of no value whatsoever. His forays into this field are superficial, as are those into the field of history. Hammer had already remarked rather neutrally that Evliya was "an indifferent historian," which is the most positive observation and all that one can say about this aspect of his reporting. Therefore, the *Siyahat-nameh* is of little use as a source for the history of Iran; when Evliya relates what he knows or has read about past events, these reports are almost invariably not entirely correct. But then Evliya was not writing a history or even a travelogue faithfully recording his observations, but rather a light-footed literary work aimed to amuse and dazzle the educated members of Ottoman society with Evliya's wit and knowledge.

It, therefore, seems that Evliya was under the impression that he would be rewarded by the number of words that he wrote as well as by the cleverness of the use of words rather than by conveying precise meanings to them. The text, which does not make for easy reading, is often an exercise of form over substance, where the medium is the message. Evliya made up words just for rhyming purposes and also was slovenly in the use of multiple adjectives and other qualifiers to suit his literary purposes rather than convey information. This poses problems for the translators, because should they translate literally or reduce the text to its bare meaning. A case in point, be it a minor though telling one, is that van Bruinessen and others have pointed out that the term *qibla* does not always denote the same as *janub* or south, and the same holds for the terms *shomal* or north and *yildiz*.[10] Although we do not disagree with this appreciation, we nevertheless have

---

9. On this subject see Jean Aubin, "Le témoignage d'Ebn-e Bazzaz sur la turquisation de l'Azerbaydjan, *Studia Iranica* 7 (1989), pp. 5-17.

10. Van Bruinessen et al., *Diyarbekr*, p. 201, n. 2.

ignored these alleged differences as Evliya often had only a very general idea in which direction he actually was travelling, and sometimes he had no idea at all. Therefore, it is rather futile to try to be precise, as being precise was not of great interest to our traveler.

The importance of the *Siyahat-nameh* therefore lies in Evliya's own observations, although in the case of his second Iranian journey it is not always clear what he had seen himself and what he had collected from hearsay. Nevertheless, his incidental observations about social customs, food dishes, 'Ashura ceremony, and educational system (the manner of the learning of the alphabet) are of great interest, as these are not to be found elsewhere. Also, his reports on the discussion with several Khans are of great interest, as they shed light on the type of conversation people carried on with one another. Also, of great interest are Evliya's reproduction of poems and the mention of locally known poets, most of whom are entirely unknown. As such, he gives us an insight into what kind of other poems literate people were interested in.

One of the recurrent items in Evliya's reports is that he is very much interested in beautiful boys, for he reports about their allure in every city in Iran (and elsewhere) that he visits. When in Bitlis, while looking at Kurdish boys who were hugging and romping as they skied down the hill, he remarks: "And quite a few of us old lechers were having fun watching their antics."[11] This homo-erotic interest of older males in adolescents was quite a normal aspect of social life in the Middle East and adjacent areas as well as in its literature.[12]

Observations on the Translation

We have tried to translate all Ottoman Turkish terms into English, although this sometimes poses problems. For example, the term *qal'e* as used by Chelebi may denote a castle, a fortress, a fortified city with walls as well as the walls themselves. Depending on the context this term therefore should be translated as castle, city, walled city or walls. However, we have translated the term everywhere as 'castle' as it is not always clear which aspect of the term Evliya meant.

When Evliya used the word *jame'* we have translated that as 'large mosque', unless it occurs in combination with the name of its builder (e.g., Uzun Hasan mosque), and *masjed* as 'small mosque' to avoid confusion, especially when they occur in the same sentence. *Jame'* sometimes is translated as Friday mosque, when that function is clear from the context. Whenever the term Persia or Persian is used it means that Evliya used respectively the term *'ajam* or *'ajami* to distinguish these from his use of the words Iran or *Iran-zamin*, which we have translated as Iran. Similarly, whenever Evliya uses the word *Qizilbash* to denote Persians we have not translated that term, but used it as such.

To avoid cluttering the text with transcriptions of titles, names and functions in Ottoman and Persian in the text, we have added a short glossary of terms used more than once, so that the reader knows that we, for example, have translated the term *kalantar* as mayor and that of *dizdar* as castellan. When reference is made to a person or to a jurisdiction, then we have capitalized Pasha, Khan and Beg (Malek Pasha; Ganj 'Ali Khan; Khan of Tabriz, Beg of Shushik); when reference is made to the generic title, then these words are written as pasha and khan. The Ottoman Sultans are often referred to as Khan (e.g., Murad Khan), but to avoid confusion with other khans

---

11. Robert Dankoff, *Evliya Chelebi in Bitlis* (Leiden, 1990), p. 361.

12. On this aspect see, e.g., Floor, *A Social History of Sexual Relations in Iran*, chapter four.

we have referred to them in all cases as Sultan. The names of persons have all been Persianized, thus no Mehmet or Muhammad, but Mohammad.

The system of transliteration of Persian words used is simple and as follows:

Long a and short a	= a
Long u	= u
Short u	= o
Long i	= i
Short i	= e

Last but not least we would like to thank the people who were so kind as to help us with difficult parts and/or words in the *Siyahat-nameh*. Iraj Afshar (Tehran) was so kind to help us resolve the meaning of some obscure Persian words, while Mohammad ʿAli Taj-Ahmadi (Paris) was always ready to answer our questions concerning obscure words or difficult parts of the Ottoman-Turkish text, while he also provided us with the text of Fuzuli's bathhouse poem. We also would like to thank Rahim Ra'is-niya (Tabriz) who provided us with the abridged Persian translation of the *Siyahat-nameh* concerning Tabriz by Hajj Nakhjevani as well as with the Turkish translation of Dankhoff's *Evliya Chelebi glossary*.[13] Furthermore, ʿAbbas Javadi (Prague), Grigol Beradze (Tiflis) and Hamid Algar (UC Berkeley) also provided helpful support. Finally, we wish to express our great appreciation for Keith Openshaw, who was willing, once again, to edit our English and make it look as if we know our way around in that idiom. Thanks are also due to Guus Floor who drew the maps.

Evliya Chelebi's Itinerary

To make it easier to follow Evliya's travels we have provided this Table, which gives the names of his point of departure and arrival each day and, where known, the travel time as well as the travel direction.

---

13. Robert Dankoff, *Evliya Chelebi glossary. Unusual, Dialectical and Foreign Words in the Seyahatname* (Harvard, 1991) translated into Turkish by Semih Tezcan, *Evliya Chelebi Seyahatnamesi Okuma Sözlü ü* (Istanbul, 2004).

First Journey to Iran In 1647

Table 1

From	To	Travel time	Direction
Maku	Iliyeh	7 hours	?
Iliyeh	Yaylachik	8 hours	?
Yaylachik	Barut-khaneh	?	east
Barut-khaneh	Doshu kaba [Dushkaya]	?	east
Doshu kaba [Dushkaya]	Chaglagort [Chaghla Gurna]	13 hours	east
Chaglagort [Chaghla Gurna]	Karshi [Karish]	?	east
Karshi [Karish]	Kendimasir	13 hours	?
Kendimasir	Kendrukh Khan [Zuchan]	14 hours	?
Kendrukh Khan [Zuchan]	Uch Kilisa	7 hours	?
Uch Kilisa	Near Mt. Shelon	?	east
Near Mt. Shelon	Zangi-nahri	12 hours	?
Zangi-nahri	Sedreki [Sidirgi]	10 hours	east
Sedreki [Sidirgi]	Ahmad Bey Tekesi	?	east
Ahmad Bey Tekesi	Qarabagh	16 hours	?
Qarabagh	Nakhjevan	?	north
Nakhjevan	Kesik Gonbad	8 hours	south
Kesik Gonbad	Aras River	7 hours	?
Aras River	Qarabagh	1 hour	?
Qarabagh	Kerkene	6 hours + 34 hours	south
Kerkene	Zenose [Zonuz]	9 hours	south
Zenose	Tesuy [Tasuj]	10 hours	south
Tesuy	Marand	12 hours	south
Marand	Kahrin [Kahriz]	?	south
Kahrin [Kahriz]	Sahlan	7 hours	south
Sahlan	Tabriz	3 + hours	?
Tabriz	Ajisu	5 hours	west
Ajisu	Sham Khazan	4 hours	?
Sham Khazan	Valiyan	?	west
Valiyan	Qumlah	5 hours	west
Qumlah	Seravrud	?	north-west
Seravrud	Dusht	?	east
Dusht	Jevlandoruq [Chulanduruk]	6 hours	?
Jevlandoruq [Chulanduruk]	Alqabandelis	?	?
Alqabandelis	Lakdrukh	?	?
Lakdrukh	Koj-abad	?	?
Koj-abad	Rudqat	?	east

From	To	Travel time	Direction
Rudqat	Maragheh	?	?
Maragheh	Turnachayiri	?	?
Turnachayiri	Sitekez [Setgiz]	?	?
Sitekez [Setgiz]	Ujan	?	?
Ujan	Mehrani-rud	?	?
Mehrani-rud	Sa`idabad	?	?
Sa`idabad	Manmah	7 hours	south
Manmah	Kahravan	?	?
Kahravan	Band [Shahband]	?	south
Band [Shahband]	Ardabil	9 hours	?
Ardabil			
Tabriz	Hajji Harami	?	north
Hajji Harami	Sufiyan	?	north
Sufiyan	Mazid Khan	?	north
Mazid Khan	Keremish	7 hours	north
Keremish	Kandushlah [Kend-e Veshleh] River	?	north
Kandushlah [Kend-e Veshleh] River	Khoy	2 hours	?
Khoy	Churus	3 hours	?
Churus	Milelli [Ravan]	4 + hours	east, then north
Milelli [Ravan]	Tur Alimi [Tut alusi]	8 hours	north
Tur Alimi [Tut alusi]	Qafaj [Qaghaj]	?	north
Qafaj [Qaghaj]	Afsharli	?	north
Afsharli	Shurehgel	7 hours	?
Shurehgel	Sharab-khaneh	10 hours	?
Sharab-khaneh	Seyf al-Din	?	?
Seyf al-Din	Tilfirak	5 hours	north
Tilfirak	Erevan	?	?
Erevan	Khvajeh Baghi	?	north
Khvaheh bagh	Damirji Hasan	8	north
Damirji Hasan	Ganjeh	?	?
Ganjeh	Kalak Hazar Ahmadi	?	north
Kalak Hazar Ahmadi	Makuchorud	?	north
Makuchorud	Aras	?	?
Aras	Sheki	2 stages	?
Sheki	river Kanut	a day's journey	east
River Kanut	Qoyun Kechdi	?	north
Qoyun Kechdi	Mahmudabad	3 + hours	north
Mahmudabad	river Gilan	?	north

From	To	Travel time	Direction
river Gilan	Niyazabad	?	north
Niyazabad	Kur Khoda-bandeh	?	north
Kur Khoda-bandeh	Til-chay (Göksu)	?	north
Til-chay (Göksu)	Aqsu	7 hours	north
Aqsu	Shamakhi	?	north
Shamakhi	Pir dar Kuh	?	north
Pir dar Kuh	Pir Marizat Sultan	6 hours	north
Pir Marizat Sultan	Quzeli	7 hours	north
Quzeli	Alta Aghaj	?	north
Alta Aghaj	Khezr Zendeh	?	north
Khezr Zendeh	Regal	?	?
Regal	Baku	?	north
Baku	Shaberan	?	north, east
Shaberan	Darband	?	south
Darband	Kureh (Daghestan)	12 hours	south
Kureh (Daghestan)	Sarir al-Alan	3 days	?
Sarir al-Alan	Khatan	?	west
Khatan	Zakhur	?	?
Zakhur	Zukhuriyeh	?	?
Zukhuriyeh	Kahkt	?	?
Kahkt	Khudray Khan	?	south
Khudray Khan	Tiflis	?	?
Tiflis	Kusakht [Kuh-e sakht]	4 hours	south
Kusakht [Kuh-e sakht]	Suran	?	?
Suran	Azghur	4 hours	west
Azghur	Akhiskha	?	?
Akhiskha	Valghar	?	west
Valghar	Ardahan	?	west
Ardahan	Kuleh (Guleh)	?	west
Kuleh (Guleh)	Marmedan	?	west
Marmedan	Id	?	west
Id	Qara Konaq	?	west
Qara Konaq	Umudum Dedeh	?	?
Umudum Dedeh	Erzerum	?	?
SIDETRIP			
Erzerum	Hasan Qal`eh	11-12 hours	east
Hasan Qal`eh	Meydanjoq	9-10 hours	east
Meydanjoq	Mazhankerd	10 hours	east
Mazhankerd	Barduz	?	?

From	To	Travel time	Direction
Barduz	Kajqovan Dudman	?	south
Kajqovan Dudman	Qars	?	east
Qars	Akhiskha	3 days	?
Akhiskha	Kaghezman	?	?
Kaghezman	Maghahberd	?	?
Maghahberd	Zarshod	nine hours	east
Zarshod	Talish	nine hours	east
Talish	Qara Teybi	?	?
Qara Teybi	Uch Kilisa	12 hours	?
Uch Kilisa	Erevan	?	east

Second Journey to Iran in 1655

From	To	Travel time	Direction
Van	Zekuk	?	?
Zekuk	Vanak Verek	3 hours	?
Vanak Verek	Hundusten	5 hours	?
Hundusten	Khoshab	>5 hours	?
Khoshab	Do Ab; Davadan Davdan	5 hours	?
Do Ab; Davadan or Davdan	?		
?	Pasik Agha	5 hours	north-east
Pasik Agha	Pinyash	6 hours	east
Pinyash	Rubajiq	?	east
Rubajiq	Qotur	6 hours	?
Qotur	Albaq [Iran]	4 hours	?
Albaq	Jelva [Jolu	5 hours	north
Jelva [Jolu	Khasun/Khanasun/Sanasun	3 hours	east
Khasun/[Khanasun/Sanasun	Karniyareq	7 hours	?
Karniyareq	Hobash	4 hours	north
Hobash	Berduq	4 hours	north
Berduq	Hoseyneh	3 hours	east
Hoseyneh	Harir	?	?
Harir	Ghaziqeran	3 hours	?
Ghaziqeran	Kuyah Darreh	5 hours	south
Kuyah Darreh	Jevlan Sultan	5 hours	?
Jevlan Sultan	Pirehdus Sultan	6 hours	south
Pirehdus Sultan	Enzeli Sultan	5 hours	south
Enzeli Sultan	Habbena	5 hours	south
Habbena	Harir Sultan	3 hours	south
Harir Sultan	Kharman-e Shahi	7 hours	south

From	To	Travel time	Direction
Kharman-e Shahi	Urmiyeh	5 hours	?
Urmiyeh	Jevlan	4 hours	south
Jevlan	DomDomi	6 hours	south
DomDomi	Ushnuyeh	7 hours	south
Ushnuyeh	Urmiyeh	7 hours	east
Urmiyeh	Qochagha Baba	7 hours	?
Qochagha Baba	Domboli	6 hours	?
Domboli	Shahsevan	7 hours	west
Shahsevan	`Ali Yar	6 hours	?
`Ali Yar	Urmiyeh	?	?
Urmiyeh	Imam Reza	7 hours	north
Imam Reza	Shah Nabun	5 hours	north
Shah Nabun	Bichor	3 hours	north
Bichor	Yazdanbash	5 hours	north
Yazdanbash	Salmas	5 hours	?
Salmas	Kojanabad	2 hours	north
Kojanabad	Tasuj	3 hours	east
Tasuj	Qumlah	6 hours	?
Qumlah	Sunjah	?	east
Sunjah	Sheikh Safi	?	?
Sheikh Safi	Sujeh Jan	?	?
Mazid Khan	Sujeh Jan	?	?
Sujeh Jan	Bandemahi	?	east
Bandemahi	Shebteri	?	?
Shebteri	Tabriz	?	?
Tabriz	Mehranrud	5 hours	east
Mehranrud	Jevlanduruq	?	?
From here onwards unlikely that Evliya actually visited these places			
Jevlanduruq	Alaq Bulaq	?	south
Alaq Bulaq	Sarjam Khani	?	?
Sarjam Khani	Sultaniyeh	?	south
Sultaniyeh	Samedehon	?	south
Samedehon	Kajabad	5 hours	south
Kajabad	Qarehqan	?	?
Qarehqan	Maragheh	?	south
Maragheh	Turnachayri	?	south
Turnachayri	Kahravan	?	south
Kahravan	Shahbandar	?	south

From	To	Travel time	Direction
Shahbandar	Kharzavil	?	?
Kharzavil	Tarom Khalkhal	?	?
Tarom Khalkhal	Serah	?	south
Serah	Ardabil	?	?
Ardabil	Masuleh	?	?
Masuleh	Sahand	?	?
Sahand	Nehavand	?	?
Nehavand	Sayyedlar	?	south
Sayyedlar	Hazrat-e Sa`d-e Vaqqas	?	south
Hazrat-e Sa`d-e Vaqqas	Kangavar	?	?
Kangavar	Sorkh Bid	?	?
Sorkh Bid	Bisotun	?	?
Bisotun	Hamadan	?	south
Hamadan	Aveh	7 hours	?
Aveh	Kermanshah	2 days	south
Kermanshah	Dargazin	?	?
Dargazin	Pilevar	?	east
Pilevar	Dinavar	?	east
Dinavar	Jam-Janab	?	?
Jam-Janab	Dast-Pol	?	east
Dast-Pol	Qasr-e Shirin	?	east
Qasr-e Shirin	Hulvan	?	?
Hulvan	Qazvin	?	?
Qazvin	Alamut	5 hours	north
Alamut	Deylam	?	east
A number of places are described, but clearly were not visited by Evliya. From here on it is likely that Evliya actually passed through these places			
Kermanshah	Fajarkhan	3 hours	south
Fajar Khan	Sohrab	7 hours	south
Sohrab	Sarkhaleh	5 hours	south
Sarkhaleh	Raq-e Giray	8 hours	south
Taq-e Giray	Dartang	2 hours	south
This is the border of Iran with the Ottoman Empire			

We have not provided an itinerary for Evliya's visit to Basra, because apart from crossing the Shatt al-Arab between Manavi and Gordolan he did not visit any of the places that he mentioned.

Mehmet IV, Ottoman Sultan during Chelebi's travels

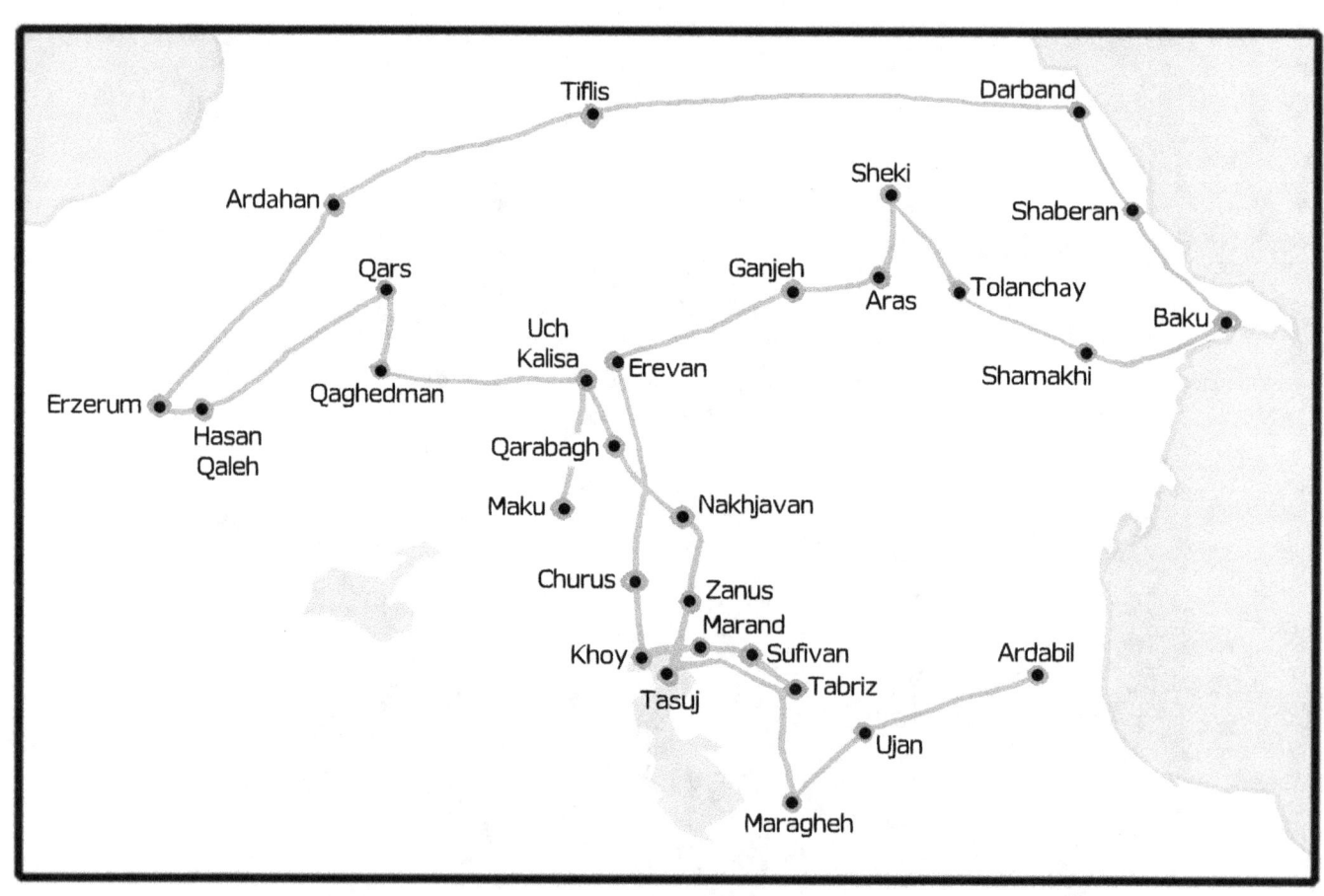

The route of Evliya Chelebi's first journey through Iran in 1652

THE FIRST TRAVELS

Travel to Shushik Castle situated in Kurdistan in the province of Erzerum

The castle of Maku. Although nothing is left of the [original] castle its construction is attributed to Anushirvan.[1] In the year [-], when the Kurds were under Sultan Sulayman[2] this place was given as a gift to the Mahmudi Beys.[3] Later the Persians acquired it through a trick. Once again one of the Mahmudi Beys was the Bey of Malazgird.[4] In the year [-] when Qara Mostafa Pasha, grand vizier of Murad [IV], the conqueror of Baghdad, had conquered Baghdad,[5] he made Darna and Dartang part of the border, and our master Malek Ahmad Pasha, when he was still governor of Diyarbekr, went with him to Darna and Dartang[6] and established the border [with Iran]. In accordance with the peace treaty, they destroyed the castle of Zalem Ahmad in the Ottoman district of Shahrezur.[7] The Persians destroyed the castle of Qotur in the Van region. Then the Ottomans destroyed the castle of Maku, which is near Revan[8] and put its Bey in Malazgird. When

---

1. Khosrow I (r. 531-579) the Sasanian king more commonly known as Anushirvan the Just was the most famous ruler of this dynasty. Apart from his just rule his name is also associated, rightly or wrongly, with the building of many cities in his realm.

2. Sulayman I (r. 1520-1566), known in the West as the Magnificent and in the Ottoman Empire as the Lawgiver (*Qanuni*).

3. The Mahmudi (Mahmudi Begi), Mehemdi or Khoshab Kurds were an influential Kurdish tribe, whose chief held an independent fief from the Ottoman Sultan, situated south-east of Lake Van.

4. Malazgirt or Malazgird is a town in Mush province in eastern Turkey.

5. Qara Mustafa Pasha, a Hungarian by birth, was enrolled into the Janissaries where he rose to the rank of *kapudan pasha*. Murad IV (r. 1623-1640) made him grand vizier after the conquest of Baghdad. He was a reformer, which brought him into conflict with the Janissaries that led to his dismissal and death in 1643. On the events and chronology of the conquest of Baghdad in 1638 see Claude Huart, *Histoire de Baghdad dans les temps modernes* (Paris, 1901).

6. These are border villages near Qasr-e Shirin and are discussed in more detail at the end of the travelogue; see p. 238.

7. Zalem Ahmad Qal`eh is in the Shahrezur border district, situated between Zohab and Sulaymaniyeh.

8. Revan is Erevan, at present the capital of the republic of Armenia. In the remainder of the text we will give the name Erevan, although Evliya Chelebi consistently uses Revan.

the Bey of the castle of Shushik[9] was in revolt the Persians seized this opportunity and cleverly in one night brought Mazandarani (soldiers) and made the Maku citadel into a fort strong like Qahqaheh.[10]

THE DESCRIPTION OF THE CASTLE OF MAKU. It is situated next to the river; its lower part is narrow and the upper part is a vast plain. It is like a mushroom, slender in stem and rises to heaven, and it is difficult to access from every side, unconquerable and unique. It is connected by wooden bridges to the rocks around it at the lower parts. There is only one gate and from there like the stairs of a minaret, its staircase is cut into the rock and goes up. Inside there are about seven hundred houses. But they are not very prosperous. If it were repaired it would be a unique citadel like Qahqaheh.[11] It is the seat of a sultan within the khanate of Erevan. There are some two thousand Mazandarani musketeers in it. Every night they raise the bridge over the river. The rock of the castle stands like an island. They lift water to the higher parts of the castle with one hundred water-wheels to quench their thirst. The khan of this castle, who resides in the upper part, came down with about one thousand royal slaves and gave a grand feast to our party. After the banquet, our general Baqi Pasha asked for the Bey of Shushik and guaranteed that no harm would come to the soldiers, and trusting in God he brought the bey in one day to his castle and handed him over to Sayyed Ahmad Pasha. The latter came on the seventh day to Hinis Qal`eh[12] and handed him over to the governor of Erzerum, Mohammad Pasha, our master. All the governors-general, emirs, soldiers, Ahmad Agha of Avenik and others begged him not to kill him, and he was imprisoned. In the end, after he had given forty thousand sheep, forty horses, seventeen strings of mules, twenty Georgian slaves and fifty purses of goods, he was set free. But his castle was given to the Bey of Malazgird, Mohammad Bey, who gave twenty purses, twenty strings of mules, innumerable lynx and tiger skins, and seven pieces of armor, helmets and neck-protectors. All Moslem warriors of the faith returned safely and victoriously to Erzerum with their booty.

That day, after traveling for seven hours, we alighted at the village of Alajalar. It is situated on the banks of the Aras River in the district of Bayazid Qal`eh; it is a village of three hundred Armenians and Moslems. Here our master gave a great feast and cordial letters to Qasem Khan, the emissary of the Khan of Erevan, to Taqi Khan, the emissary of the Khan of Nakhjevan, and to Seyf `Ali Khan, the emissary of the Khan of Tabriz. To each one he gave a full-blood horse, a rosary made of coral, a bow and arrows, and some Genoese and Venetian porcelain. He said to all the envoys:

> We Ottomans do not believe in doing anything contrary to the peace; we reduced
> the Bey of Shushik, Mostafa Bey, and ravaged his district and gave his castle to

---

9. Shushik is situated about 25km south east of Karakilissa on the Murad Chai in Turkey.

10. For the history of Maku see V. Minorsky, "Maku," *Encyclopedia of Islam II*; Mir Asadollah Musavi Maku'i, *Tarikh-e Maku* (Tehran, 1376/1997); Hoseyn Qoli Eftekhari Bayat, *Tarikh-e Maku* (Tehran, 1381/2002).

11. Qahqaheh fort was a very strong fort located near the old Alamut castle of the Assassins and served as a prison during the Safavid period. Evliya Chelebi uses this fort as a model for any strong and impregnable fort. For a description and its remains see: Ehsan Eshraqi, "Cheshmandsai beh Qal`eh-ye Estakhr va Qahqaheh dar dowreh-ye Safaviyeh," *Honar va Mardom* 142 (1353/1974), pp. 16-23; Rostam Behrad'razi, *Qal`eh-ye Qahqaheh: zendan-e siyasi* (Ardabil?, 1375/1996).

12. Hinis Kalesi near Erzerum.

another bey. Our brother, the Khan of Erevan, had complained about him. Now, in accordance with the peace treaty, you have to remove the troops that you have put in the castle of Maku and destroy the castle, otherwise my general [13] who bears the royal standard will come with soldiers innumerable like the sea and plunder the regions of Erevan and Nakhjevan.

When he said these reproachful words the three emissaries bowed and said: "Upon our eyes." Because of this each one was given robes of Persian beaver. The *kilerji* Vali Agha,[14] accompanied by Qasem Khan, the emissary, went to Erevan. Alaja-atli Hasan Agha, the emissary, went to Nakhjevan with Taqi Khan. Because I was the Clerk of the Customs, and the merchants were coming to the customs-house, they gave this humble author the letters.

A Persian Breakfast

A bejeweled saddled horse, a purebred horse with cover and saddle, a good royal handkerchief, a rosary of pearls, and one quiver with arrows were given to Seyf ʿAli Khan, the emissary of the Khan of Tabriz. This humble author was given the same. Our master the pasha said: "My Evliya, may God protect you," and he entrusted us to the good care of the emissary, saying: "Please send the caravans to our customs-house," and letters to that effect were written to the Khan and were given to this humble author along with money for the road, one set of clothes, and for the eleven servants with me, who each were from a different group, he likewise gave to each five or ten people. Totally we were forty-five persons. All our friends bade us farewell and trusting in God we went to Erevan and Nakhjevan.

---

13. Cevdet, vol. 2, p. 229 has rightly read this to be *sardar-e moʿazzamim*, meaning 'my general.'

14. Vali Agha was a eunuch attached to the imperial larder or pantry (*kiler*), hence his title of *kilerji* or butler.

Description of what we saw of strange things on our journey going from the banks of the Aras River to the land of Persia and coming to Erevan, Nakhjevan and Tabriz

A View of Erevan

From the banks of the Aras River we went that day to the east for five hours[15] and we reached

The village of Yaylachik.[16] This is in the administrative district in Avenik, a half Armenian and half Moslem village, and its Moslems are Mahmudi Kurds. It has one large mosque. Then we went again to the east, along the banks of the Aras.

The stage of Barut-khaneh. This is subordinate to the castle of Shushik and is situated on the side of a valley. The village has three hundred houses, cultivation and pastures. It is a prosperous village. There is saltpeter in its soil. That's why they call it Barut-khaneh.[17] From here again towards the east we traveled for nine hours and reached:

---

15. Hammer, *Narrative*, vol. 1, p. 123 and Cevdet, vol. 2, p. 230 have 8 hours.

16. Yaylachik (Latitude: 40° 38' 60 N, Longitude: 42° 49' 0 E) is a village situated north-west of Qars.

17. Saltpeter is one of the ingredients of gun-powder, hence the name of the village Barut-khaneh or gunpowder magazine.

THE STAGE OF THE VILLAGE OF DUSHKAYA. It is a village in ruins. In a valley called Avah, near a sweet water stream, we pitched our tents and pavilions in a pasture full of tulips and had a good time. After twelve hours of travel towards the east we reached:

THE STAGE OF THE VILLAGE OF CHAGHLA GURNA. It is a prosperous village. All the people are Shushik Kurds. On our left side we could see the castle of Shushik upon steep rocks. They fired seven cannon salvos to greet us and their bey brought us much food and drinks as a gift. Here we parted company with Qasem Khan, the emissary of the Erevan Khan, and the *kilerji* of Nikasa[18], whose name was Vali Agha, who went to the left towards Erevan. This humble author with our emissary of the Khan of Nakhjevan went to the right and crossed the mountains to Nakhjevan. Going to the east, we passed several summer quarters, mountains and orchards, and after thirteen hours we reached:

THE STAGE OF THE CASTLE OF KARISH, which is the very first castle in the Persian kingdom. This castle was built by the son of Timur Khan, Shahrokh Mirza.[19] Later it came under the authority of the Sultan of Azerbaijan, Uzun Hasan.[20] Now it is part of the province of Erevan and one of the towns of Azerbaijan. The castle is situated on a hill and it is so high that hawks and eagles nest there. It is a quadrangular building made of rock and a delightful strong Azerbaijani castle. Inside it has one thousand royal slaves (*dizchokan tulungi*). When the head of the garrison offered presents to the emissaries who were with us, he displayed his joy by firing salvos from the seventy or eighty cannons. The sound of the cannons was booming from left and right like thunder from the sky. We pitched our tents below the castle and visited at our leisure the town outside the wall. The town is not very prosperous, but in the past it was. However, in the year 1043 [1634], when Sultan Murad IV was marching to Erevan, the soldiers from Erzerum, Akhiskha,[21] Qars and Van revolted, plundered the city and enslaved its people.[22] Since then the suburb has remained in that ruinous situation. It has up to seven large mosques with minarets, three bathhouses, small bazaars, and many orchards and gardens. The town's water and climate are very pleasant, because it is situated on the banks of the river. They cultivate rice. This river comes from Mt. Sukun and falls into the Aras River. The castellan (*dizdar*) invited the emissary and this humble author. With difficulty, we and our horses managed to get to the castle in half an hour. When we looked down the whole sight was as multi-colored as the feathers of the turkey. The chief of the royal slaves (*dizchokan aghasi*) had decorated the Safavid Sufi hat (*taj*)[23] which was on his head with plumes and came to us. He said: "May I be your sacrifice. Welcome. You gladden my eyes, you gladden

---

18. Niskar is a city in Toqat province. It is located at 40°35' north latitude and 36°58' east longitude.

19. He reigned from 1405 to 1447 and held most of Iran and Transoxiania.

20. Uzun Hasan of the Aq-Qoyunlu dynasty reigned from 1453 to 1478 over western Iran, Azerbaijan, Armenia, eastern Turkey, and Iraq. Evliya Chelebi later also refers to him as king of Erzenjan. For more information see John E. Woods, *The Aqquyunlu. Clan, Federation, Empire* (Minneapolis, 1976).

21. Akiska is situated in the Black Sea province of Sinop; its geographical coordinates are 41° 35' 0" North, 35° 4' 0" East.

22. Murad IV (r. 1623-1640). On this campaign to Erevan see *Cambridge History of Iran*, vol. 6, pp. 283-85.

23. On the Safavid Sufi hat or *taj* see Floor, *The Persian Textile Industry, Its Products and Their Use 1500-1925*. pp. 277–89.

my face."[24] Saying this he invited us to his house which had views on every side. He showed very good hospitality and quickly spread a calico as a tablecloth in front of us. Eleven types of pilau were brought: cilantro-mint chutney rice (*abshileh*), rice omelette (*kuku*), sweet saffron rice with pistachio and almonds (*mozaffari*),[25] rice with aloe (*'ud*), oven-baked rice (*shileh*),[26] rice with stew [?] (*khosh*),[27] steamed plain rice (*chelow pilau*), perfumed rice (*mo'ambar*), garlic rice, *koseh* rice,[28] twice-steamed plain rice [?] (*duzde*), twice steamed rice [?] *beryani* with roasted vegetables, *namakdan*, cilantro-mint sherbet,[29] yogurt soup (*mastaba*), and delicious boiled wheat puddings; we ate well from everything and had a nice conversation. After the feast he gave presents of beautiful lynx skins to the emissary, this humble servant, and Alaja-atli Hasan Agha. We came down to our tents. Later he sent us about fifty sheep, about one thousand loaves of white bread, seven or eight mules loaded with fruit and cilantro-mint sherbet. That night we had a grand feast and stayed two more days. We looked at the mansions which were near the river Karish and viewed the beautiful buildings on the two sides of the promenade and went to the paradisiacal Kalantar garden, and there we had another feast, and he gave valuable gifts to the emissary and this humble author. When we returned from the garden we looked at the outside of the Sultan Owhadollah Mosque, which is truly a beautiful, peerless large mosque with one well-proportioned minaret. Near it is the Taj al-Din Monshi bathhouse, where there were seven guesthouses. Because of the enchanting quality of its water and climate, the bewitching eyes of the women and the youths are such that when they look at their lovers, they give life to more than a thousand others. The next morning, at sunrise, we left the city, with three hundred Qizilbash ruffians and Mazandarani scoundrels. We traveled for thirteen hours towards the east and came to:

THE STAGE OF THE VILLAGE OF MASIR. The word *kent* (village) in these parts is used to denote a small town (*qasabeh*). It is situated on the slopes of Mt. Masir and has about one thousand mud houses, with orchards and gardens. It is a prosperous town with clear water and mountain streams; it is a beautiful village. It has seven large mosques, three bathhouses, and about three hundred small shops. It is part of Erevan province under a chief (*kalantar*). In that beautiful place we were guests for one night and then departed from there, and after traveling fourteen hours we reached:

---

24. Both Cevdet, vol. 2, p. 231 and Kahraman, vol. 2, p. 116 read this sentence wrongly by separating *qorban* and *to*. The sentence should be read as: *Hey qorban-e to, kheyr maqdam*, which is Persian. The rest of the sentence is Turkish: هی قربان تو، خیر مقدم! یوز بصه بصه، گوز بصه بصه صفا گلدکز!

25. This rice is cooked with syrup, butter and saffron.

26. A type of *tahchin*, where the meat is cooked first, then the rice and vegetables are added. Another type of dish, also called *sholeh* is made of meat, wheat and chickpea puree; these wheat purees are still made in Mashhad.

27. *Khosh pilau* perhaps is *khoresh pilau* or rice with a stew. Later, p. 171, Evliya mentions *khoshk pilau*.

28. *Kuseh pilau* perhaps is a writing error for *kufteh pilau*, rice with meatballs.

29. *Ab shileh*, according to the *Karnameh va Madat al-Hayat* ed. Iraj Afshar (Tehran, 1360/1981), p. 110 is prepared as follows: "They mix unripe grapes with coriander and mint, mix it with water and then put ice or snow and sometimes they add unripe plums or mint araq and make in into a beverage." The same source mention many kinds of *kuku* or a kind of an omelette (Ibid., index). The other dishes are not mentioned in this Safavid cookbook. For an overview of modern Persian dishes see Batmanglij, *New Food for Life*.

The small town of Zuchan. This town is in the region of Nakhjevan and forms part of Nakhjevan province. It is a very prosperous town with many flowers. The guide was very gracious. Persian youths came from this town and served us; they were good singers. When they were singing in the Khorasani style, one's soul was delighted.[30] We went to the east again for seven hours, through a wide valley with impressive trees, and then reached:

The stage of Uch Kilisa.[31] This place is on the border with Erevan. On the top of three high mountains there are three large monasteries; in each of them there are a couple of hundred Armenian patriarchs, monks, and priests. There are very beautiful Magian[32] youths, who stand to serve whomever comes and goes. One of these convents was built by Anurshirvan, one by the Byzantine emperor, and one by an Armenian lady, in which there are more than five hundred virgin maidens, who eat nothing but broad-beans. In these convents they serve all travelers and pilgrims and give them milk, dates and sweetmeats and provide them with gilt sleeping clothes and take care of all their horses. Among the Christians, the Armenians have great faith in these convents and from all over the lands of the infidels they bring offerings, and it is very well endowed. Each one has five to ten guest-masters and forty to fifty cooks, whose wheat boiled with meat and boiled-wheat pudding are famous over the world. The chief priest, accompanied by two hundred priests, gave a great feast to the emissaries and the humble author with presents after the banquet.

A view of Uch Kalisa

---

30. About Persian music and the various singing styles see Lloyd Miller, *Music and Song in Persia. The Art of Awaz* (Salt Lake City, 1999).

31. For a short historical overview see S. Peter Cowe, "Ejmiatsin," *Encyclopedia Iranica*. Uch Kilisa is the Turkish name for this town.

32. It is a bit odd to have Zoroastrian youths serve in an Armenian convent.

THE CURIOSITIES OF UCH KILISA. At the grand convent built by Anushirvan, every year about forty to fifty thousand infidels come from the lands of Europe. In Uch Kilisa, on the top of the mountain, they spread out an old rug in a pasture.[33] In the summer, in these mountains, they gather whatever useful plants and herbs that are of medicinal value and put them into a big cauldron. On the rug they make a big fire using a tripod from which they hang the cauldron. Whatever herbs are in in the cauldron, they boil them for more than one hour, but the fire does not burn the rug at all, and several thousand people watch it in wonder. Then they divide the food made of these herbs among all the infidels.[34] Some people take that food to Europe as a blessing; some eat it there and they praise and enjoy it. This humble person asked its secret from the priests. They said:

> By God, this is the same carpet on which Jesus fell issuing from his mother's womb; when he was confined in a cave with his twelve disciples out of fear of the Israelites, they gathered all these herbs, made a fire on the carpet and cooked them. And the Israelites on asking for a miracle from the prophet Jesus, he restored a dead king to life on this carpet. As a miracle, he had [the disciples] cook a meal on this carpet and gave dinner to the Israelites. Later this carpet passed into the hands of Nebuchadnezzar. Then from him it came into the hands of Anushirvan the Just, who, every year after building this convent, cooked food on the carpet, cleaned it and then wrapped it in a bundle and safeguarded it. Sultan Sulayman during his Nakhjevan campaign[35] came and prayed making two genuflections on this carpet.

It seems that the wondrous rug is neither made of silk nor of cotton or wool. It is like a large prayer rug in the color of some kind of squirrel. It is very heavy. According to the deficient intelligence of this humble person, it is made of some kind of stone which comes from a big mountain on the island of Cyprus.[36] By God's wisdom, when they pound it with a mallet it becomes like linen and then they make it into handkerchiefs, beautiful and elegant dresses and shirts, which they take as gift to the great men of Istanbul and the kings. Murad IV said in jest to [his sister] Kaya Sultan, [the lady] of our master [Malek Pasha]: "My Kaya (My Rock) I am giving you a shirt that is made of rock." And he gave her a shirt and a dress. For a time, Kaya Sultan used to wear this shirt made of rock, and after it had become dirty she used to put it into the fire and it came out clean and white. It was a fancy and fine shirt. Among the nobles there are many of them. Kaptan

---

33. Hammer, p. 125 translates: "to witness the solemnity of an old carpet being spread on the top of the mountain."

34. Uch Kilisa (meaning Three Churches) refers to the complex of Ejmiatsin (the Holy See of the Armenians and the Mother Cathedral–together with the churches of Hripsime and Gayane). It was founded by St. Gregory the Illuminator in 301 according to Armenian tradition. The herbs are gathered and put in a large silver caldron and then blessed with the spear that pierced the side of Christ and other relics and prepare the Holy Chrism (meron), an oil which is then sent to all Armenian churches in the world for blessing in various ceremonies. It is not eaten, but used to make the sign of the cross on the forehead and lips.

35. The Nakhjevan campaign took place in 1548-1549.

36. The rock referred to is asbestos, which already was woven into cloth during Antiquity. In Persian it is called *adharshast* or *adharshab* and cloth made from it was called *shekasteh*, according to al-Biruni. He also reported that wealthy Persians amazed their guests by throwing the table cloth into the fire to clean it. Dehkhoda, q.v. *adharshast*.

Husamzadeh gave a kerchief of this kind to this humble person. Whenever it became dirty it was burnt in front of Malek Ahmed Pasha and it became very clean white. God knows best; it could be said that this rug is made of Cyprus stone. That is it.

After visiting Uch Kilisa we started towards the east, passing many prosperous villages and beautiful places, gardens and mountains, and plains with fruitful lands. We did not see one cubit of empty saline soil and after nine hours we reached:

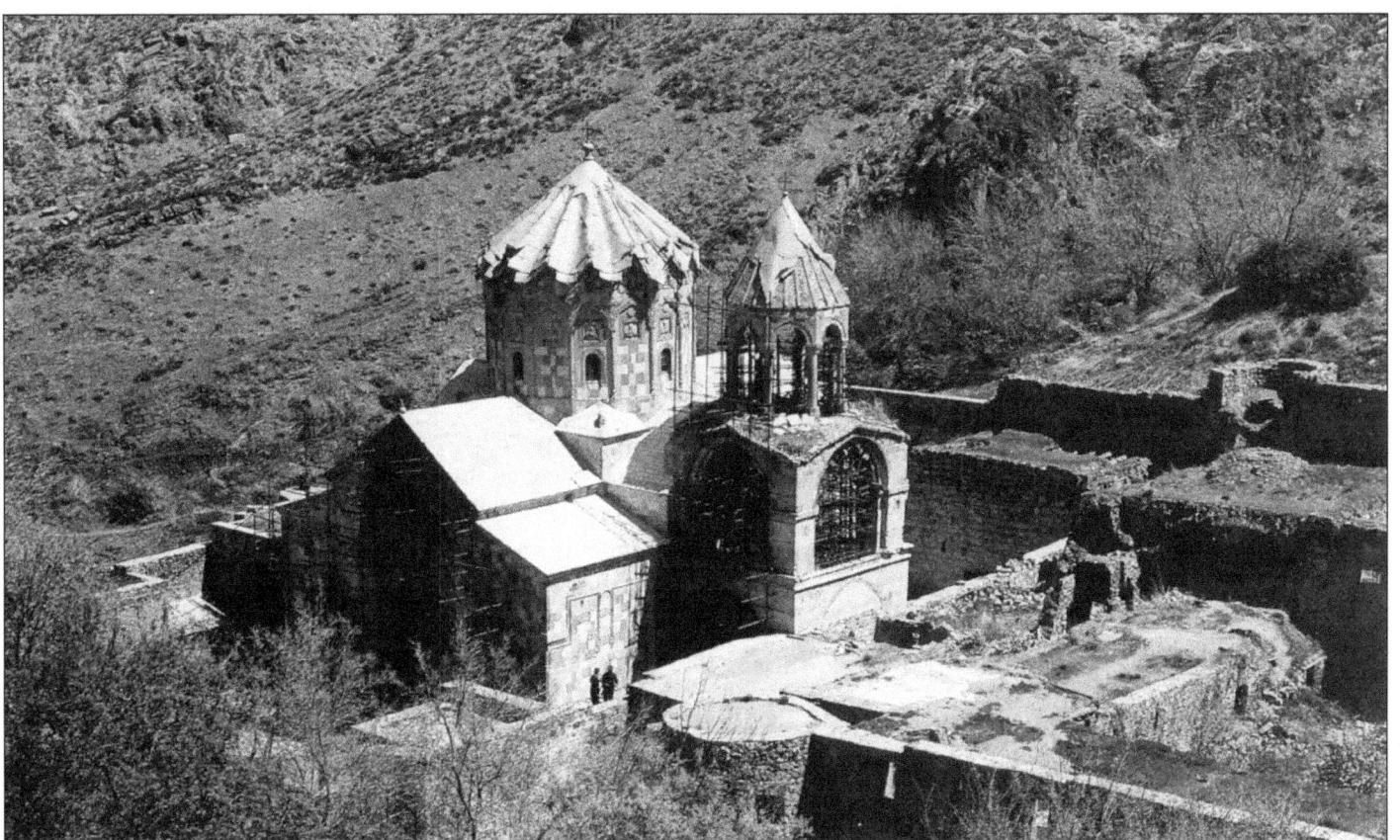

A view of St. Stepanos, Jolfa

THE VILLAGE OF SUKUN. It is situated near Nakhjevan at the foot of the Mt. Sukun. It is a prosperous village, which you would call a big town. You could see eleven minarets. But this humble person, being a little indisposed, could not properly see it.

DESCRIPTION OF THE PILGRIMAGE [OF THE TOMB OF] MOHAMMAD SHAM GHAZAN.

This is a great Bektashi convent of which the town of Sukun is an endowment.[37] It has more than three hundred bare-headed, bare-footed, and unadorned dervishes. They came to welcome us with beating drums and tambourines, flying banners, blowing horns and trumpets and cymbals and shouting "God is great." Truly, they are lovers of the holy family, gnostics, true dervishes, who have abandoned the world and they are a crowd of true lovers, kings of religious contemplation,

---

37. The Bektashi Sufi order was founded in the thirteenth century. See R. Tschudi, "Bektashi," *Encyclopedia of Islam II*.

they are bewildered by the beauty of the beloved, drunk with divine love. We put several *'abbasi*s and *bisti*s under their candles and benefiting of the good prayers of their Sheikh Ne'mat-Dedeh, by God's grace I was restored to health by him. The next day, early in the morning, we arose and traveled in this endless plain for thirteen hours. Three times en route we rested in pastures. Then on the southern side of this plain, at the end of this pasture, we reached:

THE STAGE OF THE BIG RIVER ZANGI. We pitched our tents on the river bank. By the grace of God, all over this plain people were yelling "the Ottomans have come". With extreme joy they brought much food and beverages and they showed extreme hospitality. The horses were in front of our tents and ate much grass, trefoil and clover such that their bellies swelled like royal wine-skins. The river Zangi issues south from the Haran Mountains and flows towards the north and it irrigates hundreds of towns and villages. Then it joins the Aras River, which falls into the Kur and then runs to the Sea of Gilan (the Caspian Sea). We continued towards the east and we traveled on the plains, while hunting hares, for about ten hours. Then we reached:

THE STAGE OF THE TOWN OF SIDIRGI. It is part of Nakhjevan province and an endowment of Imam 'Ali Reza. It is exempted from all taxes; it is a prosperous and lively town with one thousand houses, many gardens and orchards and a very good climate. All its inhabitants are Shi'ites.

THE SIDIRGI HOT SPRINGS. Outside the city, adjacent to gardens, there are hot springs with high domes. There are three hot springs and in each one there are big ten by ten [cubits?] basins. Persian youths swim like silver-bodied fish in the *shafe'i* basin and without any inhibition embrace each other. They sing love songs and have wonderful voices. Most of the inhabitants of this town are Gökdolaqs and weavers.[38] Again we traveled towards the east and after 13 hours we reached:

THE STAGE OF THE CONVENT OF AHMAD BEY.[39] It is part of Nakhjevan [province] and it is a prosperous city with five hundred houses, gardens and orchards. It has three large mosques. When the Ottoman [general] Zal Pashazadeh Ahmad Pasha was governor of Nakhjevan, he built a large, beautiful mosque with minarets in the Istanbul-style. This is why the Persians call it the *zaviyeh-ye Ahmad Pasha*. Now this town is the endowment of the mosque. After sixteen hours, having passed through many prosperous towns, we reached the big city of Qarabaghlar.

DESCRIPTION OF THE BIG CITY OF QARABAGHLAR.[40] The city was built by Manuchehr and is an ancient city. It is a separate sultanate in Nakhjevan. In former times it was an important city. In the year 1012 [1603-04], in the time of Mohammad III,[41] when it was in the hands of the Ottomans, it was conquered by the Persians. In the year 1045 [1635-36], the conqueror of Erevan, Murad IV, after conquering Erevan came to this town and stayed here; the city which was

---

38. Gökdolaq is a term that Evliya Chelebi uses to denote various different (Armenian, Persian, Turkic) groups, which distinguish themselves from other groups by wearing blue pieces of clothes. Bulut, p. 282 (*gök* means blue and *dolaq* means putties).

39. Ahmedbeyli is situated at longitude 390 33' 46N and latitude 370 33' 4E.

40. On the history of Qarabagh see C.E. Bosworth, "Kara Bagh," *Encyclopedia of Islam II*; Jamal Janvanshir Qarabaghi, *Tarikh-e Qarabagh* translated into English as *The History of Qarabagh* by George A. Bournoutian (Costa Mesa, 1994) and Ibid., *Two Chronicles on the History of Karabagh* (Costa Mesa, 2004).

41. Ottoman Sultan who reigned from 1595 to 1603.

like the fabled city of Eram of ancient times, was destroyed by him completely and its people were massacred, so that now only its ruins and destruction can be seen. Timur had winter quarters in Qarabaghlar and spent pleasant times here. It is a very prosperous, beautiful and a vast city. Sultan Sulayman, three times, and other commanders, several times, had winter quarters here with innumerable troops and lived there in great affluence for five to six months. This place is now recovering from the havoc wrought by Murad IV, but in comparison it is not a shadow of its former self. Our servants counted forty minarets there. God be praised that we were gladdened by the nature and climate of the city. We mounted our horses with some of our friends to see the city. According to what our conductor-of-guests said, it has around eleven thousand houses with gardens and orchards, seventy mosques, forty of which have minarets. There are many caravanserais, bathhouses and bazaars, but they are not properly maintained. It is a land of plenty both of food and beverages. Because of the mild climate you see good-looking youths and women. The goodness of its fruits, food, and beverages are not to be found in other places. If we call it Black Gardens (Qarabaghlar) there is a reason for it. While the emissary and I were visiting a garden, a gardener called Yazdan Quli, brought us twenty-six different kinds of juicy delicious pears. When you eat these pears, which are known as *melejeh*, *'abbasi*, and Ordubadi, their juice flows like clear sugary syrup [in your mouth]. It has very delicious pears and ruby-colored pomegranates. In the royal bazaars there are very clean cooks, who prepare various kinds of Erevan rice and wheat-boiled pudding, which are extremely delicious and well-scented. The cooks are very clean, because they are Moslems. In the whole of Persia there is no Rumi (Greek orthodox) or Armenian among the vendors of edibles.[42] Indeed, there are no infidel Greeks here, unless they come as merchants, but there are many Jews, Shi'ites, Tabarra'is, and Qurayas.[43] There are many atheists, heretics, Ja'faris (Twelver Shi'ites), Jabris[44] and Qadaris,[45] Hurufis,[46] and Zaminites.[47] There are very many such heretics. After visiting Qarabagh we traveled to the south and after 9 hours we reached the castle of Nakhjevan.

THE DESCRIPTION OF THE CASTLE OF NAKHJEVAN.[48] In truth, it is a world-renowned and colorful city. Some call it Nakhjevan and others Nakhshevan. Its existence is an honor to Iranian cities. It is situated on the border of Azerbaijan. It is a separate khanate and its Khan

---

42. This was due to the fact that as non-Moslems Christians and others like them are ritually unclean and at that time the Shi'ite Iranians did not want to soil their bodies or clothes by coming into contact with foodstuffs that had been handled by non-Moslems.

43. Jevdet, vol. 2, p. 235 has Qarabi. We think this perhaps is a writing error for Karami, who were followers of Abi 'Abdollah Mohammad b. Karam, a Sunni group who were anthropomorphist. See Karamustafa, pp. 30-31.

44. Those who believe in predestination. W. Montgomery Watt, "Djabriyya," *Encyclopedia of Islam II*.

45. Qadaris were believers in free will, see J. van Ess, "Kadariyya," *Encyclopedia of Islam II*.

46. An unorthodox Muslim sect of Gnostic-cabalistic tendencies founded by Fazlollah of Astarabad in Iran at the end of the 8th/14th century. See A. Bausani, "Hurufiyya," *Encyclopedia of Islam II*.

47. This Zamini sect is unknown to us. Evliya also mentioned this group in his description of Diarbekr. Van Bruinessen, p. 204, n. 18.

48. On its history see Rauf Mammadov, *Nakhchyvan shaharinin tarikhi ocherki: orta asrlar dovru* (Baku: Elm, 1977). For its remaining monuments see B. Salamzade and K.M. Mamedzade, *Pamyatniki Nakhitshevanckoi Azerbaizhanskovo Zodtshesva* (Baku, 1985).

has the largest number of soldiers. There is a grand vizierate,[49] clerk of the mayor,[50] police chief,[51] chief of the royal slaves,[52] chief of the raw flesh eaters[53] and all of these functions are part of government. It also has a qazi and a *sheikh al-Islam*.[54] This city was built by king Afrasiyab[55] in ancient times. The domes under which its ancestors are buried can still be seen. Under his rule Nakhjevan was so prosperous that in all its plains one pace of uncultivated land could not be found. Then in the year 691 [1292] the Mongols came and brought countless soldiers and out of greed they destroyed this world-famous city and turned its castle into dust. Then Shah Esma`il came and rebuilt it. {After that, in the year 912 [1506-07], during the reign of Mohammad III,[56] the erring shah sent Dhu'l-Feqar Khan to seize Nakhjevan and he did so.[57]} Then in the year [-] Murad IV's soldiers came and Tabaniyassi (Flatfooted) Mohammad Pasha conquered this place. The affairs of the world are like that, as they say:

> They destroy a thousand works
> They bring forth a thousand movements
> This work is wondrous, because
> He who makes it cannot be found.

---

49. Evliya Chelebi is mistaken. There was only one grand vizier in Iran, who was the head of the government. At that time in Iran there were two types of provinces, *khasseh* (royal) and *mamalek* (state). The former were governed by a royal vizier, which is what he must have meant, the latter by a governor or *hakem*. For the organization and functioning of the Safavid government see Floor, *Safavid Government Institutions*; Floor and Faghfoory, *Dastur al-Moluk. A Safavid State Manual*; and Nasiri, *Titles and Emoluments in Safavid Iran*.

50. *Kalantar* or the mayor of a city (or of a large village), see Floor, "Kalantar," *Encyclopedia Iranica*.

51. *Darugheh* or chief of the police, see Floor, "The Secular Judicial System in Safavid Persia," *Studia Iranica* 29 (2000), pp. 9-60.

52. Evliya Chelebi invariably uses the term *dizchoken aghasi* to denote the chief of the soldiers. *Diz chokan* literally means 'he who kneels,' but he also uses it as a synonym for the Turkish term *yenicheri* or Janissaries, and therefore the term may refer to the Safavid counterpart of the Janissari corps, to wit that of the *qollar*s or *gholam*s. On the latter see Floor, *Safavid Government*, pp. 166-75.

53. Under the early Safavids their fanatic Sufi soldiers aka Qizilbash practiced ritual cannibalism. Whether as an outgrowth of this or not, but under Shah `Abbas I (r. 1586-1629) so-called *chi yayin* or raw flesh eaters served as executioners. These men, who were all big, strong and revolting to look at, served under the *jarchi-bashi* or chief herald and wore a peculiar dress such as a thick Sufi hat (*taj*) measuring one ell (*dhar`*) without turban, which was embellished with crane feathers. See Floor, "The khalifeh al-kholafa of the Safavid sufi order." Evliya Chelebi is the only source to mention them as not only existing after Shah `Abbas I, but also as being attached to a governor's staff in a great many cities.

54. In Safavid Iran the qazi and *sheikh al-Islam* both were religious judges, the latter official, who had a similar function to that of the qazi, was higher in rank, see Floor, "The sadr or head of the Safavid religious administration, judiciary and endowments and other members of the religious institution."

55. Afrasiyab was the king of Turan, one of the chief figures in Iran's national epos the *Shah-nameh*. For those interested to read this text see Ferdowsi, *Shahnameh: The Persian book of Kings*.

56. The year 912 must be a writing error for 982 as the regal dates of Mohammad II are 1566-1603.

57. Dhu'l-Feqar Khan Qaramani was one of the generals of Shah `Abbas I, who at the beginning of the campaign to retake Azerbaijan was governor of Azerbaijan and Ardabil (1593-1605). From 1606-1610, he was governor of Shirvan, Baku, Darband and Shamakhi, but not of Nakhjevan. See Nasiri, *Titles & Emoluments in Safavid Iran*, pp. 148, 155, 160, 263, 286.

As the poem indicates the state of the world sometimes is ruinous and sometimes is prosperous. As is said clearly in the Koran: "All things perish."[58] After Murad IV this place never prospered. It has eleven thousand two hundred mud houses, seventy large mosques and places of worship, forty small mosques, twenty hostelries, seven beautiful bathhouses, and about one thousand shops. Most of the buildings are beautiful. In truth, it is situated in the fourth clime, in the middle of the eighteenth latitude; its climate is rather severe. Because it has few orchards and gardens it does not have many fruits.

It has seven types of cotton(*zagi*, *molayi*, *zafrani*, *la'li*, *khass*, and *bayaz*) and its wheat is famous. Every kind of craftsman can be found there. Its Bahrampuri chintz and printed fabrics for tablecloth are famous. All its plains are very wide and pleasant. Four *oqqeh*[59] of its black barley is enough for one horse. Its barley is nourishing and its orchards have water cisterns and produce melon and water-melon. Because of its temperate climate the complexion of its male and female beauties is white. The men wear a Safavid pleated Sufi hat[60] and a long turban wrapped around it, and a chintz *peshk-push* dress. They wear colored felt trousers, and green, red, orange and mandarin-colored footwear. The women wear pointed skull-caps, white gauze over their face, and on their feet colored boots. Its beauties wear different blue sheepskin Isfahani caps, they walk pleasingly and swaggering like *mirza*s (scribes), they converse nicely and they talk wittily and politely and are pleasant in conversation with people. But the men have little inclination towards boys. Left amongst a group of lovers of women there is an abundance of neglected beauties and youths.

Its people are all Shafe'is, but in reality they are very Qizilbash. "We are from the Shafe'i school," they boast. But it is a lie, they are Ja'faris.[61] At the time of the call to prayer five times they pray, but they don't pray communally at all. There are many large mosques amongst which many very wondrous ones; each one of them is like paradise. Among them, the Ahmad Pasha mosque, the Farhad Pasha mosque, the Guzel 'Ali Pasha mosque, the Jaghal-oghlu mosque, and the Khadem Ja'far Pasha mosque are decorated with multi-colored Chinese style tiles. The cupolas of some of them are covered with tiles. They have thirty-three minarets in the Istanbul style. The mosque of Ahmad Pasha is similar to the Rostam Pasha mosque in Istanbul.

The Janab bathhouse is very pleasant, has a good ambiance, is well-lit and it is tiled all over. Its floor is covered with rose-colored marble. All its bath-towels have a chess-pattern design. All of its masseurs are exquisite beauties with eyes like deer from Khotan. In the place we stayed in the Zal Pasha bathhouse, they serve you while their crystal-like bodies are wrapped in indigo-colored loin-cloth.

Near our guesthouse there was the Zal Pasha bathhouse, which one should visit. It has an agreeable atmosphere, with pleasant masseurs and other excellent servants; it is a delightful bathhouse. The entire interior is covered with Chinese-style tiles. Its floor is totally covered with beautiful jasper, sumac-colored marble, and granite of various hues. It is so well-lit, because all its glass windows are made of crystal of Najaf. Right under the center of its high dome it has a big basin

---

58. Koran 28: 88 (al-Qasas).

59. One *oqqah* equals 400 *dirham*s of 3.207 gram each or 1.28 kg.

60. The term used is *zurzuvileli taj*.

61. Ja'faris or those who follow the Shi'ite school of jurisprudence named after the sixth Shi'ite Imam Ja'far al-Sadiq. They constitute the majority of Shi'ites and are also referred to as Twelvers, after the twelve Imams, whom they believe to be divinely appointed leaders.

of ten by ten [cubits?]. And all the beauties are swimming like naiads. Every day the bath-keeper pours a basketful of rose-petals into the basin, so that it looks as if all the bathers are swimming in rose water; the rose-petals cover their white silvery bodies, their rose-colored faces shine and their rose-colored lips become like Badakhshan rubies. All the beauties in the basin playfully and freely throw peacock and dove feathers, they play and have fun, and meanwhile by covering their private parts they preserve their dignity and play. In short, in praising this beautiful bathhouse; its beauty and cleanliness, Hesan, the famous Arab poet,[62] and Sahban[63] cannot do justice to it, and neither can this poor Evliya. In the royal bazaar there are rich merchants and wealthy traders. Each one of them possesses more than one hundred thousand *tuman*s in goods and they are rich like Croesus, who trade on land and sea.[64] All the people of the city are given to pleasure and merry making and spend part of every day in each other's gardens. The Khan of Nakhjevan, Reza al-Din Khan,[65] when he came to greet us, took his emissary and this humble servant to a garden, where the cordial letters were read. All the notables of Nakhjevan were present and he ordered a party of music and poetry, attended by singers and musicians as if it was a party of Hoseyn Beyqara.[66] One would say that the Khan was a man of pleasant conversation and of friendly disposition. He was a Georgian boy who became chief treasurer when Shah Safi [I] gave Sultan Murad [IV] Baghdad.[67] In his manners and thoughts he is Aristotle-like. His name is Dowlat Mirza Khan. After this party in the garden, he first gave to the one who had come from the Pasha our master as emissary, Hasan Agha Alajeh-Atli, and this humble author a robe of honor, tens of *tuman*s as bathhouse money,[68] one horse, and he gave a robe of honor to his own emissary. In this way he was a generous khan. He has about forty or fifty knowledgeable men with foresight and many boon companions, who possess every kind of knowledge.

The people of this city speak the Dehqani language, but the learned poets and the refined boon companions speak the Pahlavi and Mongolian language in a refined and polished manner, which are old languages. The cities are old and its inhabitants use these languages. First, the Dehqani language, then the Dari language, the Farsi and Parsi language, the Ghazi language, and the Pahlavi language; we will mention them in their proper places.[69]

---

62. Hesan b. Thabit (563-674), a famous Arab poet.

63. Sahban (d. 674) was a famous poet and preacher.

64. Qarun a figure of Moslem mythology; the same as the biblical Qorah (Croesus).

65. No particulars are known about Reza al-Din Khan.

66. Hoseyn Beyqara ruled over Khorasan from 1469 to 1506. His court was an important cultural center for men of letters and artists and his parties were exemplary.

67. He is not mentioned in contemporary chronicles concerning the reign of Shah Safi I.

68. Bathhouse money or *garmabeh baha* is first mentioned in 1030 in the *Tarikh-e Beyhaqi*, see Dehkhoda, q.v. *garmabeh baha*. This custom continued into the nineteenth century: "The King had hitherto been in the habit of immediately allowing a settled sum of money to all Europeans who appeared at his Court, under the name of 'bath-money.'" Moritz von Kotzebue, *Narrative of a Journey into Persia ... in the year 1817* (Philadelphia, 1820), p. 236.

69. The Dehqani language is not a language; Evliya Chelebi probably means to say that the people talk the vernacular or like peasants as is suggested by his remark that courtiers spoke a refined language. The Durri language probably refers to Dari, which is just another term to denote Persian or Farsi. The Ghazi language is unknown to us, while with the term Pahlavi language Evliya probably denotes the Tati language, a northwestern Iranian language.

Whirling Dervishes

It has been mentioned in the *Tafsir-e Deylami*[70] that the prophet (PBUH), asked the Archangel Michael: "Has God almighty said anything in Persian?" He said: "Yes, O prophet of God, in the books of Abraham, (PBUH).," he said: "What shall I do with this handful of sinners other than sending them the Message." The prophet (PBUH) said: "Whoever ridicules the Ghazi language is an unbeliever, by God." And the prophet said (PBUH): "The language of the people of Paradise is Arabic and Dari-Farsi."[71] [Concerning the Persian language], Kamal Pasha-zadeh writes in his work *Daqayeq al-Haqayeq* [the meaning of some words]:[72]

---

70. Evliya's *Tafsir-e Deylami* most likely is the important study by Abu Mohammad Ruzbahan b. Abu Nasr Shirazi Deylami (522-606), *Kitab al-`Ara'is al-Bayan fi Haqa'iq al-Qu'ran*. Alternatively, this could be the *Ferdows-e Deylami* or *Mostanadd-e Deylami* by the 5th century scholar Abu'l-Fath Deylami. This Tradition has been quoted in al-Kafi as being a 'weak' one.

71. The script below is from Chelebi's original text with some minor fixes of the typographical errors:
سأل رسول الله صلى الله عليه و سلم عن ميكائيل عليه السلام هل يقول الله تعالى شيئاً بالفارسيه ؟ قال نعم، يا رسول الله يقول الله فى صُحف ابراهيم(ع.م.) چه كنم با اين مشت خاك ستمكاران جز آنكى پيام آرم. قال النبى عليه السلام من طعن حركة الغازى فهوه كافر بالله و قال النبى عليه السلام لسان اهل الجنه العربيه و الفارسيه الدريه.

72. Kamal Pashazadeh (d. 1534), see Christiane Bulut, *Evliya Chelebis Reise von Bitlis nach Van* (Wiesbaden, 1997), p. 281.

Yek (one)	*du* (two)	*seh* (three)
char (four)	*panj* (five)	*shesh* (six)
haft (seven)	*hasht* (eight)	*noh* (nine)
deh (ten)	*yanezdeh* (sic; *yazdah* – eleven)	*davazdah* (twelve)
sanzdeh (sic; *sizdah* – thirteen)	*chardeh* (fourteen)	*ized* (God)
yezdan (God)	*khoda* (God)	*parvardegar* (God)
peyember; peygambar; payambar (prophet)	*nan* (bread)	*ab* (water)
gandom (wheat)	*arzan* (millet)	*khvab* (dream)
mast (yogurt)	*biya, marow ey pesar* (come, don't go my boy)	*berow* (go)
marow (don't go)	*beguy* (say)	*Ey pedarema* (O my father)
Ey baradarema (O my brother)	*kaseh* (bowl)	*kuzeh* (cup)
sabu (pitcher)	*ham* (sic *khom*--earthenware jar)	*jarub* (broom)
zin (saddle)	*namad* (felt)	*tang* (narrow)
tank (girth)	*bardom* (sic; *pardom* – crupper strap)	*sineh-band* (breastband)
havid (camel pack-saddle)	*fitrak* (back of saddle)	*rekab* (stirrup)
legam (reins)	*afsar* (halter)	*peshmagand*[1] (saddle cloth)
taziyaneh (whip)	*jameh* (dress)	*pirahan* (shirt)
dur-riseh; (sic; *duz riye* flax spindle)	*kutlan* (goat-hair spindle)	*motreb* (string instrument player)
pilevar – peddler)	*'asalak* (mastic)	*'asalak Rumi* (Turkish mastic)
valizeh (black mastic)	*gundurud* (daily)[2]	*serih* (honey)[3]
angard (honey[4])	*angabin* (manna)	*abkameh* (bread stew)
baha (is a food made of lamb feet aka as *pacheh*);	*sigba* (sic; *sikpa* – stew with vinegar)[5]	*haygine* (sic; *khakineh* – omelette)
kuzat (rice stew)	*kachi* (porridge; but in Persian it means: sweetmeat like halva)	*chengal khast* (dried bread mixed with butter and cheese[6])
lozineh (almond confection)	*batileh* (sic; *patil* – confection cauldron)	

1. *Pashmagand* refers to any fabric made of wool as *qazagand* does the same in the case of silk.
2. This word does not exist in Persian.
3. A word *serih* meaning honey does not exist in Persian; it means 'flowing, moving fast.'. The author perhaps wanted to write *sarish* or glue.
4. Chelebi gives honey as the meaning. *Angazhd* is a bad smelling tree product, aka *samgh* that like *angabin* or manna is an exudation of certain plants and used like honey. For more information see Floor, *Traditional Crafts in Qajar Iran*. pp. 370-75.
5. *Sikpa*, from *serkeh* (vinegar) plus *ba* (= *ash* or soup). It is made as follows. They grind wheat and then soak it in vinegar and let it dry. Then when the soup is prepared this vinegar-soaked wheat is added to it.
6. *Chengal, chengali* or *chegal khast* is a food which is made of pieces of bread, hot oil, and honey.

Drink from this date wine, it is sweet like halva
That keeps you away from the blame of the fasting Sufi
Because I saw his very delicious and life-inspiring food
And I set this chronogram, may his bounty continue.

مرين بنگ خور ما خور که در حلواست جای او
همیشه در امان باد از طعن صوفئ صائم
چو دیدم قوت او شیرین روان از جان و دل حقا
بگفتم بهر او تاریخ بادا "نعمتش دائم"

Which means the year 923 [1517].

They have more sayings and maxims, but this much will suffice. In the villages around us, among the Gökdolaq and Mongol ethnic groups they have many different dialects, which, God willing, will be explained in their proper place.

In the plains of Nakhjevan there are strong castles. We saw many of them. We could not properly look at them, because we only came across them when we were hunting. The names of these castles are:

First of all, the strongest and best among them is Alinjak Van built by Mullah Qotb al-Din, then the castle of Seran, and next the castle of Susushmarvan. The very last one was built by the Ommayad Caliph Marwan Himar, and therefore it is called Sus-e Marvan.[73]

It is interesting to note that all the castles of Persia have very similar names to those of Erevan, Shirvan, Hamadan, Nakhjevan, Gilan and Mazandaran, Van of Azerbaijan and Isfahan.

But the names of the castles of Tabaristan are like Bigh kerman, Cherkez kerman, Yar kerman, Qersh kerman, Taman kerman, Shahin kerman, Arbat kerman, In kerman, Ghazi kerman, Doghan kerman, Ozi kerman, and Aq kerman.[74]

[The names of Polish castles are Kamanikaa and Alunjissa. The names of the castles in Trasylvania terminate in ár, as Sakmár, Sakswár, Oivár, etc. The German castles are Iran, Comoin, Tata, Papa, Santmarton, Posononium, Bedj (Vienna), the latter is the residence of the German Emperor. Amongst the names of Ottoman towns, those of the Holy land are the most sounding. The whole Ottoman Empire consists of seventy seats of Begler-Begs, three hundred and sixty sanjak Begs, and thirteen hundred and eighty strong castles. May they all remain in the power of the Ottoman family until the end of the World: Amen! The names of the Persian castles will be given in the course of our travels.][75]

---

73. Marwan b. Mohammad b. Marwan aka Marwan II (r. 744-750) was the last Ummayad caliph. As of 732 he had been governor of Azerbaijan and Armenia, where he remained until shortly before his becoming caliph.

74. Kerman means castle.

75. As the text between [ ] does not concern Iran we have not translated it, but have offered Hammer's abridged translation of this part of the text. Hammer, vol. 1, p. 129.

We departed after having seen Nakhjevan in this way, and having received from the Khan ten *tuman*s in '*abbasi*s, fifty full and long robes with sleeves, one Qarachuboq horse and letters for the Khan of Tabriz.

Description of the journey to Tabriz

First, coming from Nakhjevan, we went for eight hours towards the south and arrived at:

The stage of Kesik Gonbad (Broken Dome). It is a town with one thousand houses, gardens, orchards, three large mosques, a caravanserai and a bathhouse.

The pilgrimage to the tomb of Mirza Reza, son of Hoseyn Beyqara. The people of the town say that this tomb is of the son of Hoseyn Beyqara. On the box of the tomb has been written: "This is the unfortunate son of Bahador-e Shaghad b. Hoseyn Beyqara." It has a high dome with nine arches. The attendant of the tomb is also from the family of Hoseyn Beyqara. They said: "This town is an endowment to this tomb." From there we left, and after seven hours of travel we reached:

The big Aras River. The northern part of it issues forth from the mountains of the Pinyanish Kurds in Van province, flows towards the North and merges with the Zangi River. You can cross it on horseback. We traveled for one hour from here through blooming gardens, and prosperous villages and reached Qarabagh.

Description of the city of Little Qarabagh. It is one of the cities of Azerbaijan and its founder was [-]. The great general Khoja Farhad Pasha, the vizier of Sultan Mohammad III, the conqueror of Egri,[76] destroyed this place. Now you can still see traces of the ruins. After that it prospered, and in the year [-], because of disobedience of its people, Murad IV destroyed it again when he returned from Erevan. At present, it is gradually becoming prosperous. It is a sultanate within the governate of Tabriz and has one thousand soldiers. It has a mayor, a police chief, a clerk, a commander of one thousand and a chief of the royal slaves. The city is situated on a plain like the Garden of Eden. It has three thousand houses, seven large mosques, seven bathhouses, three caravanserais, and six hundred shops. It is a very enjoyable city in a vast bountiful district. It has pleasant and attractive shrines. The beauties of both sexes are pretty and pleasing. It has many farms; its products are plentiful and it is a small prosperous town. It has an excellent climate, with many streams with clean and delicious water. Its gardens and orchards are spread out over the plain as if without limits. Among its fruits and beverages twelve types of juicy, ruby-colored grapes are famous, as well as good wine, cherry juice, *shelesi* juice, and eighteen types of plums and juicy and delicious pomegranates. In particular, quinces as big as a man's head are famous. Its waters flow under the ground via subterraneous channels, and in summer it has icy water.[77] The domes of the small and the large mosques are in the old style and are pointed. They are covered with blue and indigo-colored tiles. Altogether we saw eleven minarets in the city. But the people say that there are seventy mosques. To make the city prosperous the people of this city have been

---

76. Mohammad III took part in one campaign, namely that of 1596, in which the Hungarian town of Erlau (Egri) was taken by the Turks (September 1596).

77. This is a reference to the use of *qanat* or *kahriz*, subterraneous canals that transport water from the mountains to towns and villages in the lower lying areas.

exempted from all customary taxes, but as a gift they send one hundred camel loads of dried *melejeh* and *'abbasi* pears, apricots, nectarines, hybrid peaches, quinces, dried grapes and many other fruits every year to the king of Iran. In conclusion, in Azerbaijan there are three [towns called] Qarabaghs, and each one is like a garden of paradise. We departed from the city and went towards the south, and with a thousand difficulties we crossed in the place where the rivers Aras and Jan merge. These rivers issue from the Pinayesh Mountains in Van, the Biredus and Abagay Mountains and passing from there into the Nakhjavan plains after three *farsakh*s they come to the Aras River, which goes to the Kur River, and from there to the Terek River, and that one ends up in the Caspian Sea. When we passed all these rivers, we traveled for six hours and reached:

THE STAGE OF THE TOWN OF KERKENE.[78] It is part of the province of Tabriz, in the district of Marand. It is a prosperous town with three hundred houses, a large mosque, a bathhouse, a small bazaar, but its inhabitants are extremely uncivil, rowdy and uncouth Qizilbash.[79] The cotton they cultivate in the plains is very good and produced in large quanties and therefore, the people are weavers making a coarse cotton cloth.[80] They also make twilled cottons in a variety of colors. Then for nine hours we proceeded towards the south and we reached:

THE STAGE OF THE TOWN OF ZENUSEH.[81] It is a personal fief of the Khan of Tabriz. It is a prosperous town with about one thousand good houses, ten large mosques, caravanserais, bathhouses, decorated bazaars, gardens and orchards. But its water all comes from wells. From there we went for ten hours to the south and we came to the town of Tesuy.

DESCRIPTION OF THE TOWN OF TESUY. It is in the province of Tabriz, in the district of Marand, on the banks of the Aras River.[82] The town has three thousand mud houses, seven large mosques, three bathhouses, six caravanserais, and small bazaars. Its governor is a Sultan.[83] Its gardens and orchards are spread everywhere. It was destroyed by Sultan Murad [IV] and it is now recovering from its destruction. From here to the city of Marand is twelve *farsakh*s. Its climate and its beauties of both sexes are famous throughout the world. It has different juicy fruits. All of the people are Shi'as, who make their living from horticulture. Then we went towards the south and passed through arid plains. We drank very delicious water from wells, because most of the water of these places is flowing underground. After having traveled twelve *farsakh*s we reached Marand.[84]

---

78. Perhaps it is Gerger, which several travelers mention as the first station after having crossed the Aras. See, e.g., Morier, *A Second Journey Through Persia*, p. 393.

79. The Ottomans in derogatory fashion called the adherents of the Safavid shahs *qizil-bash* or red heads, because the Sufi hats that they wore were red in color.

80. This very common cotton cloth was known as *bez*, *bazz* or *karbas*, see Floor, *Textile Industry*, pp. 160-62.

81. Probably Zonuz, situated between Jolfa and Marand. See Khamachi, *Farhang*, pp. 338-41.

82. Tesuy is the old name for what is now called Tasuj and is situated north of Lake Urmiyeh, about 80 km n.w. of Tabriz and most certainly not on the river Aras. Mustawfi, *Nuzhat al-Qulub*, p. 83; Khamachi, *Farhang*, pp. 295-97.

83. Safavid Iran was divided into a number of large provinces that were governed by governor-generals or *beygler-beyg*s. Each province was divided into a number of governates; the larger ones were governed by governors who held the title of khan and were referred to as *hakem*, while the smaller governates were held by governors who held the title of Sultan. Floor, *Safavid Government*, pp. 96-97.

84. Marand is situated between Khoy (west) and Maku (northwest), Russia (north), Arasbar (east) and

DESCRIPTION OF THE PARADISIACAL CITY OF MARAND – THE THRONE OF ELVEND KHAN. It is one of the cities of Azerbaijan, and a separate governate. It has ten thousand soldiers. It has a qazi, a mayor, a clerk, a police chief and a chief of the royal slaves. There are fourteen *farsakh*s to Tabriz. In between there is no fallow land. All of it is gardens and orchards. The town is to the east[85] of Tabriz. In former times it was the hunting ground for the son of Timur, Shahrokh, one of the kings of Azerbaijan and it was very lush and prosperous like a rose garden. Ghazi Sultan Murad, despite the Qizilbash, destroyed it and leveled its houses; however, it become prosperous again. It has three thousand beautiful houses, seven large mosques, three caravanserais, five bathhouses, and six hundred shops. There is no drapers' hall,[86] seminary, or elementary school.

But praise must be given to its seventy walks, gardens and recreational areas, each of which outrivals the Gardens of Eden. It has juicy fruits in plenty, because of its pleasant climate. The beloveds of both sexes are eloquent and well-spoken, both youths and women. When they speak, their magical words are like those of Jesus; when they walk their gait is life-inspiring. Most of its inhabitants are soldiers and retainers of the khan, but all of them are Shi`as. They are damned cursers. But being an old city, Hoseyn Taftazani, one of the great ancestors of `Allameh Taftazani, as well as `Ali Handi, Sheikh Susmari, and `Ala' ul-Din Marqadi are buried on the southern side of the town. We received gifts from the Sultan of this city. Accompanied by the emissary of the Tabriz Khan we went towards the south through plains for thirteen hours. Both sides of the public road were covered with thick and tall weeping willows and plane trees, so that we saw hardly any sunlight. We stopped at some wells and drank very good water and then we reached:

THE STAGE OF THE TOWN OF KAHRIZ. It has one thousand houses and it is the town of the secretary of the Khan of Tabriz. It has six large mosques, three bathhouses, and two hostels. It is a prosperous town with many gardens and orchards. May God destroy it!, because all of its people are Shi`ites and Tabarra'is, because for the first time in Iran I heard them cursing the blessed Omar.[87] "May God forgive me" and I almost lost my temper. But I had no choice, although I was beside myself, and killing that accursed curser was an easy matter, because in Persia envoys coming from Rum have a free hand, if they kill four cursing Qizilbash for the love of the Four Chosen Ones they are forgiven.[88] At any rate I exercised patience and we went to the south for seven hours and we reached:

THE STAGE OF THE TOWN OF SAHLAN.[89] It is the personal fief of the Khan of Tabriz situated on a flat plain and has about one thousand houses, gardens, orchards, seven large mosques,

---

Tabriz (south). Khamachi, *Farhang*, pp. 465-72.

85. Evliya is mistaken. Marand is to the northwest of Tabriz.

86. *Bedestan* or *Bazzazestan*, originally meaning the drapers' bazaar, is a covered and central part of the bazaar that can be closed, and where all shops with precious goods were kept. Elsewhere in Iran it was also known as Qeysariyeh.

87. *Tabarra'* is the Twelver Shi`ite doctrine obliging to hate those who hate `Ali and to curse those who reject the primacy of religious leadership of `Ali and his descendants. The Safavids instituted the cursing of especially Abu Bakr, `Omar, `Othman and A'ishah to which end, in addition to cursing by the common believers, professional ritual cursers (*tabarra'iyan*) also were employed, see Rosemary Standfield-Johnson, "The Tabarra'iyan and the Early Safavids," *Iranian Studies* 37/1 (2004), pp. 47-71.

88. This is hard to believe, and no Ottoman envoy ever availed himself of this alleged privilege.

89. Sahalan, a village near Tabriz, according to Morier, *Second*, p. 393 or Sahilan, Johnson, *Journey*, p. 218.

a caravanserai, a bathhouse, and a useful and small bazaar. The streets of this town are lined with weeping willows and plane trees. The people of Tabriz have summerhouses, gardens and orchards around here. The people live according to the Shafe'ite rite, but they still are cursed Rafazis (Shi'ites). Its climate and its youths of both sexes are liked by everyone. When we departed from here we saw on the right-hand side the dome of Sham Ghazan Mohammad Shah towering into the skies, visible at six hours' distance. We said a *Fatehah*[90] for his blessed soul, alighted in a pasture and sent a messenger to Tabriz. After three hours we mounted our horses and with the envoy of Tabriz, who was fully armed, we proceeded side-by-side. Before the emissary marched his well-dressed soldiers, and before me the forty retainers of this humble servant. Meanwhile in front of us innumerable soldiers appeared, who were coming to us. It was the deputy[91] of the Khan of Tabriz who had come to welcome us. Going with him, stirrup to stirrup, we entered the city of Tabriz with great pomp. In the bazaars and thoroughfares of the city many thousands of people had gathered to welcome us. This humble author was also looking at them. From one side of the city to the palace of the Khan took a full two hours. The honorable Khan, Kalb 'Ali Khan,[92] came forward and took this humble author to his lofty audience hall. We sat knee-to-knee. There was a grand reception. The royal kettle-drums, the Afrasiyab-like trumpets, flutes and the Jamshid-like hautbois were played three times with much pomp and ceremony. Armed youths with plumed and turbaned heads were standing in rows with folded arms.

After the drums were beaten, this humble author stood up and took the cordial letters of our master the vizier of Erzerum, Daftardar-zadeh Mohammed Pasha, from my bosom, kissed them and gave them to the Khan. He stood up and received the letter, kissed them and put them on his head and gave them to the secretary. The master of ceremonies led this humble author to his place, where I stood in accordance with Moslem custom. The secretary showed more respect by kissing the letter and started reading it in a loud voice. When in the letter the name of the holy prophet and his four caliphs were mentioned everybody got to his feet and showed respect to the holy prophet. But at the mention of his four friends some quickly sat down.

After reading the content of the letter the Khan began to speak as follows:

> God willing, if God helps us and gives this humble servant enough time in life, I will send one thousand head of horses and one thousand head of camels to my brother, the vizier of the royal realm of the Emperor within this month. Upon my eyes and head! You are welcome. Again, you are welcome and *bienvenue*. Apple of my eyes, light of my life.

We sat knee-to-knee and he talked pleasantly to this humble author and gave a splendid party. After eating, they brought rose water and incense burners. From among the presents of the Pasha, this humble author offered a fine rosary, a bow string, and Genoan and Venetian glasswork. Then I said: "Our honorable brother the Pasha sends his greetings, and not to come empty

---

90. The first surah of the Koran.

91. In Persian, the term *kadkhoda* usually refers to a village head or a head of a city quarter, but in Ottoman Turkish it refers to the deputy of an important official. Such a deputy was referred to as *na'eb* in Safavid Iran.

92. At that time the governor of Tabriz was Pir Budaq Khan Pornak Turkman, see Nasiri, *Titles*, p. 156.

handed he sends these things to you as a gift." He was delighted with the fine rosary and the bow-string and said: "I like them very much," and I said: "To your Excellency he has sent two purebred horses, may you enjoy them."

He got up and came to the side of the audience hall. This humble author signaled, and they brought the first horse, which had a golden and bejeweled saddle. God be praised, when that Arabian horse, walking like Rakhsh (Rostam's horse), displaying its pie-bald body, turned its head and prancing came to the field of friendship. It impressed all those present in the hall. This humble author said: "In the name of God," and gave the horse's bridle to the Khan and said: "May you enjoy it." The Khan mounted the horse without stirrups; from the field of friendship he galloped into the field of eloquence. Then I brought in the second horse and he was no less satisfied and handed it [to an equerry]. Then the Khan ordered his pages to serve all our men cilantro-mint sherbet. Then, after rose water and incense, the great Khan handed us over to the conductor of guests,[93] the chief of the guards, the police chief and the mayor. With much pomp we went to Kalantar garden and stayed there. It was a beautiful paradisiacal garden. The Khan sent after us as a gift forty *tuman*s in *bisti*s as bathhouse money and two purebred horses and one fully gilded, accoutered Qarachuboq horse, one grey-reddish speckled horse, and seven camel loads of beverages and food, and we went to our lodgings.

Later the public criers cried throughout the city: "The Ottoman embassy is here and they are Sunnis. It is the Shah's and the Khan's command not to curse; if you curse, the Sunnis will kill you, and you cannot claim blood-money. So you know." God be praised that there was no cursing of the Four Chosen Friends.[94] The blessed Abu Bakr and the blessed Othman, they definitely don't curse, but their problem is the blessed Omar. May I be forgiven of reporting that they slander him. That day the Khan gave ten fine youths dressed in gold-stitched chintz coats walking in the Isfahan fashion like peacocks. Our conductor of guests led them to us and they all kissed our hand. It seems that it was the Iranian custom that the khans sent the Ottoman envoys ten slaves for every kind of service. One is called Javan-ara, one Sadeq Jan, one Ramesh, one Mirza Khan, one Yazdan `Ali, one Kakunch, one Qorban Bey, one Sohrab, one Mazid Khan and one Yarqulu. Each one of them, like a youth of paradise, was an exceptional and delightful youth. Thereafter, we started the sight-seeing of Tabriz.

Description of the great city, the old castle and old emporium of Tabriz, the capital of Azerbaijan in the land of Iran

In the Mongol language it is called Tivris. In Darri it is Tivriz, in Dehqani[95] it is Tabriz, and in Persian it is Tibriz. In all of them it means 'fever.' In truth, when a person from another country with fever comes to Tabriz and drinks from the waters of Ujan his fever will drop and he will recover from the fever, hence Tabriz. Inside the castle of Egypt (Cairo) also no fever occurs, it is a pleasant city. In the year 175 [791-92] the founder of the fine city of Tabriz was the wife of Harun

---

93. On the role and function of the *mehmandar* see Mirza Rafi`a Jaberi-Ansari, *Dastur al-Moluk – A Safavid State Manual* translated by Floor and Fagfoory, pp. 155-58.

94. The so-called four chosen ones were the first three caliphs, Abu Bakr, `Omar, `Othman, and the prophet's youngest wife, A'isha. For this cursing practice see note 88 supra.

95. Dari just means Persian and Dehqani refers to the vernacular and/or rural dialect.

al-Rashid, Zobeyda Khatun, who was pleased with its climate, its good earth and the pleasant location, and built a palace when pregnant with the caliph al-Ma'mun. Afterwards, many thousands of *tuman*s and much wealth was spent and a large city was built, and the `Abbasid scholars called it Tebriz. It became so big that it took three days to go around it.

Later, in the year [-], during the reign of Mutawakkil bi'llah [r. 847-861], there was a major earthquake and Tabriz was destroyed, and because of it forty thousand people were buried under the debris. Thereafter, the caliph Mutawakkil came with countless soldiers from Baghdad to Tabriz and spent much wealth and rebuilt the city and enlarged it. In this way he became its second founder. On one side of the city is Mt. Ujan, on the other one Mt. Sahlan [i.e., Sahand], on the third side is Mt. Seyhan and on the fourth Qizildagh.[96] The walls of Tabriz have become larger, stronger than before.[97]

DESCRIPTION OF THE CASTLE OF TABRIZ. Its circumference is six thousand paces.[98] Now you can still see its old remains. It had three hundred towers, three thousand battlements, and six gates. The gates are: the Darvazah-ye Ujan, Bab-e Berservan, Darvazeh-ye Sarzud, Bab-e Sham Ghazan, Bab-e Sarv, and Bab-e Tabriz.[99] In each one of these gates five hundred watchmen keep guard day and night.

Then Hulagu [ca. 1217-1265] became its third founder, and he resided for seven years in Tabriz, which was his capital. He wanted to become the ruler of all kings. Later, in the year [-] Sultan Mohammad Khodabandeh,[100] the son of Arghun Shah, loaded the city that Hulagu Khan had built on the backs of one thousand camels and took it to the city that he built [i.e., Sultaniyeh]. All of its wood consisted of aloe and cypress wood carved like the book of *Arjang*[101] in such a way that one's eyes would become bewildered. But after that all the buildings of Tabriz are covered with porcelain tiles and built with plaster and mortar; and it is a beautiful city.

Later, the fourth founder, in the year 694 [1295] was Sultan Mohammad Ghazan (r. 1295-1304) on account of his justice and fairness it became extremely prosperous, so that the city extended to the mountains of Liyan, Senjan, Ujan, Sahlan [i.e., Sahand], and became a unique city, with a large population and an ornament to the world. Mohammad Sham Ghazan built walls all around it, and it would take somebody four days to circumvent it on foot. The walled city, which was built in the time of the `Abbasid Caliph Mutawakkil bi'llah, became the inner town. After that Tabriz passed through the hands of several rulers and kings, sometimes it was destroyed,

---

96. He refers to Sorkhab, see p. 36.

97. For the history of Tabriz see, e.g., Ayub Niknam Laleh and Fariborz Dhowqi, *Tabriz dar Godhar-e Tarikh* (Tabriz, 1374/1995), pp. 13-46, 417-21; Shafi` Javadi, *Peyramun-e Tabriz* (Tabriz, 1350/1971); Sayyed Aqa `Ownollahi, *Tarikh-e Panjsad Saleh-ye Tabriz* translated by Parviz Zagh Shahamrasi (Tehran, 1387/2008); Vladimir Minorsky, "Tabriz," Encyclopedia of Islam II.

98. This has been copied from Mustawfi, *Nuzhat-al-Qulub*, p. 79.

99. These names of the gates do not correspond with the names reported by other contemporary travelers, see, e.g., Laleh and Dhowqi, *Tabriz*, pp. 77-84. However, it seems that these names have been copied from Mustawfi, *Nuzhat-al-Qulub*, p. 79 who mentions Ujan, Ahar, Sharvan, Sardrud, Sham, and Saravrud as the gates built by Ghazan Khan in the second wall of Tabriz.

100. Sultan Mohammad Khodabandeh aka Oljeytu (r. 1304-1316).

101. The most important book of the third century prophet Mani (ca. 210-276) was referred to as *Arjang*. It was embellished with beautiful painted illustrations.

A view of the castle of Tabriz – Ark

sometimes it prospered and it became the capital of Azerbaijan. {But in the year 959 [1552], Sultan Sulayman plundered it and brought the people of Tabriz under his rule and gave its governorship to the Persian prince Alqas Mirza.[102] But in the year 994 [1586], the cursed Qizilbash reconquered these places.} In 994 [1586], in Murad III's time [r. 1574-1595], he sent one of his viziers, Ozdamir-oghlu Othman Pasha, as commanding general of the Persia campaign with an immense army; Cheghal-oghlu Senan Pasha, who was commanding the vanguard, conquered several castles. With the help of Shah-e Mardan (`Ali)[103] the great Othman Pasha wrested Tabriz from the hands of the sons of Heydar Shah of Ardabil; with innumerable troops he entered the city.[104] In order to control all of Azerbaijan, he built in the center of Tabriz, alongside the Khiyaban-e Shah, a quadrangular castle of rock, which seems as if it had been built by Farhad. Its circumference was twelve thousand seven hundred builder's cubits.[105] Its bastions and walls were so strong and solid that it was like a new Alexander's wall against the Yagog. The anagram that is inscribed on the Sham Ghazan Gate is as follows:

Ozdamir-zadeh captured Tabriz [in the year 993]

---

102. Alqas Mirza, younger brother of Shah Tahmasp I, rebelled against his brother in 1549 and fled to the Ottomans. He joined Sultan Sulayman when he invaded Iran and caused much havoc. He finally surrendered to his brother in 1549, who imprisoned him in Qahqaheh castle, where he shortly thereafter died. C. Fleischer, "Alqas Mirza Safawi," *Encyclopedia Iranica*.

103. The mention of Shah-e Mardan, one of the many titles of Imam `Ali by a fanatic Sunni such as Evliya is most unusual.

104. On this campaign see Abu Bakr `Abdollah, *Tarikh-e `Othman Pasha. (Sharh-e yuresh-e `othmani beh Qafqaz va Azerbayjan va tasarrof-e Tabriz) 993-996 qamari*. Edited by Yunes Zirak and translated into Persian by Nasrollah Salehi (Tehran, 1387/2008).

105. The *dhira` al-mi`mariya* or the builder's cubit measured 79.8 cm. Farhad the master builder, famous for his architecture and his love for Shirin, was immortalized by Nezami in his *Shirin va Khosrow*.

Another date is: In the path of Faith, Tabriz was captured in the year 993.

When 'Othman Pasha built this castle he became the fifth founder of Tabriz. In thirty-six days he completed the construction of the castle with his innumerable troops. He placed armaments and other necessary equipment inside it and assigned about forty thousand troops to guard it. But unfortunately, by God's will, Ozdamir Pasha could not perform even one Friday prayer in Tabriz; for after having said his night prayers, he passed away. The entire army of Islam accepted Cheghal-oghlu as its commander, and the news of the death of 'Othman Pasha together with the keys of the castle of Tabriz were sent to the High Porte. Immediately, from Istanbul a *kapichi-bashi*[106] was sent to the vizier of Tripoli in Syria, Khadem Ja'far Pasha, that he had been appointed as commanding general and he came post-haste to become the independent governor of Tabriz and commanding general. Spreading justice, he made Tabriz many times more prosperous than in the days of Mohammad Sham Ghazan.

According to the writings of the famous Tavashi (eunuch) Ja'far Pasha, three hundred thousand people inside the city and five hundred thousand in the province were enumerated. Then later, because of the revolt of the army and Janissaries in the Ottoman Empire, the Iranian ruler took advantage of the occasion and captured places like Ganjeh, Shirvan, Shamakhi, Demirkapu (Darband), Erevan, Nakhjevan, and Tabriz.[107]

Later Murad IV our master, in order to conquer Shirvan, Shamakhi, and Tiflis came to Iran. In seven days he destroyed the castles of Erevan, Nakhjevan, Marand, and Qarabagh and paused one week in Tabriz. He treated Tabriz roughly, and then he went victoriously to Van and from there to Istanbul. On the other hand, Shah 'Abbas I came to Tabriz with the army of Iran and Turan and consoled the people and made the city whole again.

NOW FOLLOWS THE DESCRIPTION OF THE BUILDINGS OF BEAUTIFUL TABRIZ. It is the capital of Azerbaijan and under the rule of the Iranians. It is a governorship held by a khan. Several times it has become a governate-general.[108] He has ten thousand soldiers. There are muftis, a chief of the sayyeds, mullahs, a mayor, clerks, a police chief, chief of the guards, chief of the royal slaves, chief of the raw flesh eaters, and the chief of the ushers, staff bearers, and conductors of guests. All these officials guard the peace and quiet of Tabriz, and they govern justly. No one suffers injustice as much as a mustard seed.

DESCRIPTION OF THE MOSQUES OF TABRIZ. There are three hundred and twenty mosques. Nineteen of them are mosques made by past kings. Fifty of them have been built by khans and Ottoman viziers. The others have been built by notables of the country. The oldest is the Zobeyda mosque, an old-style mosque. Its dome and all doors and walls are covered with tiles, and it has one beautiful minaret. The Mutawakkil bi'llah Mosque is an old-style mosque and covered with tiles. But as time passed and it was repaired by people of good will, it lost its original name. Now

---

106. Chief chamberlain; a title of courtiers attached to the High Porte.

107. This occurred in 1603 and 1604.

108. Evliya Chelebi uses the term *khanlar-khanlegi* as a synonym of the title *beygler-beygi* or governor-general, which title since the mid-sixteenth century was usually bestowed upon the official appointed to the government of Tabriz. See Nasiri, *Titles*, p. 154-56.

An Ottoman janissary

it is called the Damascus Mosque. In the old days the Sultan Mohammad Sham Ghazan Mosque was inside a heavenly garden, but now it is in a narrow place. It is an old one-minaret mosque. The

Shah Amin Mosque looks like the Arch of Khosrow,[109] you could say it is like the mosque of Baybars in Egypt.[110] It has one minaret, a beautiful garden, is covered with tiles, and its dome is rising to heaven; all its doors and walls seem as if they are worked finely with white and shining Chinese paper. It is a beautiful mosque, for whoever goes in does not want to leave. But the Shi`ites do not frequent it. Opposite of its prayer niche there is a beautiful thoroughfare, even Ahmad Pasha has not seen its like in the world. Various flowers provide fragrance for the people. Melodious birds with their songs enliven sad people. In the land of Iran this building is called *Hasht Behesht* (eighth paradises).

The Sultan Hasan Mosque was founded by Sultan Uzun Hasan, one of the kings of Azerbaijan. When Uzun Hasan was defeated by the Conqueror,[111] he fled to Tabriz and died there. His tomb is next to this mosque. Inside and outside and all around as well as its dome have been completely covered with tiles, the prayer niche and pulpit, and the place for the muezzins are very finely worked; it is unique in itself and cannot be outdone by others. Its windows are all decorated with ironwork and marble stone from Najaf and are polished and shining. The four sides of the gate facing the prayer direction are decorated with various beautiful forms: stalactite vaults, arabesques, writings, medallions, Rumi writings and designs, and each one is magically bewildering. The craftsmen have shown incredible skill. Beautiful writings are all over the doors and windows. All are in the style of Yaqut Mosta`sami.[112] On the two sides of the prayer niche there are two uniform yellow pieces of stone, [the cost of] each one is equal to the revenues of Iran and Turan. There are no similar pillars in any other country.[113]

Apart from this, there are about nineteen royal mosques. Each one of them is designed and built in a special way and covered with beautiful marble and different kinds of tiles and adorned with various patterns. But the poor mosques[114] are not frequented by the people like in Anatolia and Arabia, where there are many people inside the mosques; but here they don't pray in congregation. As soon as the call to prayer is sounded, everybody comes, of course, to the mosque and says his five-time prayers and thereafter he does not stay and leaves. In this way the mosque is empty of people.

In front of this Uzun Hasan mosque is the Shah Esma`il mosque, which is beautifully decorated. Near the mosque of Sultan Hasan there is the beautiful Shah Maqsud b. Sultan Hasan mosque.[115] [Other mosques include:]

The large mosque of Charmenar, which is an old mosque.[116]

---

109. The *Taq-e Kesra* or Khosrow's Arch is the only monument remaining of Ctesiphon, the capital of Seleucids, Parthians and Sasanis. It is situated near the town of Salman Pak in Iraq.

110. The mosque for Sultan Baybars I, the first Mamluk Sultan of Egypt, was constructed under the Atabeg Faris al-Din Aqtai and the vizier Baha` al-Din `Ali ibn Hinna in 1267-69.

111. The Conqueror is Mehmed II who took Constantinople and defeated Uzun Hasan in August 1473.

112. Named after the court calligrapher of the last `Abbasid caliph al-Musta`sim, Yaqut al-Musta`simi. It refers in particular to a kind of *nesih* with emphasis on the vertical elements.

113. See Javadi, *Peyramun*, p. 147.

114. Hammer, vol. 1, p. 135 has "These five mosques" instead of these poor mosques.

115. The quarter in which it is situated is still called Maqsudiyeh after this mosque, which still exists.

116. This mosque still exists.

The large mosque of Shah ʿAbbas I, situated at the beginning of the *Sarraj-khaneh*.

The High Mosque is one large mosque, because from the door facing the prayer direction you can hardly see a person at the prayer niche. It is supported by two hundred pillars and built with bricks. Apart from these large mosques there are many more small mosques.[117]

DESCRIPTION OF THE MADRASEHS OF TABRIZ. There are forty seven large madrasehs, which now are thriving places of learning, where every kind of science is taught. Their teachers are among the scholars of this period.

The biggest one is the Shah Jahan Madraseh.[118]

DESCRIPTION OF THE KORAN READING HOUSES. The city has about twenty Koran reading houses. But the Iranians have not been blessed with the ability of reading the Holy Koran with the proper pronunciations. Most of them pronounce it wrongly. Their reading of several Koran verses is defective.[119]

DESCRIPTION OF THE HOUSES OF TRADITIONS. There are about seven Houses of Traditions. Their scholars are not renowned for their learning of Traditions. They follow the Sayings of His Holiness ʿAli and the Twelve Imams. They say: "The blessed ʿAli, May God's prayer be on him, said," and quote the blessed ʿAli's words. Sometimes they recite good Traditions, but the sayings of ʿAli are more acceptable to them. They have several thousands of books with Traditions of Morteza [i.e., ʿAli].

DESCRIPTION OF THE ELEMENTARY SCHOOLS. There are about six hundred elementary schools for children. The Sheikh Haqqi school, the Hasan Meymandi school, the Taqi Khan school, the Sultan Hasan school and the Sultan Yaʿqub school. They give robes of honor to the children each year.

DESCRIPTION OF THE CONVENTS FOR DERVISHES. There are in total about one hundred and sixty convents for dervishes. The most famous among them are: the Shams-e Tabrizi convent, the Bulduk Khan convent, the Zeynab convent, the Aqil convent and the Mir Heydar convent.[120] The Bektashi convent is in the quarter of Rig, {which is also in the Azerik quarter.}

DESCRIPTION OF THE RUNNING WATERS. There are altogether six thousand springs and streams. The source of all of them is the Mt. Sahand. Apart from these, inside and outside the city there are nine waterways and underground tunnels. They are good for the digestion.

DESCRIPTION OF THE WATER DISTRIBUTION BUILDINGS. There are in total one thousand and forty public fountains. They are situated in beautifully decorated buildings. The Gol-e Rostam Khan fountain, the Shah Esmaʿil fountain, the Kur Khodabandeh fountain, the Khvajeh Shah fountain, the Reza fountain and the Yar ʿAli fountain are all famous.

---

117. For an overview of the older mosques that still remain see Laleh and Dhowqi, *Tabriz*, pp. 231-47.

118. For an overview of the madrasehs see Laleh and Dhowqi, *Tabriz*, pp. 276-77.

119. Evliya Chelebi, himself a trained Koran reciter, refers to the art of *towjid*, which stipulates the correct articulation of the Arabic letters in the Koran. There were ten correct ways of recitation of the Koran, as transmitted by tradition. See van Bruinessen et al., *Diyarbekr*, p. 215.

120. This convent still exists under the same name (Heydertakiyesi).

DESCRIPTION OF THE CITY QUARTERS. {In this region, they call city quarters *darvazeh*. There are one thousand sixty city quarters in total. They are: Dimashkiyeh, Pol-e bagh, Sinjaran (Meykhvaran), Verdichuk,[121] Shotorban, and Rik,[122] in which is found the Khan Serai. [Further], the Khiyaban and, in the north of Tabriz, Sorkhab, Amir Qiz (Khiz)} and Sardab, which is a big quarter, which was cleaned by Ozdamir 'Othman Pasha. [Further], the Chahar Manar, Mir Mir (Miyar Miyar), and Darvazah-ye Saray.[123]

DESCRIPTION OF THE MANSIONS OF THE NOTABLES. There are about one thousand and seventy. In the Amir Qiz quarter, there is the mansion of Allahverdi Khan, in the Rey quarter the mansion of Rostam Khan, again in the Rey quarter the mansion of Shah Bandeh Khan, once again in that quarter, the mansion of Pir Budaq Khan, and near the Sultan Hasan mosque, there is special mansion of the Khan is famous.}

DESCRIPTION OF THE CARAVANSERAIS. There are about two hundred caravanserais that function as hostels and guesthouses: [to wit] The Zobeyda, Shah Jahan, Shah Esma'il, Pir Budaq, and the 'Alam Shah Begum, the daughter of Shah Jahan, caravanserais.[124]

THE BUILDINGS OF THE MERCHANTS. There are bout seventy mercantile courts (*khan*). The Ja'far Pasha, the Shah-bandeh in the hat makers' bazaar, the Begum Khan and Baba Haqqi caravanserai.

HOUSES FOR TRAVELERS AND BACHELORS. In total there are about one hundred buildings for travelers and bachelors. They include the Mostaqim, Farhadiyeh, Ja'fariyeh, Firuz Khan, Gowhar, Cheghal Pasha and the Kalantar buildings.

THE NUMBER OF BAZAARS AND DRAPERS' HALLS. There altogether seven thousand market streets. Most of them are built of brick in the style of Aleppo. Every type of good is sold there. There is one big Drapers' Hall, where many merchants do their business and trade. {There is a large drapers' hall with a dome built of stone that does not have its like anywhere.}[125]

DESCRIPTION OF THE COLOR OF THE FACES OF THE YOUNG AND OLD. Because of the climate all people, young and old, are lively and healthy. They are tall, rosy-cheeked, black-eyed, the color of the faces is like that of blossoming roses, their lips are like carnelians, and their mouths small like small jewel boxes.

---

121. Probably Vijuyeh a.k.a. Varjih.

122. Probably Dik, short for Dikbashi quarter.

123. Laleh and Dhowqi, *Tabriz*, pp. 85-114 only mention Demashqiyeh, Shotorban, Chahar Manar, Sorkhab and Amir Khiz quarters. The other quarters all have different names and their number of thirty is much smaller than the fantastically high number given by Evliya Chelebi.

124. For an overview of the currently existing caravanserais, among which the ones mentioned by Evliya Chelebi do not figure, see Laleh and Dhowqi, *Tabriz*, pp. 220-27. Shah Jahan must be Jahan Shah of the Qara-Qoyunlu dynasty.

125. For a detailed analysis and plan of the bazaar of Tabriz see Günther Schweizer, "Tabriz (Nordwest-Iran) und der Tabrizer Bazar," *Erdkunde* XXXVI (1972), pp. 33-46.

Description of the youths of both sexes. They are white of color, handsome, but proud, and haughty and in their relations with one another they are very graceful and their conversation is sweet. As they say, "the old ones are sweeter than the youths."[126]

Description of the notables and grandees. They come from all groups, but there are many from the Afshars, Domdomis, Dumbulis, Lahijanis, Turkmen and Gökdolaq. They are rich like Croesus. All of them are Shi`ites and heretics.

The number of physicians. There are about two thousand phlebotomists, eye doctors, and surgeons. But, because of the good clime people are healthy and they are not in need of good doctors. Yet, again there are many physicians. [Most of them are looking for herbs in the mountains].

Description of the Saints and Sheikhs. There are more than seven thousand pious and God-fearing preachers as well as consolers and sheikhs. In this land they have especially respect for old and experienced people. People listen to them, but their religion is unknown.

Description of the writers and poets. There are seventy-eight poets, who have *divan*s; they are eloquent, have a fine delivery and are men of learning. First [there are], Yavari and Shabi, and Sa'ebi is the Orfi of his time,[127] [further] Adhami, Shakeri, Jabi, Razi, Sayyed Vahedi who has a *divan*, and the owner of our house Yazdan Aqa, Mardan Aqa Jan, Qorban Qoli, Khoja Naqdi, Pir Bash Agha, Mirza Bay, Hosam Ata, Alvand Aqa, Reza Bay and Kalb `Ali.[128] Of the mystics and hermits there is one named Dede Shurimi, who is always in ecstasy and no person ever saw him eating, drinking, lying down, sleeping or performing any of the natural acts of life for seventy years. Other famous mystics are Shah Kend, Shun Jahan and Dede Jan.

Description of people's clothing. The nobles and notables wrap a multi-colored and red head-band around their heads. [This is the reason for the expression of Qizilbash.] But most of them wear it in the style of the Persians, who wear white Mohammadi turbans. But on the quilted turbans they put a pointed Safavid Sufi hat. The Sufi hat of the scholars is more than two palms high. The common people wear one of one palm, and these are not bejeweled. The notables wear blue sable, and others wear woolen capes.

{**Description of the Persian taj.** In the year [-] in Iran, someone called Sheykh Ebrahim dreamt that a donkey was copulating with him, while braying, and he bore a child to this donkey that had seventy fingers. He related this dream to Sheikh Safed [sic; correctly Safi], who interpreted it as follows: "Good tidings to you, for you will become Shah of Iran and seventy of your children will rule there." He interpreted it that the one who copulated with that donkey was

---

126. This sentence has been inspired by Mustawfi, *Nuzhat-al-Qulub*, p. 80 who wrote: "They are tall, rosey-cheeked, white of skin, handsome, but proud and boastful."

127. Hammer, vol. 1, p. 136 has "Yari and Shabi are the Saib and Unfi of their time," which makes more sense. Sa'eb (1601-1677) was a famous poet from Tabriz and Orfi (not Unfi) was originally from Shiraz (b. 1555). See E.G. Browne, *A Literary History of Persia* 4 vols. (Cambridge, 1953), vol. 4, pp. 163-65, 241. For Yari-ye Tabriz aka *Khordehforush* (haberdasher), see Sam Mirza, *Tadhkereh-ye Tohfeh-ye Sami* ed. Rokn al-Din Homayunfarrokh (Tehran, 1347/1968), p. 144; Sayyed Vahedi probably is Mowlana Rajab `Ali Vahed-e Tabrizi (d. 1080), Mohammad Taher Nasrabadi, *Tadhkereh-ye Nasrabadi* (Tehran, 1317/1938), p. 1084. Shabi Siyalkuti probably was the younger brother of Molla Sarabi. `Abdol-Rasul Khayyampur, *Farhang-e Sokhanvaran* (Tabriz, 1340/1961), pp. 263, 655.

128. Adhami might be Adham-e Qazvini, of which there are two, see Nasrabadi, *Tadhkereh*, p. 48 and Dehkhoda.

Male and female dress ca. 1670

Sheikh Ebrahim b. Heydar, who then said: "If I become king, then I will wear on my head the phallus of the donkey that copulated with me as a 'crown,' and I will make the sound of the music of my drum and trumpet like the braying when he was having me," and by God's will he became Shah and made that phallus his crown and the braying of the donkey the sound of his trumpet, and this is the origin of the Persian crown (*taj*).}

DESCRIPTION OF THE PEOPLE'S LANGUAGE. The Turkmen and the Afshar speakers have a special dialect of which are examples.

> *Heze tanimamishem* (I have not known him)
>
> *Menimchun khatirmande olupdir* (he has been in my mind)
>
> *Darjunmishan* (I am heart stricken)
>
> *Yavuncimisham* (I have become the enemy)
>
> *Apar gelen chaqeri* (bring the wine)

But the people of learning speak Persian.

DESCRIPTION OF THE IMPORTANT BUILDINGS. The Sultan mosque,[129] the Shah Ya'qub building, the Shah Khiyaban building and the palace of Sahlan, the Shah Jahan building, the Khadem Ja'far Pasha building, the wonderful palace of Sham Ghazan are the ones known to us. But {in the Miyar Miyar quarter is the Arch of 'Ali Shah which is like the Arch of Khosrow, the building of Emir Khan, near the Shah Esma'il mosque, is in ruins. In front of the Shah Esma'il mosque is the Khadem Ja'far Pasha castle, which is in ruins. The Rashidiyeh castle is on the slopes of Mt. Sorkhab, which was built by one of the viziers of Mohammad Shah Ghazan, and is situated in the north-east.} Although there are several thousand [other] wonderful and strange buildings these suffice.

DESCRIPTION OF THE GOOD CLIMATE. In this country a wind blows, which is called *bad-e nasim*, which gives people eternal life, and therefore there is no fever in this country. Some men become so old that they live to the age of one hundred and seventy, and they are people of Aristotle-like intellect and sharp wit.

DESCRIPTION OF THE PURE WATER. All of its water comes from Mt. Sahand and waters the buildings inside and outside the city, and they issue from springs, and in total there are nine hundred subterranean canals that water the gardens. The water of the Mehranrud and the weather of Tabriz are rather cold. The water aids digestion, it is as if it gives new life to a man.

DESCRIPTION OF THE WATER WELLS OF THE HOUSES. In Tabriz, apart from nine hundred subterranean canals, there are seven thousand wells. Only, the water of the subterranean canals is much more delicious than that of wells. The depth of the wells is between thirty and forty cubits. In the heart of winter their water is lukewarm and in summer it is cold.

---

129. For a description see JChardin, *Voyages*, vol. 2, pp. 322-24.

DESCRIPTION OF THE CLIMES OF THE CITY. The city is in the fourth clime at the eighteenth latitude. The climate is temperate.

THE AUSPICIOUS CONSTELLATION UNDER WHICH THE CITY OF TABRIZ [WAS BUILT]. All the astronomers believe the wrong supposition that Tabriz was built by its founder Zobeyda Khatun under the auspicious constellation of the house of Scorpion when ruled by Mars. Therefore, several hundred times it has been subjected to disturbances like in the time of Murad IV. It was destroyed by Timur and Chengiz Khan.

DESCRIPTION OF THE NUMBER OF BATHHOUSES. There are twenty-one delightful bathhouses, and in each one of them there are two *shafe'i* basins with benches and fountains with free spouting water. All these have nice water and atmosphere. There are very chaste masseurs and angelic-faced youths. The Sultan Hasan bathhouse, the Pish-Koshk bathhouse, the Lusa bathhouse, the Jahan Shah bathhouse, near the Jahan Shah mosque and near the Miyar Miyar quarter; [there are also] {the Darvazeh-ye Sar quarter bathhouse, [in] the weavers bazaar the Zarju quarter bathhouse, the Pol-e bagh quarter bathhouse, and the water and ambiance in the bathhouses is very pleasant. Behind the Sultan Hasan mosque is the Shotorban quarter bathhouse, the bathhouse of Darvazeh-ye Rey, the bathhouse of the Khiyaban quarter and the bathhouse of the Sorkhab quarter.}

DESCRIPTION OF THE PRIVATE BATHHOUSES OF THE NOTABLES. There are a total of seven hundred bathhouses in the mansions. In each one of them beauties like fairies and angels with indigo-colored loin-cloths wrapped around their naked bodies swam in the *shafe'i* basins like angels and fairies of the sea, and they [the notables] intimately embraced the youths. On the tiles of the walls of the bathhouses the bathhouse poem by Fuzuli is inscribed.[130]

DESCRIPTION OF THE PULSES AND PRODUCTS. Around the city in the seven districts in the plains of Tabriz, seven types of wheat are produced that are very large-grained. Beans and barley are aplenty and seven different types of cotton are cultivated. Other vegetables are plentiful and it is a large and fertile land.

DESCRIPTION OF THE CRAFTS. The like of the master craftsmen of Tabriz—painters, designers, jewelers, and tailors—is nowhere else to be found. The master of every kind of craft is to be

---

130. Fuzuli (1483?-1556), a poet who wrote with equal skill in Turkish, Persian, and Arabic, and who was very influential in Persian and Divan poetry. The translation of his bathhouse poem is as follows:

found in this city. Especially the expensive fabrics that are made here and the silken materials that are found here, which are exported to other lands; its bath-cloths and *dara'i*[131] are well-known.

DESCRIPTION OF THE FOODS. Its, white loaf, pebble bread, barley bread, buttered rings, puffy three-cornered pastry, fancy Yazd bread, partridge kebab, flaky pastry filled with thin layers of chicken, forty different types of musky and fragrant pilaus, cream wheat soup (*hariseh*)[132] *mastaba churbasi*,[133] *duzde beryani* and fresh *paludeh*[134] are famous foods and in abundance.

DESCRIPTION OF THE FRUITS. There are several thousand[135] colorful fruits which are famous, but the most famous are its *najm-e khalaf* pears, *peyghambar* pears, Milani apples, sugary apricots, *najm-e Ahmadi* (apples), small-grained grapes, *razaqi* grapes, *maleki* grapes, *tabarzeh* apricots, *Jazireh-e Majd ol-Dini*s, *bakrani*s, yellow plums, *zananeh* [woman-like] pears and other types of fruits that cannot be found in Syria, unless they are found in Istanbul.[136]

> That cypress-statured one strolled into the bathhouse at day break
> His bright face lit up the whole bathhouse
> His body could be seen through the slit of his shirt
> He took off his dress and again he made his full moon appear
> He wrapped his bare body in an indigo-colored bath-towel
> As if inserting a peeled almond inside a violet
> The lip of the basin was honored by kissing his feet
> By his blessed sight the eye of the cup became enlightened
> It was as if each drop of perspiration on his body was a pearl to be sold
> Then they touched their purse tempted to buy them
> When he combed his hair the air was filled with musk perfume
> The scattered strands of his hair made the place ambergris-scented
> The cup kissed his hand and out of envy my liver melted away
> The water touched his body and envy gave me no rest
> Coming out of the bath, my glance covered him like a silken wrap
> And he put himself comfortably within the corner of my eyes
> The pupil of my eyes poured water at his feet
> Because water should be poured at the feet of the cypress constantly
> O Fuzuli, I would give my soul as the entry fee for the bath
> Let that cypress-statured and silver-bodied one not spend gold.

From Hamid Arazli, *Kolliyat-e Fuzuli* 6 vols. (Baku: Azerbaijan Nashriyati, 1996), vol. 1, p. 235. The Persian third case does not make a difference between male or female. However, since mixed male-female bathing was and is not allowed in Iran, Fuzuli clearly had a male youth in mind as the subject of this poem.

131. *Dara'i* is a figured or non-figured fabric woven from simple silk, or a mixture of silk and cotton.

132. It is a kind of *halim*, a thick and smooth soup like a pudding, usually made with wheat to give it a cream color.

133. A type of soup; dressed with sour milk or yogurt.

134. A sweet beverage containing fibrous starch jelly.

135. Evliya is exaggerating, again.

136. The text has *sibet milanisi*, which we have interpreted as apple of Milan, a township in Azerbaijan. For a detailed list of the fruits in Tabriz see Nader Mirza, *Tarikh va Joghrafiya-ye Dar al-Saltaneh-ye Tabriz* (Tabriz, 1323/1905-06), pp. 212-14.

A woman pounding grain

IN PRAISE OF THE VARIETY OF BEVERAGES. First, the wine made of Muscat grapes comes in seven colors, it is a very good wine.[137] Then wine made of *maleki* grapes, [and further] *koknar*,[138] pomegranate juice,[139] rose petal juice, cilantro-mint sherbet, Sahlan juice, sour cherry juice, honey mixture juice, and among the common people fermented millet and rice beer (*boza*) are well-known.

DESCRIPTION OF THE PUBLIC KITCHENS. The Shah Ya'qub, the [Caliph] Sultan Mutawwakil, the Zobeyda Khatun and the Sultan Hasan are large buildings, but in the hands of the ill-omened Qizilbash, they have become public kitchens without food.

THE RECREATION SITE OF SORKHAB, I.E., QIZILDAGH. It is situated on the [northern] side of Tabriz. In the afternoon at the very top of it you can see Lake Urmiyeh. It is one *farsakh*, or less, from Tabriz. You can go there on foot in one day.

IN PRAISE OF THE GARDEN EXCURSIONS. There are a total of forty-seven thousand gardens, orchards and recreation sites. Among them the garden of Shah Ya'qub is near the large mosque of the same name. Our great Khan gave a banquet in the honor of this humble servant the like of which I have never seen. One day during this wonderful feast, seventy singers, players and musicians playing in the Khorasani style and dancers displaying themselves like Venus, performing in such a way as if it was a party of Hoseyn Beyqara. This is a beautiful garden that has no equal in the world. One of the viziers of Murad III, Koja Farhad Pasha, when he was governor of Tabriz,

---

137. Evliya allegedly did not drink wine; so how did he know this was a good wine?

138. *Koknar* is a drink prepared from a mixture of opiates, hydrocarbons, protein, resin, oil, and pigments.

139. At present *nar-sharab* or pomegranate spice is used in the Republic of Azerbaijan as a seasoning for the preparation of fish dishes and it is available in restaurants and elsewhere to be used on fish dishes just like ketch-up.

A woman churning

became infatuated with the atmosphere of the Ya`qub Shah garden; he constructed many beautiful kiosks, rooms, courtyards, and promenades and made it very prosperous. Murad IV, when he destroyed the city of Tabriz, ordered Chiftehchi Othman Aqa to protect it. Now it is a garden like the garden of paradise. The last line [of the writing on the wall of] the kiosk where we had the banquet was written as follows: Farhad built this palace for Shirin, in the year 983 [1575].

THE RECREATION SITE OF SHAH SAFI which cannot be described.

THE POLO MALL. In the middle of it two tall pillars of Juniper wood are attached together, and on the top of it there is a silver bowl. Every Friday, the shah's servants, riding in the Polo Mall on fast galloping horses perform games and shoot arrows at the abovementioned bowl, and all their friends watch them.[140] Especially on New Year's Day of Khvorezmshah[141] they bring horses with them that have been kept in darkness for forty to fifty days and have been properly prepared, and they make them fight against each other. The fights between camels are also very interesting to see.

---

140. The game referred to is *qebeq-bazi*, see Carl Diem, *Asiatische Reiterspielen* (Berlin, 1942), pp. 66-68 and Willem Floor, *Games Persians Play* (Washington DC: Mage, 2010).

141. Apparently Evliya Chelebi has confused the Jalali with the Khvorezmian calendar. For details see Antonio Panaino, Reza Abdollahy, Daniel Balland, "Calendars," *Encyclopedia Iranica*.

Female buffalo-, ram-, donkey-, dog-, and cock-fights are exciting. In short, all these happenings on New Year's Day are very entertaining, and it is peculiar to Persia.[142]

A STRANGE AND ODD EXCURSION SPOT. Every year on the tenth of *Moharram*, on the day of 'Ashura, the nobles, notables, young and old, pitch their tents in this Polo Mall. For three days and three nights they have a special get-together. For the sake of the souls of the martyrs of Karbala they cook sweet pudding (*'ashura*) in one hundred thousand cauldrons and give it to the poor and rich. The spiritual rewards of it will go to the souls of the martyrs of Karbala, who were killed by the hand of Yazid.[143] Also, on the same day in that Mall they distribute sherbets in gratefulness. The water carriers pour sherbets and good cold water from their water sacks into crystal, rock crystal, moraine, and lead crystal cups as well as in Yemeni cornelian and Balgami turquoise cups and serve it to the people, while crying: "drink up for the love of Hoseyn of Karbala," and some others shout: "Their Lord shall make them drink a pure drink,"[144] and some others: "Drink it with enjoyment."[145] On this day, several notables hang a water sack on their shoulder and distribute water without shame for the sake of the soul of Hoseyn. The greatest spectacle was, of course, that the Khan of Tabriz pitched his multi-colored pavilion there, and all the nobles of Tabriz gathered there, sitting close together, knee-to-knee, just like when they recite the *Birth of Prophet*[146] on the pulpits in Turkey (Rum) and they recite the *Death of Hoseyn*. All the lovers of the house of 'Ali sat overcome with grief and listened intensely and heaved heart-rending sighs. When it was said: "The innocent blessed Hoseyn was martyred in this way by the accursed Shemr," at that moment from behind the curtain the white body and head of a man is brought in, which is bleeding. [Likewise] from behind the curtain in the field, they bring in the pure and holy bodies of the children of the Imams, who are martyred, having been deprived of water. By the greatness of God, a dreadful shout arises from the crowd. Everyone is beside himself and looses his senses. At that time, hundreds of barbers come amongst the sincere lovers [of Hoseyn] and with their razors that they have in their hand they slash the arms and get blood from whoever wants to shed his blood for the love of Hoseyn. The green meadow is stained with blood and becomes a tulip field. Several thousand of the lovers [of Hoseyn] have their heads and arms branded with the scarifications of Hasan, Hoseyn and Aqil,"[147] and they wound themselves and shed their blood for the sake of their love. Then they lift the effigy of Imam Hoseyn from the field, and with thousands of lamentations and professions of faith they bring the presentation of the *Death of Hoseyn* to an end. Then the *'ashura* dish is served and for three nights and three days they talk sincerely with one another.[148]

---

142. In Tabriz, there is still a *Qut Meydani* or Wolf Square, where in the past wolf-fights were staged.

143. This refers to the slaughter of Hoseyn b. 'Ali, grandson of the prophet Mohammad and third Imam of the Shi'ites, and his troops by the Ommayad Caliph Yazid 10 October 680 in the plains of Karbala. The 'Ashura dish is a special kind of sweet pudding made with grains, nuts, dried fruits, sugar, rose water and milk, made during the month of *Moharram*. In Turkey today this pudding is prepared with great ceremony. It is called *Asure* or 'Noah's pudding' and prepared in tens of thousands of cauldrons and given to the poor and rich.

144. Koran 76: 21 (al-Insan).

145. Koran 4:4 (al-Nisa).

146. The *Mowled-e Nabi* a very popular elegy in verses lauding the prophet Mohammad.

147. Aqil b. Moslem was one of the followers of Hoseyn and was killed with him at Karbala.

148. For the development and enactment of the 'Ashura festival see Floor, *The History of Theater in Iran*. pp. 124-211.

It is a very good place for entertainment and for walking. Because of its weather there are countless promenades and gardens in the city, its recreation site is like the legendary gardens of Eram, Aspoza, Maram and Sudaq. Its kiosks are wrought in Persian style and are like the palace of Shirin and the castle of Vameq and Azra',[149] and people still talk about it. In the mansion where we stayed in the Kalantar garden, the date of its construction was written in the writing of Qotb al-Din Mohammad Yazdi: "This is the place of Shirin high above the pavilion."[150] There are many similar buildings, but describing the ones that are not well-known will bring tediousness. That it why this suffices. God be praised that for two complete months we enjoyed and traveled in beautiful Azerbaijan, which is half of the world.

Describing the Visit of the Environs of Tabriz as well as of its Villages and Castles in the Company of H.E. the Khan

Around Tabriz there are as many as seven prosperous districts. With one thousand soldiers, falcons, hawks, and well-trained hounds and Afshar hunting dogs we went to hunt, while the drums were beaten and the Jew's harps were blown. First, [we went to]:

Mehranrud district. This is to the east of Tabriz and five *farsakhs* away from the gate of Tabriz.[151] Kundur Rud,[152] Esfeheh[153] and Sa'idabad,[154]–these three aforementioned villages are town-like emporia. They have many large mosques, caravanserais, bathhouses, small bazaars, gardens and orchards.

Seravrud district[155] is situated to the west of Tabriz, and it is close to the gardens of the city. It has eighty prosperous Azerbaijani villages. Jevlandoruq, Elqabendilis,[156] Lakdirih[157] and Koja-abad[158] are prosperous villages that are like small towns with large mosques, bathhouses and small mosques. The arable land is near Seravrud's water and has a rich soil.

---

149. A famous couple of lovers in Persian literature and who have been eternalized by the poem of Azraqi.

150. Kahravan vol. 2, p. 130, n. 1 observes that the hemistich gives the date as 701 (1301-02), whereas in the text 982 (1574-75) is given. The hemistich is incomplete. We have preferred to read *vala* as *bala*.

151. Mehranrud is to the southeast of Tabriz. Razmara, *Farhang*, vol. 4, p. 513.

152. Locally pronounced as Kunduri.

153. Esfeh perhaps is Esfenaj, a small town in Mehranrud district. 'Ownollah, *Tarikh*, p. 96.

154. Khamachi, *Farhang*, pp. 362-64; Razmara, *Farhang*, vol. 4, p. 270.

155. This probably is Sardrud, which now is called Sardari. Khamachi, *Farhang*, pp. 357-58 (Sardrud).

156. Probably Alqalandis, a village 20 km north of Osku, on the road between Tabriz and Maragheh. Razmara, *Farhang*, vol. 4, p. 41.

157. Nakhjevani, p. 284, n.1 suggests reading Nuk Dizaj.

158. Now it is called Kujuvar or Kojovar, about 14 km west of Tabriz.

A view of Tabriz ca. 1670

Dideherder the third district[159] is situated four *farsakh*s from Tabriz to the southwest and altogether it has twenty-four villages with large mosques, bathhouses and paradisiacal gardens.

Urdnik the fourth district[160] is situated west of Tabriz at a distance of one *farsakh*. It has about thirty villages. Each one has a large mosque, a caravanserai, a bathhouse and a bazaar.

Rudeqat the fifth district[161] is behind Mt. Sarhadd, situated to the north of Tabriz. It is about a distance of one *farsakh* from Tabriz. It has one hundred prosperous market towns.

Hanumrud the sixth district has twenty villages.

Bedustan the seventh district[162] is situated north of Tabriz. It is behind the Rudeqat district and it has seventy prosperous villages with large mosques, caravanserais and bathhouses. If we describe our hunts and pleasure in the company of the Khan during twenty days in these districts as well as all the daily events of Tabriz, God knows that it will become a big volume. There is no other city like beautiful Tabriz and Isfahan, half of the world, the most famous city in the land of Iran. It is an old city with a good climate, beautiful people, excellent buildings and is endowed

---

159. In some manuscripts its name is written as Vandehar (Nakhjevani).

160. The proper name is Arvanaq, now known as Guni. Khamachi, *Farhang*, p. 161.

161. For the district of Rudeqat see Khamachi, *Farhang*, p. 337.

162. This probably is the district of Bedowstan, situated between Ahar and the district of Mehranrud. Razmara, *Farhang*, vol. 4, p. 83.

with many good and splendid things. May God entrust it again to the house of Othman, because now it is falling into ruin. We enjoyed ourselves in this land, and we returned with the Khan to the city, and each time that we had the pleasure of the Khan's company it was a great pleasure for us.

ABOUT A CURIOUS CONVERSATION. One day during a conversation with the Khan, he offered this humble author a good wine. I said: "By God, and again by God, by the great soul of the blessed ʿAli, since I was born I have not tasted anything that is forbidden and anything that makes you high and intoxicated. Since our great ancestor, the Turk of the Turks, Khvajeh Ahmad Yasavi b. Mohammad Mehdi[163] there is nobody among my forebears who has indulged himself in partaking of such intoxicating things. Please excuse us in this wonderful party." The Khan said: "O brother, you are like my own soul to me. O apple of my eyes and delight of my heart, Mirza Shahan stood up especially for you and gave you a glass of wine. For goodness sake, who are you afraid of? If you are afraid of the Caesar of the World, the king, he is at a distance of five months' travel from you. If you are afraid of your Khan, Tabriz is at a distance of forty stages from Erzerum. Thus, whom are you afraid of? Of me, Kalb ʿAli Khan, the khan of khans of the Shah of Iran and Turan? My king, whose bread I eat, has said: 'If you drink I will rip open your chest,' but not caring for the royal command, I throw parties with music and wine, and drink it. So, who are you afraid of? You should drink wine." Then the humble author said: "My beloved Khan. If the king of Iran has prohibited you to drink wine, my king, the king of kings (i.e., God almighty) has ordered me not to drink, for he clearly says in the [Koran] verse: "Date wine, gambling, dedication of stones

---

163. Khvajeh Ahmad Yasavi (1106-66) was a Turkic poet and mystic, who founded the first Turkic Sufi order (the Yasaviyeh), which had a major influence among the speakers of the various Turkic languages.

and divination by arrows are an abomination of Satan's handwork,"[164] saying this he has even forbidden me to drink one drop. I am afraid of that almighty God who has created all beings from nothingness. I do not go against his order and don't drink."

When I said this the Khan said: "By God, he is very pious and bigoted." The humble author said: "By God, my Khan, I am not a bigot, but I am a follower of Nu`man b. Thabit,[165] a world traveler and pure of faith, companion to all people, and a devotee of the family of the prophet." The people who were present in the party and the boon companions were dumbstruck about what I had said. The Khan kept insisting; he stood up with his all his beloved pages and came to me and said: "Apple of my eyes, for goodness sake Evliya Aqa. Take this wine from me and I will give you as a gift whomever you want from among my slaves; Mirza Shahi, Firuz, Parviz, `Ali Yari, Zevalizi, Shahland, Seyf Qoli and Khal Khan. If you love Red Morteza `Ali and the twelve Imams, come and drink a cup of wine from the hands of my boys. Let our heads be warm and our hearts be tender, and in this party let us enjoy ourselves and live for the moment." Saying this, he came with all his sun-like beautiful boys who embraced me and I embraced them and we kissed each other lustily. But again I asked the help of God and said: "O Khan. Is this good companionship that Khoja Naqdi has drunk one cup of wine and is drunk and senseless and, God forbid, passes wind and makes noises in your presence? Is this the way of merry-making in Iran?" When the Khan heard me he beat this Khoja Naqdi with his fist on the head, kicked him and sat down at the head of the party. In spite of being drunk Khoja Naqdi recited this poem:

> I am so drunk that I do not understand what the world is
> Who am I? Who has become the saki? What is the pure wine?

At that time, the Khan once again pressured me and this humble servant said: "O Khan, you drink wine so that you become intoxicated end ecstatic, but divine ecstasy is the true one. Order a tambourine to be brought so that I will show you spiritual pleasure." The Khan said: "Hey, Yar `Ali, for the love for `Ali, bring a tambourine for my brother Evliya." They brought a tambourine, whose skin was made in India. When I took it from Yar `Ali, I sang the following in the Anatolian (Rumi) style and improvised it in *segah* mode:[166]

> Your love gives every sign of eternal life
> As if every afflicted one in this world gives up his life.

I sang the poem in three quatrains and one couplet in the *sema`i* style and ended it.[167] The people present in the party were astonished. The Khan took off his Persian-style sable robe and with his own hands put it on me and gave me a Georgian slave-boy and bestowed upon me a thousand praises, and said: "A hundred bravos! O you, lover of the Caesar of the World." He gave me ten *tuman*s in *`abbasi*s as a gift, and a Qarachuboq horse fast as the wind. He said: "Rest assured, I will not make you drink." We enjoyed ourselves for one full month, where every night was like the

---

164. Koran 5.93 (al-Ma'ide)

165. This is Abu Hanifa (699-765), the founder of the Hanafi school of Islamic jurisprudence.

166. On this term see van Bruinessen et al., *Diyarbekr*, p. 219.

167. The *sema`i* style is a rhythmic pattern with three beats, a form special to vocal music used by minstrels in folk music.

Night of Power and every day like the Festival of Sacrifice.[168] We had similar get-togethers, and we went around and saw what was worth seeing in the beautiful city of Tabriz. Their system of justice, safety and caring for the people and administration, keeping the bazaars clean, and maintaining the price regime of Sheikh Safi, are really praise-worthy. Because all the people are men of taste, but you do not see a single person drunk in the streets. All the people of the city are very polite. This poem describes them well:

Tabriz is like paradise, and its people pure	تبریز چو هفت قومش ز صفا
Like the mirror that is clear of all stain of rust,	چون آینه اند پاک از رنگ جفا
Thou sayest that they are not sincere in their friendship,	گفتی که بدوستی نه صادق باشند
But the mirror only can give back what it reflects.[169]	از آیینه جز عکس نگردد پیدا

IN PRAISE OF BEAUTIFUL TABRIZ. First, one of the good things is that, because there are many running streams, they sweep the streets day and night in such a way that not even a speckle of dust rises to your nose, because they sprinkle them with water. Similarly, the bazaars are as clean and cool as a cellar at the beginning of the month of July, when people come into the royal bazaar and their soul is revived and one is bewildered of looking at the beautiful faces of the youths among the artisans.

The second good thing is that they never give the maidens of the noble family of Mohammad to slaves and sayyeds, but they give them to their equals. They raised with this humble author the following question: "You marry an infidel woman, [because] from the point of the seed [the child] is in essence a Moslem. You say this, and you marry infidel women, and it is acceptable practice. But if we do not give our daughters to their equals, but to somebody who has converted to Islam, then there is the possibility that he secretly becomes an apostate. If we only take the seed into consideration, what would the child be? Perhaps he leaves those who are begotten on sayyed women and escapes to the land of the Infidels? Then we can not call his children kin of the prophet. But in your religion you say the essence is seed, and you marry infidel women. In this case children born to a sayyedah are apostate children, for what is their ancestry?" This humble author said: "God almighty makes the children who are born from the loins of his different peoples, be it Jews or Christians, born to Islam; but it is the father and mother, who make them Christian or Moslem. Then I quoted the following Tradition: "Every one is born in the faith of Islam, then his parents make him Jewish, Christian and Zoroastrian."[170] I said the prophet of God has spoken the truth. After hearing this Tradition, all of them could not say anything.

---

168. Evliya refers here to two important religious festivals, that of *Laylat al-Qadr*, the night when the Koran was sent down, and `Id al-Adha, to commemorate Abraham's aborted sacrifice of Isaac. See M. Plessner, "Ramadan,"; G. H. Bousquet, "I`tikaf,", and E. Mittwoch, "`Id al-Adha," *Encyclopedia of Islam II*.

169. This poem has been copied from Mustawfi, *Nuzhat-al-Qulub*, p. 81. In Chelebi's text the first line is different as follows: "In purity the Tabrizis are seven in number." (*Tabriz chu haft qowmash z safa*). Both Kahraman and Jevdet have misunderstood the second line, which should be read as follows: "*Chun ayineh* and *pak az zang-e jafa*."

170. This is a Tradition in Bukhari's *Sahih*, Volume 6, Book 60, Number 298. "Narrated Abu- Huraira: Allah's Apostle said, "No child is born except on Al-Fitra (Islam) and then his parents make him Jewish, Christian or Magian, as an animal produces a perfect young animal: do you see any part of its body amputated?" [http://www.usc.edu/dept/MSA/fundamentals/hadithsunnah/bukhari/060.sbt.html#006.060.298]

The third good thing is that according to the law of Sheikh Safi all their trade in the bazaars is done with Persian money, *bisti*, *'abbasi* and gold.[171] In their country money of other countries is not accepted. In seven places they coin money. The first one, which is the old capital, is Ardabil. It says: "Struck in Ardabil." Also, "Struck in Hamadan, Baghdad, Isfahan, Tiflis, Nehavand and Tabriz." On one side is written: "There is no God, but God, and Mohammad is his prophet and `Ali is his regent." On the other side they strike the name of each king. For example, on a coin struck by Shah `Abbas in Tabriz is written: "The slave of the dog of `Ali Shah `Abbas."[172] But on *qazbeygi*s, is written "Struck in Tiflis" and "Struck in Tabriz." On the other side they strike a picture and the year. They call copper money *qazbeygi*s. These are all the coins in circulation. On all their measures and all their weights, and on the sewn clothes and expensive dresses, "There is no God, but God," is written. The name of God is written on the *derham*s of the districts. Woe to the person, who cheats in buying and selling, which is based on "there is no God, but God." They blind him by passing a hot rod over his eyes, put a heated bowl on his head and incapacitate him. In all the shops of the royal bazaars and in the squares there are scales hanging from yellow bronze and iron chains and they are never taken away. Whoever wants to buy any food, drinks and herbs puts them on the scale and, after properly weighing them, gives the money to the seller. Because his coin is pure he buys the best of goods. All meat, bread, vegetables, barley, wheat, flour, chicken, pigeon, walnut, hazelnut and whatever foodstuffs are cooked in the bazaars, and for all edibles and drinkables their prices are fixed in accordance with Sheik Safi's price regime, and they sell them by weight. For wheat, rice and other cereals they do not use the *kileh*;[173] they sell all of them by weight. Woe to the man who cheats against the divine words that have been written on the coins. They sell fabrics by the royal cubit.[174] Quadrupeds and captives are sold at a price set by estimators, in accordance with Safi's law.[175] They have estimators of good faith who implement it accordingly. This is the law of the shah.

The fourth good thing is that they cannot open the cooking shops in the royal bazaars unless they have cooked all the dishes and have cleaned all the tiles, copper pots and pans, and China utensils, which are hanging from the walls and the doors. In the morning, they open their shops with a prayer and praise, and then they cook rice with stewed meat (*hariseh pilau*), *duzde pilau*, rice omelette (*kuku pilau*), *chelow pilau*, saffron flavored rice, rice with cilantro-mint chutney (*abshileh pilau*); in short, the most popular are *pilau* and *hariseh*. They weigh the food, and beautiful young servants serve it. On the side of the copper bowls, which are made shining like silver with tin, they have inscribed Traditions like: "And give them food;" "the honor of the place is with the man who sits there;" "the honor of the house depends on its inhabitants;" "the honor of the person depends on his generosity." After eating they bring towels, clean basins and ewers to wash

---

171. For a discussion of the monetary system of Safavid Iran see Floor, *The Economy of Safavid Persia*. pp. 65-85. See also the glossary.

172. On coins struck under `Abbas II the motto "*buvad kalb-e `Ali `Abbas-e thani*," occurs, but without *fa aghlan* as Evliya has it. *Fa aghlan* perhaps is *astan* and thus the text could be *astan-e Kalb-e `Ali*. See H.L. Rabino di Borgomale, *Coins, Medals, and Seals of the Shahs of Iran, 1500-1941* (n. p., 1945), p. 36.

173. The *kileh* was equal to 25.656 kg in seventeenth century Istanbul. In the provincial towns the weight was usually lower. In Iran the *kileh* was 8.33 kg. Hinz, *Islamische Masse*, pp. 41-42.

174. Hinz, *Islamische Masse*, pp. 55-62 lists 28 different *dhira*`s or cubits; see also Floor, "Weights," q.v. *dhar*`.

175. Evliya is the only source that makes mention of this system of price regulation and related implementation rules allegedly formulated by Sheikh Safi, the ancestor of the Safavid shahs.

the hands of the notables. But lower class people and servants wipe their right hand under their left arm and their left hand under the right arm like a dog urinating [lifting his leg] in the field. Their manners are like this.

BAD HABITS OF THE PEOPLE OF IRAN. According to the ancient law of Azerbaijan, out of love of the twelve Imams, they have organized the military into twelve groups, who number in the thousands. There are twelve groups of ulama and other notables who cook at home. In the homes of all the other people it is less likely that they make a fire and cook food. But if they make a fire to prepare coffee, tea, fennel, salep, and *mahaleb* (St. Lucia cherry) cordial and for washing clothes they are not prevented from heating water. All servants and soldiers, the unemployed and unmarried ones buy and eat food from the bazaar. Therefore, the life of the uncouth Qizilbash is really bad in this respect, but it is cheaper, and a man can eat whatever he wants. For the people who have to watch what they spend (*hesabi*) and unmarried men, this is better. Even the soldiers, if they eat for three months in the bazaar, when the king's rations (*donluq*) are paid, the cook says: "I am the cook of the royal soldier," and he gets the soldier's rations and goes. He does not get one grain more or less. The cook who cheats in this respect has his tongue taken out. Then that cook feasts the soldier who has the rations for twelve days for free. This is their law. {If the shah or the general takes to the field, throughout the army camp kitchens are established in tents made of felt in a number proportionate to the number of soldiers, because they are in need of cooks}.

REPREHENSIBLE BEHAVIOR OF THE PEOPLE OF IRAN. According to the laws, they don't kill or hang criminals, but the police chief and market inspector take the guilty ones to the public punishment square, where, God forbid, the cruel executioners don't let them rest, and the master executioners torture them for three days and nights with three hundred and sixty variations of torture.[176] First, they give them three hundred strokes of the lash and horsewhip. Thereafter, they break their knees; then they put reeds under their nails. Next they brand them all over their body; then they force them to swallow greasy rags with a rope attached, which, if dragged out again, would bring the stomach and bowels with it; and the man, of course, had no choice but to confess. They make him swallow an oily sponge, and they press his temples between gazelle knucklebones and put horse and hoof nails to his temples and forehead, and they drill holes in the elbows and knees, and with a musketeer's ramrod they drill a hole from his knees down to his heels. Thereafter they put heated lead in a pan and then pour it into the holes so that the lead runs out with the marrow. They tie the four first fingers and toes tight together, and hang him from a noose and torture him with burning sulphur and asses' urine under him, so that the poor man's cries pierce the skies; they squeeze his testicles and put pointed thorns into his nose, put a heated cup on his head, and blind his eyes, and they bring out his penis from his anus. From several of them they take out their navel through their anus. May God forgive us! They take out the gall bladder from under his arm, they hamstring thieves, and someone who has given false testimony, they brand him and cut his nose and ears. They cut the hands and feet of thieves. They hang a man from hooks in seven different ways for three days and nights and in this way make him an example for others. The Khan, having one day glorified himself with these cruel tortures in my presence, this humble author asked: "O Khan, what is the purpose of torturing a man to this extent?" The Khan said: "O my brother, their elimination has been established by just witnesses. After having proven his guilt, we torture him in this manner, in spite of what people say, as an example so that he may not kill

---

176. For the punishments meted out as well as the role of the *mohtaseb*, who was in charge of controlling prices, weights and measures, see Floor, "Secular Judicial System," pp. 9-60.

again and becomes an example for the forgetful. There is no one more cruel and rebellious than a human being. The case in point is that man rebelled against God and said: 'I am your almighty God.'[177] That is why we torture in this way." This humble author said: "This is against Islamic law, and therefore it has no use for the edification of the people. According to Islamic law, *hadd* punishments are obligatory. The text of the Koran is this: "the hand of the man or woman who steals should be cut, for what they have done and should be punished by God, for God is wise." It also says "If a man kills he should be killed."[178] And further on "and what we prescribed to them in that life is for life."[179] If the punishment is in accordance with that would the people then live in fear?" I asked. The Khan said: "You are right." He accepted my words; but having this excessive kind of torture is necessary to keep people under control because they are rebellious, irreligious and belong to heretical sects. So they established it as a law.

In Tabriz there are forty-two Armenian churches.

CONCERNING THE SITES OF PILGRIMAGE OF IMPORTANT, GREAT AND HOLY MEN IN THE WONDERFUL CITY OF TABRIZ. First, the cemeteries of Sorkhab, Cherandab, Kachilab,[180] Dolyan-kuh[181] and Heyjan. Apart from these there are many other shrines. In the aforementioned places there are many authors, writers and sultans. Among the great men buried there are: Imam Hafedane, Sheikh Ebrahim Kuvanan, Sheikh Shukur-khvan, Baba Farrokh,[182] Baba Hasan Meymandi, Sheikh Shoja`, Kalin, Sheikh Malin-e Tabrizi, Sheikh Hasan Belghari, Sheikh Badr al-Din Kermani and Sheikh Nur al-Din Bimarestani. In the cemetery of Sorkhab the poets who are buried there are: Anvari,[183] Zahir al-Din Faryabi,[184] Falaki-ye Shirazi,[185] Shams al-Din Sobhasi and Falaki-ye Shirvani.[186]

SAINTS AND SUFIS BURIED IN THE VILLAGES AROUND TABRIZ. The men of God who are buried in the villages around Tabriz are: Khvajeh Mohammad Kajijani[187] in the village of Kajijan; in the village of Sabadabad[188] there are about seven hundred graves of great writers and scholars, may God have mercy on them.

---

177. Koran, 79: 24 (al-Nazi`at).

178. Koran, 5: 38, 45 (al-Ma'ida). In case of offenses directly against Allah mentioned in the Koran, Islamic law imposes certain obligatory, so-called *hadd* punishments; see the article "Hadd," *Encyclopedia of Islam*.

179. Koran, 5: 45 (al-Ma'ida).

180. This is now called Gajil.

181. This is Valiyankuh and is now known as Veylan-kuh.

182. This should be Baba Faraj, a famous Sufi.

183. Owhad al-Din Mohammad Anvari (1126-89). His dates are approximate, while his place of burial is disputed. According to Dowlatshah it is in Balkh, while according to Mostawfi it is in Tabriz.

184. Zahir al-Din Faryabi (ca. 1156-1201).

185. This poet is unknown to us.

186. Abu'l-Nezam Mohammad Falaki Shirvani (thus not Shirazi) (1122-61).

187. He was a famous Sufi who died in 778 (1376-77). See Mohammad `Ali Tarbiyat, *Daneshvaran-e Azerbaijan* ed. Gholam Reza Tabataba'i-Majd (Tehran 1378/1958-59), pp. 417-18 (q.v. Khvajeh Mohammad Kaj-jani).

188. Its official name is Sa`idabad, but locally known as Seydava.

Near Tabriz, on Martyr's Mountain, general Osama b. Sharik, one of the Prophet's companions, is buried.

The blessed `Ajlak Sariyat al-Jabal, the older brother of Hamzeh, the Lord of the Believers, was sent to take the field at Nehavand, where he was wounded and came to Tabriz and died here.

Apart from this, the tombs of the blessed Sheikh Saghuji and the blessed Sheikh Salami Reyi are there.[189] In the cemetery of Sorkhab there is the grave of the blessed Ommaya b. `Omar b. Ommaya. The tomb of the blessed Sheikh Sayyed Jan Memi, who was a mine of learning and a receptory of divine secrets, is here. He was without rival in old and modern learning. He had devoted his blessed life to the learning of the unity of God. There was no end to his learning and no bounds to his beautiful aphorisms, may God bless his grave.

Near Memijan, on the tomb of `Ali, the outstanding among the scholars, this line was written:

> The Heir of the Gnostic Knowledge of the Prophet
> The Unique Pillar of the High (`Ali) Divine Law

After having visited the tomb of the heir of the heir of science and solver of problems, the blessed Sheikh Taqi, this humble author wrote these lines on his tomb:[190]

> The wayfarer of the people of the Sufi path
> Whose Guide is Pir Shafiq.
> He lit the light in Rey and Bokhara
> May the heavenly abode be his resting place,
> May God make his soul ever happy
> And may this Evliya always depend on him.

In the quarter of Sinjaran[191] [two] sons of the blessed `Ali are buried. Two of the Prophet's family, to wit: `Eyn `Ali and Zeyn `Ali are buried on Sorkhab Mountain. In the Sardeh quarter gates the head of Afrasiyab, one of the ancient kings of Iran, is buried. Sheikh Nasrollah, the son of Aq Shams al-Din, who was the master of Abu`l-Fath Mohammad Khan, is also buried here.

Outside and inside Tabriz there are several hundreds graves of great men, but to avoid prolixity in our travelogue this suffices.

Description of the outing we undertook with the great Khan to Sham Khazan and visiting the castles there

First, we moved from Tabriz with one thousand horsemen, and after traveling for five hours towards the west and passing through gardens and orchards we reached:

The stage of the village of Ajisu. This village is halfway to the castle of Qumlah.[192] It is a village of two hundred houses and well-developed and prosperous gardens; it is part of the

---

189. The section about the cemeteries is from Mustawfi, *Nuzhat-al-Qulub*, p. 81 with some additions by Evliya Chelebi.

190. We have translated Jevdet's text here (vol. 2, p. 264), because Kahraman's text (vol. 2, p. 133) is defective and incomplete.

191. The official name is Sinjaran, but its local name is Idaleh.

192. According to Nakhjevani, p. 289 this village probably is Qaramalek.

Khan's personal fief. It has one large mosque and three Sufi convents. The waters of the plains of Tabriz are subterraneous canals [and flow from village to village. On the main roads there are thousands of domed deep wells (*sardab quyi*). Since the water of this place is brackish, it is called Ajisu (bitter water).][193] The village chief (*kalantar*) gave a good feast for the Khan. In the early morning after traveling for four hours we reached Sham Ghazan.

DESCRIPTION OF THE TOMB OF MOHAMMAD SHAM GHAZAN. In the time of the dynasty of Chengiz Khan this place was a paradisiacal garden. Since it was like Syria and was in the direction of Syria, it is called Sham (Syria). In the year 694 [1294-95], Mohammad Shah Ghazan built a strong castle here, which is called Sham Ghazan. He settled about ten thousand of his subjects in this place and exempted them from the usual taxes. Then, he built a beautiful mausoleum for himself here the like of which has not been seen by the architects and engineers of Persian, Arabian and Dadiyan Iraq. It is like Istanbul's Galata tower, a tower which rises high to heaven. At the time that this humble author saw it some part of the side of it had been destroyed because of an earthquake. It is worth seeing; it is a big building and an old shrine. God be praised, we visited it with the Khan, paid our respects and read a *Fatihah* for his blessed soul. On the marble sarcophagus the following was written: [lacuna]

Now it is a Bektashi convent in which there are more than two hundred sincere bare-footed and bare-headed devotees. Outside the door of the shrine there is a big pyramid made from thousands of heads of sacrificed sheep, of which they had put their horns together. Since all the people of Iran have a great devotion for Mohammad Sham Ghazan, they send votive offerings of thousands of sheep every year. It has a well that is ten cubits deep, and in the middle of the summer its water is as if it were a piece of ice. Truly, it is like the fountain of life. They call it the shrine of Sham Ghazan. An explanation for its original name is that in the Mongol language '*shanb*' means 'grave.' *Shanb* in Persian means dome. Since the man in the tomb is a Mongol king called Mohammad Ghazan, it is called Shanb-e Ghazan. Then it was erroneously softened to Sham Ghazan. But the correct name is Shanb-e Ghazan. This huge shrine on Mount Valiyan, on its slope, called Sham Ghazan, is a strange and wonderful shrine, which is now in ruins. May God bless his dear soul. We departed from here and traveled towards the west on the slopes Mount Valiyan and we reached:

THE VILLAGE OF VALIYAN, which is a village with three houses, a beautiful large mosque, a caravanserai, a public bath, a guesthouse; it is a prosperous villages. All the endowments and charities are by the Vizier Sa`id Khoja Rashid al-Din Donboli.[194] We departed and again we traveled towards the west, and in five hours we reached Qal`eh-ye Qumlah.

DESCRIPTION OF QUMLAH CASTLE. This castle was built by Koja Farhad Pasha, the vizier of Sultan Murad III, in the year 998 [1589]. It is a quadrangular castle constructed with stones on the slope of Mount Valiyan.[195] Its circumference is about three thousand and eighty paces. It has

---

193. Nowadays this river is called Ajichay, which rises to the east of Sarab, near Ardabil and after watering Sarab and Badavistan districts passes by Tabriz and flows into Lake Urmiyeh. The text between brackets is from Jevdet, vol. 2, p. 264, which is similar to that of Hammer, vol. 2, p. 143. We have added these lines, because the Kahraman text does not make sense.

194. This is Rashid al-Din Fazlollah Hamadani (1247-1318). See Birgitt Hoffmann, *Waqf im Mongolischen Iran* (Stuttgart, 2000).

195. Now known as Veylan Kuh, Beylan Kuh or Kuh-e Valiyan: Latitude: 34.2166667 – Longitude: 49.45.

seven towers and two gates, one to the east and one to the west; the western one faces Rum, the eastern one faces Tabriz. When Khadem Ja`far Pasha was the commander of the troops at Tabriz, he fled from the Persian troops at Tabriz and took refuge in the castle. The Persian troops then besieged Qumlah castle. One night, Ja`far Pasha breached the wall facing Tabriz and with seven thousand choice troops attacked the Persian soldiers who were deep in sleep and killed them and pursued the rest to Tabriz. The soldiers arriving at the castle of Tabriz realized that they were going to be annihilated by the firing of the big caliber guns (*balyamez*)[196] of the castle of Tabriz, which had been taken by the deputy of Khadem Ja`far Pasha, and from behind by Tavashi Ja`far Pasha, who was coming with the army of Kurdistan. Finally, all of them were sent to the realm of non-existence. Khadem Ja`far Pasha again became independent commander, and the part where he had breached the wall he made into a big gate and called it the Breach Gate or the Tabriz Gate. It is a well-built gate and a strong castle. Within the castle there are seven hundred houses and one large mosque. Outside in the suburb, which is the original town of Qumlah, there are numerous gardens and orchards. The grapes, plums, *'abbasi* and *meleche* pears of Qumlah are very famous. There are seventy mosques, of which eleven are large mosques. Among them is that of Farhad Pasha, a beautiful building. Outside the town there are large mosques, caravanserais, bathhouses, markets and bazaars. This town, within the province of Tabriz, is a separate sultanate (*soltanliq*). It has one thousand soldiers, a mayor, a police chief as well as a qazi. We had great parties here, and we received gifts from the Sultan. In these places a *sanjaq-bey* is called a sultan, and an *amir-miran* is called khan, and a vizier of three horse tails is called *khanlar-khan*,[197] and a *daftardar* is called E`temad al-Dowleh,[198] and a *sardar-vazir* is called *sepahsalar*, a *quruji-bashi* is called *qapuchi-bashi*,[199] the *ra'is al-kottab* is called *monshi*,[200] an *alay-bey* is called *kalantar*,[201] a *su-bashi* is called *darugheh*,[202] an *alay-chavush* is called *yasavol-aghasi*,[203] a *yenecheri-aghasi* is called *diz-chokan aghasi*, a *yenecheri* is called *dizchokan*,[204] a conductor of guests (*mosafer kondur*) is called *mehmandar*.[205] These aforementioned officials are charged with governance and administration,

---

196. For more information on this large caliber cannon see H.J. Kissling, "Balyamez," *Encyclopedia of Islam II*.

197. *Khanlar-khan* or governor-general of large province.

198. Evliya Chelebi is mistaken. E`temad al-Dowleh is the title of the grand vizier. The Safavid counterpart of the *daftardar* is the *mostowfi*.

199. Chief of the guards at the palace doors.

200. A *monshi* was a clerk who indeed corresponds to the Ottoman function of *ra'is-kottab*.

201. A *kalantar* is the main local official in a city or large village. He is usually a local notable and not a military official as was the *alay-bey*, a title which von Hammer translates as 'colonel', while Bulut translates it as 'chief lieutenant.' The *alay-bey*, a feudatory official, i.e., a holder of a *ze`amat*, was the highest officer, below the provincial governor, mustering and commanding the *sepahi*s on campaign. H.A.R. Gibb and Harold Bowen, *Islamic Society and the West* (Oxford, 1963), vol. 1, pp. 51, 146-47.

202. The *darugheh* was the chief of police.

203. An *alay-chavush* is an usher or *chavush* who directs the march on the occasion of public processions (*alay*). Gibb-Bowen, vol. 1, p. 263.

204. *Yenecheri* or Janissaries were infantry troops formed of the Sultan's household troops and bodyguards. They were mainly recruited among Christians, who had to convert to Islam. The Safavid *gholam* or *qollar* corps was recruited in a similar way, see Floor, *Safavid Government*, pp. 166-76.

205. See Floor & Faghfoory, *Dastur al-Moluk. A Safavid State Manual*. pp. 155-58.

such is the law of Iran. Traveling from here through gardens and orchards we reached after seven hours:

The village of Seravrud, a big village, situated northwest of Tabriz. It has a caravanserai, a bathhouse and a large mosque. Its chief came and gave a party for the Khan. We spent a delightful night there, and we departed the next morning. We went hunting through gardens and orchards towards the east along the river Seravrud and reached:

The village of Dusht, where we ate and rested. It is a village in the district of Seravrud with a bathhouse, caravanserai and a large mosque. It is a prosperous village. We continued for six hours and we reached:

The village of Chulanduruk. It is situated on the banks of the river Seravrud and it is a village with one thousand houses with a caravanserai, a bathhouse, gardens, orchards and a large mosque. Then we moved to:

The village of Elqabendilis, which has three hundred houses, simple Armenian peasants, and three churches and three thousand well-built houses; it is a village with nice gardens and trestled vineyards.[206] We proceeded from there and reached:

The village of Lakderukh. This is the personal fief of the wife of Shah Safi. It is situated on the banks of the Seravrud River and has two thousand houses; it is a mixed Moslem-Armenian village, who are all weavers. There are two hundred houses altogether, and a large mosque, bathhouses and three Sufi convents. On Mount Seravrud there is a ruined castle. We proceeded from there to to the west and reached:

The village of Koja-abad,[207] which has five hundred houses, a large mosque, a caravanserai and a bathhouse. From here we proceeded towards the east and reached:

The district of Rudeqat. This is situated to the north of Tabriz on the other side of Mount Sorkhab.[208] It is a district with one hundred villages. For three days we were hunting in these town-like villages.

Description of the big city, the ancient capital, and the trade emporium of Maragheh

It is a separate sultanate in the region of Tabriz, in the land of Azerbaijan. It has about one thousand soldiers. It has a qazi, a mayor, a police chief and a secretary. It is the first capital of Azerbaijan and was built by Hushang Shah.[209] It is a well-known city with many beautiful gardens and orchards. In its trestled gardens and vineyards there is an abundance of fruits. There are many accomplished scholars there. From the city to Tabriz is a distance of eleven *farsakh*s. There are a total of seven thousand and sixty mud houses and eleven large mosques and forty caravanserais, sixty

---

206. Hammer, vol. 1, p. 144 has the village of "Kanidlis, 300 Moslems houses and a mosque; the Armenians have three churches and three thousand houses."

207. Now it is known as Kujuvar.

208. Kuh-e Sardab is situated at Latitude: 36.283333 and Longitude: 51.116667. Rudqat or Rudeqat is situated east of Marand.

209. According to Ferdowsi's *Shah-nameh*, Hushang aka Pishdad was the second king to rule the world.

mosques, and forty Sufi convents, and eleven beautiful bathhouses and three thousand shops. Its people are mostly drapers and weavers, who manufacture excellent Livornian bogassins.[210] The male and female beauties of Maragheh are praised all over Iran. From the time that this city was destroyed by Sultan Murad IV it has not yet recovered. In the time of the Ommayads, Marvan b. Mohammad al-Himar built this city, which comprised eighty thousand houses and extended to Mount Sahand. Some of its buildings can still be seen. [It has seven thousand one hundred mud houses, eleven mosques, forty caravanserais, sixty mosques, forty Sufi convents, eleven beautiful bathhouses and three thousand shops.] It was destroyed in the time of Chengiz Khan's Mongols, when Hulagu conquered Baghdad and dethroned the caliph, Mustansir billah, and destroyed that city. Several times after that the city was destroyed.[211] The buildings are distant, because Mount Sahand impedes the Northern wind from coming and makes the air heavy. Therefore, they do not build inside the wadi. In spite of this, all of its water comes from the high plateau of Mount Sahand and waters many gardens and orchards. Inside many thousands of houses, the water goes to fountains, ponds and reservoirs.

The Blue Dome – Maragheh

---

210. Twilled cottons used for linings.

211. For the history of the city see Yunes Marvarid, *Maragheh 'Afrazehrud' az nazar-e owza`-ye tabi`i, ejtema`i, eqtesadi, tarikhi* (Tehran, 1360/1981), pp. 611-40.

Its juicy grapes and other fruits, produce, pomegranates, different kinds of cotton, and vegetables are famous. Its people are very white-skinned, with beautiful eyes, who speak nicely, and have bright faces. Most of its people are in secret from the Hanafi school, and many of them are inclined to Sufism. Most of them speak the Pahlavi language, and they are eloquent and articulate. The province has eight districts.

First, the district of Serachun, [and then] Panachum, Benachum, Derjerut, Kardul, Hashtrud, Behsand, Ranguran and Qiziloren.[212] These districts have some eighty to one hundred prosperous villages. In total there are five hundred and sixty villages. But sixty of them are like a town having large mosques, caravanserais, villas, bathhouses and bazaars. It has seven castles in good condition. If we describe each of the castles separately it will be a book by itself.

DESCRIPTION OF THE PLACES OF PILGRIMAGE OF MARAGHEH. [lacuna]

We left this city and went to:

THE STAGE OF TURNACHAYIRI. This is situated in very lush and green place with two hundred houses in the district of Ujan. Its people are gardeners and weavers. Then we went to:

THE STAGE OF SETGIZ. This is a prosperous village with one thousand houses situated in the district of Ujan. Then, we proceeded to Ujan.

DESCRIPTION OF THE ANCIENT CASTLE AND CITY OF UJAN.[213] It was a big city situated on the eastern side of Mt. Ujan, which is a barrier to Tabriz. It was destroyed by Hulagu. Its first builder was Bizhan, son of Gayomarth, son of Gudarz.[214] It was a beautiful city on the border of Azerbaijan. Gradually it fell in decay and its people were transferred to Tabriz. In the year [-] Mohammad Sham Ghazan, of Chengiz Khan's line, built a quadrangular castle on the slope of Mount Sahand. Its circumference is one thousand paces; it has an iron gate opening to the east. Inside there are one hundred houses; there is no garrison, but in its suburb there are many houses. According to the mayor, there are altogether three thousand mud houses. It has seven large mosques, three bathhouses, seven guesthouses, and six hundred shops. Its products are wheat and lima beans, which are abundant. The water of Ujan comes from the mountain, but its fruits are not plentiful. Its people are Shafe'is, but they are people who hold to the saying: "Cover your gold, your religion and your path."[215] However, it is not clear what their secret religion is. They are merry fellows, but not religious. Of the Christians there are a group of infidel Armenian Christians; they have two churches. After having visited this town, we went hunting towards Mt. Seylan.

---

212. This section has been borrowed from Mustawfi, *Nuzhat-al-Qulub*, p. 88 ("the people here are fair-skinned, and of Turk race, and for the most part of the Hanafi sect. They speak a Pahlavi (Persian dialect) mixed with Arabic"). Currently the jurisdiction of Maragheh includes the following districts: Saraju, Banaju, Dizjarud, and Gavdul, which correspond with the first four districts mentioned. The last four: Hashtrud, Behsand, Anguran, and Qizilqoran are not listed among the names of the modern Maragheh districts. Marvarid, *Maragheh*, pp. 41-110.

213. The city of Ujan was situated at about 60 km southwest from Tabriz on the road to Tehran. The city probably was destroyed in the 18th century. Now the name refers to a rural district. Behruz Khamachi, *Farhang-e Joghrafiya-ye Adharbayjan-e Sharqi* (Tehran, 1370/1991), p. 214.

214. This is literally from Mustawfi, *Nuzhat-al-Qulub*, p. 83.

215. Meaning that they dissembled.

THE DISTRICT OF MEHRANRUD.[216] It is to the east of Tabriz at a distance of five *farsakh*s. It has sixty prosperous villages, but Kanderud is town-like. We crossed it and went to:

THE VILLAGE OF ESFEH. We passed from there and reached the village of Sa`idabad. In the time of Shah Tahmasp, it was founded by Vizier Sa`id and hence the name Sa`idabad.[217] In the year [-] Sultan Sulayman destroyed this village when he was marching to Baghdad, but it escaped the havoc of Sultan Murad. It is a big village inside many beautiful gardens, with one thousand houses, seven large mosques, a caravanserai, a bathhouse and bazaars. We stayed there one day and the next day we went to the south for seven hours and reached:

THE STAGE OF THE VILLAGE OF MANMAH. It was built by Kur Khodabandeh's daughter. It has one thousand houses. After nine hours we reached Kahravan.

THE DESCRIPTION OF THE CASTLE OF KAHRAVAN IN AZERBAIJAN.[218] This was built by Seyf Qoli Khan, one of the Khans of the Afshars, in the time of Shah Tahmasp out of fear for Sultan Sulayman. He was neither a subject of the Ottoman nor of the Persian kings. In the end, in the year [-], when the governor of Tabriz, Koja Farhad Pasha was going to Baghdad, this Sultan of Kahravan, whose name was Meymandi Khan Afshar, was attacking and plundering the vanguard and the rearguard of the army of the Moslem fighters for the faith, and then he took refuge in his own castle. Farhad Pasha closed his eyes to this and reached Baghdad in safety. Then he immediately sent Solak Farhad Pashazadeh with the army of Baghdad, and they besieged this castle for seventeen days and battered it with cannons. But it was not conquered, and he returned without victory to Shahrezur, but Farhad Pasha remained as chief commander of Baghdad. On the other side, this governor of Kahravan, Meymandi Khan, feeling emboldened, attacked merchants and travelers coming from Baghdad to Tabriz, and that irreligious and ill-behaved man taunted and misbehaved towards many Moslems. On one occasion, he mustered forty to fifty thousand rabble soldiers and plundered the surroundings of beautiful Tabriz. Then Ja`far Pasha, issuing from Tabriz, suddenly attacked him with twelve thousand soldiers and destroyed his army as well as all of his Yazidi Kurds and Turkman followers. The unfortunate Meymandi Khan fled almost alone to Kahravan castle. Ja`far Pasha safely returned to Tabriz with seven thousand heads and five thousand tongues and about ten thousand horses and camels and other plunder. In Tabriz they made a huge celebration by firing cannons and guns. The following day he went with seventy thousand troops and attacked Kahravan castle with seven big siege guns and forty royal cannons and he besieged it for three days, and by the grace of God he took the castle. Inside the castle Meymandi Khan was brought out alive into the presence of Tavashi Ja`far Pasha. First he cut off one of his ears and gave it into his hand and said: "O cursed one, see what a Tavashi (eunuch) governor of Tabriz can do. Look. Now we have destroyed your army. We came after you, took and destroyed the castle, captured and chained you and cut off your ear and like me you were made a eunuch." Then he called the executioner. Immediately the {ruthless} executioner came and joined the advisors saying: "Before killing him, it is better to get his property." [With tricks and promising him his freedom] he got one thousand bags [with money] and one thousand loads of cloth and then he killed him and hung Meymandi Khan from the gate. "Well done," [Tavashi Ja`far Pasha] said

---

216. Khamachi, *Farhang*, p. 497.

217. Locally it is known as Seydava.

218. This may be Goravan.

and on the one hand announced this to the shah, on the other hand he cut off the head of the Khan and sent these with the keys of the castle and 200 hundred camel loads of plunder to Sultan Murad III. Inside the castle there is a large mosque named after Sultan Murad. For eleven years it was in the hands of the Ottomans. It is a circular stone castle on the road to Baghdad. Its circumference is six thousand paces, and it has two gates, one to the north and one to the south. The one that opens towards the south is called the Ardabil Gate and the one opening towards the north is called the Tabriz Gate. It is the seat of a Sultan, with one thousand soldiers, a qazi, a mayor, a clerk and a police chief. The suburb has gardens, orchards and seven thousand houses. It has altogether sixty mosques, but only in eleven of them Friday prayers were performed. But now people do not frequent them. It has seven bathhouses, eleven caravanserais and eight hundred shops. Although every craft is represented, their chintz, comforters and bed sheet covers are famous all over; its gardens and orchards embellish the world. Due to its pleasant climate there are many beautiful people of both sexes as well as singers and musicians. We left the city towards the south, and after traveling for five hours we came to:

THE STAGE OF THE VILLAGE SHAHBAND. In the land of Ardabil it is a prosperous village with one thousand houses, with large mosques, caravanserais, villas and bazaars. There is a large mosque built by Cheghal-zadeh, which one has to visit. After nine hours to the south we reached the city of Ardabil.

DESCRIPTION OF THE ANCIENT CAPITAL OF IRAN, THE CITY OF ARDABIL

It is situated adjacent to [Persian] Iraq. In the land of Azerbaijan it was the first capital of the Persian kings, and the seat of the Sheikh Safi. In the year [-], in the time of Sultan Sulayman, it was once conquered and was the seat of a governor with the rank of Khan.[219] Later it fell into the hands of the heretics and several times the castle was destroyed, the houses were leveled and the people suffered. Then in 1039 [1629-30], the chief general of Murad IV, the lion-hearted Khosrow Pasha, plundered the environs of Hamadan, Dargazin and Ardabil. Eventually it prospered again, and now it is in the hands of Iran and is the seat of a khan. It has three thousand soldiers, a police chief, a mayor, a clerk, a qazi and a *sheikh al-Islam*. It is at one day's distance to the town of Jabal-e Sahlan.[220] From all sides it is one day's travel to the top of the mountain. The town is situated exactly in the middle of a vast fertile plain; on one side of it there is a small lake whose water is like the water of life. The first founder is one of the Armenian kings, called Ardabil son of Ardamani, the Greek.[221] After the conquest of Basra by the blessed 'Omar, when Sheikh Sariyat al-Jabal was general of Nehavand, it was built out of fear of the Caliph 'Omar. In the time of the blessed 'Omar, throughout the period of his caliphate, he battled with the Kharejites in the land of the Persians; and that is why they dislike 'Omar, while they do not mind Abu Bakr and Othman. Ardabil in former times was a very big city, and on one side it reached Mount Sahlan. Now there is a distance of two *farsakh*s, and since each *farsakh* is twelve thousand paces, this comes to twenty-four thousand paces. At the top of this mountain there is eternal snow. Now in the middle

---

219. This is correct, see Nasiri, *Titles*, p. 148.

220. This is now called Sabalan.

221. We have not been able to identify this person.

of summer, ice like a blessing appears like silver at the top of the mountain. Therefore, all the water of Ardabil comes from this mountain and waters all the fields, which is life-giving. Since it is very helpful to the digestion,[222] it enables the people of Ardabil to feast like Ma`dikarb,[223] and because of the good climate the people of both sexes are very lazy and healthy. All the women are Shafe`is, but they lie. Shah Esma`il called upon them to convert to the untrue sect of the Ja`faris (Shi`ites), and when Sunnites were converted to Shi`ites they became fickle of faith. Between Tabriz and Ardabil is twenty-five *farsakh*s. With a horse without a load it takes two days. Its climate is very much like that of Erzerum. The winter, in spite of being very harsh, provides plentiful grains and pulses, and some of its wheat harvest is left for the following year. One *keyl* of seed yields eighty *keyl* of produce. Because of the severity of the winter, there are no gardens, orchards and fruits, but there are trestled gardens and flower gardens.

DESCRIPTION OF THE LAKE OF ARDABIL. It is a clear water lake on which there are several hundred fishing boats. Its eastern side is close to Tabriz. Its western side is at a distance of one *farsakh* to Urmiyeh. Between Ardabil and this lake there is a considerable distance. Between Ardabil and the lake are promenades and forests and prosperous villages. In this lake there are seventy different kinds of fish and each one is like the bounty of Moses. The boats on the lake are used by merchants and traders with their goods, and they take them to the village where they want to go and also go to the cities on the west side, to Urumiyeh, Domdomeh[224] and Domboli.[225] The circumference of this lake is bigger than that of Lake Van. Those on foot can barely walk around it in ten days. The water of Lake Van is bitter like poison,[226] but the water of this lake is sweet and delicious. Its depth is seventy fathoms. This lake appeared the same night that His Holiness the Prophet was born, and it was on that same night that Khosrow's Arch, the idols of Mecca and the dome of the Aya Sofia were cracked. On that night when the lake appeared, around it forty-five small and big streams started running.[227] The river Sahlan waters Ardabil and then flows into this lake like the river Kehran. The names of other rivers are unknown, and I have not observed them.

{**DESCRIPTION OF THE STONE QUARRIES OF SEYLAN** (Savalan). In Mt. Seylan there is a quarry, and the stone that it yields is like Badakhshan cornelian. But since it is not profitable, it has been abandoned after the time of Shah `Abbas I. But if it were processed now, it is a jewel that has no peer. It has a separate governor. Mt. Seylan is very big and the honey that is produced in this area does not have its equal in Rum, Arabia and Persia.}

---

222. This sentence is also inspired by Mustawfi, *Nuzhat-al-Qulub*, p. 84.

223. He was a Himyarite (Yemeni) king (500 BCE) and uncle of `Amr al-Qaysh, the famous pre-Islamic Arabic poet.

224. Domdomeh is situated 30 km west of Ardabil. Razmara, *Farhang*, vol. 4, p. 218. For a description of the Domdom castle, which was built around 1608 by the Baradust Kurds, see Savory, vol. 1, pp. 990-91, 995-96.

225. Refers not to a town, but to the tribal area assigned to the Donboli tribe between Salmas and Khoy.

226. Evliya has confused Lake Van with that of Urmiyeh, the latter has bitter water and no fish, the former has fish and freshwater. There is no lake near Ardabil.

227. There are many streams and hot springs around Ardabil near Mt. Sahand.

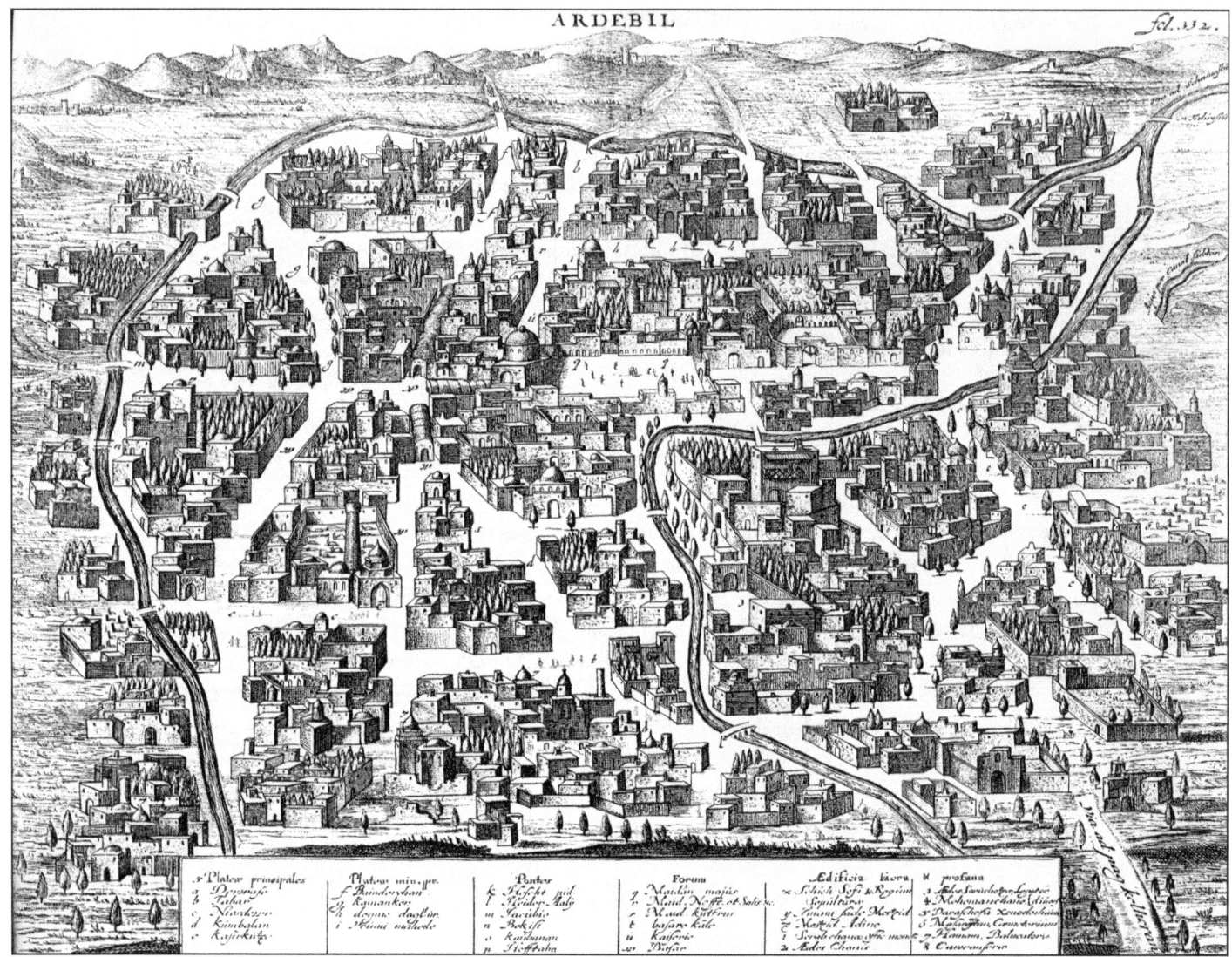

A view of Ardabil in 1637

ACCOUNT OF THE RAIN-PRODUCING STONE. In Ardabil, outside the city, there is a round and black stone that is heavier than iron. It weighs about three *qentar*;[228] it is polished and shining. Ancient priests and sages have written many inscriptions in Hebrew characters on the black stone. Truly, as if it is carved in marble, there is a picture of a person who has opened his arms towards heaven. When there is no rain in Ardabil, the notables, the high and the low and everyone roll this rock to the city. By the grace of God, it rained for three days and nights in Ardabil and all the fields, villages and towns were showered with God's merciful rain. Then they roll the stone again to its place, and the rain stops.

ANOTHER ODD AND STRANGE PHENOMENON is that when the people take this rock from its place and bring it nearer to the city the rain becomes harder. If the stone remains near the city,

---

228. The weight of a *qintar* varied per country, but in the Ottoman Empire it was equal to 56,443 kg. Hinz, *Islamische Masse*, p. 27. The entire tale about this stone is from Mustawfi, *Nuzhat-al-Qulub*, p. 278, who quotes the *History of Maghrib* and reports that the weight of the stone was 200 *mann*. Its existence is not quoted in later literature and not even discussed in Safari, *Ardabil*.

the blessed rain does not stop at all. The people of Ardabil cannot open their eyes because of the rain.

ANOTHER STRANGE SECRET. When the black stone is taken out of the city, if it stays outside, the lake of Ardabil becomes stormy, and it starts to inundate the province.

OTHER SECRETS. When this rock is taken from its permanent place, under it there is a big quadrangular rock, which is like flint stone and that also has many writings on it in Hebrew, Imrani[229] and Syriac. This quadrangular rock has twelve holes in it. [When the black stone is lifted from it], from each hole [of this quadrangular rock] a kind of water rushes forth, and until the black rock is put back it continues spouting water. It is a strange talisman. {Some of the scholars of Ardabil believe that this is the same rock that blessed Moses struck with his staff twelve times in the Sinai desert and twelve streams appeared. The Koranic verse that mentions this is: "He struck with his staff on the rock and from it came forth twelve streams."[230] It is the miracle of the prophet Musa that when he struck these streams appeared.}

Some of the people of Ardabil have this wrong belief that Sheikh Safi, who is the forefather of the kings of Iran, and who is buried in Ardabil, has made this talisman. Truly, this a miraculous talisman. Although Sheikh Safi was a wonderworker, after him in the year [-] the ill-famed Shah Esmaʿil led the people of Iran astray, and he accorded them with the despicable name of Qizilbash. May God save them. By God's wisdom, since in Ardabil cats do not live long there are many mice.[231] The number of mice in Ardabil is greater than in other places. The people of Ardabil have woolen clothes and robes that are in tatters because there are so many mice, and that is why in this

---

229. As far as we know there does not exist an Imrani script, which must be one of Evliya's concoctions. He probably took the name of the third surah (Ali ʿImran), which refers to Moses and his brother Aaron, who were sons of ʿImran, thus suggesting that they used an ancient script.

230. Koran 7: 160 (al-Aʿraf).

231. "Curious spectacle. Nowhere in the lands of the Rumi, Arabs and Persians does one find cats so graceful, so friendly that it makes you crazy, such good hunters and punishers than the cats of Divriji. This holds, even though the cats of the cities of Elvah in Egypt, Trabson and Sinob are also very well-known. But the cat of Divriji is fat, corpulent, with a shining fur like that of a thousand-colored Cymbeline. One even brings them as presents from Rum to the city of the province of Ardabil, in the land of Iran. In the land of Iran, they are carried around in cages on the head of criers and they are sold at auction in the royal bazaar and the bazzazestan, while crying: "One tuman! Two tumans!." If it is a cat of Divriji and in particular a castrated one, it is priceless, for, because the cats do not thrive in Ardabil, the mice of Ardabil are very famous. Although the people of Iran have a well-developed beard [jimberis xxx], because the rats consume all their moustaches, they buy the cats from Divriji at high prices. The sales pitch of the street criers of Ardabil is:

O you who seek the cat, the preying cat, the punisher and hunter, companion and amuser, enemy of mice, but not a thief! It is the companion of the grieving.

Chanting this in the Bayati style, the criers of cats walk with the cats of Divriji on their head and sell them. Due to the nuisance of mice the clothes of the inhabitants of Ardabil are patched up like the cape of the dervishes. That is why, in the city of Ardabil subject to calamity, the *hirre*, i.e., the *gorbeh*, i.e. the *quta*, i.e., the *sennure*, i.e. the *merrabeh*, i.e., the *machi*, the *pistan* and the *mestan*, i.e., the cat (*kedi*) is so valuable and is auctioned off in the markets of Ardabil. Such is the fame of the cat of Divriji. But the poor among the qazis of Divriji nurture an extreme hostility towards the poor *hirre*. Each year, in secret, they cause thirty to forty cats to be killed, have the skins tanned, and, in winter make a pelt with which they cover themselves. There is absolutely no difference with the furs of the squirrel of Muscovy. One does not see the difference between the reddish fur of [these cats] and those of the fox of Azak." Jean-Louis Bacqué-Grammont, "Un félidé anatolien oublié: le chat de Divrigi," in Daniel Balland ed. *Hommes et Terres d'Islam* 2 vols (Paris-Tehran, 2000), vol. 1, pp. 339-42.

city they sell cats for money. There are dealers for cats who put them in cages and sell them; they are in great demand. {In particular,} Divriji cats are sold for one hundred *qorush*.[232] But still they do not live long. The cat sellers, while selling them, cry the following chant:

> O seeker of cats
> > Of hunting cats
> Punisher and attacker
> > Companion and amuser
> Not a thief but a friend
> > An enemy of mice.

This is very amusing, but we do not want to give details of it.

THE PLACES OF PILGRIMAGE OF GREAT SHEIKHS. First, the pillar of the spiritual world, Sheikh Safi al-Din b. Sheikh Khvajeh `Ali b. Sheikh Sadr al-Din b. Musa b. Sheikh Safi al-Din Abu Eshaq Ardabili. He is the founder of all the kings of Iran and Turan. He began in Ardabil, and he is buried there under a very beautiful dome.[233] There are hundreds of dervishes, who are the custodians of his tomb. Day and night he bestows his blessings upon his pilgrims and he has extensive endowments.

Sheikh Safi came out and ruled the kingdom of Iran, and later on he was succeeded by his son Sheikh Heydar, and his son, Sheikh Ebrahim, saw in his dream that he was copulating with a donkey. He reported this to his grandfather Sheikh Safi, who interpreted it and said: "O Ebrahim, you will become a great king in the land of Iran." In fact, Sheikh Ebrahim was the first to strike coins and have the *khotbeh* read in his name. But his grandfather, Sheikh Safi and his father, Sheikh Heydar, did not strike coins and have the *khotbeh* read in their names. From Sheikh Safi to Shah `Abbas I, five kings have struck coins, and that's it.[234]

We left Ardabil and went to the north for nine hours and reached:

THE STAGE OF THE VILLAGE OF ARAMSHAH. It is a village with six hundred houses, without gardens and orchards. Then we went for eight hours to the north and we came to:

THE VILLAGE OF YAR `ALI, which has three hundred houses, no mosque, caravanserai, or bathhouse, but it has many markets. There is a weekly bazaar at a permanent location. Then we left, and after six hours we arrived at:

THE VILLAGE OF DHAT-E `EMAD. It is situated in the district of Dideherder and is a prosperous village with eight hundred houses. We traveled for seven hours from there and entered the beautiful city of Tabriz. We stayed there for several days and enjoyed ourselves. The mayor, police chief and the conductor of guests organized a caravan consisting of one thousand animals.

---

232. One *qorush* is 120 *aqches*.

233. For a description and pictures of the shrine see, e.g., Sayyed Jamal Torabi Tabataba'i, *Athar-e bastani-ye Azerbaijan* 2 vols. (Tehran, 2535/1976), vol. 2, pp. 122-91. Sheikh Safi al-Din was not a king, only the leader of a Sufi order, see F. Babinger-R. Savory, "Safi al-Din Ardabili," *Encyclopedia of Islam II*.

234. Shahs Esma`il I, Tahmasp I, Esma`il II, Mohammad Khodabandeh and `Abbas I.

Tomb of Sheikh Safi in Ardabil

Letters were written to the khans of Khoy, Behestan, the castles of Churs and Erevan, so that they would take care of this humble servant and that at every stage good guides would be provided. To our master, the great Pasha, cordial letters were written and ten strings of camels loaded with rice, raisins, dried *'abbasi* pears, pomegranates, two pureblood Qarachuboq horses, four piebald post horses and two Georgian slaves were given as gift. The two Georgian slaves brought with them brocade, gold brocade, gold-threaded tassels, raw musk and ambergris and beautiful clothes. To this humble author were given ten *tuman*s in *'abbasi*s, two *tuman*s in *bisti*s, one Georgian slave, one sable fur, one Persian-style dress, two sheepskin furs, six headdresses, one camel load of Erevan rice, one Qarachuboq horse and one piebald Uzbeg post horse with its Persian accoutrements. That day we bade farewell, and the next day the great Khan with his troops came out and the kettle-drums were beaten and the horns blown, and he accompanied us outside Tabriz to:

THE RECREATIONAL SITE OF `EYN `ALI,[235] which is the name of a quarter. And in that delightful spot he gave us a party that cannot be described. In this place of recreation he gave this humble author five *tuman*s in *'abbasi*s and twenty *tuman*s in *aqche*s to my servants as travel money, and to each of our friends one Kashani bathing-gown, three pieces of Gujarati *atlas*, and three pieces of Mohammadi turbans. He gave me three hundred chosen horsemen and one chief usher and told the latter: "O chief usher. You take my brother Evliya Agha via the good roads that the Caesar of the World, Sultan Murad IV, traversed from Erevan to Tabriz and safe-guard his

---

235. The `Eyn `Ali shrine is situated at the top of a mountain, northeast of Tabriz. Chelebi describes here the area next to the riverbed of the Mehranrud, which runs below this mountain; the `Eyn `Ali quarter is on the slope of this mountain and the river runs through it.

caravans well." He mounted his horse and accompanied us for half an hour. Then we kissed, and he returned to Tabriz and we with all our equipage went to Erevan.

Journey from the province of Tabriz in Azerbaijan to the province of Erevan and the description of its villages, small towns and castles

First, in God's name, we went from Tabriz to the north and passed through a well-developed plain full of gardens for four hours and reached:

The halting place and village of Hajji Harami. It is a prosperous and well-developed village with promenades in the land of Tabriz. It has three hundred houses with gardens and it is part of the endowment of the blessed Sham Ghazan. The tomb of Sham Ghazan can also be seen from the village. Here our conductor of guests entertained this humble one. The next morning we departed from here with two hundred horsemen and we said good-bye to the mayor and we traveled again to the north for [-] hours through well-built villages to:

The halting place and village of Sufiyan.[236] In former times it was a big village, but the Mongols destroyed it. Then Sultan Murad IV destroyed it even more than the Mongols. It is now a village of one thousand houses with paradisiacal gardens in the land of Tabriz; it is a small town with running streams. A number of people from Khorasan and notables of Persia and great writers and poets are buried here. We paid respect to them; only we did not know their names. There were more than twenty blessed domes. Every year, in the month of 'Ashura, several hundred thousand people gather here to cook 'ashura. They read the *'Death of Hoseyn'*,[237] and this is celebrated with great pomp. All of its people are Shafe'is, but in secret there are many Hanafis. We went from here to the north for six hours to:

The halting place of Mazid Khan. It is a prosperous village, bordering on Tabriz, of five hundred mud-covered houses with gardens, orchards and springs welling up from the earth. It has two large mosques; it has a well-built and prosperous caravanserai, one bathhouse and a royal market. We went to the north through a prosperous plain with villages and gardens for seven hours and we reached:

The halting place and village of Keremish. It is on the border with Nakhjevan, and it has one thousand houses, seven large beautiful mosques, caravanserais, bathhouses and bazaars. We took two hundred riding animals and went towards the north, and we passed through marshlands for [-] hours and reached:

The halting place and village of Veshleh Chayi, where we pitched our tents on [the river's] banks and rested and stayed there for several days. This river issues from the mountains of Nakhjevan and merges with the Aras River. From there we traveled through sandy places, and black dust was constantly rising up. In two hours we reached [the castle of Khoy].

---

236. A village about 36 km north-west of Tabriz on the road to Khoy. Khamachi, *Farhang*, pp. 390-91; Razmara, *Farhang*, vol. 4, p. 318.

237. The book referred to was a so-called *maqtal-nameh*, which was a text in which the story of the martyrdom of Imam Hoseyn at Karbala was described. It was used by panegyrists and elegists to edify the people, in particular during Moharram, the Shi'ite month of mourning, because Imam Hoseyn's martyrdom had taken place on the tenth of that month.

DESCRIPTION OF THE FINE CASTLE OF KHOY. It is an orderly city and beautiful like Marand. It is separate seat of a Sultan in the land of Azerbaijan, which has up to one thousand soldiers. It has officials like a qazi, mufti, overseer of the sayyeds, secretary, mayor, police chief, watchmen, royal slaves and a conductor of guests. Khoy is to the west of Manand[238] at a distance of ten *farsakh*s. It is a beautiful, well-built quadrangular stone castle situated on a flat plain. Its circumference is twenty thousand paces. The moat around it is not very deep. It has two gates, one in the south facing Tabriz, the other in the west,[239] which is called Bab-Manand [sic; Marand]. Inside the castle there are one hundred houses and one large mosque. The builder of the castle was Farhad Pasha, but the founder of the old city is Shah Heydar Karrar (the attacker).[240] This city has been destroyed many times and rebuilt; outside there are seven thousand houses covered with good earth; the city has seventy mosques, eleven of which are Friday mosques, two bathhouses, seven caravanserais and about one thousand shops. It is surrounded by orchards and gardens; it is a well-ordered city with beautiful people. The circumference of the city is thirteen thousand paces. Our slaves measured it. Since Murad IV destroyed the city, it has not been prosperous. The major crop of the entire plain is large-grained rice, and the climate is moderately hot. It produces cotton and juicy grapes. The river issues from Mount Salmas and flows into the Aras. Its gardens and orchards are famous. Among its famous fruits are the *peyghambar* pear, which is sweet, juicy and delicious and there is nothing like it. Because of the good climate, the countenance of the people is very white. Some historians call this city Turkestan, Afsharestan or Iranistan. It is an ancient city and major emporium, and altogether in its district there are one hundred and eighty prosperous villages.[241] Most of its people are Shafe`i Sunnis. Shah Esma`il made them pay a tax because of their long beards.[242] But now from the time of Shah Safi they have been exempted from this tax. In spite of the fact that they keep their long beards, they do not pay tax. There are many beautiful youths.

{**PILGRIMAGE TO THE TOMB OF SHAMS-E TABRIZI**}[We paid respect to the tomb of Shams-e Tabrizi[243] as well as of Amir Bughay. This person was from Turkman stock, and after he had been defeated by the Franks he fled to Isfahan, where he died in the year 495 [1102]. His tomb can be seen outside Khoy.[244]]

---

238. This must be Marand.

239. This is wrong; the gate faced the east. Riyahi, *Tarikh*, p. 104, n. 47.

240. No historical source makes mention of this Heydar Shah. Riyahi, *Tarikh*, p. 105, n. 50 suggests that Evliya Chelebi may have had Sheikh Heydar, the father of Shah Esma`il, in mind. However, the problem is that there is no evidence that he ever was in Khoy and the city is much older.

241. Evliya Chelebi copied the data concerning the products, the climate, the looks of the people, and the number of villages of Khoy from the *Nozhat al-Qolub*.

242. It was a characteristic of the adherents of the Safavid Sufi order that they were clean shaven and only wore a moustache. The tax on beards aimed to provide an incentive to Sunnis to convert to Shi`ism.

243. This is not the famous Shams-e Tabrizi, the companion of Jalal al-Din Rumi, but a certain Shams al-Molk, one of the ancestors of the Donboli khans, who is buried in Khoy. Riyahi, Tarikh, pp. 70, n. 6, 552-53.

244. According to Mohammad Amin Riyahi, *Tarikh-e Khoy*, p. 104, n. 44 this concerns a certain Qavam Karbugha, who is not buried outside Khoy, however. Riyahi suggests that Evliya Chelebi may have read in an old history that this person was buried near Khoy and that he reported it as a fact without verifying it.

Here we gave our letters to the Khan of Khoy, and we stayed there for two days and enjoyed ourselves. With several gifts and two hundred armed guards we went towards the north, and after nine hours of a pleasant journey we reached:

THE HALTING PLACE OF THE TOWN OF BEHEHSTAN. It is one of the dependencies of Khoy. It has a separate chief. Formerly, it was a city like Tabriz, but Hulagu's people destroyed and set fire to it. Now it is a small town with one thousand houses, three large mosques, a caravanserai, a bathhouse and a small bazaar. It does not have an important drapers' hall. But there is no end to its gardens and orchards. From there we traveled for three hours and we reached Churs.

DESCRIPTION OF THE CASTLE OF CHURS.[245] It is a separate seat of a khan on the border with Nakhjevan. It has two thousand soldiers, a qazi, and for the love of the twelve Imams, it has only twelve officials. Its pentagonal castle is on top of a hill; it is not a strong building with a simple wall in the form of a pentagon. It was built by the ruler of Azerbaijan, Uzun Hasan. It was attacked by Murad IV, and now the holes in its walls have been filled and it is brick building like a redoubt. Although it is on a hill, the hill itself is on the slope of a mountain. It has a gate facing the south. Inside the castle, except for the large mosque of Rus Hasan Pasha, there is no other building; but outside the town there are seven thousand houses that are newly built. It has eleven large mosques, among them the very ornate ones of Ozdamir Othman Pasha and Farrokhzad Shah b. Timur Khan. It has three bathhouses, seven caravanserais and two hundred thriving shops. Its climate is very clement, and its women are very beautiful, chaste and of good character. Its various kinds of grains, pulses, and produce are famous all over Azerbaijan. It has very beautiful, newly built villas and mansions. The young people are extremely pretty, with eyes likes the does of Khotan, and are sweet-voiced with beautiful faces, and accomplished, who make their lover swoon. When they put on their Isfahani caps, Persian chintz dress and the embroidered red overcoat and stroll like peacocks of Paradise, they make all their lovers lose their wits; and sometimes, when they cast a glance and smile at their eager lovers, they make as many Majnuns of them.

We stayed for three days and nights with the Khan of this town, Ayyub Khan, because he is a very likeable, humorous, well-spoken and sociable man. All this while, day and night, musicians, singers and minstrels performed; with his easy-going and likeable young boon companions we had get-togethers like those of Hoseyn Beyqara. On the fourth day, after receiving one fold of a full and long robe with sleeves (*lepache*), several types of silk fabrics, one woolen blue cloak, several headbands, striped fabrics, and three *tuman*s in silver *'abbasi*s from the Khan, we said farewell to all the friends that we had associated with and with two hundred riding-animals left the town. We went to the east and after four hours we reached:

THE QAREH CHEPOGH RIVER. This river issues from the Churs Mountains and, after watering several villages, falls into the Aras river. In the summer its water becomes less, and even animals like goats and sheep can cross it. We crossed the river and continued to the north passing through prosperous villages for seven hours until we reached:

THE HALTING PLACE AND VILLAGE OF MILLILI.[246] This is a prosperous place on the border with Erevan with five hundred houses, gardens and orchards and a large mosque; it is situated

---

245. Churs is situated at 7 km south-west of the Ziya al-Din village near Khoy. Razmara, *Farhang*, vol. 4, p. 163.

246. Hammer, p. 150 has Kent Halli.

on the banks of the Millili River. It is a small river issuing from Mt. Sepand, and it falls into the Aras. From there we traveled to the north through vast pastures and plains covered with plane trees, Chinese sumac trees and weeping willows flanked with promenades, and after eight hours we reached:

The stage of Tut alusi.[247] It is a pasture full of tulips and it has several hundred thousand shady trees. There are no buildings and people. It is a pasture and farmland. The police chiefs and mayors of the adjacent villages brought us all food necessities and beverages. We stayed in this pleasant place for one night and then went to the north to the banks of the Aras River, and we crossed the Aras and reached:

The halting place and village of Qaghaj.[248] It is a small town on the eastern bank of the Aras with a large mosque, caravanserais, bathhouses and three hundred houses. Its produce is rice. It is part of Erevan and a beautiful village. Going to the north on sandy roads after four hours we reached:

The halting place and village of Afsharli. It is part of Erevan and a prosperous village with one thousand houses, with a large mosque, caravanserais, bathhouses and a small market. It produces rice. Its inhabitants are Sunnis, Turkmen of the Afshar tribe and that it why they are called Afsharli. It has a separate mayor and conductor of guests. From here we passed for seven hours on the banks of the Aras and we reached:

{**The town of Shurehgel.**[249]} It once was a big town, but now it is not all that prosperous. It is the seat of a Sultan with one thousand soldiers. It has a large mosque, a caravanserai, a bathhouse and a small bazaar. After five hours we arrived at:

The halting place of Sharab-khaneh. It has five hundred houses, a large mosque and a caravanserai; it is a prosperous village. We then went to:

The village of Seyf al-Din, [-]

The halting place of Seyf al-Din Khan is on the border with Erevan situated on the banks of the river Aras. It was built by Seyf Qoli Khan, one of Khans of Erevan; it is the personal fief of the Khans of Erevan. It is a small village with one hundred eighty houses, one large mosque; it produces rice, has gardens and orchards. Five hours further north along the Aras is:

The halting place and village of Tilfirak.[250] This has one thousand houses, a large mosque, a Sufi convent, a caravanserai, a bathhouse, and its produce is rice. When Murad [IV] laid siege to Erevan he cut seventy thousand huge trees, which were used as gabions at Erevan, but since then such an innumerable number of large trees were grown in the gardens of this village that you cannot count them. From this village we sent people to the Khan of Erevan and the next morning we went to the north, crossed a river, and rested in a pasture. When we mounted

---

247. Hammer, p. 150 has "Tuto-lumi, where there are some hundred shady trees, but no village."
248. Hammer, p. 150 has Kagaj.
249. Shurehgel was a border district situated in Erevan province.
250. The name probably is Delferaq.

our horses a great procession of people appeared in front of us. It was Alvand Aqa, the deputy of the Khan of Erevan. After embracing, we went to the castle of Erevan with this great procession.

Description of the castle of Erevan of Azerbaijan in the City of Khoja Jan

When we entered the city they welcomed us by firing a twenty-gun salute. We went with the procession to the Khan's palace. There was no one. It was a completely empty building. It so happened that the Khan had given his sister in marriage to the Khan of Baku, which is situated on the Gilan Sea [sic; the Caspian Sea]. The Khan had gone to the party. The deputy sent us to the palace and bade us eat and drink. We enjoyed ourselves. We handed over all the caravans that had come with us from Tabriz as well as the camels with their loads. The Georgian slaves, and post horses and all the other presents from the Khan of Tabriz to Hasan Bey went to Erzerum with our letters. This humble author remained in Erevan and with the people of the caravan went sight-seeing as much as possible round Erevan.

The story of the building of the city of Erevan.
In the year 810 [1407] one of Timur's rich merchants, named Khvajeh Khan Lahejani, set foot here and a found a fertile land. He settled there with all his family and day by day became wealthier by cultivating rice, and he made it into a big village.[251]

Afterwards, in 915 [1509-10] the king of Iran, Shah Esma'il ordered one of his khans, called Revan Qoli Khan, to build a fort there, which he completed in seven years, and that is why it is called Revan. It is situated on the southeastern bank of the river Zangi and the castle, made of brick and stone, is beautiful. It is single-walled. Then, in 921 [1515-16], Sultan Sulayman, having undertaken an expedition against Nakhjevan, after having conquered Erevan with the army of Islam, plundered it. He totally destroyed its small and useful castle and returned to his Abode of Felicity (Istanbul) with an immense booty.

Later, in 990 [1582], in the reign of Murad III, the grand vizier Farhad Pasha was sent as chief commander of the Persia expedition with innumerable troops, and he plundered the environs of Ganjeh, Shirvan, Shamakhi, Erevan and Nakhjevan. He destroyed the beautiful mansions, gardens and orchards of the king, his errant son, and their other faithless followers and did not leave a stone unturned. He shaved the unshaven heads of several thousand uncouth Qizilbash with the Ottoman sword, and several times he fought with that rabble army. Then Koja Farhad Pasha came to the old castle of Erevan and pitched his tents, and to conquer Erevan he consulted all the fighters of the faith, following the text of the Koran: "Consult them in the affairs."[252] In the land of Erevan he built a palace called Tuqmaq Khan, which was like a paradisiacal garden. On the banks of the Zangi, from south to north, he began digging a big ditch.[253]

A hundred and fifty thousand soldiers of Islam did their best in forty-five days for the sake of the holy religion and finished the castle. In another forty days they completed other buildings

---

251. Erevan is a much older city and the 'modern' city Evliya saw had its origins in the 12th–13th centuries and its name is not derived either from Revan Khan. For a brief history see Eric Kettenhofen-George Bournoutian, "Erevan," *Encyclopedia Iranica*.

252. Koran 2: 159 (al-Baqara).

253. The next paragraph is headed as: Shape of the castle of Erevan, which does not make any sense here and therefore we have removed it.

and an arsenal. Its first governor was Cheghal-zadeh Yusof Pasha, who had been brought up in the honorable harem of Sultan Sulayman and had been given the rank of vizier. Farhad Pasha put seventy thousand soldiers to guard it, and then he repaired the castle of Shurehgel in the province of Erevan and left soldiers there. After that he repaired the castle of Qars and filled it with soldiers of Islam. He also conquered the castle of Ardahan, repaired it and put a garrison there. He further repaired the castle of Akhiskha like a shining pearl and put three thousand soldiers there. He made the son of Tomris Khan vizier of that place and returned to the Abode of Felicity (Istanbul). While the vizier Cheghal-zadeh Yusof Pasha governed the province of Erevan with justice and magnanimity and gave the city [of Erevan] even more prosperity than it had enjoyed in the time of Sultan Sulayman, under Laleh Mostafa Pasha and throughout [the province] each village became a big town, and all the subjects were treated with justice, and he made them prosperous. Most of the people enjoyed themselves. Then in the year 1012 [1603], after having taken Ganjeh and Shirvan the uncouth Qizilbash stormed Erevan for seven months. Because no help came from Erzerum, the castle's Moslem warriors of the faith suffered hunger and thirst and were forced to surrender the city to the Persian general Tuqmaq Khan. Leaving their arms, they went on foot to Qars and from there came to Erzerum. Later, in 1037 [1627], the Redheads were in the castle and it became even more prosperous than before. But the uncouth rabble of troops of Amir Guneh Khan, who were in the castle, infested the environs of Kaghezman, Qars, Cheldir, Akhiskha and Ardahan. The governors of Akhishka and Georgia, and the *vali* of Erzerum[254] sent complaints and requested assistance from Murad IV. Immediately envoys were sent to[255] the king of Iran and the imperial standard was erected in the garden of Scutari (Uskudar).[256] All governors-general of the provinces of Rum and Anatolia, confidantes and gate-keepers gathered to muster the army. The grand vizier, Tabaniyassi Mohammad Pasha became the commander-in-chief and marched one year ahead to Erevan. In the year 1044 [1634], Sultan Murad IV in his royal pavilion assembled a huge army of forty thousand Janissaries, twenty-two thousand *sepahis* in front of the garden of Uskudar, in accordance with all Ottoman requirements, rules and regulations, and prepared all the necessary equipment and heaped presents on them, {leaving Beyram Khan as his deputy in charge of the state,} and marched on the fifth of Shavval [24 March 1635] from Uskudar, traversing these stages to the city of Konya and Keyseriya to Sivas. In this halting place, he appointed the royal boon companion, the arms bearer, Mostafa Pasha, as his second vizier; but he kept his boon companionship, and the arms bearer Musa Pasha was appointed as the quartermaster general of the royal pavilion. Then the Neshanji Pasha[257] became arms bearer, and Malek Ahmad Agha became first lord in waiting. When he entered the castle Erzerum, Sultan Murad was told that "two hundred thousand soldiers had been added to the army." From Rumelia alone, the governor, Jan Pulad-zadeh Mostafa Pasha, had mustered an army of thirty-one thousand. The Sultan was told that: "From all provinces one thousand seven hundred caparisoned, hennaed and white-spotted thorough-bred Hasani and Hoseyni horses with their flank armor have been brought as lead horses." Khalil Pasha, the governor of Erzerum, fell in disgrace and his enemies, Selehdar Pasha and Morteza Pasha, rejoiced. [The governorship of] Erzerum was conferred on the vizier of

---

254. "and from the Begs of Georgia," Hammer, p. 151.

255. Hammer, p. 151 has "were sent from the Khan of Persia."

256. Hammer, p. 151 had added, "as the signal of Asiatic war."

257. The *neshanji* was the head of the chancellery, although his authority changed over time. Gibb-Bowen, vol. 1, pp. 124-30

Damascus, Kuchek Ahmad Pasha, except for the barley-money[258] of the entire province, which was given to the weapons-bearer Mostafa Pasha. Then the army marched in three days from Erzerum to Hasan Qal`eh and from there via Qars went to Erevan. On the twenty-first day[259] he pitched his tents at Erevan with two hundred thousand troops. With long guns the Redheads (Persians) were able to inflict damage on the army of Islam in this place, which, not caring about the booming guns of the Qizilbash, crossed the river Zangi. An unfortunate archer in the Sultan's guard, while crossing the river on foot, was carried away by the water. Having seen this, the Sultan, from the back of his horse, grabbed him by the waist[260] with his left hand and saved him. This story is much celebrated in Azerbaijan.[261] After having crossed the river, the Moslem fighters of the faith started making trenches in broad daylight. With the *zagharji-bashi*[262] and Jan Pulad Mostafa Pasha, the troops of the Rumelian province entered the trenches from the side of the Tabriz Gate. On the right, the vizier of Anatolia, Gurji Mohammad Pasha, with the provincial[263] troops and twenty battalions of special palace guards entered the redoubts. The grand vizier, Tabaniyassi (Flatfooted) Mohammad Pasha,[264] and the gate keepers with twenty battalions of special palace guards entered the trenches in between the Anatolian and Rumelia troops and started fighting. The commander of the Janissaries, Qara Mostafa Pasha, with the deputy of the Janissaries and ten battalions of special palace guards from the side of the river Zangi entered the trenches and with twenty guns started battering the castle day and night. From five sides with twenty cannons they fired and gave no rest [to the enemy]. One day, Sultan Murad himself entered the redoubt of the Rumelian troops and aimed a cannon named *Qarahbali* and fired a good shot at the Khan's palace. The governor of Erzerum, Kuchek Ahmad Pasha, battered the inside of the castle and the towers from the north with fifty royal cannons from a high redoubt and did not allow the Redheads (Persians) to raise their heads inside the castle and destroyed it. Qapudan Deli Hoseyn Pasha bombarded the castle of Erevan, both inside and outside, day and night, from the Mohnad Hill. You could neither stay on the battlements or shooting holes, nor in the bazaars, or even in the cellars of the castle because of the damage done by the cannons. Morteza Pasha and the district *sepahis* were placed as ushers on the side of the mud castle. Musa Pasha and Kan`an Pasha with the *motafarriqas*[265] were charged with guarding the imperial pavilion. The castle was surrounded at a distance of five hours by a sea of people who kept watch, so that not a single person had the nerve to destroy those two provinces. Every day, several thousand Sunni subjects came with gifts and asked for mercy. With this effort the castle was watched every moment and on the ninth day, the uncouth Qizilbash appeared on the bulwarks and ramparts crying, "Mercy, mercy,

---

258. *Arpaliq* was the term to refer to civil holdings, whose "revenues were supposed to pay for the barley consumed in the stables of officers and officials, and for the slippers of the Harem ladies." Gibb-Bowen, vol. 1, p. 188, n. 4.

259. Hammer, p. 152 adds, "after having left Erzerum."

260. Hammer, p. 152 has "by the necklace."

261. The text has Azerbaijan of Ujan, which does not make any sense, apart from the fact that it rhymes.

262. One of the three officers that formed the divan of the Janissary corps.

263. Hammer, p. 152 has "Asiatic troops."

264. He was grandvizier from 18 May 1632 to 2 February 1637.

265. *Motafarriqa*s were feudal guards attached to the service of the grand vizier. Gibb-Bowen, vol. 1, p. 362.

O you chosen of the house of Othman," and submitted[266] the keys of the castle to the Sultan and asked for mercy. They came to surrender to the Sultan. The next day in the morning, the army of Islam took over the fort. The following day, the commander of the musketeers, Mir Fattah, and the Mazandarani soldiers were allowed to kiss the feet of the Sultan and were sent with guards to Nakhjevan. On the aforementioned day, the governor of Erevan, Amir Guneh Khan, who is a Georgian by birth, came to perform the royal foot kiss with seven khans, and each one received a pavilion and became guests of the vizier. From the towers of the castle the Mohammadan call to prayer was heard and the ramparts and bulwarks were embellished with flags for seven days. After each of the five prayers, three times the shout of "God is great" was heard, and three times they fired guns and muskets, and during dark nights a great number of candles and lamps lit the tents and pavilions. By continuous shouts of "Allah, Allah," Persia was full of fear. In this manner, in forty days the castle was again repaired and Morteza Pasha became the governor of Erevan. Forty thousand Moslem fighters for the faith were left to guard it. Emir Guneh Khan, the khan of Erevan, and other khans who were captives of Sultan Murad set out on the road. {On the way, the Sultan gave the governorship of Aleppo to Amir Gunehzadeh, but because [later on] he killed his deputy, he was dismissed and the province of Aleppo was given to Kuchek Ahmad Pasha. Amir Guneh Yusof Pasha came to the High Porte and became an imperial companion. When Sultan Murad died, Qara Mostafa Pasha killed Amir Gunehzadeh.} In Erzerum, Tabaniyassi Mohammad Pasha and Jan Puladzadeh gathered seventy thousand troops to serve as the garrison of Erevan, and they started from Erzerum and, after passing many stages, reached Nakhjevan and the Qarabaghs and {the castle of Shurehgel, Churs, Behestan, Khoy, Ordubari (sic; Ordubad) and Tabriz, which were pillaged during seven days and nights, together with the castles of Bagh-e Jenan, Ujan, Kehran, Qumlah, Marand, and Salmas, after which havoc they returned via Van, Bitlis and Diyarbekr to the Abode of Felicity and there was much merry-making.} Then, the evil king of Iran came with one hundred thousand troops and battered the castle of Erevan for seven months and did not leave them any hope. Since Tabaniyassi Mohammad Pasha was an enemy of Morteza Pasha, who was besieged, he did not help Erevan. {When he heard of the accursed shah's movement he came to Erzerum to help Erevan}. In seven months whatever stores and gunpowder were inside the castle were exhausted. Eventually, one night, Morteza Pasha swallowed his diamond ring and died. The following day the Moslem troops came out of the castle without arms asking for mercy and surrendered the castle to the shah, but most of the Moslem fighters for the faith were martyred by the uncouth Qizilbash and some {drowned} and some were saved by Sunni families and taken out of the Aras and fled to the castles of Qars and Bayazid. On hearing this sorrowful news, Murad IV girded himself on two sides with the sword of religious zeal and high enterprise and decided to try to liberate paradise-like Baghdad from the hands of the rabble Qizilbash, a city where the tomb of our great Imam No'man b. Thabet is.[267]

As of the year 1045 [1635], Erevan for twelve years has been {in the hands of the Persians} and prospered and thrived. But since its walls were not strongly built it could not resist a strong attack from the Ottomans for seven days, because its walls were only one-fold.[268] This castle is situated on the bank of the river Zangi from south to north, and having so little width that the balls fired by Sultan Murad from big siege guns destroyed the wall at the Tabriz Gate, and balls

---

266. Hammer, p. 152 has "Emirguneh brought the keys."

267. Meaning Abu Hanafi, the founder of the Hanafi school of jurisprudence, which was the official school adhered to by the Ottoman Empire.

268. Many castles and cities had double or even triple walls, van Bruinessen et al., *Diyarbekr*, p. 210, n. 64

came out from the other wall and even now the marks of the balls can be seen on the walls of the towers. The castle of Erevan that Farhad Pasha built has a height of forty royal cubits; but the castle built by Tuqmaq Khan has a height of fifty cubits and a width of twenty. Although it has no moat on the side of the river Zangi, there are many shooting holes. On the southern, eastern and northern sides there are moats. However, since they are in a marshy place, they are shallow. Some parts of the moat are as wide as hundred fifty cubits. There are three strong iron gates.

The Tabriz Gate is to the south and the Meydan Gate to the north, which is also called Yeyla Gate. They play polo on this site. To the west, there is the Bridge Gate, which the Persians call Darvazeh-Pol. There are about seven hundred pieces of small and big guns left by the Ottomans and innumerable other stores and arms, because this is the border of Azerbaijan in Iran, and it was conquered by the Redheads with difficulty. About three thousand men are in the castle, three thousand of the Khan and seven thousand provincial levies. Several times it has become a governorship-general. It has a qazi, a mullah, an overseer of the sayyeds, a mayor, a police chief, a clerk, a chief of the ushers, a chief of the royal household troops, a master of ceremonies, a chief of the royal slaves, seven conductors of guests and chiefs of the merchants. This is the best border city of Iran. Inside the city there are about two thousand mud-covered houses and the most outstanding among them is the palace of the Khan, which has been repaired and enlarged by Emir Guneh. Close to this palace, on the right side, there is the mint, which coins *abbasi*s and *bisti*s. The suburb outside the Yayla Gate is called the old city. It has a caravanserai, a large mosque and a bazaar. Near the bridge there is the garden of the Khan, and there are many large mosques, caravanserais, bathhouses and bazaars.

In short, the inside and outside of the city's royal bazaars are impressive. In the year 1045 [1635], when it passed into the hands of the Persians, they built a three-fold wall of clay and straw on the east side that is stronger than stone.

While I visited the town a messenger came from the Khan of Erevan inviting this humble person to a feast.[269] His deputy gave ten *tuman*s in *abbasi*s for my travel expense so that it would cover my cost on the road, and with forty servants and companions I left to Baku.

Observations on the Journey from Erevan through the Provinces of Shirvan, Shamakhi, Tiflis, Termenis and the Castles of Arash and Baku

We first traveled from Erevan to the north through rice fields, along the river Zangi, and after five hours traveling through prosperous villages we reached:

The village of Koja Baghi, which is a personal fief of the Khan of Erevan. It is a big village of five hundred houses with a large mosque and a bathhouse. From there we continued to the north for six hours through gardens and along the banks of the river Zangi and reached:

The halting place of the village of Demirji Hasan,[270] which formerly was a Turkman city, but now they only come there in winter; it is a big place. Murad IV destroyed it. Going from there to the north after six hours we reached Ganjeh.

---

269. Hammer, p. 154 adds, "to assist at the ceremony of the circumcisions of his sons."

270. Hammer, p. 154 has "Demiji Hassan."

An Ottoman sepahi

A view of Shamakhi in 1637

DESCRIPTION OF THE CASTLE AND THE WONDERFUL CITY OF GANJEH.[271] It was wrested from the hands of the king of Iran, Shah Tahmasp, in the year 990 [1583],[272] by Koja Farhad Pasha. And in the year 1014 [1605], while the deputy of Sari Ahmad Pasha, whose name was Mohammad Pasha, was its governor, the evil king of Iran besieged it for seven months, and they fought day and night. Since there was no help coming, the Moslem fighters for the faith had no choice but to surrender the castle, and the unarmed Moslem troops were martyred. This was made known to Mohammad III, the Conqueror of Egri,[273] [who made some effort to retake it, but without effect]. Now this important city is in hands of the Persians. But the shah destroyed its castle. Now it is a prosperous city, with six thousand houses, gardens and orchards, mosques, caravanserais and mansions, a drapers' hall and royal bazaars. The city is filled with gardens and orchards and situated in a plain. The Kurun river flows through its gardens and orchards and joins

---

271. For a brief history see C.E. Bosworth, "Ganja," *Encyclopedia Iranica*.

272. Shah Tahmasp I died in 1576.

273. Mohammad III took part in one campaign, namely that of 1596, in which the Hungarian town of Erlau (Egri) was taken by the Turks (September 1596).

with the Kur. Towards the south there are mountains, which are covered with gardens, and their juice grapes and the Ganjeh silk are very famous. All around it there are seven districts with infidel villages, where cotton, rice and silk are cultivated. Here are very rich Magians, i.e., Armenians, and their Khotan gazelle-eyed children are famous. Their female beauties are famous. {The horse shoes as well as iron of Ganjeh are as famous as its silk.} It is the seat of a Khan. It has three thousand soldiers, a clerk, a mayor, a police chief, a qazi, and for the love of the twelve Imams, there are a qadi and officials. When, for the first time, the Ottomans held it, Khadem Hasan Pasha became its governor, who took the castle of Barda` and took Heydar Mirza, Shah Tahmasp's nephew hostage, and concluded peace.[274] Farhad Pasha brought this Mirza to the High Porte.

THE TOMBS OF THE MARTYRS OF EREVAN. Twelve thousand Moslem fighters of the faith were put to the sword by the merciless shah, in spite of his emphatic oath, when they came out unarmed asking for mercy. Now they are buried outside the city in a place called 'The Martyrs of Erevan.' Several times the people of the province have seen divine light descending on their graves. We became the guests in the caravanserai of the city, and then with fifty of our companions traveled north to Ganjeh. When going to the north, there was on our right side Lurestan,[275] which is a khanate. After four hours and passing through its environs we reached:

THE HALTING PLACE OF GULUN [?] HAZAR AHMADI.[276] In former times it was a town; now it is a prosperous village of seven hundred houses with gardens and orchards. It has large mosques, a caravanserai and a bathhouse, and it is the personal fief of the Khan. Its fine silk is well-known everywhere. We went for nine hours to the north and after nine hours reached:

THE VILLAGE OF MEKUCHUVUR.[277] This is situated on the banks of the river Kur. It is a Moslem village with seven hundred houses, a large mosque, a caravanserai and a beautiful bathhouse. There are absolutely no infidels; its silk is famous. On the other side of the Kur there is an Armenian village called Kendere. They cross in boats and come to Mekuchuvur for the weekly bazaar.[278] These villages are on the border with Ganjeh. We left and crossed the mountain pass of Qushlunja and after [eight] hours we reached Aras.

DESCRIPTION OF THE HALTING PLACE OF THE IMPORTANT CASTLE AND TOWN OF ARAS. It is situated in the province of Shirvan in the land of Persia. It was built by king Gayomarth in ancient times. In the year 985 [1577] it was conquered by Laleh Qara Mostafa Pasha, one of the viziers of Murad III. Later,[279] a forty thousand strong army of uncouth Qizilbash, the ir-

---

274. Heydar Mirza son of Sam Mirza, brother of Shah Tahmasp. For details see Savory, *History of Shah `Abbas the Great,* vol. 1, p. 482.

275. There is no Khanate called Lurestan in this region. Evliya probably referred to Luri, a Khanate situated in Qarabagh. Nasiri, *Titles*, p. 236.

276. Hammer, p. 154 has "Gilkzar Ahmedi," and Jevdet, vol. 2, p. 287 has Klk (Kelek?) Hazar Ahmadi.

277. This probably is modern day's Mingecevir.

278. Jevdet, vol. 2, p. 287 has "to cause mischief."

279. Hammer, p. 155 has "Emir Khan arrived with forty thousand men to succour the town."

religious enemy, arrived to help, found that the castle had passed into the hands of the Ottomans. They besieged the castle and fought until noon. The brave Laleh Pasha attacked the Persians with the Moslem fighters of the faith and killed thirty thousand of them. Their commander, Amir Khan was captured and the remainder of his army, consisting of Turkmen, Gökdolaq and Georgian knights, fled. They were faced by the deputy of Ozdamir-oghlu Othman Pasha, who was coming with the army of Shirvan at the bank of the Kur, and he killed all of them. Several thousand of them, out of fear of the Ottoman swords, stormed the bridge over the river Kur and caused it to collapse, and by God's wisdom, all the uncouth and ill-mannered Qizilbash drowned in the Kur. Their bones still may be seen and the bridge that was broken is still there. Now, they have put planks of pine trees and cross over it. Later, the Moslem fighters of the faith returned with an abundance of Persian plunder. Then the great commander, seeing that this city of Aras was a very important and strategic city between Ganjeh and Shirvan, gathered all the fighters of the faith and other workers and builders on the banks of the Aras River, including a garden called Shah Khiyabani, which was outside the town, and built a wall around it and made a wide and deep moat, with three gates and seven redoubts, and with mortar made a strong castle. Its circumference is nine thousand six hundred paces. The general finished it in forty days and gave its governorship to Qeytas Bey, who had been brought up in the harem of Sultan Murad. Laleh Pasha himself went to the High Porte. Now this beautiful town on the slopes of Mount Shah is very similar to Bursa, with a pleasant climate, and is filled with gardens, orchards, rose gardens and trellised vineyards. It has about ten thousand well-maintained mud houses[280] and about forty large mosques; among them are famous the ones by Murad III, Farhad Pasha and Qara Senan Pasha and many others, but I do not know them and some of them are not frequented by people. The name of the city is Aras. But in the Persian, Turkmen and Daghestani Qomuq languages it is pronounced as Arash. When Sultan Murad acceded to the throne, this place passed into the hands of the Persians and it is prosperous just like Marand. It has forty quarters and forty mosques as well as madrasehs, Sufi convents, elementary schools, sixteen bathhouses, eight hundred shops, seven coffeehouses and a merchant's caravanserai. It is a beautiful city ornamented with gardens and orchards. Its boys and girls have beautiful Khotanese gazelle-eyes with faces shining like the sun, because their women were born of Georgian, Dadian, Achiq bash and Shavsheti people. Because of its climate they are beautiful. Mt. Shah has several thousand running streams that waters its gardens and orchards such that it does not need the Aras river. Around it there are seven big districts, each one with one hundred prosperous villages.

Of the region around Aras, that of Levand district is the most prosperous. Both the Sultanjiq district and, on crossing the bridge of Ozdamir-zadeh Othman Pasha, the Great Pilevnay district are prosperous as well.[281]

The district of Shayi` is prosperous, and on a hill there as is castle, since I do remember its name I have not written it. There are several [other] prosperous districts. Opposite the city on Mt. Shah the Turkmen people have their large summer quarters. In the region of Aras, the district of the castle of Sheki is prosperous,[282] but occasionally the ruler of Daghestan occupied it. Now it is

---

280. Hammer, p. 155 has "houses with terraces."

281. Hammer, p. 155 has instead, "On crossing the bridge of Uzdemir-oghli Othman pasha, the traveller arrives at the district of Palvana, and the district of Shair Abadan, where a castle is seen on a rock, the name of which I do not remember."

282. Hammer, p. 155 has instead, "The royal mount, opposite the town, is the summer abode of the

in the hands of the Khan of Aras. Because the Khanate of Aras is an important khanate between Daghestan and Georgia, it has three thousand and twenty soldiers. It has a qazi, a clerk and twelve officials. We stayed three days in this city and received gifts from the Khan. With two hundred Mazandarani musketeer companions, we departed from here to the north and after two stages we reached Sheki:

DESCRIPTION OF THE CASTLE OF SHEKI. This castle was built in ancient times by one of the rulers of Georgia and Shavshad called Alexander Khan. Then it passed to the rule of the Bey of Daghestan.[283] Then it went to the Persians, and in the year 986 [1578], after the vizier of Murad III, Laleh Qara Mostafa Pasha, had conquered it, he gave its governorship to Erekle Bey, the son of Levand Khan. Later, during the accession of Sultan Mostafa, it fell into the hands of the uncouth Qizilbash, and it is now the seat of a Sultan with one thousand soldiers. It is a beautiful stone castle on a hill in the province of Shirvan. Its circumference is three thousand paces, but since it is built on an impassible mountain there is no moat. There are two gates, called those of Shirvan and Ganjeh. It is a prosperous castle on the border of Daghestan, but it is considered to be part of Georgia. It has three thousand houses and seven large mosques. In the market is the large mosque of Mirza `Ali Bey; in the castle the large mosques of Laghosh-oghli Ahmad Bey and Sultan Murad III are famous.[284] It has caravanserais, bathhouses and a small bazaar. In its gardens and orchards peerless[285] silk is produced. At one day's journey east of this castle we crossed the river Kanut that flows into the Zangi river. While we were going north we crossed the river Qabur via the Ozdamir-oghli Othman Pasha bridge and arrived at a place called Qoyun Gechdi (Sheep-crossing).[286] Here in a cellar we saw piles and piles of human bones. I asked our companion Yavar `Ali Agha: "What are these?" He said:

> Laleh Mostafa Pasha, the general of Murad III was surrounded in this place by Amir Guneh Khan of Tabriz, the khans of Moghan, Lur, Nakhjevan, Qarabagh-Qazan, and Qazaq and of Ansar Khalifeh Sharaf Khan, in short nine khans. All the generals of Iran and commanders of the Redheads with more than twenty thousand men surrounded Laleh Mostafa Pasha and gave battle. The general ordered the Moslem fighters for the faith to shout 'God is great,' and from one side Ozdamir-oghli and from another side Mohammad Pasha, the governor of Aleppo, and from the third side Mostafa Pasha, the governor of Mar`ash, attacked simultaneously. And he himself attacked as well, and in a short they killed ten thousand uncouth Qizilbash, and the remaining troops, like a flock of sheep going to the sheepfold, went to the place called Qoyun-gechdi and drowned. Some fled and drowned in the river Kenek and some in the river Kabur. The result was that in this great war forty thousand followers of the shah (Shahsevan) were killed by Laleh Mostafa Pasha.

Turcomans."

283. For a brief history see V. Minorsky-C.E. Bosworth, "Shakki," *Encyclopedia of Islam II*.

284. Hammer, p. 157 has instead of 'are famous' the following text, 'is falling into decay.'

285. Hammer, p. 157 has instead, "great quantities of."

286. For this battle see, Abu Bakr b. `Abdollah, *Tarikh-e `Othman Pasha* translated into Persian by Nasrollah Salehi (Tehran, 1387/2008), p. 71.

"Curse be on the Ottomans!" said my friend, "These are the bones of those men." After saying this they recited a *Fatiha* for those dead and crossed. This humble servant passed Qoyun-gechdi and going to the north after three hours crossed the river Aqsu, which the Persians call Gilan-chay. It comes from the mountains of Aras and falls into the Kur River. After crossing it and having traveled for three hours we came to:

THE HALTING PLACE OF THE DISTRICT OF MAHMUDABAD.[287] It is in a vast plain with two hundred prosperous and well-developed villages with promenades, which each year produce one thousand camel-loads of silk. Each village is a small town by itself with a large mosque, bathhouses and royal markets. Its villagers are Armenian, Gökdolaq, Turkmen, Mongol and Qomuq. One of the tribes is called It-til.

ACCOUNT OF THE IT-TIL TRIBE. In the Mongol language *it-til* means 'tongue of dogs.'[288] In battle they howl like dogs like "aw, aw" and "wow, wow"; they are a stubborn lot. Near Mardin, in the mountain district, which I entered with Malek Ahmad Pasha Efendi, there are about twenty thousand unclean and faithless Kurds, who are [like them] without religion, ill-mannered, corpse-eating, ass-riders and a disgusting people. If you ask them they say: "We are followers of blessed Hamzeh."[289] But they know nothing of fasting, prayer, hajj and *zakat*,[290] and they know nothing about what God has decreed upon them. Seven or eight men marry one woman. If the woman gives birth to an illegitimate child, all her seven or eights adulterers gather and the mother gives an apple into the bastard child's hand; the man to whom the child gives it is considered to be his father, and thereafter it is decided that the woman belongs to that man and nobody may lay a claim to her. In the land of Iran this famous accursed tribe is called the Candle Extinguishers.[291] I have not seen or heard of similar behavior anywhere else. But it is a fact that they drink out of the shoes of their shah, to whom and to their khans they are very obedient.

{DESCRIPTION OF THE TRIBE OF THE QEYTAQ.} There is a tribe called Qeytaq who number about twenty thousand and they live on the border with Daghestan.[292] They come to the cities of Aras and Sheki to trade. They are a very strange looking people, like the beast of the Day of Judgment. They are men with heads like kettles, long hair, brows two fingers broad, shoulders so square that a man can easily stand on them, with broad chests, thin waist, fat thighs, flat feet, round eyes, red-colored and round-faces. They claim to be Shafe`is and are very stout people.

---

287. Mahmudabad was built by Shah `Abbas I, it is now called Hajigabul.

288. *Il* in Turkish means dog, and *til* or *dil* means language and tongue.

289. This probably refers to Sheikh Hamzeh Baba, a saint buried near Diyarbekr, see van Bruinessen, p. 185.

290. *Zakat* or obligatory alms for the poor given to charity as a certain percentage of one's income. It is one of the five, so-called, pillars of Islam.

291. The same accusation was made against all "heterodox religious groups, who were accused of organizing mixed male-female gatherings with so-called light-extinguishing ceremonies (*cheragh-koshan*) as part of their ritual. During this period of lights-out they allegedly were engaged in sexual debauchery, for which accusation, like that of the earlier group marriage, never any piece of evidence was and is proffered." See Floor, *A Social History of Sexual Relations in Iran*. p. 68; Matti Moosa, *Extreme Shiites. The Ghulat Sects* (Syracuse, 1988), pp. 126-27, 136-38. See also p. 159 infra.

292. On the Qeytaq see Floor, "Who were the Shamkhal and the Usmi?"; Gmelin, *Travels through North Persia, 1770-1774*, pp. 303-10.

When they come to the markets of the castle of Aras and Sheki they come on foot to the plain and then get onto wagons of Sheki, because of their huge weight, which is like that of an elephant, cannot be borne by a horse or mule. The wagons are drawn by special buffaloes. On their heads are turbans large like a dome and headbands around them are like that of a Crimean qazi, with shaven moustache and long beards; they greet people on both sides in a dignified manner, and they look like the people of the Anti-Christ. They are a very strange looking people of Oghuz extraction. They are ridiculed by the people of Gilan, Shirvan, and Shamakhi. They are a very Oghuz-like people.

THE LANGUAGE AND EXPRESSIONS OF THE QEYTAQ, WHO ARE A SECTION OF THE MONGOL PEOPLE

Mori (horse); *achra'a* (stallion); *güvan* (mare); *utġan* (foal); *qulun* (colt); *nev* (moon); *toqa'* (dog); *tavlay* (rabbit); *susar* (weasel); *qafa* (pig); *germun* (squirrel); *yelġan* (sable); *cumran* (mouse); *ceyran* (deer); *vet'an* (elephant); *utem* (ermine fur); *hesine* (wolf); *şivlasun* (lynx); *temgen* (camel); *lavşe* (mule); *hüker* (steer); *miġun* (cat); *ahhin* (spider); *buvasud* (louse); *qomriqa* (ant); *besleqen* (crocodile); *helye* (kite); *deqaq* (hen); *deqavun* (rooster); *siġirça* (starling); *laçin* (peregrine falcon); *tilkü* (goshawk); *itavun* (partridge); *betuqçin* (vulture); *çiġa* (unfledged chick); *ciġa* (crane plume); *çaq cay* (Qipchaq Steppe); *surhen* (name of a ruler); *cav* (enemy); *şenp* (graveyard); *şenbet bay* (gravediggers).[293]

There are so many other expressions, but in the two days that I was among them I could only collect these, but this much I wrote down. The Qeytaq people are originally Mongols from the province of Maghan,[294] but they themselves are Turkish-Mongols, speaking Mongolian. When they say Mongolian they mean Turkish. It is an old language unlike any other one. We saw these people in the district of Mahmudabad, and then having traveled to the north for (-) hours we reached:

THE HALTING PLACE OF GILAN-CHAY.[295] It is situated on the banks of river Gilan in the province of Shirvan. It is a prosperous village of Oghuz and Turkmen with gardens and orchards with six hundred houses. Again moving towards the north in the plain after [-] hours reached Niyazabad.

DESCRIPTION OF THE TOWN OF NIYAZABAD.[296] It is situated on the border with Shirvan. It was founded by king Yazdegerd.[297] In ancient times it was a big city. Now the ruins of its buildings and the [once] high sky-scraping arch can be seen. Then the Mongols united with the tribes of Daghestan, the Qeytaq and Qomuq, invaded the town and destroyed it.

---

293. We have adopted the transcription as given by Dankoff, *Glossary*. The Qeytaq do not speak Mongolian, but an Ibero-Caucasian language of the Dargino-Lak group. This entire sample of words was copied from Mustawfi, *Nuzhat al-Qulub*, see Paul Pelliot, "Le prétendu vocabulaire mongol des Kaitak du Daghestan," *Journal asiatique* 210 (1927), pp. 279-94; Ibid., "Les formes turques et mongoles dans la nomenclature zoologique du *Nuzhatu'l-kulub*," *BSOAS* 6 (1930-32), pp. 555-80.

294. Both Jevdet and Hammer have Mahan, which seems to be the correct form. It probably is a region in Central Asia, near Merv. See Bulut, p. 324.

295. This river is also known as Aqsu.

296. Niyazabad, port south of Darband. For a description see Müller, *Sammlung*, vol. 4, pp. 103-07.

297. Yazdegird I (r. 399-421) was one of kings of Sasanian Iran.

Later, Koja Farhad Pasha, the commander-in-chief of Sultan Murad III, made this town his winter quarters. Then on the Khvarezmshahi New Year, when he was going to Shirvan, he destroyed it and turned Niyazabad into Kharababad and then went to Shirvan.[298] Now it is the frontier between Iran and Daghestan. It has forty mosques and forty quarters. There are large mosques, a caravanserai, bathhouses and a royal market. It is the seat of a sultan. It has one thousand soldiers and twelve officials, a qazi included. According to the mayor, it has more than one thousand gardens and orchards. It is a vast, well-developed province with good people, with fine tombs. It has many farms, with an abundance of products, many running streams and it is a prosperous city. But the castle which is in the center of the town is in ruins.[299] If God should give the Ottomans possession of it then it would be easy to repair and become a Qahqaheh-like strong castle. The city is surrounded by a plain, which is covered with villages and gardens.

The tomb of Afshar Baba. He was one of the deputies of the blessed Khvajeh Ahmad Yasavi, our great ancestor, the Turk of Turks.[300] Since the Persians greatly respect him, there are more than hundred dervishes in the Yasavi convent occupied in prayer and devotion. Pilgrims are well-treated and fed in this convent. The tomb is visited by high and low. Most of the people of the city are Hanafis, because it is part of province of Shirvan, which for seventy or eighty years was under Ottoman rule.[301] We took some companions from this town and went to the north and after [-] hours reached:

The village of Farrokhzad. It is on the border with Shamakhi, on the bank of the river Aqsu and has five hundred houses. It has a large mosque, a caravanserai, a bathhouse and a small market. The conductor of guests was very kind to this humble servant. We left this place and went to the North, and after [-] hours through shady groves we ate at the royal hunting lodge of Shah Kur Khodabandeh, and from there we went to the village of Nil-chay, which is also called Göksu. It is a life-giving stream that comes from Daghestan and joins the river Kur.

{**In praise of Mount Elburz.**[302] By God's wisdom, all the rivers issuing from Mt. Elburz, which is on the southern side of Daghestan, fall into the river Kur. Those rivers that flow towards the North drain into the Caspian Sea. Those coming from the south of Mt. Elburz drain into the Black Sea. Those from the north side in general join the river Kuban. This river drains into the Black Sea near the island of Taman.[303] Mt. Elburz is a large and high mountain, which does not

---

298. Hammer, p. 157 has instead: "and levelled the castle, when he left in the spring." Kharababad means 'ruined place.'

299. Hammer, p. 157 has instead, "It is a pity that its strong castle lies in ruins; if God should again grant that it be restored to the Ottoman power, it might be easily repaired, and become a very strong castle. This town is surrounded by an endless plain on all four sides."

300. He was born near Tashkent, one of the popular Sufis, who died in 1166. Between 1397-99 Timur built a mausoleum for him in the town of Turkestan (now Yasi) in Kazakhstan, which still exists.

301. The Ottomans ruled most of Azerbaijan, including Niyazabad, for 23 years, between 1583 and 1606.

302. Mt. Alborz or Elbrus is situated in the Western Caucasus in Circassia, near the Georgian border and is 5,642 meters high, being the highest peak in Eurasia. Its glaciers are the source of the Baksan, Kuban and Malka rivers.

303. The Kuban flows 870 km north and west from its source near Mt. Elburz and eventually issues into the Sea of Azov. Taman is Taman peninsula.

Two views of Niyazabad, south of Darband

have its like on the earth, and all around it there are five kings, and to the south are the Abaza tribes.[304] Its length is eighty stages. The Abazas are settled on its eastern side. On the slopes of the mountain, Mingrelians, Georgians, Achiq bash, Shavshetis, Guril and Dadians[305] are settled, the length of [the settled area of] these tribes and Georgia is forty stages. The winter quarters of Georgia, at the border with Persia between the province of Tiflis and the Throne of the Alans (Sarir-e Alan), is on the other slope of Mt Elburz and its length is nineteen stages. From here, towards the north of Mt. Elburz is the kingdom of the uncivilized Circassians, with the tribes of

---

304. The small Abaza ethnic group lives in the foothills of the main range of the Great Caucasian Mountains on the upper reaches of the Big and Little Zelenchuk, Kuban and Kuma rivers. The Abaza language belongs to the Abkhazo-Adyghian group of the Caucasian languages.

305. On these terms see below pages 99, 107

Kabartay, Besti, Bolatkay, Khatukay, Mamushukh, Bozodoq, Taqaqu, Zana, Shagaki[306] and other Circassian tribes. Each are living separately on the mountain slopes for a length of eighty-one stages. According to this calculation, the circumference of Mt. Elburz is two hundred and forty stages. It is a huge mountain and its summit can be seen from every side at ten days distance. In the world, God has created one hundred and forty-eight mountains, of which twelve are the highest. Mt. Elburz is the highest among them. After that there are Mount Bingol, Mount Demavend, Mount Subhan, and then Mount Kamar at the source of the Nile and at the source of the river Danube the German mountains; then, in the land of Erdel at the source of the river Turla [Dniester] and Tise [Zeiro], Mount Sahansamur [?]. After these the other mountains are smaller. But there is nobody who has ever climbed half the height of Mt. Elburz. There are all sorts of animals on this mountain. Even during this journey when we were passing the border of Shirvan into the kingdom of Daghestan, its highest peak was visible wrapped in dark clouds.

We decided to return. We had stopped [the description] at the aforementioned village of Gokchay, which is a big village with a mayor and a conductor of guests, with seven hundred houses, gardens and orchards. Its silk is very famous. Its people are Sunnis and paid beard tax during the reign of Shah Esma'il. But now, in the time of Shah 'Abbas II, they are exempted from customary obligations; they are Moslems. In the land of Shamakhi it is one of the most prosperous villages. We traveled from here to the North in the plains for seven hours and reached:

The halting place of the village of Aqsu, in the land of Shamakhi. It is a prosperous and beautiful town with gardens and orchards, one thousand houses, a large mosque, a caravanserai and a bathhouse. The river Aq passes through it and joins the river Kur. Its origin is in the mountains of Shirvan and after watering the rice fields in the plain of Shamakhi it falls into the river Kur. From here, we traveled north, and after [-] hours we reached Shamakhi.

Description of the province of Shirvan, i.e., the castle of Shamakhi, may God protect it

Its original founder was the Persian king Yazdegerd in the year [-]. It is an ancient land, which has passed through the hands of many kings. It consists of seven khanates. Some say that its name Shamakhi comes from a contraction of *sham akhi* (brother of Damascus) and some say *sham ahi* (the sigh of Damascus). They say Shamakhi, because the original inhabitants of this place came from Syria (Sham); some say Shamaki. The Daghestanis call it Shemekhi, and the Gilanis call it Sham aqi. Its proper pronunciation is Shamakhi or Shamaqi. It is a prosperous and large province with forty khanates, forty-eight judgeships, forty quarters, seventy castles, about one thousand three hundred prosperous villages, large like towns, and it is an old and prosperous city. Two of the viziers of Sultan Sulayman, Ulama Pasha and Piri Pasha, the governor of Qaraman,[307] came to the city with a letter of Sultan Sulayman, and the Sunni notables, after consultations with each other, handed over the keys of the castle to Piri Pasha, and the province of Shirvan surrendered. When this situation was reported to Sultan Sulayman, he gave the governorship to Ulama Pasha.

---

306. According to James Stuart Olson ed. *An Ethno-historical Dictionary of the Russian and Soviet Empires* (West Port-London, 1994), p. 150 the Cherkess included the following 'tribes': Adyghas, Kabards, Abadzag, Beslenoi, Bzedugh, Gatjukai, Jererukoi, Kemgoi, Kheak, Nadkhoknadzh, Shapsug, Temirgoi."

307. Qaraman, province in south-central Turkey, 100 km south of Qonya.

Thereafter, Shah Tahmasp besieged the castle of Shamakhi for seven[308] months and granted mercy to the Sunnis inside and gave its governorship to his younger brother Alqas Mirza. Alqas Mirza was governor of Shamakhi for three years. Then in the year 954 [1547] he became fearful of the erring Shah's behavior towards him and left the governorship of Shirvan in 954; and in the night with his retinue of brave, courageous and valiant men, along with his valuables, he left Shamakhi for the Ottoman court. After forty days of traveling through the Heyhat desert,[309] he arrived in Kafa [in the Crimea]. He then boarded a ship and came to Edirne to kiss the noble feet of Sultan Sulayman. Since he spent several days in the company of the king, {the date of the coming of Alqas Mirza is: "Alqas Mirza became the subject of Sulayman of the Time," which gives the year 954 [1547].

Thereafter, comes the date when Alqas Mirza destroyed the land of Persian Shirvan:

On Laleh-ye Mostafa Pasha's advice
The king of kings went against Tahmasp, which equals the year 956 [1549]}

He was sent to the royal city of Constantinople and made his abode in the palace of Pertev Pasha. Later, Sultan Sulayman came from Edirne with a huge procession and entered Istanbul via the Edirne Gate. Near the great mosque of Shahzadeh,[310] Alqas Mirza watched this great procession and said: "O son of Othman. How is it that you, with this pomp and power, have not been able to defeat the king of Iran and Turan and have not uprooted the evil Qizilbash." He was overcome by the sight of the innumerable Ottoman soldiers. Later, when Sultan Sulayman invaded Azerbaijan and Van, he took Alqas Mirza with him. From Tabriz, Laleh Mostafa Pasha was appointed chief commander of the province of Shirvan, and Alqas Mirza, who was the former governor of Shirvan, went to Shirvan and ravaged the cities of Nakhjevan, Erevan, Ganjeh and Shirvan. On their return they received news of the death of Shah Tahmasp.[311] They then besieged the castle of Shamakhi and, with the power of Laleh Mostafa Pasha, they wrested the castle from the hands of Shah Tahmasp's son. They put sufficient troops and equipment in there and repaired it. After Laleh Pasha became the governor of Shirvan, he appointed Alqas Mirza as governor of the district of Mahmudabad in the province of Shirvan. Alqas Mirza, because of the grudge that he bore, ravaged the Persian provinces as far as the environs of Isfahan. The news of this as well as the good news of the conquest of the castle of Shamakhi, together with the keys of Shamakhi, were sent to Sultan Sulayman. Several times [both sides] fought over Shirvan. Eventually, in 991 [1583] in the time of Sultan Murad III, Ozdamir Othman Pasha conquered Bab al-Abvab, i.e., the Iron Gate (Darband) and granted mercy to the people of Shamakhi and repaired its castle. Later in the year [-] it fell into the hands of the Persians, but was retaken by Farhad Pasha in the time of Murad III, and it remained in Ottoman hands until the time of Murad IV. Eventually, the uncouth Qizilbash conquered Shamakhi and Demirkapu (Darband), and granted mercy to the Pasha of Demirkapu and his retinue, who returned to the High Porte. From that time onwards

---

308. Hammer, p. 158 has, "three months."

309. The Heyhat desert (or Plain of suffering) is situated roughly between 47° and 48° N and 32° and 33° E at present day Prichernomorskaya Nizmennost', see Fuat Sezgin, *Mathematical Geography und Cartography in Islam and their Continuation in the Occident* (Frankfurt a/M, 2000), map 155a.

310. The Shahzadeh mosque was built by Sultan Sulayman during 1544-48 using the services of the great architect Senan, which was his first major building.

311. This is incorrect, Shah Tahmasp I died in 1576.

it has remained in the hands of the Persians. It is now the seat of a khan with a qazi and twelve officials. The castle is on a hill on the banks of the river Kur; it is very strongly built with stone. Its inside is very strong and well-built, but the exterior of its lower part has many holes. There is a castellan, a chief of the royal slaves, with about one thousand soldiers. Inside the town there are about seven thousand well-built houses with stone walls and roofs covered with mud, and each house has a well. It has innumerable gardens and orchards.

It has twenty-six city quarters. The Meydan and Shaburan quarters are situated in the castle. Being in the best part of the town, the houses are very nicely built.

It has about seventy large mosques. There is the mosque of Div `Ali, which is an old one. Formerly, he was one of Shah Tahmasp's khans. He was a Sunni, and he built this large mosque. But in the suburb there is a large mosque, which looks like the Arch of Khosrow. It is frequented by many people and was built by Shah Safi. It is a very elegant building. In the court yard (*haram*) there is a *shafe`i* basin and fountains, surrounded by cells for the students. Because the Farhad Pasha mosque has no endowment, its gates are closed. It is built in the Ottoman style and is a beautiful mosque. The Ozdamir Pasha Mosque is now a madraseh; the mufti of the city teaches there.

Apart from these large mosques there are Sufi convents. Seven seminaries and a soup kitchen are of Shah Khodabandeh's foundations. There are forty elementary schools for children. There are seven beautiful bathhouses.

Altogether its climate is pleasant; the buildings are well lit. The Shahburi bathhouse, because of its ambiance and situation, is the best one. It has numerous private rooms in the midst of basins and fountains. Silver-bodied Shirvani youths with Khotanese gazelle eyes and indigo-colored wrap-arounds are its masseurs. The Meydan, Qazaq Khan and Faraj Khan bathhouses are situated outside, but near the castle, the bathhouse of Khosrow Khan is the most famous. Apart from these, in each garden there is a bathhouse and a *shafe`i* basin.

Inside the city there are forty-four brick-built caravanserais, in each of which reside rich merchants, who own goods worth many thousands of *tumans*. All the conductors of guests are good people. Everyone who has a shop in the caravanserai closes the door without locking and leaves his goods there, which are guarded by watchmen; such is the security in the land of Shirvan. Though there are twelve hundred shops, yet it has no stone drapers' hall, despite the fact that they contain many valuable goods. The coffeehouses as well as the barber shops are very beautifully decorated and are frequented by and full of witty people.[312] Its climate is mild and coastal, because it is situated at the extreme end of the fifth clime. The produce of its land is: rice, cotton, seven types of grape, *`abbasi* and *melejeh* pears and melons. Its male and female youths are famous all around the world. The people are mostly Sunnis, and it has many Hanafi ulama and devout people, who perform their Friday prayer in secret.[313] We were hosted by Taqi Khan, the Khan of Shamakhi, for seven days and enjoyed it; he enjoys the society and good company of his friends. Taqi Khan is a generous, poetically talented, Persian speaking, and considerate man. He is also a good horseman and brave. Among the good companions that we associated with were Shahverdi Aqa, Qolu Aqa, Sohrab Aqa, Koja Yazdan-shir, Imirza Ma`sum and Rostam Aqa, and we received

---

312. Hammer, p. 160 has, "meeting-places for wits and learned men."

313. The Shi`ites had a serious internal religious conflict about the legal status of the Friday prayer. For a discussion of this problem see Rula Jurdi Abisaab, *Converting Persia* (London, 2004), pp. 112-14, 124-26.

several silken fabrics, ten *tuman*s in *'abbasi*s and one Qarachuboq horse, and all of our retinue received gifts. Being himself invited to the wedding party of the Khan of Erevan in the castle of Baku, he left from the castle of Shamakhi with one thousand soldiers, and while hunting, he went to the north.

PILGRIMAGE TO THE BLESSED PIR DARKUH SULTAN. He is outstanding among the saints of Khorasan, and his large shrine is strongly built of bricks. It is a fine promenade for all the people of the city to divert themselves, because you have a good view of all the buildings of Shamakhi. Around this Sufi convent there are three hundred prosperous villages with many gardens and orchards. Most of the inhabitants of this village [of Pir Darkuh Sultan] are Bektashi dervishes. Its Sheikh, called 'Ali Quch Dedeh is a commentator of the Koran and a relater of Traditions, a Sufi of great perfection and a perfect Guide as well as extremely saintly and a man of God. God be praised that we were blessed by his prayers. From here we went north for six hours through a cultivated country and arrived at:

THE HALTING PLACE OF PIR MARIZAT SULTAN. We stayed in the house of the mayor; this humble servant became a guest of the Pir's shrine. They call him Pir Meri-zad, but the common people call him Pir Merza, and some call him Pir Mirza. However, the correct form is *Marizat*. He is also known as Diri Baba in the land of Iran and Turan. *Marizat* in Persian means 'bent over'.[314] Indeed, this saintly Pir on the slope of this high mountain in his great convent is always on his prayer rug; his blessed face is covered with a woolen robe, and he sits squatting on his heels in a corner facing the direction of prayer, while leaning with his noble head against a stone in the convent. His blessed body, being white as cotton, has not decayed and is still fresh. All his servants consider him alive and take pleasure in serving him day and night and attending to him. They clean the shrine, and every night they fill the ewer and basin of that beloved one with pure water, and in the morning they find them totally empty. For the last one hundred years no speckle of dust has set upon his blessed robe.[315] In his joyous convent the senses of the visitors are perfumed by the scent of ambergris and aloe wood. Sheikh Safi came from Ardabil to make a pilgrimage to this place and spent ten units of treasures[316] of Azerbaijan on this Bektashi convent, so that in decoration and beauty only the shrine of Imam Reza in Mashhad may rival it. Whoever enters its blessed door is overcome by awe and humility, like culprits before a king; it is such a spiritual place. God be praised that we made a pilgrimage and recited 'Ya Sin'[317] in his blessed memory and asked for help from his blessed soul. I am unable to report the date of his death, as there is no chronogram on the gate. But a certain dervish, named Khvajeh Salah al-Din, free from all worldy attachments, described his genealogy, and this I will say about him.

According to him, that blessed saint was the muezzin of Sheikh Ebrahim Shirvani. He had exerted himself so much in devotion that when he raised his voice in the call to prayer an answer came from high heavens. Sheikh Ebrahim touched his back and said: "Marizat, Marizat," (Bravo, bravo). This is why his blessed body has not decayed, is well-preserved and sits in prayer position

---

314. *Marizat* in Persian means "May it last" or "bravo."

315. Hammer, p. 161 has instead, "his dress is thus always washed white without the least dust upon it."

316. In Ottoman usage a *khazineh* or treasure was equal to 36,000 purses or *kiseh*.

317. This is Surah 36.

on the prayer rug as if he is still alive like an ascetic in meditation. Whoever makes a pilgrimage to his tomb and recites the *Fatiha* will have his spiritual needs fulfilled within seven days. Up to now several miracles and blessings have become manifest from him. May God bless his resting place. From this shrine we traveled for one league to the north through gardens and orchards, and we reached the village of Kharaj.[318]

PILGRIMAGE TO THE BLESSED SHEIKH MERZA SULTAN. This saint is the Sheikh of Diri Baba and his convent is the place of pilgrimage of high and low. Khodabandeh, one of the Persian kings, has built a big dome over it. There are many endowments attached to it. Departing from here and traveling for seven hours to the north over promenades we reached:

THE STAGE OF THE CARAVANSERAI OF KOZLU. There is no village. Inside the beautiful garden there is a big caravanserai founded by Shah Esma'il. From here we went to the north, and after seven hours we reached:

THE STAGE ALTI AGHAJ, which the Persians call Shesh Derakht (six trees), which is situated in a big meadow with a caravanserai. The village is in ruins. This place is on the border of Darband in a beautiful district. Again we went to the north and after [-] hours we reached:

THE PLACE OF PILGRIMAGE OF KHEZR ZENDEH. This saint rests under a big dome.[319] His noble body is still unspoilt. Ozdamir-zadeh Othman Pasha had such great faith in him that while hunting he came to his tomb and ordered it to be repaired. Now it is a place of pilgrimage for Shirvan. Going into the distict of Mushkur near the town of Shaburan, after [-] hours we reached:

THE TOWN OF RUKAL (Regal). Another Regal is also found in the vicinity of Shamakhi, but that one is a small village. This one has a large mosque, a caravanserai, a bathhouse, markets, gardens, orchards and some three thousand beautiful, mud-covered houses. In the past it has always been under the governorship of Bab al-Abvab, i.e., Demirkapu (Darband); but now it is under the governorship of Baku and it is a very nice small town. Its inhabitants are mostly nomadic Turkmen Sunnis. The Qeytaqs and the natives of the towns of Daghestan, Enderi, Tarkhu, Kovin and Tabeseran (Tabarsaran) are Sunni subjects that are exempted [from taxes]. They were not dualists.[320] Dualism is one of the heretic beliefs which [people in these parts] are suspected to adhere to.

Again we went from here to the north and after [-] hours ate and rested on the banks of the river Regal.

THE KHAN OF SHAMAKHI. Our friend sent somebody to the Khan of Erevan in the castle of Baku. After having eaten we departed from the banks of the river Rukal, and after [-] hours traveling through plains we suddenly came across a great troop of soldiers coming from the side of the Caspian Sea;[321] and what did I see?

---

318. Hammer, p. 161 has, "Khardjeh."

319. For a description in 1693 by Engelbert Kaempfer, *Die Reistagebücher Engelbert Kaempfers*. Ed. Karl Meier-Lemgo (Wiesbaden, 1968), p. 43

320. I.e., believers in two creators, good and bad.

321. The text has Bahr-e Haraz, which does not refer to any known sea and must be Kahravan's misreading of Bahr-e Khazar or the Caspian Sea.

I saw a number of Iranian Khans, first those of Erevan, Ganjeh, Lur[i], Baku, Gilan, and Moghan and [several words omitted].

Several sultans dressed in party clothes proceeded with pomp with more than ten thousand hastily collected irregular troops of Turkmen, Mongols, Boghol, Qimiq, Qomuq, Qalmaq, Gökdolaq, Moghan, and Qazaq, who were dressed in different ways, outfits and arms, and were sounding the trumpets of Afrasiyab and beating the royal kettledrums and the falconry drums. Then they were playing the Jew's harp and the small-sized bagpipe in such a way that you cannot describe. From this procession of soldiers the Khan of Erevan, while trotting on his horse, came forward and my friend, the Khan of Shamakhi, said: "Hey Evliya Aqa! Look, the Khan of Erevan is coming to me." He came and first greeted and embraced me while still on horseback. Then we exchanged greetings with the Khans of Erevan and Gilan. During the three hours' ride, until we arrived at the castle of Baku, we got better acquainted. When we arrived at Baku, so many guns were fired from the towers and the walls of the castle that it seemed that the old castle of Baku was left inside the fire like a salamander.[322] It was at the occasion of the arrival of the Muscovy envoys from the west side of the Caspian Sea, from the castles of Astrakhan, Balkhan, Saray, and Heshdek[323] and Turk, who had brought gifts. These welcoming salutes were fired to show them the strength of the arsenal and its power. Thus we entered the castle of Baku on Friday, the first of Moharram of the year one thousand fifty-seven [6 February 1647].

THE DESCRIPTION OF THE CASTLE OF BAKU ON THE PERSIAN BORDER WITH THE PROVINCE OF SHIRVAN

A lengthy Mohammadi tablecloth was spread, and after eating I gave the letter of our master Daftarzadeh Mohammad Pasha, governor of Erzerum, together with a fine rosary, wavy silken European fabrics and a sword.[324] He said: "You are welcome" and paid me compliments. I delivered the letters of the Khans of Tabriz and Nakhjevan, complimenting him profusely on his wedding party. In these letters the humble author was very much praised. The Khan of Erevan entertained me as a guest in his sister's palace. The festivity lasted for ten days and nights.[325] The friendly letters of our master and the presents were appreciated by all the khans who were present, and he showed the pearl rosary to all the Khans and Sultans. That day he gave this humble author a Persian robe and ten tumans in royal *bistis*.[326] [Afterwards] I went to see the town with my companions.

The castle of Baku was built in the year [-] as protection against the Muscovy ruler. It was built by Dara Shah[327] on the banks of the Caspian Sea on the top of a high hill. It is a beauti-

---

322. Many salamanders tend to dwell inside rotting logs. When placed into a fire, the salamander would attempt to escape from the log, leading to the belief that salamanders were created from flames. As a consequence there are many myths and legends about salamanders purporting that they sprang forth from fire, hence their name, which comes from the Persian *sam* (fire) and *anderun* (inside).

323. Balkhan is Balkan, situated in Turkmenistan on the Caspian Sea. Its capital Balkanabat is situated at 39°30'42"N 54°21'54"E. Saray is the old capital of the Golden Horde, situated 85 km east of Volgograd. Heshdek was the name of the territory of the Bashkirs near Kazan.

324. Hammer, p. 162 has instead, "beads of pearls, Irak stuffs, and a fine sword."

325. No festivities or marriage take place during the month of Moharran. Evliya must have made a mistake here.

326. Hammer, p. 162 has here, "ten tomans of Abbasi, and ten tomans of Bisti."

327. Dara or Darab Shah, the son of Bahman, was the eighth legendary Kayanid king of Iran. See

fully built quadrangular castle. The inner castle has a gate, which faces the west, and is made of Nakhjevan iron. Its circumference is seven hundred paces. It has seventy towers and six hundred battlements. The height of the walls is forty royal cubits. Since it is built on a rock there is no moat.[328]

Inside the castle there are up to seventy old houses. There is a large mosque, called Heydar Shah, which has no minaret. There is no caravanserai, bathhouse or market. But on the sea coast in the big suburb, there is a nice town with up to one thousand houses, gardens, orchards, large mosques, caravanserais, bathhouses, markets and bazaars; this is protected on three sides with walls, and it has three gates. To the north is the Gilan Gate, to the south the Darband Gate, and towards the west at the coast there is the Harbor Gate.[329] Here, seven minarets with step-like recessions[330] can be seen, the names of which were unknown.

It has three bathhouses, of which the Mirza Khan bathhouse is very well-lit and has a good ambiance. Its bazaar is not very well decorated. Since it is on the border with Muscovy there are many Shahsevans and royal slaves.[331] It is situated in the province of Shirvan; it is a separate khanate with three thousand soldiers and twelve officials. It has a separate judicial jurisdiction and seven districts. Several times the Muscovy Cossacks, coming from the Volga River (Edil), have pillaged the districts of Gilan and Baku. At the other side at a distance of three hundred *mil*[332] there is the land of Muscovy. Even so, in the year when Ozdamir-oghlu Othman Pasha conquered it and Qobad Pasha was its Ottoman governor, the Persians encouraged the Muscovy Cossacks to come and lay siege to the castle of Baku and all the infidels were put to sword. Now their bones can be seen on a hill on the coast.

The climate of the city is pleasant and coastal, because rice and cotton are cultivated in its districts, and it has gardens and orchards. Its cotton is very good, but its water smells of naphtha oil. In seven places near the city there are naphtha mines, each one of a different color: yellow, red, black, etc. The inhabitants of the districts of Muskir[333], Sendan and Rineb, do not use wax candles or lamps with grease, but they only use black naphtha, and they use it in lamps. The people are extremely healthy and stout. Occasionally there are beautiful people among them of both sexes, because it is situated in the eighteenth clime. The people are mostly Sunnis.

Between this castle and that of Demirkapu (Darband) is a four days' journey going via the sea coast. Between them the villages of Mushkur are prosperous and each one of them is like a city. Its people are nomadic Turkmen. They pitch their felt tents here during winter and then they migrate. The town of Shapuran, to the east[334] of Baku, is at a distance of three days' journey. The

---

Ahmad Tafazzoli, "Dara," *Encyclopedia Iranica*. There is also a prose romance about his adventures aptly called *Darab-nameh*, see William L. Hanaway, "Darab-nama," *Encyclopedia Iranica*.

328. For a brief history of Baku see S. Soucek, "Baku," *Encyclopedia Iranica*.

329. Given the fact that Gilan is situated to the south-east, Darband to the north, and the Caspian Sea to the east of Baku 'north' should be south, 'south' should be 'north', and 'west' should be 'east.'

330. The term used is *pas-payeh*, which probably comes from *pas-payegi*, meaning 'set back, recessed.'

331. The term Shahsevan refers to those 'who love the shah.'

332. One *mil* is two km, being one third of one *farsakh*, which is about 6 km.

333. This is the coastal district of Mushkur, north of Baku, situated between the rivers Samur and Balbal. Müller, *Sammlung*, vol. 4, pp. 99-100.

334. Properly Shabaran, which was situated to the north of Baku.

castle of Shamakhi is at a distance of five days' journey in the east.[335] The town of Gilan is to the north of Baku at [-] days' journey.[336] Baku is the port of Shamakhi. Envoys and rich merchants constantly come from China, Tatary, Khotan, the City of Women,[337] Kalmukia, and Muscovy, who bring merchandise. The Muscovite envoys come regularly to Baku as security. To Persia they mostly bring beaver pelts, tusks of walrus, squirrel pelts, and Bulghar leather and many other kinds of goods they bring to Gilan and Baku. In return, they take to Moscow salt, naphtha, saffron and silk from Baku. Saffron and silk come from Lahejan, which has very soft raw silk, and from Anatolia very good saffron. In the districts of Baku there are salty places where, if you stand for a while on your feet or on a horse, your feet will burn. The people of the caravans dig up earth at some places and put a saucepan over it and the food cooks very quickly that way.[338] This is an incredible wisdom of God. To the north of the town in a nearby district the river Kur drains into the sea. Some of the Muscovy Cossacks often enter the river in boats made of reed and pillage the Persian provinces and the enslaved captives are sold in the bazaars of Gilan without any problems. Its river is broad like the Danube but not as deep.

We stayed in the city of Baku for several days and visited places, while we enjoyed the festivities of the parties of the Persians and witnessed the life of the notables. If we describe the ceremonies of the wedding of the sister of the Khan of Baku with the Khan of Erevan, Taqi ʿAli Khan, it will be a book by itself. We stayed for fifteen days and enjoyed ourselves. From Taqi Khan, the Khan of Erevan,[339] and from Ashraf Khan, the Khan of Baku, we received Persian sables, Georgian slaves and Tavusi camels. The Khan of Erevan, moreover, pledged to send to the customs, one hundred caravans and gave to our master the Pasha a sable robe, ten pairs of Gilani bow strings, six Georgian slaves, ten tusks and three pieces of ambergris. He wrote a cordial letter and gave this humble servant ten *tuman*s in *bisti*s as travel money and to our 45 man retinue ten *tuman*s in ʿ*abbasi*s. We took leave of all the notables of Baku and the Khans, and the Khan accompanied us out of friendship, and we left the castle Baku going to the south.

Our Journey from Baku Castle to the province of Georgia and the description of the stages, villages, towns, castles and provinces

The Khans of Baku and Erevan gave us one hundred armed retainers, and we went to the south along the coast over salty land, where we saw different naphtha mines in seven places.

Description of the naphtha oil mines. It bubbles up from the earth on the seashore or in the Mushkur district by God's command. It bubbles up like hot springs, and the patches of

---

335. Shamakhi is situated to the northwest of Baku.

336. The province, not the town, of Gilan is situated to the southeast of Baku.

337. The *shahr-e zanan* is a mythical city allegedly situated in India or East Africa, whose people and its ruler were women, see Dehkhoda, q.v. *shahr-e zanan*.

338. For a discussion of the use of naphtha and natural gas as lighting and cooking fuels in Baku and other parts of Iran see Floor, *Traditional Crafts in Qajar Iran*, pp. 134-48.

339. Evliya Chelebi is mistaken. During this period there was no governor of Erevan who was named Taqi Khan, see Nasiri, *Titles*, p. 172. He earlier mentioned that Taqi Khan was the governor of Shamakhi, which perhaps is the person whom he meant.

A view of Tarku in 1637

naphtha oil settles on the surface of the water like cream. It is a separate concession that yields seven thousands *tumans* for the king.[340] The naphtha concessionaire's people go to these small ponds and collect the naphtha in goatskins. Then the merchants buy it and take it to all parts.[341] Naphtha comes in seven or eight types. But the yellow one is the best. Black naphtha is the royal type that is transported all over Persia, Uzbekistan, Hindustan, Iraq, Kurdistan, and the Ottoman Empire, Georgia, Mongolia, Daghestan, and it is taken to the castles at their borders. In dark nights they use it for lighting. When the army of Islam attacks them they throw all kinds of blankets and other items on them and set fire to them. The castles and the cities need it as weapons. Even in the presence of the shah and in all the great houses the torches are lit by the naphtha of Baku. It is a great work of God that it is heavy. The naphtha is guarded day and night by guards, because if it catches fire it will burn forever. This is why near the naphtha mines heaps of earth are piled up like mountains for extinguishing [fires]. If a spark gets to the mine everybody rushes there and throws earth to extinguish it. There is no other alternative. There are also naphtha mines in caves and in rocks in several places, which, however, I have not seen. What we described is the naphtha of Baku. Again, we traveled south along the coast for [-] hours and stayed in the district of Mushkur

---

340. This figure seems to be correct, see Floor, *Fiscal History*, pp. 175-76.

341. Naphtha was bagged in sheepskins called *tuluq*.

in felt tents of the Turkmen. In these plains, the Mongols, Qomuq, Turkmen and Yaka Turkmen winter here in their tents and rest. They enjoy the coastal area, which is a very fertile land.

DESCRIPTION OF THE ELEPHANT-EARED WHALE OF THE CASPIAN SEA. We proceeded from here, and while we were traveling along the Caspian coast we saw a fish that had been beached by the waves of the sea. Its length was one hundred paces. It had two heads, one was at its tail, and it looked like the head of a snake. The other one was a big head like the dome of a bathhouse. Its head seemed to be like that of the dragon in the pictures. In the upper jaw it had one hundred and fifty teeth and in the lower jaw one hundred and forty teeth. Each tooth was one cubit long. It was as thick as a man's thigh; it had ears like those of an elephant; and its eyes were round as a tablecloth. It was a creature hairy like a beaver and a frightening fish. All the people from Baku, Shamakhi, and Darband came to see it. Koja Sari Khan, a voyager of the Caspian Sea, told me the following:

"This fish is a special whale of the Caspian Sea, which the sailors call the elephant-eared whale. All the fish are afraid of it." In fact, such carcasses that you find along the coast of the Caspian Sea cannot be found on any other coast. The shore is covered with bones and carcasses unlike any seen at other coasts. There are quadrangular or pentagonal creatures with round heads and thin tails. The *kepi* and *mina* are very colorful, and their length is one cubit. There are fish like *lipata*, red-bodied fish (*sorkh andam*), green fish and silver fish and several thousand other types of colorful fish, but what is known and eaten are several types only.[342] According to sailors, the Caspian Sea is one and a half times bigger than the Black Sea. Its circumference is four thousand *mil*. It is not connected to another sea. It is a big sea. Unlike the Black Sea, it has no islands. In the Mediterranean there are small and big inhabited islands, – in total two thousand forty islands. Out of those, forty are large. For example, the island of Cyprus, Crete, Moria, Rhodes, Mytilene, Limni, Tinos, Cos, Chios, Naxos, Zanilsa [?], Kefalonia, Sicily, Corsica, Sardinia, Malta, and there are others like them. In each one of them there are from five or ten to seventy or eighty strong castles and big rivers. But in the Caspian there is not one island.[343] But there are many ports and the movement of the waves is stronger than in the Black Sea. It extends to the land of China, and it is at the extreme end of the seventh clime. In the west it is bounded by Muscovy, in the east by Persian Gilan, the Uzbegs, Bulghars, Qalmaq, Chinese and the Kazaks. Because of the severe winter, the sea between the Kazaks and Muscovy is frozen for seven months; the Qalmaq and the Tatars walk over the frozen ice and plunder the Muscovy lands and make captives and sell them in China and Khotan, and they become rich. In Gilan, Baku, Darband and that of the Terek castles, this Caspian Sea does not freeze at all, because of its coastal climate. At this side, at the end of the sea, at what is called Bab al-Abvab, there is a bay to the south of Demirkapu. On the border of the kingdom of Daghestan, at the shore of the Caspian Sea, near the land of the Avars at the banks of the Terek river, is the Muscovy castle of Tarku, where the Caspian Sea ends. It is situated from south to north, and its length is four thousand *mil*, and at its deepest place it measures three lead lines (*iskandil*), i.e., three hundred cubits. There are thousands of ships sailing on the surface of the sea carrying goods of the merchants. All ship captains are very afraid of the infidel Muscovy Cossack vessels (*shayqa*), and sometimes they fight big battles on the sea. They do not have large galleons like those of the Black Sea, the Mediterranean, the Atlantic Ocean and the Circambulant

---

342. Concerning these fish see Brian W. Coad, "Fish," *Encyclopedia Iranica*.
343. This is incorrect. There are many small, mostly uninhabited islands in the Caspain Sea.

Ocean. They have small ships with gunwales made of reed and with swivel guns. Sea battles are the prerogative of the cunning Franks and the brave Ottomans, who have galleons and men-of-war with two or three thousand soldiers and two or three hundred cannons, and they fight in the Mediterranean. But on the Caspian Sea they only have to fight the Muscovy Cossacks. We went to the east through flat fields, and after [-] hours we reached the district of Mushkur:

A view of the Dagestan coast and of Darband

Description of the district of Shaburan in Shirvan

It is a beautiful city in the province of Shirvan, but it is situated on the border with Darband. In ancient times it was built by king Esfandiyar.[344] Later, when Hulagu the Mongol came, he destroyed the city, made its people suffer and leveled all their houses. Later, it was rebuilt. Eventually,

---

344. Esfandiyar, son of Gushtasp (the fifth Kayanid King).

after Ozdamir-zadeh Othman Pasha, the vizier of Sultan Murad III, had conquered Darband, all the Sunnis of Shaburan submitted themselves, and it became the seat of a *sanjaq-bey*. Later on, early in the reign of Murad IV, the Qizilbash conquered Shirvan and took control over Shaburan as well.[345] Now it is the seat of a sultan on the border of Demirkapu (Darband). After beautiful Tabriz, the capital of this *sanjaq-bey* is the best of Iran from the point of view of the climate. It is situated in the fifth clime and now it is an average prosperous city. It has seventy mosques and seventy quarters.

Among its large mosques are the mosques of Uzun Hasan Shah, Tuqmaq Khan and Afshar Khan. There is nothing in this land like the Uzun Hasan mosque, unless the Uzun Hasan Kurd mosque in Egypt. The ceramic tiles and the ponds with fountains of this Shaburan mosque are nowhere else to be found. Ozdamir-oghli Othman Pasha would come every Friday with a great procession from Demirkapu and would worship in this mosque. It is an old place of worship that one must see. Its four walls are adorned with so many arabesques and carvings in marble that the greatest architects are left astonished when beholding it. The city of Shaburan is situated in a fertile valley in the plains of Mushkur with rose gardens, fruit orchards and promenades on the border of Shirvan. It has seven districts, and each one is named after the seven planets. For instance, the districts of Mercury, Venus, Mars, Jupiter and Saturn.

From here we went to Ladus, passing nomads in the district of Mushkur, and after six hours along the sea coast through a vast plain we came to:

THE STAGE OF THE VILLAGE OF CHARKHI. It is the personal fief of the ruler of Daghestan, the Shamkhal.[346] It was given by Ozdamir-zadeh Othman Pasha to him. Although it has passed into the hands of the Persians, it remained under the Shamkhal. It has five hundred houses, a large mosque, a caravanserai, a bathhouse, a small bazaar; it is a small town. Its people are mostly Qomuqs from Daghestan; they make good armor. We traveled further to the south, leaving the town of Regal on our left, and arrived at last in the district of Mushkur.

DESCRIPTION OF BANDAR-E BAB, I.E., THE TOWN OF BAB AL-ABVAB, I.E., THE WALL OF ALEXANDER THE TWO-HORNED, THE CASTLE OF DEMIRKAPU

According to learned historians, in the Koran God ordered Alexander the Two-Horned to build the wall of Gog and Magog: "They said: O Two-Horned, Gog and Magog are the corruptors of the earth."[347] He came to this land of Demirkapu and saw a beautiful spot on the coasts of Daghestan. He consulted with his viziers, Aristotle and Pythagoras the Unitarian, and his treasurers, Bitlis and Galenus, Hippocrates and Socrates–sage, farseeing and thoughtful wise men–and measured the elevation of Demirkapu and found that the Caspian Sea was higher than the Black Sea. He wanted to connect the Caspian with the Black Sea and sent for skillful engineers. On the third day, on the slopes of Daghestan and the Elburz Mountain, at the coast of the Black Sea at

---

345. Properly Shaberan, which was sacked in 1712 and completely destroyed in 1723 by the Lezgis, see Bakikhanov, *Heavenly Rose-Garden,* p. 112.

346. *Shamkhal* was the title of the chief of the Qomuqs, who was the most powerful ruler of Daghestan. See Floor, "Who were the Shamkhal.

347. Koran 18: 94 (al-Kahf). See further A.J. Wensick, "Yadjudj wa Madhudj," *Encyclopedia of Islam II.*

the border with Mingrelia, they entered the big river Fasha, which was the end of the Black Sea, and there they measured the altitude and found that the Black Sea was situated twenty degrees lower than the Caspian Sea. Again on the third day, they reported their findings to Alexander, who in the name of God ordered master stonecutters and diggers to start working and gave them tools and equipment, and in seventy days they went seventy thousand paces deep into the earth near Demirkapu on the coast of the Caspian Sea. All his wise men said: "O Alexander, you were charged to build the wall of Gog [and Magog], not this one, because that will take too long. A man on foot can walk the distance through the mountains between the Black and the Caspian Sea in three days, but to cut through the flint stone rocks on the slopes of the Elburz Mountains will require several thousands of treasures and the lifetime of Noah. We know by the science of astrology that your reign will last only thirty-two years and then you will join God." They said: "there are more useful things than this to be done." For they surmised that when Alexander would join the Black and Caspian Seas, he may cut the Black Sea from the Bosporus, resulting in the drowning of the cities of Macedonia and Kaydefa, situated below Uskudar and the Sara peninsula. By God's wisdom, that night Alexander had a terrifying dream and he then gave up the idea of joining the two seas. Again, by the counsel of the wise men, Alexander the Great built triple-strong walls and three moats to the Black Sea at a seven-stage distance from Daghestan. This has become the wall between the two seas, and to the east of it are the people of Iran and Turan, and to the west are the people of the Qepchaq steppe, the Bani Asfar (yellow) and Sal`at tribes, while the Crimean and the odious Russian tribes are situated in between. Now, this humble servant has seen these triple walls and three rows of moats inside the Elburz and the Dadiyan Mountains. All those who travel from the Crimea into the country of the Qomuqs see them as well. Some people say, in accordance with a tradition, that this is the wall of Gog and Magog that Alexander built. From the time of Alexander's reign to the time of the prophet of God, according to Mohammad Ibn Eshaq,[348] was 882 years.

From the time of the hijra of Prophet to our time of traveling, one thousand and fifty-seven years have passed. From the time of Alexander until now it has been one thousand nine hundred thirty-nine years. Now, some parts of the wall have been destroyed, but in other parts some towers and battlements are left. Each one is like the Qahqaheh fort. The deep moats have been filled with sand. These points are not hidden to the people who have seen them. The author of the *Tarikh-e Tohfa*[349] says: "Alexander dug an underground canal in seventy days that linked the Caspian Sea with the Black Sea, and the Caspian Sea thus ran to Phasus River, which flows underground."[350] In this way it falls into the Black Sea. But this humble author disagrees. In the year one thousand fifty, when we were going to Azaq castle[351] we stayed on the banks of the Fasheh River. Its water was very delicious, while that of the Caspian is worse than snake poison. If somebody purifies himself with that water his private parts will burn like fire. So how can it be, if the Black Sea were

---

348. Probably Mohammad b. Ishaq b. Yasar b. Khiyar (704-67) is meant; see the article under that title by J.M.B. Jones in *Encyclopedia of Islam II*.

349. Evliya also cites this chronicle in other parts of his travelogue, but so far nobody has been able to identify this work. See Bulut, *Bitlis*, p. 336.

350. In classical times the river Aras was also referred to as Phasus. Charles Rollin, *The Ancient History of Egyptian, Carthaginians, Assyrians, Babylonians, Medes & Persians, Macedonians & Grecians* translated into English by William H. Wykoff (New York, 1848), p. 217.

351. The town of Azov.

A view of Darband in 1637

connected underground with the river Phasus, that its water is so delicious? Therefore this is an erroneous idea. As they say [in Persian]:

Hearing is not the same as seeing

شنیدن کی بود مانند دیدن

We have described in our journey to Trabson that Alexander the Two-Horned built a strong castle near the wall of Daghestan on the shores of the Black Sea at the mouth of the Phasus River. He [also] built a strong wall at the shores of the Caspian Sea, which is this Demirkapu on the slopes of the Mt. Demirkapu, and it protrudes into the sea and it is the very strong fort of Bab al-Abvab.[352]

The layout of the castle of Bab al-Abvab, i.e. Demirkapu (Darband). Its original founder is Alexander the Two-Horned; there is difference of opinion whether he was or was not a prophet. Later on, in the time of the Ommayad Lord of the Believers, Yazid b.

---

352. For the romantic story of Alexander's wall see William L. Hanway, "Eskandar-nama," *Encyclopedia Iranica*. For a brief history of Darband see Erich Kettenhofen, "Darband," *Encyclopedia Iranica*.

'Abdol-Malek, Atike Khatun, the daughter of Mu'awiya, in the year 500, took it from the Khavareji[353] and all the people of Daghestan were converted to Islam.[354]

Then, suffering many sieges, it was sometimes destroyed, and sometimes it prospered. Eventually, in the year 986 [1578], Ozdamir-oghlu Othman Pasha, one of the viziers of Murad III, arrived at the castle. The Sunnis inside put in chains Cheragh Khan, the governor of the erring Shah, and killed all the heretics and cut off the heads of all the Qizilbash and sent the Khan of Demirkapu with all the heads and the keys of the castle to Othman Pasha to the camp of the army

A view of Terki in 1637

of Islam, where he cut off the head of Cheragh Khan and made his day as night. Then all the fighters of the faith shouted "Allah, Allah" and the sound of the Moslem call to prayer was raised and the good news was sent to the High Porte, and Othman Pasha became the independent governor of Shirvan and commander of the castle of Demirkapu, which he repaired and rebuilt as if so that it became a new strong iron gate. The Moslem fighters for the faith made several night attacks

---

353. The year 500 clearly is impossible and is more likely to be 50 or 670 C.E. Khavareji may be either a copyist's error for the Khazar or a confusion on Evliya's part, see Bakikhanov, *Heavenly Rosegarden*, pp. 23, 41-51.

354. The Islamization of Daghestan proceeded at a much slower pace, for only by the fifteenth century the majority of its population had become Moslems. See V. Barthold, "Daghistan," *Encyclopedia of Islam*.

on Shirvan. They conquered seventy castles, and it became a big province. One thousand janissaries, four batallions of *sepahi*s, ten batallions of armorers, ten regiments of royal gunners, sixty siege cannons, five hundred boxes of ammunition and other supplies, and five thousand soldiers[355] completed its means of defense. Three thousand soldiers were assigned to guard it, and the province of Reval had assigned fifteen thousand soldiers to it. Due to his justice and fairness, all these parts were as if they were paradise. Roads were opened with the Qipchaq steppe, Circassia, and Daghestan, and from the Crimea the Tatar army came with supplies as well as troops coming from Akhiskha, Erevan, Ganjeh, Tiflis, Tomanis and Shamakhi, and it became so prosperous as if the land was under the justice of ʿOmar. Until the year of the ascension to the throne by Murad IV, when the army and the Janissaries rebelled, the shah of Iran took the opportunity and in the year [-], since help was not coming, granting mercy he took the castle and all the Moslem fighters first went to Daghestan, then to Circassia and finally to the Crimea. Up to now it is in the hands of the Persians, and it is so prosperous that it looks like Anushirvan's castle. Now it is in the hands of the Persians and the seat of a khan and a judge. It has twelve officials, a secretary, a mayor, a chief of the ushers, a chief of the guards, a chief of the royal slaves, chief of the raw flesh eaters[356] and two thousand royal slaves. In total there are nine thousand Shahsevan soldiers, who are paid by the king. I met with the Khan of the castle, who has a beautiful, well-furnished palace at the tower of Qeytaq Khan overlooking the sea, where we stayed and enjoyed it. I gave him the cordial letters of the Khans of Baku and Erevan, and he appreciated it. Day and night he treated us nicely. He was Shafiʿ Khan Shahsevan, a grayish, energetic eighty-year-old, who was drunk day and night, but he was witty, of poetic taste, had a fine writing hand and was eloquent. He gave this humble person five *tuman*s as travel money, and every day he was providing us with our necessities through our conductor of guests.

THE SIZE OF THE IRON GATE CASTLE. The reason for its name is that in the wall that Alexander built there was an iron gate where he put guards. This gate remained until the time of Anushirvan and hence the name Demirkapu (Iron Gate). Since the castle is called Demirkapu, it is a very strong one. The second founder was Anushirvan, and the third one was king Yazdegerd. The fourth and fifth are Shah Esmaʿil and Ozdamir-zadeh Othman Pasha. It is situated on the slopes of Mt. Arghin and Mt. Duneb. Since the left side of the castle is near the Caspian Sea, the principal walls are battered by the sea. These walls, after Shah Yazdegerd, were repaired by the king of the Khazars, who built a jetty; and on its gate there is a poem in Persian indicating the date of its construction. The protruding wall built by Alexander can still be seen on the side of the sea. It is a very thick and massive wall. If the kings would desire it, it would be possible to extend the harbor from these walls to the castle. Now its tower and bulwark can be seen in the sea. From the side of the sea wall to the top of the mountain is a distance of one arrow shot, and again, from the sea to the mountain situated at the back of the castle, the width of the castle is one bow shot. The castle is built on a high hill in the form of a pentagon. It is the strongest castle I ever saw during my journeys. The master architect divided it into three parts and strengthened it three times, so

---

355. Hammer, p. 166 has here instead, "and fifteen hundred militia of Erivan."

356. The eating of people, either raw or roasted, was one of the features of the ritualistic behavior of the Qizilbash adherents of the Safavid Shah, which practice was later instituted by keeping a number of such men at the shah's court, whose services were called upon to execute some death sentences. Chelebi is the only author to mention that they also were employed in some provincial towns. See note 52 supra.

that truly they are iron gates. One side of the castle looks eastward towards Mt. Safah. The second gate opens towards the city. The wall facing Mt. Arghin has two gates, and the wall that faces the lower city has two strong gates. One is called the Mushkur Gate, which opens to the east to the Mushkur district. Those who exit from this gate go by horse-drawn carts to Shamakhi. Another gate faces the south towards the Qipchaq steppe, the Crimea, Circassia and Daghestan.[357] Horse-drawn carts do not go to Daghestan. Simple carts travel to the Muscovy Terek castle, Kazan province and the Qipchaq steppe. The third part of the castle is on the side of the sea. It is not all that well-developed. Therefore, Qarchigha Khan has built houses there for the soldiers and royal slave guards. The horse-drawn carts filled with goods of the merchants who come from Gilan and Baku are lined up in the castle. This is because the terrain is steep and rocky, and therefore horse-drawn carts are used.[358] There are several ships coming to these parts by sea. That is why it is a valuable strong castle for the region. According to my calculation, there are [-] number of gates inside and outside the castle. It is a quadrangular castle, and its circumference is eleven thousand sixty paces. There are seventy large towers, in each of which there is a mosque and a madraseh for strangers and men without family. From Baku castle, black naphtha is sent for the students for lighting, while day and night wheat soup is prepared for them in a Keykavos-like kitchen, and the horses are fed twice [per day]. In this way they have made the ulama to watch and guard the castle. Apart from the aforementioned seventy towers, there are one thousand and sixty battlements. Each dark night they light the castle with naphtha, because from the sea and the land the castle has thirteen deadly enemies. First, there are the infidel Muscovite Cossacks, who come every time and plunder its environs. But they do not come near the castle, because near the sea there are seventy big cannons. All of them are Ottoman guns, which are so polished that one can see one's face there like in a mirror. And a strong enemy to the west is the Ottomans, the Crimean Tatars and the Qalmaqs. To the south their enemy is the Circassian. Again in the south the greatest enemy is Qomuq people of Daghestan. In the east the enemy is the land of the Georgian Tomris Khan.[359] Therefore, each night soldiers and sailors keep guard in the castle and shout "*Khoda khub.*"[360] Out of fear for the enemies, fifty watchmen keep guard day and night on a high mountain called Duneb at a considerable distance from the castle, in a forested area; and whenever an enemy shows up they warn the people in the castle by lighting fires on top of the mountain.

DESCRIPTION OF THE BUILDINGS INSIDE THE CASTLE. First, the stones of all the walls of the castle are each as big as the body of an elephant, but cut square. Each one of them cannot be lifted by fifty men using the 'science' of crane lifting. Inside the castle there are altogether one thousand two hundred old style mud-covered houses without gardens and orchards. On the south side attached to the wall there is a huge hall, whose architecture and craftsmanship has no equal in the whole of Iran. Attached to that hall is a large mosque, whose minaret has fallen. Near this mosque there is a beautiful bathhouse built in the Ottoman style, whose founder is not known. There is one good spring. Near the gate of the boats, which faces east, there is the mosque of Ozdamir-oghlu Othman Pasha as well as a caravanserai and shops. Outside the castle there is a beautiful suburb. It has one thousand fine houses, with gardens and orchards on three sides, but

---

357. Evliya often confused directions. Here, "east" must be south and "south" must be north.

358. This sentence does not make sense. One would not expect horse-drawn carts on steep and rocky terrain.

359. Tomris Khan is Taymuraz I (1586-1663), see W.E.D. Allen, *A History of the Georgian People* (London, 1932), pp. 161-73.

360. Literally, 'God is good."

it has no public kitchen. There are many large mosques, bathhouses, caravanserais, markets and bazaars. There are various artisans. Most people earn their living by weaving various kinds of silk. Many Qomuqs produce well-made chain mail. Most people are Sunnis and Shafe'is.[361] There are no very wealthy people. Because of its climate there are beautiful youths of both sexes. According to Ibn Hawqal, it is in the eighteenth traditional clime,[362] but because it is on the coast of the Caspian Sea, it has a coastal climate and therefore its youths of both sexes are praised. Its latitude is seventeen hours, seven minutes and two seconds. On the other side of the sea, in the west at three hundred leagues, are the Russian provinces of Heshdek and Qazan, and beyond that the Qepchaq and Alatar steppe and the Heyhat desert. In this place, for the last twenty years,[363] Taysi Shah of the Qalmaq Tatars, Moyonjak Khan and Kuba Kalmakh Khan have wandered around these vast plains with five or six thousand soldiers. In some years, they invaded as far as the Crimea and made night attacks and martyred Gurji Mostafa Pasha, who had been dismissed from Egypt, in the vicinity of Azak,[364] on the banks of the river Gugumlu. They are Qalmaq infidels. Although they have no idea of belief and unbelief, they are desert dwellers and stout creatures. Most of the time they come peacefully to Muscovite Heshdek and Kazan to sell their butter; some of them embark on Muscovite ships and have started coming to Demirkapu. Every year, hundreds of thousands of ships come for trading to the jetty of Demirkapu from China and beyond [Ma-Chin], Tatary, Khotan, Faghfur, Muscovy and considerable customs duties are collected from them.

When it was in Ottoman hands its annual revenue from its jetty and from the province of Shirvan was two hundred and forty-seven loads of *aqches*, besides the personal fief and fodder that was given to its officials, to the Sultans in seven *sanjaqs* and for the maintenance of peace to the king of Daghestan. After the conquest by Ozdamir-oghlu Othman Pasha, according to the writings of Dal Mohammad Efendi, it was collected and justly managed. According to that document, the province of Shirvan has seventy judicial districts, seven khanates and twelve sultanates. But, in accordance with the orders of Othman Pasha, there are no *timars* or *ze'amats*. One may not confiscate the personal fiefs of the sultans and other officials. The land of Shirvan is very prosperous and well-developed. The inhabitants still say, "May God give it back again to the Ottomans!" When we were in Demirkapu, a Gökdolaq messenger came from the High Porte to spy. He said: "My Khan, last year the Ottoman Sultan sent one of his generals called Yusof Pasha to the island of Crete, and he took the castle, called Haniya,[365] and he put soldiers there. When the son of Sultan Ebrahim, who was called Shahzadeh Mohammad,[366] was born, great festivities were organized.

---

361. Hammer, p. 168 in addition has, "rich men, and fine youths."

362. The text has: "According to Ibn Hawqal, it is in the eighteenth traditional clime, but because the seventh real clime is situated in the middle of the fifth clime," which does not make sense. Therefore, we have shortened the translation. These terms refer to the seven 'real' Ptolomaean climes and the later division into 28 'traditional' climes. The real clime is determined by latitude only and was calculated with the astrolabe or by measuring the longest day (or night). The first clime includes all those regions where the day lasts 12 hours, the second clime those where it lasts 13 hours, and in each following clime the day lasts 30 minutes less. See van Bruinessen et al., *Diyarbekr*, p. 221, n. 128.

363. Hammer, p. 168 has instead "where twenty years ago."

364. Azak (Russian Azov, Venetian. Tana).

365. Cania, Chania, Khania or Haniya is the second largest city on Crete and was taken by Yusof Pasha on 22 August 1645, with an enormous loss of life. He was executed on his return to Istanbul for having lost forty thousand Ottoman soldiers.

366. He was born on 2 January 1642.

Seven days and nights the Ottoman lands were illuminated in festivity." The Qizilbash did not like that the Sunnis of Shirvan, Shamakhi and Gilan were very happy and pleased and started dancing. They are waiting for the coming of a great Ottoman general who is holding a green banner of the messenger of God.

DESCRIPTION OF THE PLACES OF PILGRIMAGE OF DEMIRKAPU. In the year 50 (570 C.E.), the Ommayad Yazid b. ʿAbdol-Malek,[367] who was born to ʿAtikah, a daughter of Muʿawiya, came from Syria with innumerable soldiers against Kharejites[368] at Demirkapu and engaged in a major battle. More than seven hundred of them were martyred. May God be pleased with them all! They are all buried in a graveyard which is at a distance of one *mil* from the west wall of Demirkapu. In the land of Persia another one came to destroy the kingdom, viz. the Ommayad Caliph Hesham ʿAbdol-Malek who came with an innumerable army from Syria and conquered the castles of Daghestan, Qomuq, Tabarsaran, Qeytaq and Bab al-Abvab (Darband). In the year that all the people were converted to Islam; the people who were martyred at Demirkapu are buried in these tombs there. On the grave stones the date and their names are given in *Tholth* and *Kufic* script. Among them there are seventy transmitters of Traditions.[369] The notables of Demirkapu feel honored that so many of them are buried there. If we transcribe all the writings of their tombs it will amount to a big tome. On the marble of the gravestones is written in bold letters that Ottoman notables are in there. On the gravestones of the ancient notables the cause of their death, names, time that they ruled and their official titles are written.

THE PLACE OF PILGRIMAGE OF THE FORTY. There are forty big tombs.

Then, **THE PLACE OF PILGRIMAGE OF DEDE KHORKHUT.** He is a great Sultan. All the people of Shirvan believe in this Sultan.[370] This is the resting place of several thousand Saints, but those that we visited and with whom we became acquainted are these. May God's mercy be upon them all!

After visiting and making the pilgrimage, the Khan of Demirkapu gave us ten *tuman*s in *qazbeygi*s, one postal horse,[371] ten Gujarati cotton fabrics, and with two hundred companions we took leave of our friends, the sultan and the khans.

JOURNEY FROM DEMIRKAPU TO GEORGIA

First, starting from this castle we traveled for twelve hours through forests towards the south on the border of Daghestan and arrived at:

---

367. He ruled as Yazid II from 720 to 724.

368. Probably the Khazars are meant.

369. Hammer, p. 168 has instead, "the inhabitants of Derbend boast that amongst this crowd of martyrs seventy-five doctors of true tradition are buried. Amongst these tombs some are to be seen with inscriptions in Jelli (great Neskhi) of Ottomans, giving an account of their lives and deaths."

370. Hammer, p. 168 has in addition, "Several thousand great Saints are buried here, but I visited and made myself acquainted with those only that I have mentioned. God's mercy upon all of them!"

371. Hammer, p. 168 has, "a horse of the race (Kadhibeg) and a trotting (Chapar) horse."

The stage of the town of Kureh. It is a big district, the capital of the Shamkhal, the king of Daghestan on the border with Tabarsaran.[372] It has gardens and orchards with one thousand fine and well-built houses and a small mosque. There are no markets or bazaars. Every Friday, people from villages in the surrounding area gather here to buy and sell, but they do not know about gold or silver money. They do business through barter. They have been doing this forever.[373] It has about ten thousand inhabitants. They are all Shafe`is, religious and devout. I did not see any women in this town. In Daghestan women do not leave the house until they die, and then they are taken to the grave-yard of the town. Women are not allowed to leave the house unless they go to make the hajj pilgrimage to Mecca. Its inhabitants are hospitable, healthy and good-humored. There are many orchards and gardens.

We proceeded from here and by mountains, promenades and a ruined castle we arrived after [-] hours in the big country of the Avars. It is a personal fief of the king of Daghestan. After three days of traveling and visiting all the villages here, we reached Sarir al-Lan.

Description of the castle of the town of Sarir al-Lan. The castle was built in ancient times by Hormuz, the son Anushirvan. Many kings fought for the possession of this town. After many battles for this town, the king of Persia, Kur Khodabandeh, wrested it from the hands of the king of Daghestan. Then the Ottomans, desiring it, conquered it and destroyed its castle, so that it might not be used as a defense against them. Now it is in the hands of the Persians in the land of the governor of the castle of Erish.[374] It is situated on the slopes of Mt. Elburz, and in ancient times it was the capital of the kings of Daghestan, and it was a large town. It has been written in the histories of Daghestan that in the beginning the prophet Solomon, when he visited Mt. Elburz together with his wife Bilqis, all Genies and innumerable troops, erected his flying throne and built this city there and that is the reason for calling this town Sarir al-Lan, i.e., the Throne of Solomon.[375] *Lan* in Persian means 'nest', and the word *sarir* means 'he who travels'.[376] In short, 'the flying nest.' That is why the town is called Sarir al-Lan. Now on a high hill, it is a Persian promenade and place of recreation, it is called the Throne of Solomon, which is correct. It is an old town between Bab al-Abvab (Darband), Shamakhi and Niyazabad. In spite of being between the three cities it is not very prosperous. Its climate is cold, and therefore it does not have many gardens. It has about three thousand mud-covered houses. There is a large mosque, which, since it is in the hands of the Persians, is not frequented by people. There are seven bathhouses, eleven caravanserais, and up to seventy shops in the bazaar. Since I was there for one night I could not see its inside. It is the seat of a khan and of a qazi. It has a mayor, a secretary, a police chief, and up to one thousand soldiers and royal slaves, who are paid by the Shah. There are many Sunnis. They weave cotton cloth. Because of its pleasant climate the beloved of Sarir al-Lan are very famous. All the streams that irrigate the cotton fields and trestled gardens issue forth on the west side of

---

372. Tabarsaran is a district south of Darband that was governed by two hereditary chiefs called Ma`sum and Qadi, see Bakikhanov (index). Until the end of the sixteenth century the capital of the Shamkhal was Qomuq, thereafter it became Tarku. See Floor, "Who are the Shamakhal."

373. Barter trade was normal in the Caucasus area and probably elsewhere in many rural areas of Iran, see Floor, *The Economy of Safavid Persia*, pp. 118-19.

374. Areshi, a town in Kakhzti.

375. The correct form is Sarir al-Alan or the Seat of the Alans.

376. *Laneh*, not *lan*, means 'nest' in Persian and *sarir* in Persian means 'throne.'

Mt. Elburz and merge into the river Kur. There are many hundreds of water mills, whose water is like that of the fountain of youth. From here we traveled towards the south, and after [-] hours we came to:

THE DISTRICT OF KHANI. It is now under the king of Daghestan; it is a district with three hundred prosperous villages that are like towns with forests and mountains, with large mosques, caravanserais, gardens and orchards. One side of it is Mt. Elburz. After three days of visiting the villages here we came to:

THE DISTRICT OF THE VILLAGE OF ZAKHUR. It has one hundred and fifty big villages that are like towns with gardens and orchards, large mosques, caravanserais and bathhouses. One of the chief lords of the king of Daghestan, Amir Yusof Bey, is governor, but he has been under the Persian yoke several times. Its people are Shafe'i Sunnis and they have up to seven thousand fighting men. We stayed one night with the Bey, who gave us fifty skins of stone-martens and of wild cats. This humble servant gave him three embroidered Qaya Sultan handkerchiefs.[377] In this village there is:

THE PILGRIMAGE OF THE TOMB OF SHEIKH AMIR SULTAN. He is a great Saint of the *Khvajegan* order. In this district the scholars of Daghestan, the commentators, the transmitters of Traditions and the divines of the community do not have their like anywhere. In this land there is no lying and backbiting, evil action and suspicion, hatred and pride, envy and enmity, except for the Shi'ites, who do not allow them into their midst and do not trade with them. Every year there is a big market here. Here ends Daghestan.

DESCRIPTION OF THE PROVINCES OF GEORGIA AND SHAVSHADISTAN

First, on the border is situated:

THE CASTLE OF URDUBAR,[378] which belongs to the Persians. Passing it on the left this humble servant entered into Georgia, and skirting the boundaries of the castle of Sheki, which formerly I had seen on my way to Shamakhi, we arrived at:

THE VILLAGE OF ZOKHORYA, which is situated in Georgia, on the border of Tamoras Khan's land; it is under the Khan of Tiflis and a big village. Its subjects are Georgians knights. There are also Armenians Gökdolaq. Then after [-] hours we entered Kakht.

DESCRIPTION OF THE ANCIENT CASTLE AND IMPORTANT CAPITAL CITY OF KAKHT

It is situated on the border of Georgia, now it is held by the Persians. Its first founder was Anushirvan.[379] When the Prophet was born, Anushirvan said: "Now, a prophet has appeared. From the aggression of his people, my people will be protected." Then he ordered this pentagonal castle to

---

377. We have not been able to identify this type of fabric.

378. Hammer, p. 170 has Ur.

379. Hammer, p. 170 has, "It was built by Nushirvan to keep the tribes of the Caucasus in order."

be built at the slopes of Mt. Elburz in a fertile open land. Because of the passage of time, some parts of its castle have been ruined. According to the measurement of the slave Khosrow its circumference is fourteen thousand paces. It has one hundred and seventy towers and three gates. Inside the castle there are around two thousand well-built houses, the large mosque is in ruins, the caravanserai, the bathhouses and the bazaar are decorated, and each house is embellished with gardens. Its climate and its beloveds of both sexes are famous. Its water is very pure and delicious. Its waters come down from Mt. Elburz in seven terraced stages across the slopes of Kakht, watering its gardens and orchards, and then they fall into the river Kur to the east. Since its climate is rather cold, its silk is not famous. Most of its people are Armenian, Gökdolaq and Georgian. Its governors are independent sultans. It has about one thousand soldiers who are Qaderis.[380] It has twelve officials and a qazi. Shah Esma'il resided three years here[381] before fighting with (Sultan) Selim in the battle of Chalderan because he liked the weather of this place. Outside the castle he built a big suburb with chessboard-like streets, which looks like the city of Kaschau[382] in the middle of Hungary. Later on, he himself was wiped out by Selim in the battle of Chaldiran, and one hundred thousand of his soldiers were put to the sword, and he himself barely escaped to Azerbaijan. Thereafter the plundering Ottoman army along with Georgian troops pillaged and destroyed the city of Kakht. Afterwards it did not prosper very much. However, its suburb is more beautiful than the other cities. When Farhad Pasha was building the castle of Aras, he took the stones from here in several thousand carts. The Sultan of the city accompanied this humble servant out of kindness for one stage. We traveled towards the south and stopped at the village of Khodray Khan. It is situated on the banks of the river Kur; it has one thousand houses, a large mosque, a caravanserai and a bathhouse. It is on the border with Tiflis and a village with a chief and gardens. From here after [-] hours we arrived at:

Description of the capital of Shavshadistan Georgia, i.e., the castle built by Bitlis, the strong castle of Tiflis[383]

According to one of the historians of Iran, the author of the *Sharafnameh*, this town was built by Bitlis, the treasurer of Alexander the Two-Horned.[384] He also built that castle of Bitlis in the province of Van. In short, several hundred times, several hundreds of thousands of rebels had come and laid siege to this castle, and it passed from king to king, Tiflis is one piece of work. Eventually it ended up in the hands of one of the Georgian rulers named Davud Khan. Fearing the Ottomans, the aforementioned khan went to the mischievous shah and obtained the [appointment to] the khanate. After many years of ruling with Anushirvan-like justice and keeping the land prosperous, eventually in the year 986 [1578], in the time of Murad III, Laleh Farhad

---

380. Qaderis are believers in the free will of human beings.

381. This is incorrect.

382. Now known as Ko ice, 200 km n.w. of Budapest.

383. The term Shavshadistan refers to the Georgian principality of Shavsheti, a mountainous district of Samtzkhe, between the rivers Choroki, Acharis-tsqali and Imer-Khevi. It was conquered by the Ottomans in 1547. Shavshat, as it is referred in Turkish, is now a town and district in Artvin province, on the border with Georgia.

384. This historian is Sharaf Khan Bidlisi, whose *Sharaf-nameh* was translated into French as *Cherefnama ou Histoire des Kourdes*, publiée par V. Veliaminof-Zernof, 2 vols. (St. Petersburg 1860-62). For the story of the foundation of Bitlis see Ibid., vol. 1, p. 2/1, p. 200.

A royal banquet in Tiflis, ca. 1670

A view of Tiflis ca. 1670

Pasha marched against Georgia with an army of innumerable soldiers and conquered the castle of Childir and seventy of its subordinate castles. He aimed to take the castle of Tiflis. When Davud Khan[385] learned that this great general was marching against Tiflis, he put forty thousand soldiers in the castle of Tiflis, prepared for war and reinforced the castle. On the other hand, the innumerable [Ottoman] army came to the plain of the castle of Shuran after having marched several stages and pitched their tents. First, the general sent a letter to the governor of Tiflis and invited him, [Davud Khan], to the True Faith, then to surrender the castle to the Sultan and to become tax-paying subjects; otherwise, according to the true faith, "you will be put to the sword and all your wives and children will become captives." In accordance with the Prophet's law, when the letter arrived, it was read and its content became known to all the infidels and uncouth Qizilbash, who gathered to take counsel. It was decided to send back the envoy with the message, "Whatever the Ottomans want let them do it," and to put themselves into a state of defense. But those who

---

385. Hammer, p. 171 in addition has, "who was then the governor of Tiflis."

were more prudent took counsel and taking into account the fact that they could not oppose the besieging army of Islam, they all abandoned the castle by night and left it empty. Hearing of this joyous news the great general pursued them with the army of Islam and near the castle of Tiflis crossed the river Kur with great speed and in one day and one night arrived at the castle of Zekim (Zagam). He overtook the Khan of Tiflis, who had taken refuge with his family and all his valuables in a big deserted place inside a rocky forested area. By the grace of God, the fighters for the faith attacked the Georgians and the Qizilbash from all sides like numerous ants attacking a snake, and a fierce battle ensued. They asked for mercy, which was denied and forty thousand Georgians and Qizilbash had their heads cut off. The army of Islam collected an enormous booty and the least of soldiers received a shield full of gold.

That victorious general sent the commander of the Janissaries with seven batallions to secure Tiflis castle, and with the army of Islam, he himself besieged the castle of Zagam, where he granted mercy and took in the year 986 [1578]. Then he went to the north and surrounded the Kerim castle. Its people not being able to withstand the attack of the Ottomans were granted mercy and surrendered the castle to the general. Those who were inside went to the abode of misery. This humble servant did not see the castle of Zagam, but while passing through the plain of the castle of Kakht I saw the castle of Kerim. But I did not go inside. The valiant general came out into these provinces hunting like a lion, and he conquered twenty-six small and big castles, some of which he destroyed and some of which he repaired, and in each one he put a castellan, an arsenal, a garrison, equipment and supplies. Then, after traveling several stages that day he reached the castle of Tiflis. There was a great festivity for the Ottomans, so that the lands of Iran and Shirvan were frightened and the Moslem call to prayer was heard.

THE CONQUEST OF THE CASTLE OF TIFLIS IN THE YEAR 986 [1578] AT THE HANDS OF QARA LALEH MOSTAFA PASHA DURING THE REIGN OF MURAD III. Then this great general made the castle so strong strong that there is no castle as strong as it in Georgia and Azerbaijan, except for the castles of Baku and Maku. Later, the victorious general liberated the province and made it a big one. He gave its governorship, with the rank of governor-general, to the governor of the *sanjaq* of Kastamonu,[386] Mohammad Pasha, the son of Solaq (left-handed) Farhad Pasha. He prepared[387] and completed all the necessaries and supplies, assigned twenty regiments of Janissaries, five regiments of armorers, five regiments of gunners and brought soldiers from hundred seventy destroyed castles. He assigned the soldiers from the *sanjaq*s of Tireh, Mantasha, Teke, and Hamid as well as from the province of Sivas as guards. After conquering forty small and large castles, destroying some and repairing others, he sent the keys of seventy of castles as well as the keys of Tiflis, Childir, Shuran, Khartin, Azghur and Tumek to the High Porte. While he was returning to the High Porte, the uncouth Qizilbash with the infidels of Georgia laid siege to the castle of Tiflis for seven months. All Moslem fighters for the faith suffered from shortage and dearness of supplies. Eventually they were forced to eat their horses, then their dogs, and gradually the corpses of the martyred ones. In seven months the infidels attacked seven times. The commander of the Qizilbash, Emam Qoli Khan, offered quarter with empty words and words of cheat and deceit. The Moslem fighters for the faith, knowing full well that they would be killed, did not surrender. The dog of somebody called ʿAli Subashi was sold for seven thousand *aqche*s and was eaten. By the grace of God, the governor of Erzerum, Mostafa Pasha, with an innumerable army marched with great speed to the besieged castle and put Emam Qoli Khan to flight. The besieged fighters for the faith enjoyed this booty and plunder immensely. When Mostafa Pasha arrived at the foot of the castle the following day, the soldiers of Islam found a new life.

Thereafter, Hasan Pasha, the son of the Grand Vizier, arrived with a caravan of three thousand camel loads of wheat and other cereals, and put them into the stores. Now there are still stores in the small castle.

In short, from the time of Sultan Murad III until that of the accession of Sultan Mostafa this castle was in the hands of the Ottomans; when the heathen Georgians, uniting with the Persians, suddenly attacked and giving no quarter to the fighters of the faith, they evicted them from

---

386. Kastamonu is a province on the Black Sea, west of Sinop province in Turkey.

387. Hammer, p. 171 has, "its works were repaired, and its stores completed. He then sent the keys of no less than seventy large and small castles to the Ottoman Court and then returned himself to Constantinople."

the castle and seized it in the name of the Shah. From that time on it has been in the hands of the Persians, and it is very well developed and prosperous.[388]

THE FORM OF THE CASTLE OF TIFLIS. It is built on the banks of the river Kur on a rock. There are two castles facing each other, one is called Bitlis and the other Tiflis, between which the river Kur flows. There is a big bridge over the rocks connecting the two castles, so that you can go easily from one side to the other. The large castle is situated on the south of the river Kur and the other to the north of it. The river Kur flows and washes the walls of the large castle, which looks over the plain and at the front of the gate that opens to the small castle. After seven stages the river Kur drains into the Caspian Sea, between Baku castle and the city of Gilan.[389] It originates in the mountains of Childir, comes up to Ardahan,[390] then to the castles of Akhiskha[391] and Azghura, and passes through Tiflis into the Caspian Sea. It is a major river, and the historians of Iran say: "One thousand sixty streams feed it." Truly, after the Euphrates the river Kur is the biggest river. The large castle that Bitlis built stands on a steep rock on the banks of this river. It has a circumference of six thousand paces, but is an old building. The height of its walls is sixty cubits, and it has seventy bulwarks and three thousand battlements, with one draw-bridge and no moat. On the river Kur there is a water tower, so that in case of a siege water is supplied from it. Inside the castle there are six hundred mud-covered houses; the mansion of the Khan is in this castle. It has a large mosque, a caravanserai, a bathhouse and a small market. Later, the small castle was built by king Yazdegerd. It is a quadrangular stone building on a steep hill. At the top of the bridge there is a gate. Inside the castle there are three hundred houses, and a large mosque, but there is no drapers' hall or other buildings. This castle is on the north side of the big castle, but its walls are stronger than those of the large castle. The castles have three thousand guards; every night the watchmen light the castles with torches and shout: "*Khoda khub*" (God is well; i.e., All's well). Although it is in Persian territory, most of the people have been Sunnis of the Hanafi and Shafe`i school since Ottoman times. There are many ulama and beloveds of both sexes.

Tiflis produces very good large-grain, a special white bread, and a red and white hybrid peach (*shaftalu*), which is famous for its juicy and very sweet taste. Because it is produced in the gardens of Georgian harems; they are very fleshy peaches. Its pulses and herbs are very good. There is no cotton and silk, but its juicy grapes are famous. These crops do not get water at all from the river Kur, for they all grow because there is sufficient rainfall. Although the river Kur from its source passes one hundred and fifty villages, it cannot irrigate each one of them and hence its name Kur (blind).[392] But the Mongols call this river Kur-e ur, which means 'useless,' but its water

---

388. Hammer, p. 172 in addition has, "It is the capital of Georgia, to which belongs sixteen Sultans, seventy judges, forty districts and seven tracts called Oimak. Three-tenths of Georgia are occupied by the province of Tiflis; the khan commands two thousand soldiers, it has also a judge and twelve public officers in honour of the twelve Imams."

389. The Caspian province of Gilan is meant.

390. Ardahan is a province in the most north-eastern corner of Turkey, north of Qars, bordering on Georgia. The Chaldir or Keldir Mountains straddle the Turkish and Georgian border.

391. Akheshqeh in Meshkhia province of Georgia on the border with Turkey.

392. The name Kur or Kura probably comes from Megrelian *kur* (water, river) or Albanian (reservoir).

is very delicious. Since it is flowing all the time in valleys, it it cannot irrigate upland places. Its bathhouses are not good, because there are hot springs in the city.[393]

DESCRIPTION OF THE HOT SPRING OF TIFLIS. On the east of the large castle a hot spring boils out of the soil by God's power without burning wood, in which sheeps' heads and feet are cooked. This is a nicely domed hot spring.

PLACES OF PILGRIMAGE IN TIFLIS. These include Imam Hosam Efendi, Rezvan Agha, the deputy of Farhad Pasha and Jam ʿAli Efendi, who were all treasure houses of knowledge. There are many places of pilgrimage, but these are the ones known to us.

Tiflis is at five stages distance from the castle of Kakht and four stages from the castles of Aras and Ganjeh. From here, with two hundred companions and after getting three *tuman*s in ʿ*abbasi*s as travel money, we went through narrow roads towards the south, and after four hours we reached Gulusakht.

DESCRIPTION OF THE CASTLE OF GULUSAKHT. It is a small square-shaped castle on a steep rock; it is under the Persians and it is in the district of Tiflis. [The castle of Luri] was to be seen on top of a high peak amongst the mountains. We did not go near it but looked at it from afar.

THE CASTLE OF LURI is near the castle Tiflis and was built in the year 990 [1582] by Farhad Pasha.

DESCRIPTION OF THE CASTLE OF SURAN. After passing there we went to the castle of Suran, which is a small castle under the Khan of Tiflis and situated on a very steep hill. Yet it is very strong with interconnected high towers and ramparts. The original founder is Anushirvan and it is one of the older castles of Georgia. Now its inhabitants are mostly Georgians, Gökdolaq and Armenians. From there we left to the west, and after four hours we reached Azghur.

DESCRIPTION OF THE OLD CASTLE AND BIG WALL OF AZGHUR OF ALEXANDER GUR. According to the learned historian of the *Sharafnameh*, this is the first castle that was built in Georgia; it is known as Azghur castle. In the Georgian language, Azgur-e gur means 'king of kings.'[394] Its foundation is attributed to Alexander the Two-Horned. Truly, this square-shaped, big, flint stone wall indicates that it was built by Alexander, otherwise five hundred men in our time could not possibly move one of these stones. Now it is an old, small, square-shaped castle situated on a high hill. The castle is situated in Georgia on the border with Akhiskha, which is under a deputy. It has a gate facing towards the south. Its governor is an *aqa*. It has up to two hundred soldiers. It is entirely standing alone. It is strongly built. {The river flowing in front of the town issues from Mt. Oda in the Akhiskha mountains. It passes through Akhiskha and waters the gardens and orchards of the town. It drains into the river Aras.} It has a large mosque, a caravanserai, a bathhouse and about forty to fifty shops.[395] Because of its pleasant climate, gardens and orchards,

---

393. Meaning that people preferred the hot springs.

394. What these words mean is not known; they certainly do not mean 'king of kings' in Georgian.

395. Hammer, p. 173 has, "forty small streets."

the beauties of Georgia are proverbial. Since this place is in the land of the Shavsheti people of Georgia, its inhabitants speak Georgian.

The language of the Georgian Shavshetis.

erti: 1; *ori*: 2; *sami*: 3; *otxi*: 4; [*liuti*: [xuti] 5]; *eksi*: 6; *shudi*: 7; *ruway*: 8; *çixray (khijrey)*: 9; *ati*: 10; *puri*: bread; *chiqali*: water; *xorc*: meat; *ghina*: wine [gvino]; *bak*: cherry; *pishali*: [pisxali] pear; *quwax*: gourd; *leghay*: fig; *qurzeni*: grapes; *itxelli*: hazelnut; *nesu*: melon; *puroçoguli*: pomegranate; *xárbucaqi*: watermelon; *pizoli*: mulberry; *qoqo*: girl; *qali*: old woman [woman]; *aqi mod bico pur camos*: Come boy let's eat bread; *dacéd bico*: sit boy; *cagma dedá moqtanis*: May dogs fuck your mother; *ar sáwides xitnam*: don't go out; *aqi patoni puri çamos*: Come sir let's eat bread; *ibizi*: it is good; *aqi mod ar sáwides*: come don't go; *dacd paton*: sit sir; *paton erti on bicem xar* (*bice mxavs*) *dacéd agdos*: Sir, I have one or two boys, will you buy?; *aqim pátrayá baqayi*: Let me see, is he little (young)?; *didi arish*: No, he is big; *ar gidos*: I won't buy; *tis mádma q[ajy bceya*: By God, he is a fine boy; *qay araris qiláxa*: He is not good, he is bad; *çixén*: horse; *çori*: mule; *wiri*: donkey; *cagli qudban*: The dog is naughty.

There are some more words and expressions, but since we could not write them [all] this much will suffice.

Concerning the genealogy of the Georgian kings

The Jewish people were the first of the heathens. Then came the Georgians, the Dadian[396] and the Shavsheti people, and from them issued forth the Guril,[397] the Achiq bash[398] and the Mingrelian people. All of them have descended from the prophet David and are Christians, and having the New Testament they have their own misconceptions. All of them talk in twelve languages. Its dialects are special and they do not understand each other, unless with the help of interpreters. According to their beliefs, the language of the Shavshetis and the Dadiyan is the most eloquent of all people. If the line of the Muscovy kings should be extinguished it is said that the Georgians are the chosen ones among the Christian nation and the descendants of Anushirvan. They will come and get a *bey* from the Shavshetis or the Dadian and make him the king [of Muscovy].[399] They are people of the Book. However, the Abazas[400] and the wretched Circassians, being a new nation and an Arab offshoot, do not have any Book or religion. The Georgian priests claim that the kings' genealogy goes back to Key Kavus and through many thousands of knights ends up with the prophet David. There was a king in Georgia. When he died he was succeeded by his daughter

---

396. Dadiani is the territorial patronymic of the ruling princes of Mingrelia. The name probably has been derived from the river Dadi.

397. This is the territorial patronymic of the Wardanisdze family, princes of Guria, a province of Imereti. Allen, *History*, pp. 120-22.

398. Achiq bash was the Ottoman name for the *atabeg*dom of Samtakhe, Meskhia, or Saatabago. In 1512 it fell into Ottoman hands.

399. This refers to the embassy of Mikhael Ignatyevich Tatishchev to Georgia in 1604-05 to arrange, among other things, a marriage between two children of Giorgi X and two of Borish Godunov. Allen, *History*, p. 165.

400. Abkhazians.

Tamarrud, who became ruler.[401] She never married anyone and ruled the country that she had inherited from her father. One night she was partying with a beautiful slave and she was drunk and she was violated and the queen became pregnant. She gave birth to a beautiful girl, whom she kept hidden and sent her to the region of Vat. On the other hand, in order not to get a bad name the queen sent the young groom who had deflowered her to hunt for fowl on a frozen pond; when the ice broke he sank and drowned. In this way all talk about the daughter came to an end. When the girl reached adulthood she was married off to a prince, who was known as Bey Divan. She bore three sons, and when they reached adulthood Georgia was divided into three parts. To the eldest prince was given the district of Kotatis, which is called the province of Bash-acheq. The origin of the people of Bash-acheq is from [this] prince Marula. The middle one, whose name was Simon, was given the district of Tiflis and the youngest one, whose name was Dadian, the district of Baht was given. The people of Dadian are descended from him. Since prince Dadian was a fine and just ruler, all the infidels became his subjects. Even now all the Georgians obey the Beys of Dadian and Bash-acheq as if they were the chief high priests. When the kings of the infidels ascend to the throne and want to gird the sword, they do it with the permission of these Beys of Dadian and Achiq bash and all the infidels support this king.[402] When Selim I was governor in Trabson, he made friends with the bey of Achiq bash and spent time amusing himself in Kotatis Castle.[403] When Selim acceded by imperial writ to the throne after his father, Bayazid, he exempted the province of Achiq bash from all customary duties, and up to our day it is exempt. Every year, they simply sent Ispiri hawks, falcons, eagles, and beautiful boys and girls to the High Porte as presents. This is the law of Selim I. Later we departed from the aforementioned Azghur castle and went towards the west and passed through prosperous villages as well as promenades, gardens, fertile lands and meadows and after for hours, praise to God, we arrived safely at Sadd-e Islam.

DESCRIPTION OF SADD-E ISLAM AND THE CONQUEST OF SELIM OF THE PROVINCE OF CHILDERAN, THE STRONG CASTLE, THE MIGHTY CITADEL, THE GREAT EMPORIUM OF OTTOMAN AKHISKHA

The name of Akhiskha is pronounced differently in each of the languages of the people in the area surrounding it, such as Ahkeska, Ahcheska, Akeska, Akhesha {and Akesha}. In the imperial [Ottoman] records it is only registered as "the province of Childir ruled by such and such Pasha." Its first founder is Anushirvan, the great monarch who built the Arch of Khosrow, and in his time the great prophet Mohammad Mostafa was born, and at that time this Anushirvan was the chief priest. He said "O, this night the last prophet, Mohammad, has arisen." Since the time of Alexander, who was the original founder of this castle, 882 years had passed. It was so well kept and maintained that every year Anushirvan came from paradisiacal Baghdad to Akhiskha and took his summer quarters here for six months, because its climate is so pleasant. Thereafter several

---

401. The queen's name was Tamara (r. 1184-1212), who was a very strong and successful ruler, whose reign is remembered as the golden age of Georgia. For her history see W.E.D. Allen, *A History of the Georgian People* (London, 1932), pp. 103-07.

402. Evliya's interpretation of Georgian dynastic troubles and the rivalry of the Mingrelian and Samtzkhe factions is a fanciful one. See Allen, pp. 152-60.

403. Kotatis, ancient Colchis, the capital of Imeretia, situated on the banks of the Phasis River.

thousand[404] kings coveted to become king of Akhiskha. If we want to expand on their possession of the castle this will become a big tome. According to the history of the *Sharafnameh*, in the year [-] of the hijra, Hesham b. ʿAbdol-Malek, the Ommayad caliph came with innumerable soldiers and conquered Aleppo, ʿEyntab, Marʿash, Malatiyeh, Diyarbekr and Erzerum. Then he went to Akhiskha and conquered it. The first bulwark of Islam in Georgia was this Akhiskha. From there he sent an innumerable army to take the castles of Tiflis, Tomanis, Ganjeh, Shirvan, Bab al-Abvab, and the province of Daghestan and conquered them all, and they were all converted to Islam by the Lord of the Believers, the Caliph Hesham. Then he returned to his beautiful capital Damascus. Then the Georgians conquered it again (Akhiskha). Then one of the rulers of Azerbyjan, Qara Yusof Shah, conquered this place and when Timur appeared, Qara Yusof could not resist him and took refuge with Ilderim Bayazid of the Ottoman dynasty.[405] Later on, this castle Akhiskha came into the hands of Sultan Uzun Hasan. Although Timur went against Uzun Hasan, the latter behaved wisely and kissing his stirrup and along with eleven kings he walked on foot while Timur was riding and Azerbaijan was saved from plunder and pillage and was again bestowed upon Hasan Shah. After this, the rule of Azerbaijan went to Shah Esmaʿil, who was from the line of Sheykh Safi. He made Akhiskha his summer quarters and subdued all of Georgia. In the time of Bayazid Khan, he ravaged the Ottoman lands and pushed his incursion up to Sivas, which was known as the granary of the Ottoman lands, and until he got there he had conquered seven provinces. At that time Sultan Selim I was governor of Trabson. Like a lion coming after this evil-acting king, he put all troops to the sword.[406] God almighty helped him and the Ottoman throne came into his possession. First he was bent on holy war and came against Shah Esmaʿil with innumerable soldiers on the plains of Childir [sic; Chalderan] and fought an incredible battle, killed one hundred thousand of the uncouth Qizilbash and shaved off their red heads with the sword of Islam. Eventually, the shah fled to Azerbaijan to safety. His escape is reported in all Ottoman histories, and there is no need to mention it here. Later on, Sultan Selim subdued the castle of Akhiskha and subjected all of Georgia.[407] The chronogram of the date of "the conquest of the castle of Akhiskha" is the year (704/1306-07):

> The oracle of the unseen puts its date
> The Sultan of Rum seized the land of Iran.

---

404. Evliya cannot help himself and exaggerates again.

405. Evliya Chelebi is as usual historically wrong. He confused Qara Yusof with Ahmad Ilkhani who sought refuge with Bayazid, see, e.g., Bakikhanov, *Golestan*, p. 71. Also, Timur had died before Uzun Hasan was born.

406. Hammer, p. 174 instead has, "and many times pursued the Persian troops." The events were somewhat different, the great rebellion of 1511-12 was not incited by Esmaʿil I and he tried as much as possible to avoid conflict with the Ottomans. It was rather Selim who chafed at being held in check by his father Bayazid II who wanted to take action against the Qizilbash, which he despite his father's will to the contrary, occasionally still did. See, e.g. *Cambridge History of Iran* vol. 6, pp. 222-23.

407. On the events at Chalderan see *Cambridge History of Iran*, vol. 6, pp. 223-25. Selim did not conquer Georgia, in fact his retreating troops were harassed by Georgian troops. Floor, *Safavid Government*, p. 131. Also, Childir (Akhaltsikhe), the first piece of Georgian territory held by the Ottomans, only became part of the Ottoman Empire in 1578.

After the conquest Sultan Selim ordered a survey, made it into a big province and gave its government to a Pasha.[408] As this town is the frontier of Georgia, Kurdistan, Turkistan, Daghestan and with Persia, it was declared a separate province.

According to the law book of Sultan Selim I, the province of Childir consists of thirteen *sanjaq*s.

There is a treasurer for the revenues, registrar of the *timar*s, an inspector of the rolls, a deputy of the *chavosh*, a commissioner and a secretary of the *chavosh*.[409]

The *sanjaq*s are as follows: First, the *liva* of Olti, Khirtiz, Ardanij,[410] Hajrek,[411] Ardahan, Posthu,[412] Makhchil,[413] Acharpenk and Akhiskha; all these are seats of a pasha. The four *sanjaqleq*s of Purtekrek, Livane,[414] Nesf (Half) Livane and Shavshat are hereditary *yurdeluq*s and *ojaliq*s.

Every *sanjaq* denotes the personal imperial fief of beys. The fief of the *liva* of Olti (200,017); Pertak (462, 190); Ardanij (280,000), Great Ardahan (300,000), Shavshat (656,000); Livane in the form of an *ojaqliq*, which consists of two *sanjaq*s in one place (365,000); Khirtiz (200,500); Hajrek (365,000); Posthu (206,500); Makhchil (20,322); Ajara (200,005), and Penk (400,000). According to Selim I's regulations, all the emirs of the entire province of Childir have thus been given their fiefs.

Description of how many *timars* and *ze'amats* there are in each *sanjaq* in the province of Childir.

In total there are 656 *timar*s and *ze'amat*s. According to the Selim I's laws, together with the armed retainers of the fief holder there are eight hundred soldiers. With the soldiers of the Pasha they become one thousand five hundred soldiers.

The *liva* of Olti has 3 *ze'amat*s and 113 *timar*s.

The *liva* of Greater Ardahan has 8 *ze'amat*s and 87 *timar*s;

The *liva* of Ardanij has four *ze'amat*s and forty-two *timar*s

Hajrek 2 *ze'amat*s and 72 *timar*s

Khirtiz 13 *ze'amat*s and 35 *timar*s

Posthu 12 *ze'amat*s and 68 *timar*s

Penk 8 *ze'amat*s and 54 *timar*s

---

408. Hammer, p. 175 has, "to a Pasha of three tails."

409. *Chavush* were officials attached to the law courts of grand vizier. Gibb-Bowen, vol. 1, p. 87.

410. Hammer, p, 175 has Ardikh.

411. Hammer, p. 175 has Khajrek.

412. Hammer, p. 175 has Postkhu.

413. Hammer, p. 175 has here in addition Acharpenik.

414. Hammer, p. 175 has instead Lesana.

Sasin 7 *ze'amat*s and 4 *timar*s

Luri 9 *ze'amat*s and 10 *timar*s

Osha 10 *ze'amat*s and 17 *timar*s

Chaqliq 11 *ze'amat*s 32 *timar*s

Khatla 18 *ze'amat*s and 7 *timar*s

Ispir 4 *ze'amat*s and 14 *timar*s

The number of *timars* and *ze'amats* are as mentioned above. Each one has an *alaybey*, a *cheri-bashi*[415] and a *yuz-bashi*.[416] If they go on a campaign, on condition that they march under the *sanjaq*, the pashas, the *mir-livas* and *alaybeys* get their expenditures paid out of the revenue of one thousand sixty villages. Every year all the *timar* and *ze'amat*-holders benefit from the revenues of one thousand sixty villages, which yield three hundred and twenty Ottoman purses.[417] In a detailed decree Sultan Selim gave this province to the Pasha of the *sanjaq* and made the governors of provinces of Erzerum, Sivas, Mar'ash, Adana and Rakka subordinate to the governor of Childir. It is Selim's law that every year they had to come to protect it. First, he granted its judgeship with the rank of mullah[418] to Ramazan Efendi of Eskelib[419] with five hundred *aqches*, and now it is three hundred for the judgeship. Every year the judge may collect seven purses in a just manner from the districts belonging to his jurisdiction.[420] The imperial personal fief of the *mir-miran* of Childir amounts to 400,000. There is a castlellan, about two thousand regular soldiers, castle wardenships (*qal'a- aqalik*), seven batallions of royal janissaries, armorers and gunners. In the year [-] the evil Qizilbash found an opportunity and conquered Childiran when it was prosperous and thriving. Later on, in the year 1044 [1634] Murad IV wrested Erevan from the Persians. After its conquest he made Koja Ken'an Pasha general over the innumerable army; he came and conquered the castle of Akhiskha in the year 1045 [1636-37] and put it in in good repair and condition, which holds to the present time.

DESCRIPTION OF THE LAYOUT OF THE CASTLE OF AKHISKHA. It stands on a steep hill, made of stone as if it is built by Farhad. It has two gates. Inside the castle there are about one thousand one hundred mud-covered houses without orchards and gardens. One gate opens to the east and the other to the west. It has a total of twenty-eight mosques; the *khutba* is read there.

The large mosque of Sultan Selim I is in the upper part of the castle. It is an old building, which is covered with mud and plaster. Inside the town there is no lead-covered soup kitchen. The minaret of this beautiful mosque has been destroyed. The large mosque of Kunbet-oghlu is also covered with mud and without minaret. In the lower castle, there is the large mosque of

---

415. The *cheri-bashi* was the second highest ranking officer of the *sepahi*s and other local feudal levies, after the *alaybey*. Gibb-Bowen, *Islamic*, vol. 1, p. 51, 53, 149.

416. An officer in charge of one hundred men.

417. One purse contains 500 *qurush*.

418. A mullah, also *mevla* and *monla*, was a qazi of the highest rank. His function and rank was referred to as *mevliyet*. van Bruinessen et al., *Diyarbekr*, pp. 208, n. 51, 209, n. 55.

419. Eskelib, or Iskib, a town in Turkey, government of Sivas, 12 m. W of Churum.

420. On the payment of qazis see van Bruinessen et al., *Diyarbekr*, p. 209, n. 57.

Khalil Agha, which is an old building and much frequented by people; it is a pleasant and joyous mosque. The people of the province are Sunnis and are devoted and true Moslems. Apart from praying five times, in each mosque the Koran and other branches of learning are studied.

Apart from this there are mosques in the quarters. There are no special schools for teaching, learning Traditions and the Koran. But in every mosque there are professors who teach different subjects, because there are many students.

Outside the castle there is a very prosperous suburb with in total [-] thriving caravanserais.

The total number of bathhouses is [-]. The bathhouse in the castle is small but useful. Situated on the east-side of the castle facing the gate, the bathhouse is a nice building with a good ambiance. Its masseurs are beautiful Georgian youths.

There are [-] number of caravanserais for merchants. The caravanserais of Deli Mohammad Aqa and of Ekmekchi `Isa Agha-oghlu are famous. It has beautiful mansions.

Although there are no orchards, there are gardens here and there. There is [-] fruit, but there are many trestled gardens and their produce is manifold. There are many streams with pleasant water, which come from the Oda Mountains and water the fields of the town and then enter the Castle of Arghun and near the castle of Kusakht they fall into the Aras. To go from this castle to the suburb you have to cross a bridge over the moat. The suburb does not have a wall around it. In this suburb there are about three hundred shops, but there is no drapers' hall.

Since its climate is somewhat cold, its people are healthy and brave. Especially its governor, Vizier Safar Pasha, who originally is Georgian, is a brave, talented and valiant warrior and his deputy, Dervish Agha, is from Georgian extraction and very generous, and Seyfi Agha and other householders are honorable and gentleman-like men.

Description of the hot spring

Erevan is six stages to the east of Akhiskha and mid-way is the castle of Qars. From Akhiskha to Tiflis is five stages to the north-east, and to Ganjeh it is five stages to the east. Georgia is situated at [-] days to the north from the castle [-]. The castle of Akhiskha is situated between them all in the plain of Childir, and it is a prosperous castle in Georgia.

Description of the Georgian castles under the province of Childir

The castle of Khirtiz, near Childir, was conquered in the year 986 [1588-89] by Laleh Pasha.

Akhilk alak[421] castle was also conquered by him as well as the castles of Purkan and Kabir Valeh, which is a small castle between two high mountains of Valeh. This was also conquered by Qara Laleh Mostafa Pasha in the year 985 [1587-88].

In the heartland of the province Georgia, the castle of Kotatis is at two stages' distance from Childir. It is the capital of Achiq bash. It is situated near Mount Perizat. It is a prosperous province and the center of the government of Georgia. When Selim I was a prince and governor

---

421. Hammer, p. 177 has Adhil. Akhalk alak is situated in the Javakh region of Georgia.

of Trabson he had come to Shavshat and enjoyed himself. Under the caliphate of Selim it became an *ojaleq*. Now it is a personal fief with 606,000 [*aqches*] and has no *ze'amat*s and *timar*s.

THE CASTLE OF HAJREK[422] is situated between Akhiskha and Ardahan. In the province of Childir it is the capital of the *mir-liva*. It was conquered by Laleh (Pasha). The personal fief of its beyg is 365,000 *aqche*s. It has an *alay-bey* and a *qazi* with five thousand soldiers.

THE CASTLE OF SHATAN, which is known Sheytan castle, was conquered in the year 990 [1582] by Farhad Pasha. It is near Childir on a steep rock, but it is a strong castle.

THE CASTLE OF QIZLAR is situated near Childir on the banks of the river Chagh on a steep rock; it has no peer and is magical.

THE CASTLE OF ALTUN was conquered by Laleh Pasha and is made of stone, and it is within the distance of three hours from the castle of Qizlar.

THE CASTLE OF ODURYA was conquered by Laleh Pasha; it is small and built on a steep place.

THE CASTLE OF AL is near Akhiskha. The castle of Posthu is in the province of Akhechkha. It is the seat of the *sanjaq-beyg*. Its personal fief, *ze'amat*s and *timar*s were mentioned above. It was conquered in the year 985 [1577-78] by Mostafa Laleh Pasha. It is a judgeship with hundred and fifty *aqche*s, an *alay-bey* and a *cheri-bashi*. Since old times in the region of Shavshat there was a governor-general with two standards. It is seven hours from Childir.

THE CASTLE OF SHAVSHAT. It is the capital of the *sanjaq-bey* in Childir province. It is steep. It was conquered by Laleh Pasha. Its personal fief, *ze'amat*s and *timar*s have been mentioned above. Its government is an *ojaqleq*. There is no *qazi*. Shavshadestan is a mountainous area full of steep precipices.

THE CASTLE OF KHARBE is near the castle of Ardanij[423] next to a valley, it is a castle in an inaccessible place.

THE CASTLE OF ARDANIJ in the province of Childir and the seat of a *sanjaq-bey*. The personal fief and *ze'amat* of the bey were mentioned above. It has been conquered by Laleh Mostafa Pasha.

THE CASTLE OF OKHCHU is the seat of a *sanjaq-bey*. In the imperial records it registered as Makhchil. It is a difficult castle to reach. The bey's personal fief has been mentioned above. There is no *qazi*.

THE CASTLE OF CHAGHISMAN is near Childir; it was conquered by Laleh Pasha, and in an inaccessible place.[424]

{DESCRIPTION OF THE CASTLES NEAR ARDAHAN

THE CASTLE OF VALE; conquered by Laleh Pasha in the year 982 [1574-75].

---

422. Hammer, p. 177 has Khajrek.

423. Hammer, p. 177 has Ardikh.

424. Kagizman is a place of famous Neolithic stone engravings, located on a breathtaking canyon.

THE CASTLE OF GUMEK; conquered by Laleh Pasha in the year 982.

THE CASTLE OF AKHARIS;[425] conquered by Laleh Pasha in the year 982.

THE CASTLE OF Pertak, near Olti, conquered by Laleh Pasha.

THE CASTLE OF SEMAGHAR, near [-] at four hours.

THE CASTLE OF MAMRAVAN and THE CASTLE OF NAZARBAT.[426] They are at three hours from Ardahan. They were built by Ghazi Sefer Pasha in the year 1053 [1643-44].

THE CASTLE OF KINZE [-] in the district of Ardahan,[427] on a hill; it is an inaccessible castle. It was conquered by Laleh Pasha.

THE CASTLE OF KAZAN is at twelve hours from Ardahan; it was conquered by Laleh (Pasha). Its water goes to Ardahan}.

Among these castles there are several strong castles situated on the major roads, which have been mentioned. Truly, Georgia is a big country.

After visiting these we received from Sefer Pasha two Georgian slaves, one horse, one pair of Georgian woolen socks and one hundred *qurush*, and we left with our companions westward towards Erzerum.

DESCRIPTION OF THE STAGES THAT WE PASSED GOING [FROM AKHISKHA] TO ERZERUM

First, from Akhiskha we passed Olghar's summer quarters and after four hours reached:

THE CASTLE OF KINNAV, which borders on Ardahan. Again going to the west through a steep forested area, after [-] we reached Qara Ardahan.

DESCRIPTION OF THE CASTLE OF QARA ARDAHAN IN GEORGIA

It was conquered by Sultan Selim I in the year [-], and it is the seat of a *sanjaq-bey* in the province of Childir. The personal fief of the bey is 300,000 *aqches*, and there are 87 *timars* and 8 *ze'amats*, an *alay-bey* [colonel], a *cheri-bashi* [captain], a castellan,[428] two hundred guards. In addition to the garrison there are the bey's feudal troops, or a total of one thousand. It is a noble judgeship with one hundred fifty *aqches*. There is no *Naqib al-Ashraf* (head of the *sharifs* or descendants of the prophet). Its mufti is in Akhiskha. It is a rectangular huge castle on a steep rock. Its circumference is [-] paces, and it is not enclosed by neighboring heights. It is two-storied, with seventy towers; it is a beautiful castle. It has three gates. One batallion of armorers of the High Porte is based here. Inside this town the family of Qaya Pasha is famous. Under the town a river flows towards the east, which merges with the river Aras. In the town there are [-] old, mud-covered houses, and there are [-] mosques.

---

425. Hammer, p. 178 has Akharsin.

426. Hammer, p. 178 has Nazarban.

427. Hammer, p. 178 has, "the castle of Kese Dusal in the district of Erdehan on a hill; its water flows to Erdehan."

428. Hammer, p. 178 further has, "are the commanding officers of the garrison."

There is no public kitchen, no madraseh and no school of philosophy, but there is a school for children. There are a few markets and here and there a small caravanserai. Because of its cold weather it has no gardens and orchards. Its fruits come from Tortum[429] and the castle of Acharis and feed the people of the town. The people of Ardahan are pious and real Moslems, Sunnis, hospitable and devout. They are mostly farmers. Some are small merchants. In the mountains there is good hawthorn fruit. This castle is five stages north of Erzerum. From Ardahan to Qars is one stage via Kargha-bazar. Again going from here towards the west we reached Gole after [-] hours, sometimes passing over rocky roads, sometimes through woods, sometimes through good straight roads amidst meadows.

DESCRIPTION OF THE CASTLE OF GOLE. It is in the land of Akhiskha. It was built by Levand Khan, one of the Georgian kings. Since the reign of Sultan Selim, it is the seat of a *sanjaq-bey* in the province of Childir. According to imperial regulations, the *bey*'s personal fief is 300,000 *aqch-es*, with an *alay-bey*, a *cheri-bashi*, a castellan and a garrison. The castle was conquered by Sultan Selim and is situated on an inaccessible rock, and it is a beautiful castle. But its circumference is unknown. It is a judgeship with one hundred and fifty *aqches*. It has [-] houses, a large mosque, a caravanserai and a bathhouse, but not a beautiful bazaar.

Again, for eight hours we went to the west.

DESCRIPTION OF THE CASTLE OF PENK. It is known by the name of its founder the Georgian king; it is a beautiful castle. It has passed through many hands. Sultan Selim I conquered it. Now, it is a seat of a *sanjaq-bey* in the province of Childir. The personal fief of the bey is 400,000 *aqches*, and it has an *alay-bey* and a *cheri-bashi*. The *ze'amat*s and the *timar*s were mentioned above. According to the regulations, the garrison and the soldiers of the bey number one thousand men. It is a small castle made of stone. It has one gate and a castellan with a garrison and a judgeship of one hundred and fifty *aqches*, but there is no royal bazaar nor gardens and orchards. Its people are very devout; they are farmers and live frugally. It has very good water, which they consume and become very pious. Its subjects are Armenians, Gökdolaq and Georgian knights.

Again from there we went west.

DESCRIPTION OF THE CASTLE OF OLTI. It was built by one of the kings of Georgia and conquered by Sultan Selim. It is the seat of a *sanjaq-bey* in the province of Childir. The personal fief of the bey is 200,017 [*aqches*]. There are *timar*s, *ze'amat*s, *alaybey*s, *cheri-bashi*s, a judgeship of one hundred and fifty *aqches*, a castellan, a garrison, notables and nobles; it is a prosperous *sanjaq*. The two-storied, huge, stone, quadrangular castle is built on a steep rock with two gates. One opens to the west and the other to the east. At the foot of the castle is the river Olti, which waters the gardens and orchards and towards the south it falls into the river Aras. Its houses are all covered with good earth. It has many large mosques, a caravanserai, gardens, orchards, and a school for boys and a few shops. Because of its pleasant climate Olti's beauties of both sexes are famous. Despite this, its people are very good Moslems. Again we went west and after three hours reached:

DESCRIPTION OF THE CASTLE OF MAMRAVAN. It was built by one of the Georgian kings and conquered by Laleh Qara Mostafa Pasha. Since olden times it is a seat of a *sanjaq-bey* and now it is a seat of a *sanjaq-bey* in Erzerum. The personal fief of the bey is 203,000 *aqches*. It has a

---

429. Tortum about 100 km north of Erzerum is famous for its waterfall.

Tomb of Sayyed Ebrahim in 1637

cheri-bashi and an *alay-bey*. There are [-] *ze'amat*s and *timar*s. The garrison and the bey's soldiers number five hundred. It has a judgeship with one hundred and fifty *aqche*s. It has a castellan, an *'azab-aghasi* and soldiers. It is a big square castle with a gate facing the south. Its circumference is unknown. It has one gate facing the south. In total it has eight hundred shabby houses. There are few wealthy people. They are Sunnis, Naqshbandis and a devout people. They have large mosques, a bathhouse and caravanserai and a small market.

Again going west, we reached after [-] hours:

The village of Iyd. It is a village in the district of Mamravan with Armenian and Moslem inhabitants; it is a *ze'amat* village. Going west through a treeless mountainous area we reached:

The village of Qara Kuneq. It is a prosperous *ze'amat* village situated in Erzerum province. Again we crosssed the pass of Georgia, through meadows and after [-] hours we reached:

The village of Umudum Sultan. It is situated on the slopes of a high mountain with one hundred houses and is prosperous. It is at the very source of the Euphrates. As mentioned previously in the description of Erzerum, the Holy Koran mentions it as "water of the Euphrates" which issues forth from a big cave in the mountains near the village of Dumli Sultan.[430] It is like

---

430. Koran 77: 27 (al-Mursalat) states *ma' furatan*, which Evliya mistakenly read as the "water of the Euphrates instead of "water sweet (and wholesome)".

Tomb of Sayyed Ebrahim in 1702

the Fountain of Youth as if the verse "To thee we have granted the Fount of Kawthar"[431] has come down. Speckled trout each of a royal cubit's length like a heavenly dish sport in it. Their bodies are colored like rubies from Badakhshan or like emeralds of Isvan, like heavenly fish. Umdudum Sultan is buried here, and his shrine is visited by everyone. No one dares to catch these fish. If you go down one *farsakh* you can catch these fish and when you eat them one's nose is filled with its fragrant smell. However much you eat it does not give you a fever or indigestion.

THE TOMB OF DUMLU DEDEH. It is a saintly place and Sheikh Ebrahim Efendi is one its saints. Again we went south through the plains to Erzerum, and after [-] hours we reached the castle of Erzerum safe and sound. We entered the castle of Erevan, and without changing our robes we went to meet the Pasha, our master, and laid the letters and presents of the Khan of Erevan at his feet. We enjoyed the honor of his company and we told him one by one of the castles and the strange places[432] that we had visited. He was very pleased and out of his gracious consideration gave a full robe of honor to this humble servant with three hundred *qurush* as bathhouse money and two purses to be paid out of the revenues of the customs house. We were one week there, when a friendly letter arrived from the Khan of Erevan, which said that "soldiers of Qars had molested our caravans and requested that one high-ranking Agha might be sent to accompany the

---

431. Koran 108.1. al-*Kawthar* means the heavenly fountain of unbounded grace, knowledge, mercy and wisdom.

432. Hammer, p. 180 has here, "an account of all the castles, towns, kents and villages, which I had seen on my journey."

caravans to Erzerum." When this cordial letter came with ʿAli Aqa, by God's wisdom I was sent again to the lands of the Persians.

Journey to the region of Erevan in the year one thousand fifty-seven [1647]

From Erzerum we traveled twelve hours to the east and reached:

The stage of the castle of Hasan Qalʿeh. This has already been described in connection the Shushik case and our journey to the region of Tabriz. Again going towards the east we passed though the plain of Pasin and reached:

The village of Badeljivanli is an Armenian village with a *zeʿamat*. After nine hours we reached:

The stage of Meydanjiq. All its inhabitants are Armenian infidels. It is a prosperous *zeʿamat* village in the plain of Pasin. After ten hours, going east, we reached:

Description of the castle of Mijingerd[433] It is situated in the province of Erzerum, in the governorship of the bey of Khorasan. The small castle is on a steep rock, quadrangular in form, with a castellan, and a garrison of one hundred fifty, with two hundred houses, but it has no market. It is a dependency of the judgeship of Pasin. There is a large mosque built by Sultan Sulayman. It has a small bathhouse and a caravanserai, but there are no gardens and orchards. In its fields there are many crops.

Again we traveled towards the east for six hours to the border of Erzerum and after passing through the valley of Khan, we reached the province of Qars. After passing a ruin called Yedi Kilisa (Seven Churches),[434] we traversed a pass, which was wooded, narrow and dark. After having traveled six hours towards the west through meadows and tulip fields we reached Barduz.

Description of the castle of Barduz.[435] It is in the province of Qars and was built by Karim al-Din Khatun daughter of Malek ʿEzz al-Din Aq-Qoyunlu. On the top of the castle in thick letters its date has been written. It is situated near a valley, and is a quadrangular stone building. It has a castellan with a retinue of one hundred and fifty, who are adherents of the Qaderi order. The daughter of the Aq-Qoyunlu amir left one hundred fifty endowments. It has large and small mosques and a small bathhouse. There are no bazaars, caravanserais, welfare foundation, garden or orchards. From there towards the south we reached after [-] hours Kejivan.

Description of the ancient castle of Kejivan, of the town of Dudiman, built by Anushirvan. This is the castle of Dudiman Kejivan, which is mentioned in some histories concerning the story of the war between Bizhan, Shaffaq,[436] and Afrasiyab. In former times this castle was destroyed by Hulagu Khan of the Mongols (during the reign of the ʿAbbasid caliph Mustansir biʾllah), who killed the people and destroyed Baghdad. Dudiman Kejivan was rebuilt by the endeavors of Qara Yusof, the Qara Qoyunlu, and became as prosperous as Erzen

---

433. Hammer, p. 180 has Mishingerd. Morier, *Second*, p. 399 has Minsingird.

434. See Lynch, *Travels*, vol. 2, p. 113.

435. Situated at 39˚95'00" latitude and 39˚51'67" longitude.

436. This Shaffaq does not occur in the Bizhan story in Ferdowsi's *Shahnameh*.

Akhlat, but it was destroyed by Timur. Later, the vanguard of the army of Islam under Laleh Qara Mostafa Pasha conquered it while Sultan Selim was coming to Nakhjevan. It is part of the governorship of Qars. Now it has improved, but it is not a commercial town. The castle is situated on a precipice; it is a small square castle. The governor is the *sanjaq-beyg*. The bey's personal fief is 153,500 *aqche*s, with [-] *ze'amat* and [-] *timar*s. It has an *alay-bey* and a *cheri-bashi*. According to the regulations, together with the bey's soldiers there are two hundred fully equipped soldiers. It has a castellan, and an *'azab-aghasi*[437] and a *gönüllü-aghasi*.[438] The castle has a garrison of three hundred men. The qazi has three hundred *aqche*s. Kejivan has seven districts and has about 1,200 mud-covered houses, three small mosques, and forty to fifty shops. From there we went to the east for [-] hours and reached Qars.

Description of the castle of Qars Dudiman, which is at the very border of the Ottoman Empire

In the Ottoman Empire there are three *sanjaq*s named Qars. One is in Silefka, it is called Qara Tashleq Qars, the other is Qars of Mar'ash and the third is Qars Dudiman. This Qars is the oldest. In the year 987 [1579], in the time of Sultan Murad III, Laleh Qara Mostafa Pasha was the general who came to Qars in the company of Ja'far Pasha, the vizier of Anatolia, Tavil Mohammad Pasha-zadeh Hasan Pasha, the vizier of Syria, and of Milanli 'Ali Pasha with about one hundred thousand victorious soldiers and remained here. He repaired Qars, which had been destroyed by the evil Qizilbash. When the repair work started under the supervision of Mahmud Pasha, the Pasha of Rumeli, a quadrangular marble stone was discovered that had an inscription in Arabic, which said in big letters:

> The foundation of this blessed castle was by Asaf al-Moluk Firuz Aqay, may God hold dear his companions, in the time of Sultan 'Ezz al-Din, may God help his fortune, with the help of the well-known daughter Sultan Karim al-Din Begum, may God illuminate her tomb. In the year 548 [1153-54].

Now this stone has been placed in the suburb near the gate facing south. Truly, how beautiful it was written and how wonderful it was cut on the marble. The [second] founder of Qars, Laleh Pasha, put these old relics with great care in that place, and informed the people in charge of foundations. From this date it appears that the old castle and the building of Karim al-Din were completed with the help of that chaste lady. The second founder Laleh Pasha finished the castle in seventy days, and he prepared the entire arsenal and all necessary things pertaining to it. During the repairs, one of the devout people, who was one of the soldiers and someone who knew the Koran by heart, had a dream, and he related it to Laleh Pasha as follows:

---

437. The `azab*s (bachelors) initially were used as infantry, later as ammunition-carriers, and finally there were incorporated in the *jebeji*s. Their local chief was called *`azab-aghasi*.

438. The *gönüllü*s (volunteers) were inferior in standing to other types of soldiers; their local commander was called *gönüllü-aghasi*.

In my dream a weak old man appeared to me and said: 'They call me Abu'l-Hasan al-Kharaqani,[439] I am buried in this place. If you want any signs and marks of mine, under your feet there is a deep well, dig there so that you will see wonders.'

After the dream had been related several hundred workers were detailed to dig that well. They found a polished rectangular red marble tombstone and while shouting, "God is great," and incantations they lifted that red stone. On it was written in a fine script, "I am the fortunate martyr Kharaqani." In the tomb they found that his body was still fresh and on his wounded arm there was a kerchief. He wore a woolen robe, and blood was coming out of the wound in his right arm. When the soldiers of Islam saw this they shouted, "God is great," and covered the tomb.

Then Laleh Pasha built a convent and a tomb over it, which is the convent of the blessed Hasan Kharaqani. The castle of Qars has been recorded as a province, and now it is in the hands of the Ottoman Empire. The imperial decree says: "The government of Qars is in the hands of my vizier, Pasha So-and-so." Dudiman is at the very border with Persia. Several times it has been given as *arpaleq* to viziers with three tails. Now its Pasha has an imperial personal fief worth 600,000 *aqches*. In the old days it was a *sanjaq* of Erzerum. According to the regulations of Sultan Sulayman, the *sanjaqs* of Pasin were added to it and the province now has seven sanjaqs. It does not have a *defter kedkhodasi*, a *defter amini*, a *timar defteri*, a *mal defteri*,[440] *chavoshlar kadkhodasi* and *chavoshlar amini*.[441] Its *sanjaq*s are the following:

Ardahan Minor, Khojajan, Zarshad, Kejivan, Kaghezman, Varishan and Qars, which is the seat of the Pasha. It has seven *ze'amat*s and 102 *timar*s. According to the regulations, the district's feudal troops and the pasha troops altogether amount to three thousand choice soldiers. Many times it has been compared to seven or eight Persian khanates. It has an *alay-bey*, a *cheri-bashi*, a judgeship with three hundred *aqche*s, a castellan, seven *'azab-aghasi*s, three batallions of janissaries, one batallion of armorers and one batallion of gunners. Most of the *chorbi-bashi*s[442] along with their men reside in Erzerum. There are one thousand eight hundred choice soldiers in the castle. In these places, the soldiers of Van, Qars and Akhiskha are famous for their bravery and chivalry.[443] The annual pay of the garrison of Qars is collected from revenues of the boats at the castle of Birejik on the Euphrates, and from the villages of Suruj and Bombuj in the province of Aleppo, amounting annually to seventy thousand *aqcheh*s. The province Qars has ten judgeships, and each one has eight districts. There is a *sheikh al-Islam*, an overseer of the sayyeds and other notables. May God increase their numbers.

---

439. Abu'l-Hasan al-Kharaqani was a Sufi (351- 352/962-964 and d. 425/1033) whose tomb is in the town of Kharaqan, which is in the general region of Bastam and which today is in the vicinity of Shahrud, within the administrative district of Semnan in Iran, received a spiritual transmission from Abu Yazid Bastami and received spiritual guidance from Sheikh Abu al-`Abbas Ahmad b. Mohammad `Abd al-Karim Qassab-e Amuli.

440. Each of these officials were responsible for keeping the registers, i.e., for the general administration, respectively, the deputy, the *amin*, the *timar* registrar, and the keeper of the accounts (*mal*).

441. The deputy and commissioner of the ushers or *chavus*.

442. The *chorbashi* was the commander of an *orta* or battalion of the Janissaries.

443. According to Dankoff 1991, the expression *benem digar nist* is a quasi-Turkization of the Persian *manam digar nist* ('I and no other') a phrase used to indicate reckless daring, ultimately derived from the Bible (Isaiah 47.8).

The Ottoman army builds a fortress

THE LAYOUT OF THE CASTLE OF QARS. At a gun-shot's distance on the north side there is a high mountain; on its slope the castle is situated on a hill. But the lower castle is situated in the plain and has five strong walls. The castle's citadel has one house. The gate of the castle looks to the east, and what is called the upper castle is in fact the middle one, and its iron gate opens to the west and is very strong. Inside the castle there is a house for the castellan, houses for two hundred soldiers and a fully equipped arsenal. But there is no bazaar, caravanserai, bathhouse or charitable foundation. Further down from this castle there is big wall around the suburb, which is a two-fold wall. It has three iron gates. Inside the gate is decorated with helmets, neck-protectors, muskets, other military equipment, and there are also gate-keepers and ushers. One of the gates on the west is the water gate, also called the gate of the troops, looking towards Erzerum. The second or middle gate opens to Kaghezman. The third one is the gate of Bahram Pasha, which faces east and Erevan. The soldiers in the guard-houses on the walls of the castle keep watch night and day, and at night they illuminate the walls and gates with torches. The wall of the suburb is not very high, but is very broad, made of stone and very strong. Around the lower castle instead of a moat {there is a lake, whose water is delicious,} which extends from the gate of Bahram Pasha to the middle gate. {It is not possible to conquer the castle from this side.} Around the castle there are two hundred and twenty very strong towers. There are two thousand eighty battlements. The entire circumference is five thousand seven hundred paces.

DESCRIPTION OF ALL THE BUILDINGS. In this castle there are about three thousand houses of notables and tradesmen. There are forty-seven large and small mosques. Only in eight of them is the Friday prayer performed. The oldest one was built by Laleh Pasha. It is the mosque of the blessed Sheikh Abu'l-Hasan al-Kharaqani, whose description was given above. He is buried near the mosque and his tomb is a place of pilgrimage for everyone.

Besides this, facing the water gate, is the large mosque of Va'ez Efendi. On the side of the square is the High Mosque, and the Sulayman Efendi Mosque, following the text of the Koran which says: "Turn your face to the Mosque of the Rock,"[444] converted it from a church to a mosque. It is a very beautiful large mosque and full of light. The Hoseyn Kadkhoda mosque, which originally was a convent named the Golden Church, was changed into a mosque by the order of the king and was saved from darkness. It is now well illuminated and many people frequent it, because the people of this city are devout in their prayers. When the evil Qizilbash conquered this castle they found the name of this mosque – the 'Omar Efendi mosque – offensive and completely destroyed this beautiful house of worship. They turned other mosques into caravanserais and stables.

At the gate of Bahram Pasha there is the Qaltaqji-zadeh mosque; it is an old and large mosque {and it has no minaret}; there are also the mosques of Tash (Stone) and of Beyram Chelebi-zadeh, and when you cross the bridge to the south into the suburb there is the mosque of Amir Yusof Pasha, which has minarets.

Apart from these are other small mosques, which are all covered with earth. They have eighteen schools for young children. There are madrasehs, where all the sciences are taught.

---

444. Koran 2: 144 (al-Baqara).

Mount Ararat

[**The bathhouses.**] Inside the water gate near the rampart there is the Amir Yusof bathhouse, which is beautiful. Its building is well-illuminated and delightful. Inside the middle gate the old bathhouse is very good.

Although there are no places for studying the Traditions or the Koran, nor is there an elementary school, yet each noble family is very generous and travelers and strangers are generously provided for. The land is very productive. There is no well-built drapers' hall, but there are two hundred shops and all the products of India, Sind, Persia and Egypt are found there. Since it is in the middle of the fifth clime, it is very cold and therefore there are no gardens and orchards.

The production of pulses is high. The people are very lively and make their living by trade and farming; a great number of them are Moslem fighters for the faith. Realizing that "Ruin follows Fame," they have humble sad two-storied houses. Near the well-built palace of the Pasha and next to it there is an Islamic court-house. Also, next to the High Mosque is the Pasha's palace. The religious court is situated below it, and not far from it is the mansion of the *alay-bey*, which is connected to the court. The houses of the deputies of the janissary and the *chavosh*es are in this quarter; they are well-built. Because the southern side of the castle is enclosed by a lake, and the side of the gate and the middle gate is also surrounded by a pond;[445] there is no moat. Yet it is a strong castle. It is not possible that an enemy would enter the redoubts from the third side and be victorious.

---

445. Evliya in fact wrote '*khalij*', i.e. a gulf or bay. The only body of water near Qars is the Qars river.

We traveled from Qars for twelve hours, passing the village of Orchivek and the valley of Bagharseq and passed the summer quarters of Ulghar in twelve hours. In three days we reached the castle of Akhiskha. From Qars through Qargabazari is one stage to Ardahan and again from Qars to the north the castle of Gole is ten hours. The day that we arrived at this castle from Qars, I gave the letter from our master, the governor of Erzerum, Daftarzadeh Mohammad Pasha, to Vali Pasha and other aghas, which was written in the most gracious manner. After the letter had been read and its contents known, all the notables present said:

> Never have we have attacked or hurt the Persian Erevan caravan. This is an absolute calumny by the Persian inhabitants of Kaghezman. Last week those of Kaghezman under the pretext of getting protection money hurt the merchants of Erevan. We have to defend their rights.

From here with the officials of Qars we rode our horses towards the south on grassland for one stage reaching the river Aras, which we crossed on rafts.

DESCRIPTION OF KAGHEZMAN CASTLE IN AZERBAIJAN.[446] It is situated on the south side of the river Aras. It is in general considered to be the border of Azerbaijan. The Aras River from the western side issues forth from the summer quarters of Bingöl (one thousand lakes). After passing several castles and towns it flows towards the east and joins the Arpa River at Mt. Aghri (Ararat) and with the Zangi River. This castle of Kaghezman, by being on south of the Aras, forms the border of Azerbaijan, but it is part of the Ottoman province of Qars. It was built by the fortunate daughter of Anushirvan and hence the name of the castle. It has passed through the hands of many kings eventually reaching those of Uzun Hasan and then of Shah Esma`il. In the year [-]

Shaping a mill-stone

---

446. The town of Kaghezman in Kars province (Turkey) at 40.1581 latitude and 43.1353 longitude.

it submitted to Sultan Sulayman and has become a separate seat of a *sanjaq-bey* in the province of Qars. In accordance with regulations the personal fief of the bey is 200,000 *aqche*s. It has nine *ze'amat*s and 178 *timar*s, an *alay-bey* and *cheri-bashi*. In total there are nine hundred soldiers. It has a judgeship with one hundred and fifty *aqche*s, a castellan and three hundred castle guards. Their wages are paid out of the taxes on salt production. On the west side of the castle there is a major salt mine and a quarry for millstones. From the mountains of Kaghezman millstones are exported to Persia and Erzerum and other places.

There is a stone called wound-stone that is used by the surgeons as a Sulaymani ointment that they put on wounds and which heals. The borax of goldsmiths, the whetstone of the barbers and the slate whetstone are produced in the quarries of the Kaghezman mountains. In accordance with regulations, the revenues of these quarries go to the castle guards. In two places there are gold and silver mines, but as cost exceeded profit they were abandoned. In short, altogether there are eleven quarries.

This impressive, strong, quadrangular castle is situated in a wasteland; it is a small castle. Inside it there is the large mosque of Sultan Sulayman. Above and under it there are seven hundred small houses. There are large mosques, a caravanserai, a bathhouse and a small bazaar. It is not a commercial town but a frontier town. Mount Aghri (Ararat), situated to west of Erevan near Qaghedman, is one of the famous mountains of the world. It is the summer quarters for the Turkmen. Since Kaghezman is on the banks of the Aras, its climate is temperate and has many gardens and orchards. Its people are well-mannered and friendly, and here and there are beauties. Most irregular troops (*levends*) sing in the Persian style; its inhabitants are beautifully voiced and poetically talented. With the notables of Qars, who were with us, we entered Kaghezman and in the divan of the *bey* there was a big exchange between the officials of Qars and Kaghezman. The officials of Kaghezman swore by God: "We did not plunder the Persian caravan. We only collected our lawful tolls." Since they denied it this humble author took the notables that were with us along with the officials (*aqas*) of Kaghezman, viz. Hasan Agha, Chaleq-Safar Agha and seven other *aghas* to prove the truth of what they said.

Description of the stages that we traveled to Erevan

From the Pasha of Qars and eleven *agha*s of Van and the *bey* of Kaghezman as well as from the notables, this humble servant received as a reward for my coming one purse with *qurush*, two Mahmudi horses and two Georgian slaves. We left Kaghezman and crossed the Aras River on rafts, and after nine hours going to the east we reached Moghadhberd.

Description of the castle of Moghadhberd. It is situated in Georgia. According to the old regulations, it is under the government of the province of Qars and is the seat of the *mir-liva*. Several times the Qizilbash conquered and destroyed it. It is one of the districts of Qars. Its castle was built by one of the kings of Iran, Moghadh Khan. Later it passed to the Aq Qoyunlu and afterwards to Shah Esma'il, and then Sultan Sulayman conquered it. Its governor is the castellan of the castle. It has one hundred and fifty soldiers; it is a deputy-ship. Its impressive pentagonal small stone castle is built on a free-standing rock.[447] It has about six hundred gardens, orchards and houses in the suburb. It is a border district with only high buildings. The Arpa River flows at the foot of this castle. This river, coming from the side of Georgia, passes this place and flows

---

447. Hammer, vol. 2, p. 184 has here "It has a mosque, a caravanserai, a bathhouse and ten shops."

into the river Aras, where Tekleti village is situated. The castle of Moghadhberd is contiguous to the territory of the Persian castle of Shurehgel. But only the castle of Shurehgel remains in Persian hands, because the entire district of Shurehgel belongs to the Qars government. Between these two, the river Arpa is the border. To the east is Persia and to the west is Qars.

Opposite to Moghadhberd, towards [-], at one day's journey is the castle of ʿAni. It is part of Qars, situated on a hill. It is a square mud castle in ruins, built by Anushirvan. At its foot there is a prosperous village, which is a *zeʿamat*; its inhabitants are Armenians. Between the castle of ʿAni and Qars there is a mountain called Iki Yahni. Beyond it is the castle of Qars, and between it and the ruined castle of Ani is one stage distance. We passed this castle and went through a large meadow for nine hours and arrived at:

DESCRIPTION OF THE CASTLE OF ZARSHOD. It is built by the Persian kings. Since the Persians suffered greatly here and were put to the sword, they called it 'Zarshod' (Calamity struck).[448] It is the seat of a *sanjaq-bey* in the province of Qars. The personal fief of the *mir-liva* is [-] *aqche*s; there are [-] *zeʿamat*s and [-] *timar*s. It has an *alay-bey* and a *cheri-bashi*. In time of war it had twelve hundred armed soldiers. Its judgeship has one hundred and fifty *aqcheh*s. There is no mufti or a *naqib*, but it has a castellan and one hundred and fifty guards. Along with the chief of Qars, they get a fixed stipend. Its castle is situated on a beautiful plain on a hill; it is a magnificent, stone, quadrangular building, but it is not that big. Its circumference is not known. Outside and inside there are three hundred houses. It has a large mosque, a caravanserai, a bathhouse, a Sufi convent and small bazaar. It is situated on the road from Qars to Erevan at one stage distance. Its climate is very mild. Again going eastward from Zarshod for nine hours we reached:

THE VILLAGE OF TALASH.[449] It is in the land of the Persians on the border of Erevan. From here we went to the village of Qara Tay'i and then going to the east for twelve hours we reached:

THE STAGE OF UCH KILISA. It was built by the Byzantine Emperors. It is by the side of three Convents; one is for the Armenian nuns, one for the Greeks and the other for the Armenians. In the Persian lands this old Uch Kilisa and those on the road to Nakhjevan Yedi Kilisa are among the most famous houses of worship. There are many strange monuments and relics worth seeing.

A must is the balsam oil called *mirun-yaghi*, which is produced here. They make a fire on a silk carpet, and they put a kettle on it and cook all sorts of herbs and plants. The fire does not harm the carpet. Then they press all these plants for their oil and pour it into flasks. They take it as a blessing to Europe and the Abode of Infidels. From those places they sent votive gifts to this convent. This balsam is used to cure all diseases and wounds, so they believe.

ANOTHER STRANGE THING. Near the convent is a big iron bar suspended under an arch, which all the time is hanging, without being supported from six sides. Truly, it is a magical work in this strange cave. According to the wrong beliefs of the Christians, this iron pillar stands suspended by a miracle of Simeon, one of the apostles of Christ. Of course, some Moslems who have seen this believe in it, because when a strong wind blows it vibrates. Some evil people, saying that

---

448. The etymology is fanciful as ever. The name of town is Zarishat, situated in Shirak province (Armenia).

449. The village of Talysh, about 20 km south of Uch Kilisa. Lynch, *Travels*, vol. 1, p. 320.

it should not be touched have built a strong wooden fence around it. According to this humble servant, this miracle can be explained.

[Concerning the explanation of the iron pillar.] The master-architect first built the arch over the iron bar, then he hung a big magnet stone in the middle of the arch and another magnet stone he placed in the ground, in accordance with the science of geometry. Then he put this iron bar in between the two magnets, and in this way this bar stayed in the middle. This is neither a miracle of the Apostle Simeon nor a talisman of Samson. Whoever comes here is amazed. This humble person with his deficient intelligence has made this observation, by the grace of God, hoping that this observation will not be in error.

This convent has five hundred priests and monks. Every night five or six hundred horsemen come either from the Persian or the Ottoman side and stay here. Without taking down the saddle and fodder bag from their horses, all the monks entertain them with date juice, candy sugar from Hama and Syrian-style food, and day-and-night they serve them. It is a strange Christian shrine. Again from here we went east, and crossing the Aras and the Zangi rivers for a second time we entered Erevan.

Description of Erevan in Azerbaijan. God be praised, the Khan of Erevan, Taqi ʿAli Khan,[450] had returned from the wedding of his sister, and in his palace there were great feasts and we became his guests. The following day the *agha*s of Kaghezman and Qars went to his divan. The *agha*s of Kaghezman and Qars said: "My Khan, they have misinformed the vizier of Erzerum and have said that we have attacked the caravan, and we have brought Evliya Agha as our interceder; is he worthy of it?" Then there was a long discussion, and eventually the *agha*s of the castles were considered guiltless and that the people of the caravan had made false accusations. The latter went to Erzerum where at last peacemakers interceded. Taqi ʿAli Khan gave a big party for the *agha*s for three days. Again he gave to this humble servant five *tumans* in *ʿabbasi*s, one horse, and to the Pasha one mule, one camel load of Erevan rice, and to the border *agha*s five to ten pieces of fabrics. We returned again with letters from the Khan of Erevan to Erzerum.

[Here ends Evliya Chelebi's first voyage to Iran. In the next section the account of his second voyage to Iran is given.]

---

450. At that time Mohammad Qoli Khan Chagatay was governor of Erevan, see Nasiri, *Titles*, p. 172.

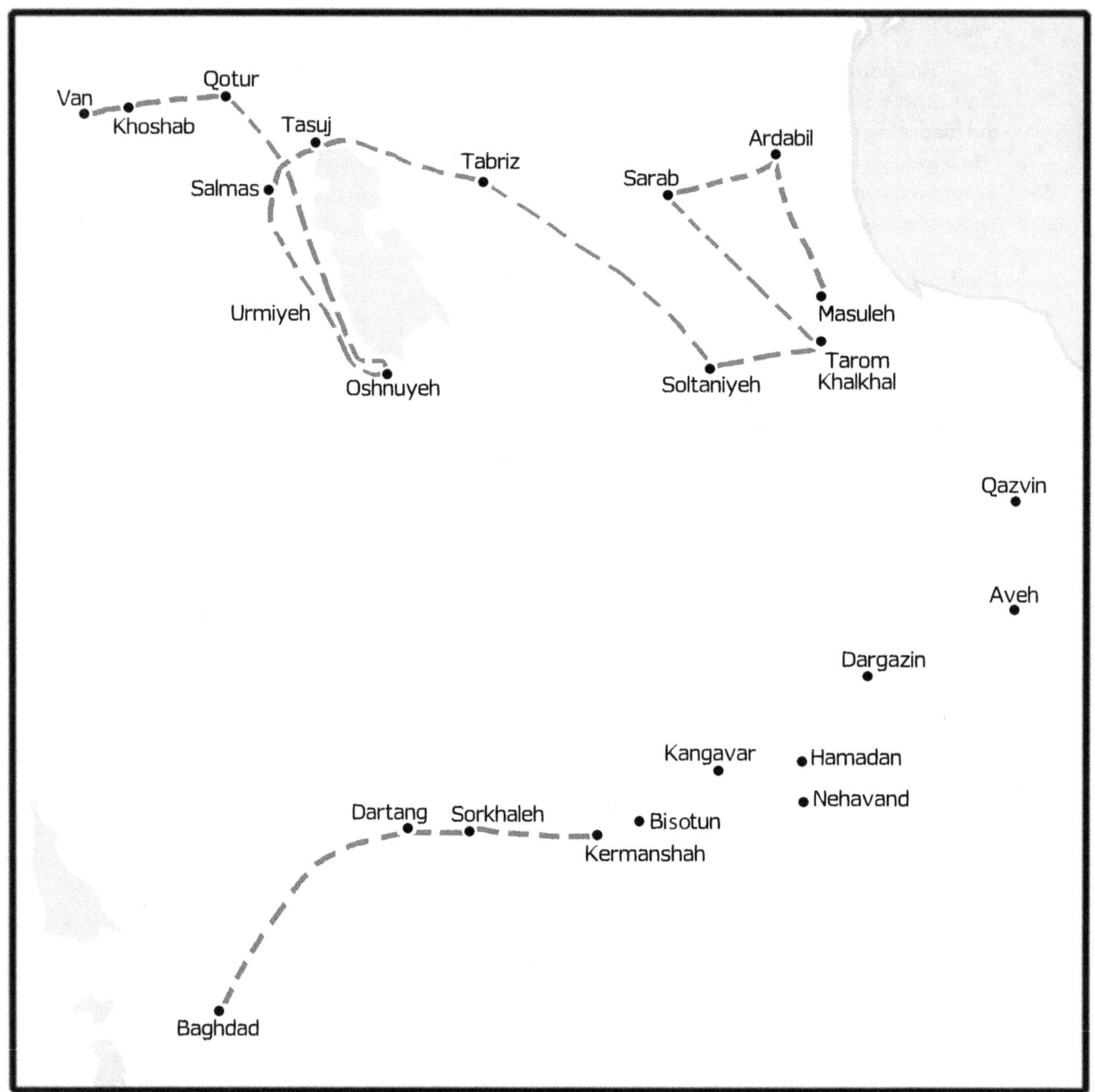

The route of Evliya Chelebi's second journey through Iran.

THE SECOND TRAVELS

DESCRIPTION OF OUR JOURNEY FROM THE CASTLE OF VAN AS ENVOY TO THE LAND OF THE PERSIANS IN THE YEAR 1065, THE THIRTEENTH DAY OF DHU'L-QAʿDEH [14 SEPTEMBER 1655], AND OUR TRIP THROUGH THE OTTOMAN LANDS AND AZERBAIJAN TO THE BEAUTIFUL CITY OF TABRIZ, AND FROM THERE TO ARABIAN IRAQ AND THE ACCOUNT OF THE CASTLES AND MAJOR TOWNS.

From the castle of Van, Sari ʿAli Agha with two hundred fully armed and choice soldiers were chosen to go to the Shah. This humble author also departed to the land of the Persians with a string of mules and one hundred pious and armed champions, who would say: "No one is braver than I." Our friend, ʿAli Agha, who was the *agha* of Mostafa Pasha, left Van with one hundred young men. Also, one hundred men of our friends the Pinyanish notables, who were complaining about sheep, came from Shirvan. When we were leaving Van we formed a large procession of five hundred people altogether. Trusting in God, we bade farewell to our master the Pasha and received his blessing, and we left the castle going to the north. The Erdermit gardens of Van were on our left side, and after three hours we reached:

THE PASS OF NERGOK. This is a steep pass. We alighted in the village of Nergok. It has three hundred houses and one church; it is an Armenian village. Its taxes, which are collected by the *defterdar,* belong to the garrison of Van. Then, going from there for three hours to the east we reached:

THE STAGE OF VANAK VEREK. Being in Armenian lands, all the churches are called *vanak*. This Vanak Verek is built on the easy slope of Mt. Verek, in an orchard full of trees with an embellished dome and an iron gate, which is unlike any old church. It has more than three hundred Armenian priests and monks, and each one is busy with a special task. That night they hosted and showed respect to our five hundred soldiers in a way that I cannot describe. Because among all Christians after the Kimame Church[1] in Jerusalem, this Vanak Verek is the most frequented church. They gave to our friends and to this humble author the furs of a lynx. As the poem goes:

> The property of an infidel is permissible to the believer.

In the morning, after having received presents, we departed and with much trouble we crossed the wooded Mt. Verek, and after five hours we reached:

---

1. Presumably the St. James Church is meant.

The village of Hundusten. This is a village in the district of Van, with three hundred houses with gardens and orchards; it is an Armenian village. Its taxes belong to the garrison of Van, and nobody interferes with them; these are collected by the *defterdar*. After five hours we reached {Van} Kulu Chayiri. This is a meadow full with clovers and plants. Then we went to:

Soleyman Bek Chayiri. It is a separate wadi full with alfalfa. We passed these villages and reached Khoshab.

Description of Khoshab Castle. Its name is derived from the river called Khoshab that flows below it. Its old name is Erchek Bala. The ʿAbbasi Hakkari (Kurds) built it, but in the year 800 [1398-99] it passed into the hands of the Mahmudis and now it is the capital of the Mahmudi Beys. Later, an important khan called Sulayman-e Zaman extended this castle by building a town on the eastern side that overlooks it. He has built a Sulaymani-like castle where each stone is as big as a Mankerusi elephant. The length of each stone is twenty paces. These are put lengthwise in the wall and the taller ones are protruding from the wall. To resist cannon fire, the wall of the castle has been made like the back of a tortoise. However many cannons are fired at it, they will not affect it, and (the balls will) slide down. In the year 1060 [1650], Mohammad Amin Pasha, son of Shams Pasha, for twenty-nine days stormed the castle, but not even one stone was dislodged, and he returned empty-handed and in disgrace. (In the Ottoman Empire) the gates of the castles are made of wood but covered with iron. If you fire on them, the wood burns and the iron melts, but each side of the gate of Khoshab Castle is made of three hundred *qentar* of Nakhjevan steel, and there is no wood. The master craftsman who made it has hidden it between two towers, so that it is not even seen. Nobody else lives inside the castle, except the castellan Mahmudi Ebrahim Bey. It is a very small castle. Its circumference is one thousand two hundred paces. Inside there is a Sufi convent, a special small bathhouse for the Bey, and a storehouse for wheat, cellars, a sufficient arsenal and ten pieces of royal cannons; its water is collected from the rain {in cisterns}. One rock is protruding like the trunk of an elephant. The late Sulayman Bey had devised iron wheels on the top of those rocks, which turn with one hundred fathom chains to draw water from the river Khoshab. For the people of the suburb looking at it from the bazaar, it is a wondrous sight.

Its castellan, Ebrahim Bey, with whom we were together in the war with the Khan of Bitlis, gave a feast to this humble author and his companions. He gave us a good tour of the castle. All four sides of it are like the pits of Hell, but it does not have a moat around it. It has a gate facing the north. Inside the gate there is a moat, which is like a pit of Hell, and its bridge is made of the wood [on which] cannons [stand].

This moat is filled to the brim with the water from cisterns. The Kurdish people call this castle Khosh-av. They call water "*av*", but those of Van call it the castle of Khoshaf. In short, {the castle} is known by the name of the river Khoshab that flows below it; it is a beautiful castle, which is pentagonal in form. Its towers are like the towers of Qahqaheh castle.

Description of the suburb. In this place a suburb is called *rebat*. This is situated inside the valley; its four sides are enclosed by mountains, and on the west side is the river Khoshab. It has forty towers and low walls, two gates, without a moat, and is four thousand paces in circumference. Inside it there are eight hundred houses, one large mosque, one dirty bathhouse and several small shops. There are no other buildings in the castle.

THE SITUATION OF MAHMUDI KURDISH FIGHTERS FOR THE FAITH. In the year 995 [1587], they submitted to Sultan Sulayman, and in the battles for Tabriz, Nakhjevan and Erevan rendered valuable service to him and, since their region was given to them, they governed it as a *yurtluk* and *ojaqlik*. Now they are part of the province of Van; they are *ojaq-beys* with drum and banner. According to Sulayman's regulations, they have their own *ze'amat* and *timar*, and the revenues are collected by the Bey. The revenues of the Bey's personal fief come from his own district. Because of their proximity, they campaign with the governor of Van. There is no *alay-bey*, *cheri-bashi*, castellan, deputy or *sardar*. The High Porte in Istanbul has appointed a judge with an income of one hundred and fifty *aqche*s. The Mahmudi tribe has eight thousand soldiers. Several times they have battled the Shah of Persia. They have many courageous, valiant and warlike fighters of the faith. All of them have beards, and they color them red, green, yellow, and crimson. They are pious Sunnis of the Shafe'i school, devout and true Moslems. If among them there is one who is proved to be a liar they say: "You are a liar," and ban him forever from the region, together with his family.

VIEW OF THE RIVER KHOSHAB. The waters that come down from the Hakkari Cholumerik[2] Mountains and the Hasani summer quarters gather at the foot of this castle and form the river Khoshab. Then it flows from here to the west into the valley of Van and passes through the gardens of Erdemit at the foot of the castle of Vastan in the Hakkari region. It flows into Lake Van. We stayed one night in this castle and the Khan gave us many gifts. In the morning we departed and after five hours reached:

THE STAGE OF THE VILLAGE OF DAVDAN. This Kurdish village has one hundred houses, and it belongs to the Mahmudis. It has one large mosque. We pitched our tents in the meadow, and that night the people of the village brought the soldiers lambs, deer, stags and wild sheep. They made a dish of milk, cereals and butter. It was called *pokhin*, and we all ate it and really enjoyed it.[3] It seems that *pokhin* is one of the famous dishes of this region, and it is cooked for every guest. But there were some rascally Kurds who came and asked: "Have you eaten *pokhin*?"[4] Some of our soldiers would say that it had a bad name and would not eat it. But in fact it was very delicious.

DESCRIPTION OF ERECHEK CASTLE. In the year [-] one of the 'Abbasis[5] mistakenly called Er gerchek, Erechek. It was built at great expense. It is a quadrangular castle situated on a hill. The upper tower on top of the hill was so high that I could not climb to the top to see it. It is held by the Mahmudi beys. In the past it was the capital of the Mahmudis. Now it is not so prosperous. But it is still part of the province of Van, and under the government of the *sanjaq-bey*. It has two thousand soldiers. The best horses of the Mahmudis are raised at Erechek. Its revenues are given as *timar* and *ze'amat* to the Bey. The Bey resides in the castle. The suburb is situated in the corner of

---

2. Also written as Julomerg, which is the name of the fort in Hakkari, the chief town of Hakkari province. Bulut, p. 313.

3. According to Faruq KeyKhosrovi, Kurd *dar tarikh*, p. 266, n., the term *pokhin* does not make sense and what Evliya has eaten in Khoshab and enjoyed was *ash-dugh* or *dukuliv*, a Kurdish dish. However, *pokhin* in Kurdish (from *pukhtan* or to cook) means a gruel made of wheat and roasted wheat ground to flour (*qavut*).

4. *Pokh* in Turkish means "excrement". *Pokhin* or a variant of this word means "his excrement."

5. Several leading Kurdish families as well as the ruler of Lurestan claimed descent from the Abbasid caliphs. See Bidlisi/Charmoy I/2, pp. 114, 132; Nasiri, *Titles*, p. 234.

the plain and has five hundred houses, gardens and orchards with poplars, one large mosque, one caravanserai, one dirty bathhouse and some ten shops. Near the castle of Erechek there is a small lake. Its trout are famous all over Kurdistan, and each one of them weighs ten *oqqah*.[6] The fishermen catch them and send them as gifts to the notables. They do not smell of fish at all. Sultan Murad IV stopped and ate beside this lake. He said, "Truly, what they call the good food of Erechek is very true (*gerchek*)." Also, to the west of this lake there is a road. You can go to Van in five hours and it is an easy road. Up to here, we were the guests of the Bey of Erechek and received gifts and guides. Although it was against our direction, we went towards the north. Passing through mountains and valleys, we traveled for a full eight hours and reached Abagay.

DESCRIPTION OF THE CASTLE OF ABAGAY. Its name is the distorted form of *abaqa'i*. "*Qay*" means "king."[7] Apparently the Egyptian governors still are called *qaytabay*, *qayabay*, and *kayagha* and similar names. Since this castle was built by a king from the ʿAbbasi clan who was named Abaqay, they mistakenly call the castle of Abagay. From the west it is ten hours to Van. This castle is pentagonal in form, built on the top of a rock and is enormously strong. Now it is under the rule of the Mahmudi Beys. From there we traveled east for seven hours and reached:

THE BLACK FORT OF VAN IN KURDISTAN. The Kurds call this fort Karaja (the black one), since most parts of the buildings are made of black stone in the time of the Abbasid caliph Ghayath al-Din al-Muqtadir bi'llah [r. 908-932]. It is very old. In the Ottoman Empire this is the sixth black fort of the Kurds. The others are: Qara Hisar of Afyon, Shebin, Develi, Antalya, and [-]; the sixth one is the Kurdish Qara Hisar. This one is not less than the others. It goes high up into the sky and is situated in a high mountain; it is a small castle. Since it is surrounded by hellish pit-deep precipices, I could not measure its circumference. But it is rectangular, and lengthwise it is long. Now it is held as a *yurdliq* and *ojaqliq* by one of the Mahmudi Beys, my namesake Evliya Bey Mahmudi, who is an honorable emir with a drum and banner. He has captivated all the emirs of Kurdistan by his generosity. He has four thousand choice and armed soldiers. He is an asset to the Mahmudis. Although he looks stout and fat, he is very agile and lively and, from the viewpoint of talent, an outstanding Mahmudi emir. Nobody in Kurdistan is equal in generosity to the Khan of Bitlis and Evliya Bey. He gave a huge feast for all our friends in the lower part of the promenade. All the sugar of its delectable dishes was from Hama. After the dinner, I had an emerald ring on my finger with an inscription in a special script, and even Hatem Tay'i could not boast to have such a one. He said: "My Evliya, let me see the seal." I said: "See my Khan" and gave the signet ring to him, and he read:

> From the chief of the pious and the prophets' seal
> Evliya has hope for intercession and appeal.

Upon reading it he became bewildered. He said: "My Evliya, of course, you will give it to me." This humble author said: "My Khan, this is auspicious to me, it might be ill-omened to others." He immediately said: "The saints and the prophets cannot be ill-omened. You and I, we are special to the Saints. We have been created under the most fortunate stars. Of course, I want the seal." Seeing his persistence this humble author said: "My Khan, you are welcome to it. May

---

6. One *oqqah* weighed 1.28 kg.

7. Perhaps this is a variant of *qay va bay*, the title of Turkic princes from Central Asia. Bulut, *Bitlis*, p. 301.

it be a blessing to you." It was as if the world was given to him and he said: "Immediately give five hundred sheep to my brother Evliya Chelebi." He also gave me one sable fur coat, one studded Sheykhani sword and one Mahmudi horse. He gave the *agha* of Morteza Pasha one horse and another one to the *agha* of our Pasha and, then we took our leave from him. We received capable guides and departed into northeastern direction and after five hours reached:

THE STAGE OF THE VILLAGE OF PASIK AGHA. It is a village of one hundred houses that belongs to Evliya Bey. It has one large mosque and many gardens. From there again we went towards the east for three hours and passing through steep rocky terrain arrived at:

THE STAGE OF THE VILLAGE OF MELAHAN. It is situated in a deep valley and is surrounded by high mountains. It has one thousand families. It is a Kurdish Moslem village with gardens and orchards. All of them are Shafe'is. Most of the Mahmudis are choice soldiers and they are under the orders of Evliya Bey. There is a stream, and at the head of it Evliya Bey has a beautiful garden, which is like the Meram garden in Qonya. The village chief came and gave us a party, which cannot be described. Again we received gifts from Evliya Bey, which included tiger skins, and I sent my five hundred sheep to Van to be sold. Then we went for three hours to Pinayesh castle.

DESCRIPTION OF THE PINYANISH CASTLE, I.E., THE STRONG HASANI CASTLE. In the year [-] Sultan Uzun Hasan, the king of Azerbaijan, built it and hence it is called Hasani Castle. Under Ottoman rule there are [-] Hasani castles. One is Hasan Barak, which is in ruins. Another is Hasan Mansur, whose name is a distortion of Hasin-e Mansur (i.e., the victorious castle). One is Hasan Keyfa. Yet another one is near Erzerum and is called Hasan Castle. Another one in Syrian Tripolis is called Hasanabad. And this one is Hasani Castle. This castle rises to heaven on the top of a rock, as if it is not the work of man. It is worth seeing, and Man could not have built such a strong wall. It is as if by divine command layer upon layer, rocks upon rocks formed its towers. It is impossible that Man could have done this, unless there were several hundred architects. Truly, it is a remnant of the time of 'Ad[8] and a unique cave made by man, but it is a small castle. Inside the caves there are ten houses, cisterns, and many supplies. The castle is towered over by mountains, but not in such a way that it is harmful to the castle. In the year 1033 [1623-24], Rustam Khan the Bald besieged it for eight months and shelled it, but could not capture it and returned dejected to Iran. It has one gate towards the south, which is accessible by a ladder. They draw up the ladder by ropes, and when the ropes are drawn it is inaccessible from any side. Except for man and birds, no animal can enter. Inside there is one large mosque, warehouses and cisterns. In the surrounding mountains there are so many tigers, lynxes and stags that only God knows how many. Knowledgeable Kurds dig pits in the mountains and cover them with leaves. When the wild sheep pass over them they fall into them, are caught and eaten. They kill tigers and lynxes and keep their skin. All of its people live off wild sheep. The tigers in these mountains are as big as a horse, and they are not to be found in the mountains of Sikifle and Qaratashliq. In the Berduq valley, which is situated below the castle, there are some six hundred Kurdish ground floor houses. There are no walls around them, only a moat. There are no gardens, but there are very many orchards. On the

---

8. 'Ad and Thamud were two tribes of idol worshippers mentioned in the Koran 89: 7 (al-Fajr) who lived in Yemen. One of the emirs of the 'Ad was named Shaddad b. 'Ad who allegedly built the legendary paradise-like city of Eram Dhat al-'Imad. Evliya invariably calls all huge buidings *shaddadi*. See W. Montogomery Watt, "Iram," *Encyclopedia of Islam II*.

banks of the river Berduq there are meadows, where there are thousands of tall poplar trees, and each one of them reaches for heaven.

An interesting spectacle. I am really amazed at the fearlessness of their children. When in spring the trees are nourished with water and are supple, about eighty or one hundred big and small children climb to the top of them. Because the trees cannot bear their weight, they bend down like the bow-string of Berejiq and come down. The tip of the tree nearly comes down to the ground. At this time, one by one the children jump down so that the weight is lessened, but still some forty or fifty of them remain. At this moment the tree wants to rise, although there are still many children in it. Suddenly about ten children jump down. The tree rises up and bends towards the other side. In this way the poor trees sway to and fro. At this moment when there are many children on it, it bends and the children cry out in their childish voices. When the tree goes to the right all of them shout: "*Halli sun, halli sun*,"[9] and joke.

When it bends to the left they yell: "*Verre run, verre run*,"[10] until the poor tree comes back to its upright position. Again they climb the same tree like spiders and make it bend so that it comes near the ground because of the heavy load. Again they climb the tree and the people who are hanging on it jump down. Those who jump down again climb the tree and cry so many times "*halli sun*" that their sound rises to the heavens. If they do not hang properly, those who are on the ground shout: "*Hey batabni batabni; hey kosni dumbelini*",[11] and they clap and joke. It is strange that in no other country is it possible to bend poplars up and down in this way.

Everyday in the afternoon, when the children are free from their teachers, they rush to the trees, have fun and play in them. It is a very strange spectacle. But the boys are very noble and grown-up. Because of it their fathers allow their boys too much freedom in this land, as it is a rocky and isolated place. In this town there is only one small mosque and one large mosque, and there is one caravanserai for travelers.

There is no bathhouse or bazaar. In their summer quarters they keep many sheep. It seems that at the instigation of the governor of Aleppo, Ipshir Pasha, the Qizilbash had stolen forty thousand sheep from these people. Since we were charged with the mission of returning those sheep, the Pinyanish paid us much respect. Under the abovementioned trees, they feasted us and we enjoyed ourselves. It has a very good climate.

The situation of the Pinyanish people. In the year 955 [1548] they submitted to Sultan Sulayman. Therefore, the bey became the *ojaq-bey* of the revenues of that same region. There is no *ze'amat* or *timar* in that place. The bey has been honored with the drum and standard of an emir. They have six thousand soldiers, and are considered to be part of the Mahmudi region. Their official title is recorded as Emirs of the Pinyanish. They are a simple-minded, sincere people, who wear daggers and swords at their belt. They are vivacious and proud, and they do not know of tricks and schemes. One hundred of the people who had come with us from Van stayed here, and I chose ten of these people to accompany me to the lands of Persia. Going towards the east after [-] hours we reached:

---

9. 'Rise up, rise up!'

10. "Go down, go down!"

11. We have not been able to find the meaning of these words.

THE STAGE OF RUBAJIQ SULTAN. When Sultan Murad IV returned from the war at Erevan, he pitched his tents here, and the location of his tent has now become a platform. Here is the border of the Pinyanish, which is part of the Ottoman Empire. {By God's wisdom} Rubajiq has a water well whose water is as delicious as the paradisiacal water of Jerusalem. Anyone who drinks it continuously for forty days by God's command will become brave and courageous. It is for this reason that the Mahmudi tribe is so valiant. Unfortunately, the roads are very difficult to travel, rocky and wooded. In their steep rocky mountains there are many wild goats and sheep as well as innumerable tigers, lynxes and beach martens. The village is not very prosperous; it has three hundred households and one large mosque. It is a Pinayish Kurdish village. Each week the villagers of the region come together here and hold a weekly market. We departed and after six hours we reached Qotur castle.

DESCRIPTION OF THE CASTLE OF QOTUR.[12] In the Mongol language they call mulish and stubborn people *qotur*. One of the Mongols of Chengiz Khan, Mohammad Shah Ghazan, converted to Islam and is buried near Tabriz. He had a stubborn vizier named Qotur.[13] Mohammad Shah Ghazan commanded that vizier: "O Qotur, build a castle in these rocky mountains." The vizier Qotur said: "Your order is my order," and he built this castle in the year 694 [1295], and it became known as the castle of Qotur. Truly it is built in a very rough place.

Another castle called Qotur is built in the *sanjaq* of Hersek[14] in Bosnia at the end of the Gulf of Novi on a very steep rock. But now it is in the hands of the infidel Venetians.

But this Qotur castle is in the hands of the Persians. In 992 [1584], after it was conquered by Farhad Pasha, it fell into the hands of the Ottomans. Later, in 996 [1588], when Cheghaloghlu was defeated in the battle of Sarab and left all his arms, supplies and all other equipment and fled, the Persians took advantage of this opportunity and occupied the castle. Now it is completely repaired, and it is strong and solid. Even in 1045 [1635-36], when Sultan Murad, the conqueror of Erevan, stopped here, they fired cannons constantly at the army of Islam so that no one could go near it.

Sultan Murad asked: "From where comes this sound of the cannons?" And they replied: "My king, this castle was ours, now it has fallen into the hands of the Persians and the sound of the cannons are from the castle of Qotur." At that time the late Sultan Murad, may God's mercy and forgiveness be upon him, mounted his horse called Noghay and went to a high point and viewed the castle and said: "May God curse it. What a strong castle it is. As winter is nearing, if we besiege it, it may become increasingly difficult for us day by day, so it is better to leave it alone. May this be a correct decision, let us hope for the best." He then returned to his tent. In the year 1048 [1638-39] when he conquered Baghdad and made a peace treaty, Sultan Murad told Qara Mostafa Pasha: "Mostafa, in this peace treaty it should be mentioned that the Persians should destroy the castle of Maku, near the castle of Erevan, as well as the Qotur castle, which is in the province of Van."

---

12. Qotur is situated some 50 km south-west of Khoy at 38.4661 latitude and 44.4422 longitude. Razmara, *Farhang*, p. 283.

13. Not known to us.

14. Hersek or Herzegovina.

In fact, his insightful observations were not carried out, for the castles of Maku and Qotur were not destroyed, but rather all soldiers were withdrawn and the castle of Qotur was left abandoned. By God's wisdom, after the treaty of Baghdad Sultan Murad died in Istanbul and subsequently the Qizilbash took advantage of the accession of Sultan Ebrahim. They went back on their word and put soldiers in the castles of Maku and Qotur and made them as strong and solid as if they were a polished piece of precious stone. Now in the province of Van, it forms the border with the Pinyanish district. Formerly, Qotur was the center of the *sanjaq* of our beys. Although the castle is in Persian hands, all the surrounding area of Qotur is in Ottomans hands. Qotur has a bey, who was with us in the battle of Bitlis.

THE LAYOUT OF QOTUR CASTLE. It is situated on a long rock at the southern end of a valley. It is a very high, quadrangular, very strong and beautiful castle not very unlike that of ʿAdeljavaz. How many paces it is I do not know, but it is small. It is on the border of Persia and a nice castle. Inside the castle there are three thousand choice Mazandarani musketeers and royal slaves. When we stayed there one night in the lower gardens, the walls and towers of the castle were illuminated with torches and the watchmen cried, '*Khoda khub,*' until morning. Truly, in the same way that the Franks are good at building castles, the Persians are good at maintaining them. The royal slaves and the ushers came to our tents; they were extremely kind and gracious to us.

In the morning they gave us about fifty royal slaves. We went to a place called Mohammad valley and then went to Shah Gedighi (royal pass). It is a low mountain and is the beginning of the Persia. When Qotur was in Ottoman hands, the Persians retook it by a trick. But if you truly look at it, the world does not stay with anyone, it seems that sometimes it is in the hands of the Persians and sometimes in that of others, and sometimes it again goes into the hands of the Ottomans.

> The world's affairs are in this way
> Don't make fun of what I say.

As the poem goes, in the hands of kings of the world all these castles pass from one to the other.

In short, in the morning of Dhu'l-Qaʿdeh 1065 [September 1655] we crossed Shah Gedighi and set foot in Persia. After three hours we reached Albaq castle.

DESCRIPTION OF THE CASTLE OF ʿALI BAQ, I.E., THE CASTLE OF ALBAQ. It is thus called because in 694 [1294-95], in the time of Mohammad Shah Ghazan, whose capital was Tabriz, ʿAli Baqi built this castle, and the Mongols and the Kurds distorted his name to Albaq. It has passed from ruler to ruler. It is a ruined crow's-nest of a castle. It is situated in between the cities of Van, Azerbaijan (Tabriz), Urmiyeh and Ujan on the slope of a mountain. It is small and quadrangular shaped. Inside there is a chief of the ushers, a chief of the royal slaves and royal slaves who are paid by the Shah. There are Mazandarani soldiers who drink wine and hard liquor from the shah [i.e., who are paid by him] and who are armed with well-equipped muskets. There are gardens and orchards. Sultan Murad, conqueror of Erevan, returning from the conquest of Erevan, alighted below Albaq and did not destroy or pillage it, but passed it. Now there are benches in a meadow at the place where he stayed. In that blessed place the people of the village gather every week and have a very great bazaar. Outside the stone castle there are a large mosque, a caravanserai, a bathhouse and a good number of shops.

SHAMS AL-DIN KHU'I. He is one of the saints of the Khvajegan Sufi order, and he has performed many miracles and is buried in this town.

Then going to the north after five hours we reached:

THE VILLAGE OF JULO. One Hakkari, called Julo, who accepted the Qizilbash hat from the Shah, developed this town, and that is why it is so called. Its people are all Shi`ites. Again we traveled for three hours to the east and came to:

THE VILLAGE OF SANASUN. It is a prosperous town situated on the border of Salmas district in a large grassland plain; it has one thousand households, gardens and orchards, a large mosque, a caravanserai and bathhouses. It has only a royal market in the place where Sultan Murad stayed, where they have a weekly bazaar. Again after seven hours we reached:

DESCRIPTION OF THE CASTLE OF KARNIYAREQ. It was built in 922 [1516] by a Khan whose name was Karniyareq,[15] and that is why it is called Karniyareq. It is under the government of the sultan of Berduq. It is a beautiful, strong castle on a high mountain and its shape is rectangular, built lengthwise. It is a small castle, but on a very high hill. When we learned that they would not allow us inside the castle, {we did not visit it}, and we do not know how many people are there. We were told, "It has one large mosque, one caravanserai, and about three hundred musketeers." But we pitched our tents near the lower rampart and stayed there and looked at the castle. Outside there is a place which has one thousand clean mud houses embellished with gardens and orchards, ponds and promenades constituting a beautiful suburb. It has many large mosques, bathhouses and a sufficient number of shops. In the place where Sultan Murad stayed and walked there is a recreation area. Nearby Mullah Shoja` al-Din Kermani is buried. Then we went towards the north for three hours and reached:

THE STAGE OF HOBASH.[16] We deviated from the road that Sultan Murad had taken. We saw the minarets of the town of Tesuy [Tasuj] on the left, passed through gardens and pitched our tents in this Hobash. The mayor and police chief (*shahneh*) of this prosperous village were very hospitable, as were all the peasants. It is near Tasuj town with one thousand households, one large mosque and bathhouses; it is a prosperous village. We went for three hours to the north and reached:

DESCRIPTION OF THE CASTLE OF BERDUQ.[17] It is inside the border of Persia and part of the province of Van, governed by the Pinyanish Kurds. Most of the sheep stolen by the Persians are from these parts. Its summer quarters borders on that of the Persian Afshars. This high castle was built in 1025 (1616) by one of the beys of the Pinyanish, Cholaq (Lame) Mir `Aziz Bey. This castle is very close to the Pinyanish Hasani castle, but considering the invitations we went to several castles, gave our letters of friendship and returned to Berduq castle. All the Pinyanish people welcomed us, and we pitched our tents in their gardens and became their guests.

---

15. Karniyareq means 'torn belly.' It is also the name of a well-known Turkish eggplant dish stuffed with minced meat, onions, garlic and tomatoes.

16. This is probably Habashi, at about forty-six km southwest of Khoy and some six km north of Qotur. Razmara, *Farhang*, p. 172.

17. Berduk, a village in the district of Urmiyeh, is situated 11 km south-west of Hashtiyan. Razmara, *Farhang*, p. 85.

THE LAYOUT OF THE BERDUQ CASTLE. It is situated in a wasteland; it is a useful and small castle and has no moat. On the east side it has a wooden gate. The circumference is eight hundred paces. Inside there about two hundred rooms, and its guards are from the Pinyanish tribe. It has three small cannons and one large mosque. It has no shops, caravanserais or bathhouses. But whatever valuable goods you want you may get without trouble, because it is adjacent to and inside Persia. On the southern side of the castle, on the banks of river Davdan, there is a prosperous suburb, which has three hundred houses with gardens, orchards and poplars. It is a small town.

It has a large mosque, which was built by Cholaq Mir ʿAziz; it has a dirty caravanserai and bathhouse. This humble servant went to the bathhouse. It is a ridiculous bathhouse which can only accommodate six persons. In this suburb there are about three thousand Pinyanish youths who have frequently gone to the land of the Persians and have defeated the shah's chief general at several occasions. They are a very brave and warlike people. They pin feathers on their turbans,[18] and these are the courageous youths that can cut the heads of five or ten evil Qizilbash with their sharp swords. Now they have become neighbors of the Khans of Urmiyeh and Tabriz. The Persian emirs sent them most of the time supplies, horses, clothes,and silk to rid themselves of their trouble.

But this time the Persians came with many soldiers and stole forty thousand sheep from the summer quarters. When they learnt that we were commissioned to get the sheep back, they wanted to come with us to the Khan of Urmiyeh. This humble author said: "We have several letters about your sheep from the vizier of Van to several Persian khans. We have traveled a great distance. You may come later to Urmiyeh." They liked this idea and gave us many gifts. I asked about this river Davdan that flows inside the suburb. They said: "It originates from the Harir Mountains and the high plateaus of Ardalan and the mountains of Hakkari, and it crosses our town and on the east side it passes from the land of the Khan of Jevlan and then it flows into Lake Urmiyeh." It is a freshwater river that is easily fordable. Then we went towards the east for three hours and reached:

THE VILLAGE OF HINE.[19] It is village of three hundred Kurdish and Armenian households, who are both under the Persians and the Pinyanish. By being under two swords, it pays taxes to both sides. We passed it and went to:

THE VILLAGE OF HARIR. These are subjects of the Ghaziqeran Kurds, but they pay tithe to the Persians. It is a prosperous village. We passed it and after three hours we reached Ghaziqeran.

DESCRIPTION OF THE ABODE OF THE FIGHTERS OF THE FAITH, THE CASTLE OF GHAZIQERAN. In the year [-] the ʿAbbasi kings of the Hakkaris built it. But its original name is unknown. It has changed hands several times between the Persians and the Ottomans. Now it is part of the province of Van and held by the Ghaziqeran beys as *ojaqliq*. Half of the people are subjects of the Persians, because their village and orchards and gardens are in their land. Because their castle was inaccessible, being in a steep place, it was left in the hands of the Ottomans. But they are Ghaziqeran, who are part of the Pinyanish Mahmudi tribe.

---

18. The text has Qizilbash turbans, which does not make sense and therefore we have deleted 'Qezelbash' from the translation.

19. This perhaps is the village of Hoseyni in the district of Maragheh, Razmara, *Farhang*, p. 176

They are called Ghaziqeran because in earlier times they were eight thousand soldiers, who, with the *ghazis* of the sultan's khans were going to help the castle of Erevan, fought the Qizilbash and put their swords to such use that none of them could save his head. And that is why they are called Ghaziqeran (i.e., killers of *ghazis*), but they are not Persian subjects.

THE LAYOUT OF THE CASTLE OF GHAZIQERAN. It overlooks the valley of Urmiyeh and is situated on top of a steep rock; it is a small and old, but a beautiful quadrangular castle. It is not known how many people it contains. Inside the castle there are ten houses and a bey's mansion. It is a richly adorned big mansion. Its bey governs it as an *ojaqleq*. He has one thousand soldiers. Its revenues are all assigned to him as a personal imperial fief. It has no separate *timar* and *ze'amat*. There is a royal order denoting that it "is free from fiscal and administrative interference,"[20] so that if the Persians would conquer it they would honor this. On Friday they read the *khutbah* in the large mosques, first for the Ottoman dynasty and then for the Persian Shah, but they love the Ottoman dynasty more. They say: "We wish that the Ottomans would return once again," because when the Persians and Ottomans made peace we became poor.

DESCRIPTION OF THE LOWER SUBURB. The un-walled environs form a suburb with houses, gardens and orchards, but it has no bazaar, caravanserai or bathhouse. Sari 'Ali Agha, who was charged to go into the presence of the Shah of Iran in Isfahan, separated from us and departed with two hundred horsemen towards Isfahan, while we went to Azerbaijan to the south. And after five hours we reached:

THE STAGE OF THE KUYAH PASS. This is in the district of the Persian Jevlan Khan, and this valley, which is situated between it and Ghaziqeran, is called Shah-Gedigi (the royal pass). To the west is Ottoman Ghaziqeran. This Shah-Gedigi is such a beautiful valley that you would say it is paradise. The air is filled with the fragrance of several thousand colorful flowers. On each side of the main road weeping willows, cypresses, firs, juniper, box and plane trees have been planted in lines. They do not let the sunlight penetrate. In this wretched valley in the year 992 [1585], as a result of the mishandling of the battle of Sarab by Cheghal-zadeh Senan Pasha, the army of Islam was defeated and, while fleeing the Persians and the Kurds pursued and killed them in Kuyah valley. They buried their martyrs at the side of the road. Apart from the tombs of 'Ali Yar Pasha, Tireli Fazli Pasha, Vasi 'Alisi Defterdar Pasha and Farrokh Bey, several hundred notables had their names and titles carved on their marble tombstones. But the khans of Tabriz and Urmiyeh removed them, saying that these were written while it was in Ottoman hands.

We went from here for five hours towards the south to the Shahrezur Mountains and the slopes of the Harir and Ardalan Mountains and reached:

THE STAGE OF JEVLAN SULTAN. This is a big village situated on the slope of a large mountain with one thousand houses, gardens and orchards, large mosques, caravanserais, bathhouses and about one hundred shops. A grey-haired man called Jevlan Sultan, the chief of the soldiers, came forward with a great procession and took us to his house for a feast and made all our people guests in his garden. He put up our friend the *agha* of Morteza Pasha, in the house of his son. This Jevlan Sultan originally is from the Ghaziqeran Kurds. Since he has received a *taj* from the Shah, he has become a Sultan. In the land of Persia they call *sanjaq-bey*s sultan. He is a grey-haired old

---

20. Evliya Chelebi writes: *mahfuz al-qalam va mafruz al-qadam*, a common technical term to denote the fiscal and administrative autonomy of a district. Willem Floor, *A Fiscal History*, p. 334.

man who has one thousand soldiers but no castle. When we gave the letter of the Pasha to him, he kissed it and after reading it he said: "By God, I have not taken any sheep from the Pinyanish, but together with the Khan of Urmiyeh I have plundered their towns." Then he said: "Therefore, after a few days I will come with you to the government house of the Khan of Urmiyeh." In the morning we received his gifts and we went towards the south and after five hours reached:

The stage of Afsharli Sultan. (The Sultan) also welcomed us and took us to his garden. We gave the letter, which he read and said: "Yes, upon my eyes. I will meet you in the government house of Urmiyeh." He behaved very nicely. He is actually a Turkmen, who fled from the tyranny of the Ottomans[21] and received a *taj* from the Shah. He has ten thousand Turkmen who make the Harir Mountains their summer quarters. They are a generous people. Its village has five hundred houses, with a caravanserai, and a bathhouse, and its gardens and orchards are everywhere. Again from here we went for six hours towards the south and arrived at:

The stage Pirehdus Sultan. The Sultan was a sick old man. His head was on a pillow, and he was shouting. His deputy welcomed and lodged us. We gave the letter, and he gave it to the Sultan, who was sleeping in his pajamas in his harem, and he said: "Be welcome; a hundred times welcome. Be welcome." He showed us hospitality. We said, "We cannot stay long." The town was very prosperous; it has five large mosques, but because of being under the evil Qizilbash, they are not frequented. There are caravanserais, bathhouses and bazaars. Then we went to the south and after five hours reached:

The stage of Enzeli Sultan. The Sultan, who was from the Kahravan region, came to welcome us. He was a favorite[22] of Shah ʿAbbas II, an early riser, and a good horseman. He took us to his own house and was delighted to read the letter, and he said: "May I be the sacrifice to this Ottoman king, the Caesar of the World." He was very complimentary about the Ottomans and said: "God willing, we will meet at the government house of Urmiyeh." After the feast we visited the suburb. It is a beautiful town with promenades, gardens, orchards, large mosques, caravanserais, bathhouses, sufficient shops and plenty of servants. There are one thousand soldiers in this town, but the beauties of Enzeli are something else. Because of the pleasant climate, the beautiful youths have great bodies, and their fingers are very dainty. They have plenty of running water, trestled flowerbeds, excellent pomegranates, plums and pears; it is like paradise. We went somewhat to the south and after five hours we reached:

The village of Habbena. It borders on Enzeli Sultan. It is an endowment by Shah Esmaʿil and has one thousand houses with garden-like promenades. It is a big village with Kurdish, Armenian[23] and Gökdolaq inhabitants. Going south from here for three hours we reached:

The stage of Harir Sultan. Its village chief welcomed us and took us to the Sultan's mansion. The Sultan was hunting; he returned with about one thousand soldiers, greyhounds and hunting dogs. When he met this humble one he said: "O my cousin, you are welcome," and spoke familiarly with me. He was a Turkmen of the Qiziqli tribe. He had come with seven thou-

---

21. This must be a slip of the pen by Evliya, perhaps quoting what the Sultan said.
22. The term used here is *cheragh-e afrukhteh*.
23. Jevdet, vol. 4, p. 285 has deleted the mention of Armenians as he does in many other instances.

sand people from Shahrezur to Persia and had received a *taj* and has become a landless[24] Sultan. When we gave our letter he put it on his eyes and face and gave it back to this humble one and said: "Read it."

I read it and when its content was understood he said: "By God, when we attacked the Pinyanish we were with twenty khans. If our king says 'give the sheep,' we will give them willingly." I said: "upon my eyes." And then he made a present of the sword that he wore on his belt to this humble author. I said: "No, I will not accept the sword. It is not done among the Ottomans." He said: "O good Ottoman, may I be your sacrifice." He gave me a Frankish sword, a Qarachuboq horse, and he also promised to come to Urmiyeh.

These seven[25] abovementioned Sultans, in the time of Sultan Ahmad and Sultan Mostafa, were subjects of the Ottomans. They were Turkmen khans with tens of thousands of Turkmen who made their summer quarters in the Harir and Ardalan mountains. Later, during the decline of the reign of Sultan Othman (II, r. 1618-1622) and when Murad (IV, r. 1623-1640) acceded to the throne, the Qizilbash took Tabriz and Urmiyeh and thus they came under the Persians and became subjects of the Shah. I asked all of them if they wanted the Ottomans to return. 'May God make it happen!' We received gifts from all these Sultans. We went towards the east for seven hours and reached:

The stage called Kharman-e Shahi. This land is all under the Khan of Urmiyeh. It is a prosperous village in the valley of Urmiyeh with five hundred houses, gardens and orchards. It has a large mosque and a bathhouse. Proceeding from here into the valley of Urmiyeh we reached in five hours the castle of Urmiyeh in Azerbaijan.

Description of the castle of Urmiyeh in Azerbaijan, i.e., the earthen fort of Ghazan

Being of Chengiz's house and having converted in the year 694 [1294] to Islam Sultan Mohammad Ghazan built this castle. After him it was transferred from king to king, and in the year 932 [1525-26] Shah Tahmasp enlarged and developed it. Later on, in the year 992 [1584], Farhad Pasha, while building Qumlah Chemeni castle, repaired this one as well. Sultan Sulayman's eunuch, Sulayman Pasha and Khadem Ja`far Pasha reinforced and rebuilt all its gates and walls.

Now we will describe how we entered into the city

One day earlier, from a place called Kharmanshahi, a city quarter, we had sent a well-spoken and respectable man to the deputy of the Khan of Urmiyeh. Our man met the Khan and kissed his hand, and the Khan said: "Please, come in the morning," and he sent three carts full of beverages, food and fruits as a gift and said, "Be welcome," and sent a cordial letter. This humble person without dissimulation, but rather in accordance with Ottoman custom, then gave his man many things, and inside a Qaya Sultan handkerchief, I put a cordial letter and sent it to the Khan. In the morning with our entire retinue, fully armed and equipped, in full festive dress, this humble

---

24. *Khoshneshin* in Persian normally refers to a class of landless peasants. Thus, the use of this term here probably indicates that this Sultan had not been given a fief of landed property.

25. We only counted five.

person along with our friend, the *agha* of Morteza Pasha, with all our animals and baggage rode together stirrup to stirrup. And with us were three led horses and two hundred armed men. While we were going in the Urmiyeh plain, we saw a black dust cloud rising in front of us. From inside of it an army appeared and the sound of shawms, flutes, trumpets, and kettle-drums filled the air. When they were coming towards us and we were going towards them, I saw that from the Persian army the Khan appeared with five or ten horsemen. This humble person along with ʿAli Agha separated from our group and galloped towards them. We kissed each other out of friendship and became acquainted. The Khan said: "You are welcome; you are a hundred times welcome." This humble person said: "Peace be upon you. I have come like a moth to render myself to the light of your candle." When he saw that the Morteza Pasha's *agha* gave no reaction, he turned his horse's head to this humble servant and said: "It is not the custom in the land of Iran that khans with their companions come to welcome strangers. Because I love Ottomans I have come to welcome you." I knew that inside him there was pride and stupidity and said immediately: "My Khan. May God preserve you from wrongs. You have followed the honorable Tradition of the Holy Prophet who has said: 'Honor the guest, even if he is an unbeliever, for you have come to welcome the guest. You have shown to have a great heart." I said several more words like this. While the soldiers were playing polo we approached the castle. At one hour's distance several thousand people came to welcome us, young and old in rows, and dignitaries on each side.

The Khan had a disorganized riff-raff army that cannot be described. All of them wore a *taj* as headdress and had feathers on their head. They were Yaka Turkmen, Ardalan Kurds, and Mongols; a miserable ragtag army. They did not like each other and this made one wonder. I saw that the Khan was a stately and magnificent young man who still wore tresses. His retinue was not bad. He had many well-dressed servants, but his music band was a different story. In short, with this pomp and cavalcade we approached the castle and the Khan rode forward, and we along with the Agha, stirrup to stirrup, turned to that earthen castle. Once more, the sound of the drums, kettle-drums, and trumpets, was heard from the walls of the castle. Big caliber cannons spouted fire; by the glory of God, from these lightings earth and sky trembled. All the people of Urmiyeh were trembling like autumn leaves. From all the battlements of the castle's parasols, banners and flags were hanging so that its ramparts looked like a wedding party. In this manner we visited Urmiyeh castle with our retinue, and with our huge crowd we visited the city and all the people, and all the beloveds of the city amused themselves and accompanied us to the palace of the Khan and again we embraced. I was at his right hand side and the *agha* of Morteza Pasha on his left. We had a friendly banquet at the Khan's table with kerchiefs and utensils.

Then were brought in China trays with twenty different types of rice and twenty bowls of stew. The head butler came in and with a serving spoon distributed the rice covered with saffron, which was in front of the Khan, to everyone. He distributed every dish among the people present. In short, except for rice, the Persians do not have any good food. They have several types of soups and roasted meat,[26] which are praised all over the world. Because they have no other good food they call them bad-living Qizilbash. In effect, because of their bad manner of living, gypsies and their poor soldiers are called "bad living" (*bad-maʿash*). Whatever type of food is eaten, man's aim is to still his hunger. Whether it is date juice, pieces of sugar candy or barley bread, all of them serve to still hunger. We ate several dishes and the table cloth was taken away, but compote

---

26. Meat or fowls roasted with oil in a large pot or in a *tannur* or oven are called *biryan*; when grilled or cooked on an open fire, they are called kebabs.

(*khoshab*) did not come, because in Persia compote and *zerdeh*[27] are not very well liked. The reason is that compote was made by the Caliph Othman. Since *zerdeh* was first made by Yazid's father, Moʿawiya ibn Abi Sufiyan in the land of Iran, these two dishes are disliked, but some people eat it in secret.

After the food, they brought a ewer to me and the Khan, and in accordance with Ottoman custom we washed our hands. The others wiped their hands with a partially soaked handkerchief. Those not of the Qizilbash wiped their right hand under the left armpit and then wiped their left hand with the right side of their skirt. They have such strange manners of eating.

Then I took the letter of the Pasha from my breast-pocket, kissed and presented it to the Khan. The Khan said: "Peace be upon you," kissed the cordial letter and put it on his head, and everybody who was present got up. He showed the letter to them and gave it to the secretary to read aloud. When its content was known, the Khan said: "Evliya Agha, you are welcome and we are delighted. You are a messenger who has been charged with a special commission. Let me inform you about the issue. Listen carefully to what I say. We were sitting comfortably in our city, and we were praising the Shah of Iran and Turan. Suddenly we saw that one night that the Pinyanish tribe attacked and that they took cattle and sheep from this castle. From the lands of Jevlan Sultan, Pirehdus Sultan and other sultans they had taken 12(,000) of our sheep.

"We were wondering, 'Is this affair against the peace, what could be the reason for it?' We discussed this among ourselves. Most of us said, 'Let's get some sheep from the Pinyanish and then ask them why they have acted as they did.' We discussed this and informed the shah. Our shah sent letters to your king and to your vizier in Aleppo, Ipshir Pasha.

"This good-for-nothing Ipshir, the valiant vizier, did not take mercy on us and said, 'I will deal with them,' but he closed his eyes to the whole affair.' Again the Pinyanish tribe attacked, beginning at Salmas and Tasuj and plundered several merchants' caravans and cut many throats. We saw that it was not possible to sit and just watch. At the orders of the Khan of Tabriz, several khans and twenty beys invaded the land of the Pinyanish with the army of Iran. We took several herds, twenty thousand sheep, and brought them safely and victoriously to Urmiyeh." While the Khan said this, the Pinyanish who owned the sheep shouted: "No, our forty thousand sheep and one hundred and fifty men are missing. You have them," and they said: "We will go to the Shah."

This humble servant said: "Hey, why are you shouting? God willing, by the favor of the Khan your sheep will be returned. Have patience and get out." In this way I got rid of all the sheeps' owners. I remained all alone with the Khan and talked, and I addressed him as follows:

The Khan and this humble servant sat knee to knee and I said: "My Khan, since we happened to be in Van I wanted to be graced by your favors. God be praised, I was graced by the beauty of your face and achieved my objective. I have a request for you. By Mohammad, if you honor his inborn eloquence or the pure and blessed soul of the lion of God, ʿAli, may God bless his face. If you love these two, now that there is no one except you and me, let us talk and take counsel. By the love of the friend of God (i.e., Mohammad) do not despair." He said: "By God, I do not despair; in accordance with custom, you are our guest, and it is as you said."

---

27. A dish of sweetened rice covered with saffron, probably the same dish known in Azerbaijan as *sareshileh*.

This humble author said: "My Khan, did not the late Sultan Murad IV, may his soul rest, conquer Baghdad and make peace with Shah Safi, the Shah of Iran? And, on what basis did the two sides do so? Is this known to your Excellency?" He said: "At that time I was not born yet, but our Khvajeh Naqdi and Hajji Qorban Qoli they know it well. Let's call them."

After they arrived, the Khan said: "O Khvajehs, on what basis did Sultan Murad make peace with Shah Safi about Baghdad?" When he said this Khvajeh Naqdi said: "O my Khan, here is the peace treaty which was made on the basis of twenty articles." Then the Khan opened the small folding desk and took out the peace treaty.

Text of the Peace Treaty

First, in the name of God; second, in the name of Mohammad, if it was not for your sake we would not have created the firmament; third, in the name of the four chosen friends (i.e., the rightly-guided caliphs), may God have mercy on all of them. Fourth, I who am the guardian of the two holy places and the ruler of the kings of Arabs and non-Arabs; and you, Shah Safi Bahador, may God Almighty bless him, who is king of the land of Iran. You have asked for a peace of forty years. I have given my royal consent for a peace treaty of twenty years based on twenty articles.

The first article is that both sides should not be engaged in robbing, plundering and stealing. If somebody does, both sides agree to return what is due.

The second article is that troops with trumpets, hautbois, firing cannons and muskets should not invade the land.[28] After these two articles had been read this humble servant said:

"O Khan, blessed be your grandfather. See, these two articles are proof and confirmation for you and me. What is your take on this peace treaty until now?" The Khan said:

"To begin with, the Pinyanish tribe has done something which is contrary to the peace. They have taken sheep and herds from the castle of Urumiyeh." This humble person said:

"O Khan, did the Pinyanish come with muskets and cannons?" The Khan said:

"No, they attacked by night." I said:

"O Khan, may your father rest in peace. You are the absolute representative of the king of the land of Iran and his chief general. Why, according to the articles of the peace treaty, did not you pursue the plundering and thieving Kurds and render justice when you had an easy excuse? However, you gathered twenty khans and forty thousand troops with cannons and muskets to make war in front of everybody, contrary to the treaty, and attacked the Pinyanish and took forty thousand sheep and three hundred herds (of cattle)? Now there are many wounded people, and their land is destroyed and their mosques were destroyed by cannon fire." The Khan said:

"By God Evliya Agha, we only fired seven cannons." I said: "O Khan, even if you did not fire the cannons, taking cannons is contrary to the treaty."

I saw that the Khan became crestfallen. He said: "What shall I do?"

This humble servant said: "By God, O Khan. When the Ottoman Sultan heard about this action contrary to the peace, he sent his son-in-law, Malek Ahmad Pasha, the chief commander, to

---

28. For the English translation of the text of the peace treaty, see J. C. Hurewitz, *Diplomacy in the Near and Middle East. A Documentary Record 1535-1956* (New York, 1956), vol. 1, pp. 21-23, which does not have these two articles.

Van. Perhaps you have not heard this. As soon as he entered Van he gathered around him one hundred thousand troops and fought with the Khan of Bitlis and destroyed his lands and killed three thousand people. He has started to make this affair more complicated. Now my dear Khan, don't be annoyed. I have broken bread with you. One day you will see that on the basis of this peace treaty Malek Ahmad Pasha will invade the provinces of Diyarbekr, Erzerum, Akhiskha, and Van with seventy or eighty thousand troops and destroy them. Especially, when the felicitous Sultan says, "if I would campaign all the time against Persia, re-conquer the castle of Erevan, which was seized by my uncle Sultan Murad and put soldiers in the castles of Maku and Qotur, because the Persians broke the peace treaty and attacked my Pinyanesh province." The glorious Sultan saying this could not master his anger and therefore went hunting day and night. Now, my Khan, the conclusion of this affair has worsened. Before the entire army attacks this area, you better collect these sheep and hand them over to the pasha, otherwise the peace treaty cannot be renewed, if this is not done then regard this as Ottoman land. For five or ten years the army will not leave this land, and the Shah will call you to account. You better consult with farsighted, unbiased people." When I said this, the Khan said:

"May Red Morteza 'Ali strike him whoever has done this to me," and his eyes became wet. Khvajeh Naqdi said: "By God, my Khan, the envoy Evliya Agha has spoken well. Truly, he has eaten your bread in sincerity. But, my Khan, you see that the Ottomans have not forgotten that we have put troops in the castles of Maku and Qotur, which is contrary to the treaty. It is better to bring together a few thousand sheep and return them to the owners. My advice is that you should reward Evliya Agha." Everybody was pleased and astonished about this advice.

This humble person said: "My Khan, I have brought letters from our vizier to the sultans who are under your authority and all of them said that 'we are under the orders of the Khan'. Early in the morning you should send messengers to them so that they come and you take counsel with them." After saying this I came to the guesthouse. Our people, the khan's people, and one thousand troops took us to our guesthouse with much honor. I told all our people to behave well.

Our 'Ali Bey said: "My Sultan, we tolerate whatever this Persian is doing, but they are cursing the four chosen companions. We should kill those cursing Qizilbash." This humble servant said to my people: "People, be polite. You can make the world a better place. For a few days just don't go to the bazaar."

Then we wrote a letter to the Khan of Urmiyeh and asked for removing the cursers and we asked for a chief of the royal slaves to guard our doors and sent the letter to our conductor of guests with the request to forward it to the Khan. At this time, inside the city of Urmiyeh the public criers were crying "the Khan has banned the cursing of the four chosen one, while the Ottomans are here. All the professional cursers and dervishes are forbidden to stay in the city." God be praised that we were freed from the wagging tongues of the unbelievers. The honorable Khan gave this humble servant a well-furnished room with twenty pillows, six eiderdowns of gold brocade, round pillows, many utensils and vessels, three bundles of clothes and different robes of honor, ambergris and aloe, six master cooks, six carts with supplies, ten carts with firewood, and six carts with all kinds of fruit. Furthermore, a very polite chief of the royal slaves came to serve as our doorkeeper. Morteza Pasha's *agha* was sent to the garden of the *shahbandar*. Similar provisions were sent to him.

Later, in the afternoon, the Khan sent the master of ceremonies. He said: "Please come, the Khan is asking for you." The letters from the *aghas* of Van, the request of Mahmudi Deli Ebrahim Bey for the return of the sheep, and our Lord the Pasha's gifts for the Khan, viz. horses with their accoutrements, with their beautifully decorated saddles, saddle blankets made of *diba* were brought by well-dressed grooms. The people of the Khan went before us and they took two full-blood horses to the Khan. When he saw the first horse with its studded tack he was beside himself and when he saw the second horse he was astounded. I said: "Pasha, these are the horses from your father the Caesar. Excuse and accept them from us. To you Khan he sends many greeting together with theses horses and (other) gifts and says that if our son, the great Khan, accepts the petition of the poor people of Pinyanish we will send him a number of full-blood horses and we will make him our son in this world and the world to come. God willing, I will ask the king for the Khanship of Erevan. May he make the land of his father prosper." The Khan became extremely pleased with these words and said: "Malek vizier is our father. He made us distinguished among our peers. May God increase his honor." When saying this he looked at the studded stirrup made of pure silver and he mounted it without using the stirrup and galloped for a while and enjoyed it tremendously. He tied the two horses with a silver leash.

He went to the Government House and said: "Evliya Agha, God willing, we will gradually get the sheep from the mouth of the seven-headed dragon. Our secretary will write letters to all of those who recently have gone with us to plunder, to the leaders of the soldiers and to all the sultans, so that they all come." This humble servant found this an opportune moment and said: "My Khan, you should collect these sheep sooner. You will be free from any misfortune. I also will send the news to your father, the pasha, that so many sheep have been collected." He said: "I hear and obey, Evliya Agha." He said this and was very pleasant with me.

Then Morteza Pasha's *Agha* came and we ate delicious dishes. After dinner, when we came to our house, the Khan gave us three hundred *qorush* as bathhouse money and sent a Qarachuboq horse with a good Persian-style saddle and bridle.

The next day, the sultans of the province of Urmiyeh all came to the government house and in three days collected twenty thousand sheep. These were given to this humble person and immediately the sheep were given to the representatives of the Pinyanish people. Ten of our men went with them and they were sent to the Pasha in Van. We said: "We take ten percent and you take ten percent. God willing, after this we will send whatever sheep we collect." I said so in a letter.

The Khan became very glad because of the letter, and he was freed from sorrow and grief. That day we went hunting with the Khan, and then we played polo. In the promenade of the Kochagha Sultan garden the Khan gave a party for me and all the sultans. After dinner he said: "For my sake, give some presents to my dear Evliya Agha, because he has been sent from the land of Caesar as an envoy and we have to honor him." Earlier he had given an admonition to the people of Urmiyeh. Those eight sultans gave eight full-blood Qarachuboq horses, eight postal horses, two panther skins, five pieces of Kashan *qatifeh*,[29] ten Gujarat cottons and twenty pieces of colored Livorno fabrics, and they all apologized for its inadequacy. In the afternoon the drummers started beating, and together with our hunted game we entered Urmiyeh.

The next day, in the morning, the Khan came to be our guest. He brought ten platters of flavored food and we ate. But the Khan was anxious and had no peace of mind.

After breakfast he said: "My dear brother, by the soul of our dear prophet Mohammad, I am a Sunni, the son of Sunnis. By his four chosen companions, I have come to our blessed

---

29. *Qatifeh* has several meanings including that of velvet and satin, but its main characteristic is that of a fabric with a long pile, hence also the meaning of bath-towel or bath-robe.

threshold. Be truthful with me and whatever you say, say it in sincerity and justly. By God, to you and the vizier {Malek Ahmad Pasha}, my father, I pay attention. If I truly say, from you and him, has any *Agha* gone as yet to our great king?" This humble person said: "Yes, my Khan. Somebody known as Sari 'Ali Agha has gone to the shah with two hundred soldiers and with four full-blood horses as a gift along with letters of friendship."

The Khan said: "Truly, the spies came early. They came in the evening and said the same. My brother, you have spoken the truth."

This humble person said: "My Khan, we are believers in one God, lovers of the family (of the prophet) and servants of the viziers. Lies are forbidden to us. Especially, the refuge of prophethood (i.e., Mohammad) has said: 'Liars are not of my people.' Therefore, we tell the truth."

The Khan said: "For goodness sake, my dear Evliya. What was written in the letter? And for what reason has that *Agha* gone? Do you know?" I said:

"By God, my Khan. This has been an affair contrary to peace and prosperity. The *Agha* has gone to the Shah, and I have come to you my Khan on account of the problem of the sheep." When I said this the Khan slapped his hands on his knees {and said}:

"Woe to me. Woe to me, O Ganj 'Ali Khan," as if he lost his mind, and he took my hand into his hand and said:

"My dear Evliya, I now know you are a man of action who is pure of heart. This is all foreign to me. The Tabriz Khan, the old Qeytemaz Khan,[30] became the enemy of my soul when these sheep were plundered. But what is the solution to this?" This humble person said: "I agreed with him from the bottom of my heart and said:

"O Khan, my soul. I have received twenty thousand sheep from the sultans when they were in the city as well as other people, and you gave me presents. For the time being I will sent a letter to the Pasha by courier that forty thousand sheep have been received. I also will write to the Khan of Tabriz that I have received forty thousand sheep from Ganj 'Ali Khan, and I will announce this. If you want, I will send a letter with my friend 'Ali Agha, who is going to the court of the Shah, saying that forty thousand sheep have been received from [Ganj] 'Ali Khan and have been handed over and that the affair with the Pinayish has been finished and that peace has been restored. Your messenger will give the letter to 'Ali Agha, and 'Ali Agha will present our letter to the shah, and from every side the entire affair will be resolved easily. At the moment only twenty thousand are left to be collected." The Khan kissed my hand and said:

"Ganj 'Ali Khan may be your sacrifice. Help me." He took five hundred Persian gold coins from his breast pocket as well as five pieces of ambergris and ten branches of Khotanese musk and gave them to me.

"By my life. I will give you more things. The letters will reach your *agha* before he even gets to the shah's palace. You write and you will see. Today I will give you, in whatever way you want, fifteen thousand sheep." He said this and went to his palace. He held court and in two days he gathered thirty thousand sheep from the notables and Sultans of the province.

By God's will, sheep were everywhere and one sheep weighing thirty to forty *vaqiyeh* was sold for one *bisti shahi*, i.e., twenty *aqches*, showing how valuable a region this is. On the third

---

30. This Qeytamaz Khan is not found among the governors of Tabriz, see Nasiri, *Titles*, p. 156.

Alkou – Lake Urmiyeh

day there was a big court session (divan), and he gave this humble servant twenty-thousand sheep from the Urmiyeh divan. He also gave the Pasha ten thousand more sheep, as well as ten Qarachuboq horses, twenty strings of male camels, five strings of female Tavusi camels, five strings of she-camels loaded with Isfahani Persian mats and carpets and five very beautiful Georgian slaves, and to this humble servant three thousand sheep, three full-blood horses, two Persian small rugs, one sable coat, three Georgian slaves, five camels, and from his own wardrobe one set of gold-stitched and printed clothes, one Asadi sword with a gilt scabbard; he distributed ten *tumans* in *aqches* among my people. He said: "I apologize."

To each one of my retainers he gave one *tuman 'abbasi*s in *aqche*s. To one hundred people he gave five hundred sheep and said: "May you enjoy it."

At the court of Urmiyeh, I gave these aforementioned sheep in the presence of the notables of the province to the Pinyanish tribe, and I counted them to be about forty-thousand. We received from the Khan of the Pinyanish a deed denoting the closure of the claim and the lawful settlement of the conflict, and a document was drawn up by the Islamic court.

This humble servant gave all the sheep, the gifts for the Pasha as well as the other gifts, a total of fifty, to my servants, and I made our 'Ali Bey their chief and told him: "Early in the morning take all these through Shah Gedigi (the royal pass) to the Ottoman lands, to the *ojaq* of the Ghaziqeran, but on no account go to the Qotur valley. You should not stop until you arrive with all sheep at Van. Otherwise the Pasha will claim tithe from these twenty {thousand} sheep, because it is lost property. First, the twenty thousand sheep which are sent will go to their owners, then you kiss the blessed hands of the Pasha." I gave these instructions and in the presence of the Khan gave them the letters to the Pasha together with the sheep. I sent fifty of my retainers with one hundred Pinyanish Kurds, and this humble servant remained in Urmiyeh with fifty people.

That day and night our people passed through Shah Gedigi (the royal pass). When the news came that they had entered Ottoman territory, I gave the abovementioned document about the closure of the claim given by the Pinyanish notables to the Khan. The Khan and all the people of the divan rejoiced. This humble servant sent a letter to the Khan of Tabriz saying: "I received all the sheep, and from the Pinyanish I received a document of the cessation of the claim." I wrote letters and gave them to the Khan, and I also gave a very eloquent and detailed letter to ʿAli Agha, who was going to the Shah, describing the good treatment given by the Khan and all his subjects. The Khan was very pleased and almost danced of joy. At that same time we sent a letter post-haste to the Khan of Tabriz and another one to ʿAli Agha, who was en route to Isfahan. Then we found joy and satisfaction and later enjoyed ourselves in the city of Urmiyeh.

One day, the Khan said:

THE QUESTION OF THE GREAT KHAN OF THE CITY OF URMIYEH CONCERNING THE REASON FOR THE KILLING OF IPSHIR MOSTAFA PASHA

"O my dear Evliya. Please tell me truly. Why do the Ottoman kings always destroy and kill their viziers? Why did they kill Qara Mostafa Pasha, Hezarpareh Ahmad Pasha, Yusof Pasha the conqueror of Hania,[31] Saleh Pasha, Koja Vizier and the like? Especially now, they killed and cut off the head of a peerless vizier like Ipshir, who was a statesman, a hero of the time, and knowledgeable concerning the Koran. In good he was good; in bad he was bad. Why did they kill him? Tabriz, nay Iran was trembling before his power like an autumn leaf. Alas, the Ottoman state spills blood unjustly. Do they neither fear God nor are they ashamed of the prophet. The injustice done to the Asaf-like Ipshir was not done to Asaf-e Barkhiya nor to the martyrs of Karbala. He was a patron of the poor, the orphans and weak, and a man of God and a great vizier. The cruel Ottomans killed an innocent vizier. It would be great if you can you explain this to me?"

This humble author said: "If my Khan asked from this humble servant the reason for the killing of Ipshir, you have to ask wisdom from Aristotle and a cure from Loqman."

The Khan said: "Yes, my life. My ears are with you, I am listening."

This humble servant said: "At one time Sultan Mohammad sent his seal to Ipshir in Aleppo, and in a letter said: 'You will come immediately and go to the island of Malta.' When the seal reached Ipshir, he said: 'The High Porte is the place of execution when they want to kill a vizier.' Due to his evil thoughts he tendered one thousand excuses and pretexts and stayed away from the High Porte for five months. When he was the master of the horse of Sultan Murad, he went to campaign in Persia, and at the foot of Erevan castle his soldiers were killed and he himself wounded and his foot became lame. Because of this he wanted to take revenge on the Persians, and as the commanding general he made elaborate preparations to go against Erevan.

In the end he realized that Persia did not offer any cause for war. Eventually when he was himself the governor of Van he sent a message to the sheep owners of the Pinyanish tribe from Aleppo saying: "I will increase your allowance if you plunder the Persians and act contrary to the peace, but do not fire and do not beat the drums." When they received this good news from

---

31. Chania on Crete was taken in 1645 at the cost of the lives of some forty thousand Ottoman soldiers.

Ipshir, the Pinyanish accepted it with joy, and these short-sighted Kurdish people started to engage in brigandage and sheep stealing from Urmiyeh. When people like you complained to Ipshir he closed his eyes. Eventually, you were forced to attack the Pinyanish tribe and plunder their property and cattle and attack their settlements with musket and cannon fire and kill a number of them, and you captured three hundred of them. Then the Kurds described their sad situation to Ipshir, who from Aleppo wrote to the Sultan: 'My king, I am campaigning against the Persians but I am not asking you for any soldiers or supplies.' When at New Year a summary report was submitted to the Sultan, saying that a campaign against Erevan is necessary, he showed it to our Malek Pasha, who said: 'God forbid, my king, never do this. The Persians have not done anything against the peace. If anything has been done against the peace it was done by the Kurds. It is absolutely necessary that Ipshir comes to Istanbul. It is better to send someone and recall Ipshir.' Instantly couriers departed with the royal decree to Ipshir saying: 'You have to come to the High Porte. If you bring the king of Persia in chains to my court I will not allow it.' When this decree reached Ipshir he had no choice but to come to Istanbul. One day the Sultan said: 'O Tutor, I sent my seal to Aleppo. Why did not you come to the High Porte in ten days like my other viziers, but stay for five months in Aleppo? Why did you want to campaign against Persia and abrogate the peace of Sultan Murad? To this question you sent me letters several times, and now you have come to the High Porte. Why did you trouble my old viziers and ask for money? Why did you instigate the Pinyanish Kurd and send them to plunder Persia?' From this reproof and criticism from the king, the refuge of the world, the army leaders knew that his attitude had changed negatively towards Ipshir. Those army leaders exaggerated and said: 'Our king, we will kill this Ipshir Pasha.' Then they took him and cut of his head and put it in the Hippodrome. The reason for the killing of Ipshir was due to this incident of the sheep and the plunder you did in the land of the Pinyanish, and originally it was because of Ipshir's opposition to the peace."

When I said this, Khoja Naqdi said: "O Ottoman, may I be your sacrifice. Don't you see that for violating the peace with Persia a wise and valiant vizier like Ipshir has been killed?" The Khan said: "If that is the case let him kill such a man who is trying to instigate trouble and is a heretic. May the hands and arms of the Ottomans be strong. Let the people that they kill always be corrupt men." Khoja Bakhtiyar said: "Evliya Agha, if this is so, the Ottomans have shown great respect for Persia by killing Ipshir. Out of fear for him we could not sleep in peace in our homes. The Shah of Iran, when he heard of the killing of Ipshir, said: 'Now, I am the ruler of the seven climes.' We won't hide from you because of the killing of Ipshir, we celebrated for one day and one night and organized an illumination of the walls and the city. We had heard about Ipshir's intention to come to Iran." From my truthful words the Khan was very pleased and grateful and became very friendly with me.

Description of the Castle of Urmiyeh, its layout and its strength

This castle in common parlance is originally called Toprak Castle (the earthen castle). But the Persian historians call it Sur-e tila-ye Ghazan (the golden fort of Ghazan), because in the year 694 [1295] Mohammad Shah Ghazan built it. The Mongols call it Urumiyeh; the Persians call it Rumiyeh-ye Kubra. Some historians call it Turkestan-e Iran because there are many Turkmen saints. Later, in the year 932 [1526], Shah Tahmasp extended it. Then Farhad Pashad, Khadem

Ja`far Pasha, Tavashi Sulayman Pasha and Cheghal-oghlu Senan Pasha all added buildings to it. It is a strong castle, all of whose buildings have been constructed with fine yellow mud mixed with wheat stalks and reed roots. The entire exterior of its gates and walls has been covered with white plaster; it is a beautiful castle like a white swan. It does not have crenellated walls. It has been outfitted all over with shooting holes, towers and bastions. In the west it has a hidden iron gate. Inside the castle there is a mansion for the Khan. There is one Ghazan mosque, but there are no mosque-goers. There are wheat warehouses, water wells and three hundred rooms, but there are no caravanserais, bathhouses and bazaars. Its circumference is eleven thousand paces. It has seven redoubts and is quadrangular. From the moat the height of the wall is seventy royal cubits. The thickness of the wall is thirty cubits. Horsemen can play polo on top of it.

It has a wide moat, which is like the moat of Famagusta castle on the island of Cyprus or like the castle of Rhodes. The master-builder first began to dig the moat and then used the excavated earth as mud mixed with other materials to build the castle in a perfect manner and at a the same time to make the moat forty fathoms deep and eighty cubits wide;[32] it surrounds the entire castle. Its circumference is fifteen thousand paces. From the shooting slits long metal bars extend over the moat. Every night, torches are hung from those bars and illuminate the castle and all watchmen, ushers and guards call *khoda khub* and keep watch until morning. Every Friday they hang pennants, flags and banners from the castle walls for decoration.

It has four thousand soldiers. The chief of the royal slaves is the holder of the key and commands all the guards. There are ushers, gunners and armorers. Since the time of Ozdamir-oghlu Othman Pasha, it has seven thousand barrels of gun-powder, four times one hundred thousand cannon balls[33] and one hundred and ten pieces of small and big cannons. In the lower storey there are seventy pieces of large caliber cannon, which are similar to the cannons that stand by the gates of Erzerum and Tabriz. But this Persian castle constitutes a protective wall at the very border with the Ottomans. Over the moat there is a wooden bridge, and every night they raise it. Inside the castle they beat small and big kettle drums, and play the trumpets, horns, and hautboy and announce the watch.

Outside the castle there are no buildings. In the middle of the Urmiyeh plain, this beautiful castle stands out like a white swan. Beside the moat there is a polo field and a small, useful palace like that of Khovarnak.[34] Except for this wall there is nothing else. The guarding of the castle is in Persian hands. Although the castle is built of mud, around the gate and walls and inside the moat no plants or herbs grow, which amazes me. To the southeast is a lake, whose water is bitter like poison. It is at a distance of one stage from the castle.

The city of Urmiyeh is situated to the north of the castle at a distance of one cannon shot. Although this castle is far from the lake, it has a coastal climate, so that summer and winter vegetables are not lacking. In winter it snows a lot, but soon disappears. From the eastern side of the strong walls until the capital of Azerbaijan, pleasant Tabriz, is sixteen *farsakh*s. If the lake is calm, it takes one day to Tabriz. This strong castle in Azerbaijan forms one separate khanate.

---

32. This would make the moat 73 meter deeps and about 38 meters wide, which is very hard to believe.
33. This is another exaggeration by Evliya.
34. The legendary Sasanian palace of Khovarnak, which No`man, Bahram Gur's tutor, built for his pupil.

Description of the Khan of Urmiyeh's troops

In the entire province there are eleven sultans, and the entire army of the Khan and the sultans consists of fifteen thousand soldiers and all of them are paid by the shah.[35] Apart from these soldiers, there are in total twenty thousand people. The city has a police chief, a mayor, a clerk, a chief of the ushers, a conductor of guests, a master of ceremonies, a qazi, a mufti and an overseer of the sayyeds. One mufti with a special feathered *taj* has been sent by the Shah to convert all the Shafe`is to the Ja`fari faith, and he was still urging people to convert to the false Shi`ite faith. All soldiers walk around fully armed, but they are not very able and brave.

Description of Turkestan-e Iran, i.e., the city of Urmiyeh in Azerbeijan

Urmiyeh is a prosperous city with gardens and orchards, whose circumference is seventeen thousand paces. With the gardens and orchards, a horseman can with difficulty go around it in a day. It is situated at one cannon-shot distance from the castle, and the lake is situated at one stage towards the east. It has no walls at all. In former times it had a moat, but with the passage of time it has filled up with earth, but it has fortified gates on all sides. It is a very old city.

Since its people are Sunnis, the Ottomans would not plunder it. Therefore, it is one prosperous and dynamic city. Its fist founder is the `Abbasid caliph Harun al-Rashid. Thereafter it passed from government to government. It has sixty quarters and six thousand wells, and the walls of the houses are made of earth, and they are covered with good-smelling earth. The palace of the Khan of Urmiyeh is like that of Eram (i.e., paradise). It has seventy courtyards, estrades and kiosks. There are rooms for servants.

There are mansions of the mayor and the clerk and Khoja Naqdi, which are named after them. The Sheikh of Urmiyeh, who is buried in Diyarbekr, has a mansion named after him and also the Urmiyeh Saray, because a Sheikh of Urmiyeh is buried there.[36] There are many (of the Sheikh of Urmiyeh's) relatives and family members who live in the city, as well as the mansion of the clerk, the chief of merchants and the judge, and other mansions with beautiful promenades. There a total of eighty mosques.

The Sultan Uzun Hasan Mosque. When Sultan Hasan was king of Azerbaijan he built it. He was defeated in battle by Abu'l-Fath Sultan Mohammad. He died in Tabriz, and this beautiful mosque was left unfinished.[37] It was later completed by his son, Ya`qub Shah. Its length is eighty paces, and its width is fifty. It has eight domes, one minaret, which is very well decorated and the door facing the prayer niche is extremely well decorated; it is a wondrous door. But the mosque is not frequented by people in this land because there is (no) just and pure Imam, and

---

35. On the system of payment of the army during the Safavid period see Floor, *Safavid Government*, pp. 128-211.

36. Apparently this family made it its business to provide Sheikhs to the Naqshbandi order. For one of them, who was quite active in Diyarbekr, where he was known as the Sheikh of Urmiyeh, see van Bruinessen et al., *Diyarbekr*, p. 227, n. 168.

37. This battle took place on 11 August 1473, see *Cambidge History of Iran*, vol. 6, p. 179.

therefore they cannot perform the five prayers. Therefore, everybody worships individually. They say "ritual prayer is the same as invocation," and without saying an invocation they go away.[38]

The inside of the mosque is so well decorated and geometrically well-built that it is hard to describe. This is true for the dome as well. In the middle of the courtyard there is a large *shafe`i* basin, whose water is like that of the *Kowthar* pond of Paradise.[39]

Around the courtyard there are various pillars that are topped by blue domes. The courtyard has three doors. While sight-seeing the mosque, the muezzin started the call to prayer and said: "I bear witness that Mohammad is the prophet of God," and then he added twice, "`Ali is the friend of God." After the call to prayer he began to say: "O enemies of the family of `Ali and martyrs of Karbala ...," and relating similar stories; but seeing us he was dumbfounded.[40]

When the muezzin came down from the minaret, I said: "Bring that curser." When he was brought down, the muezzin was whipped in accordance with Sunni traditions of beating heretics. He shouted: "Help me O `Ali. One time suffices O Vali." I said, say: "With the help of Abu Bakr, with the love of Omar and the love of Othman." I gave him one hundred extra lashes and threw the cursed one several times into the pond and thus purified him, and saying: "Let the dog go," I freed him.[41]

Apart from this we did not hear any untoward saying. In short, the Sultan Hasan Mosque is a good one, but the people are terrible.

Then there is the `Ali Khan mosque, which is beautiful, the Ja`far Pasha mosque, the Farhad Pasha mosque and the Qochagha Sultan mosque, – the mosque of the ancestor of the Sheikh of Urmiyeh. But the Kalantar mosque and the Sheikh Akay mosque are the famous ones; the other mosques are just simple small mosques. In this city no buildings are covered with lead.

There are six madrasehs, three Sufi convents, forty elementary schools for boys, eleven caravanserais and many bathhouses.

The Sheikh of Urmiyeh bathhouse is a big building and an old place of pilgrimage. If a sick man goes there he will be cured; it has a big basin which is well-lit and it has a pleasant ambiance. The Kalantar bathhouse is a beautiful bath, and its masseurs are youths. The Darugheh bathhouse and the Qurqud Khan bathhouse are among the bathhouses that have basins. Several hundred houses have their own bath.

It has two hundred royal bazaars where every shop is decorated with thousands of different colored flowers. The noses of the buyers and sellers are delighted by the variety of pleasant fragrances. In this land the barbers are called *salmani*.

All the shops of the barbers, tailors and saddlers and the shops of the bazaars are laid out like a chessboard. Like in Damascus and Aleppo it has ponds and jet fountains. In the coffeehouses

---

38. The test has "namas du`adir," thus making a distinction between *namaz* or obligatory ritual prayer and *du`a*, which is a private invocation.

39. Koran 108 (*al-Kowthar*).

40. This is the Shi`ite credo by adding that "`Ali of the *Vali* of God." It is also of interest and odd that Evliya seems to consider the martyrdom of the Shi`ite Imams at Karbala an *afsaneh* or tale.

41. This is a most incredible story, since it is highly unlikely that a Sunni Ottoman functionary on official business in the Shi`ite city of Urmiyeh beats a muezzin for pronouncing the Shi`ite formula of faith and then lives to write to write about it. *Va Allahu a`lam*.

there are singers, minstrels, musicians, dancers and young dancing boys, and they are very well decorated. They prepare coffee from Yemen, tea, fennel, jujube, milk pudding, sugar sherbet, special milk [?] (*laban-e khass*). They put a variety[42] of spices and mixtures thereof in them. In every coffeehouse the fragrance of the flowers exhilarates the spirits of the lovers and beloveds.[43] All coffeehouses are surrounded on four sides by flower gardens and orchards and every corner is a world to itself. Every shop is a very mine of wealth. There are beautiful dancing boys, who wear a headband of a flowery pattern.

One drapers' hall is like a castle, whose four gates open up to the Chaharbagh and the Kagheh bazaar. It is a beautiful bazaar adorned with domes and covered stalls. There are rich merchants. All kinds of goods are there from everywhere, such as brocade, watered silk, *dara'i*, brocade, gauze, cloth shot with gold-thread in plenty. Their cooks and bakers are out-of-this world. And also the system of price control by the governors, which is known as Sheikh Safi, as well as the management and the purity of their coins is unrivalled. They write: "There is no God but God, and Mohammad is the prophet of God, and ʿAli is the friend of God," on their *ʿabbasi*s and *bisti*s. Whoever meddles with or counterfeits these coins is not tolerated for one moment and is executed.[44] All the vendors of beverages and food stuffs sell these by the ʿAli weight. Even wheat, eggs, cooked chicken, and white bread and in short all things in vessels they sell by weighing it. Even the cooks sell soups, kebabs and rice by weight. Who would dare to cheat Sheikh Safi`s fixed prices? Because whoever cheats is immediately blinded by putting a hot needle under his eyelids or by placing a heated ball on his head; or they are cut open and have their guts taken out, and others they open and take out their heart. There is an excellent government in accordance with the rules of ʿAli. All the buildings in the city, the beautiful gardens and orchards are irrigated (by a river) and the drinking water for the people comes from the west side of the city from Mount Jevlan and the Harir and Enzeli Mountains, and after watering the city (the river) flows into Lake Urmiyeh in the east.

In Urmiyeh province there are one hundred and fifty prosperous villages. Each one of them is a big village with two and three thousand houses, gardens and orchards, a large mosque, a caravanserai, a bathhouse and royal bazaars. In total it has forty-one towns and fifty strong castles. If need be, they can raise twenty thousand soldiers from here, but they have recorded three hundred thousand peasants.

Description of the beverages and foodstuffs of greater Urmiyeh

First, there are seven types of wheat, which are as good as the wheat from Syrian Hawran, and its barley is as good as the barley of Sivas. Its beans are as heavy as two derhams; its full-grained fava beans cannot be found anywhere else. Other cereals are similar. According to the mayor, it has twenty thousand gardens and orchards. All its grapes are more juicy and delicious than the Zeyn grapes of Syria, the Muscat grapes of Bozja ada and the grapes of Bazarkoy near Istanbul. Even the people's language reflects this. If the peasants see a youth accompanied by a man with ulterior

---

42. Evliya Celebi has "several thousand" which is not possible, of course.

43. Coffeehouses were places where males went to find, among other things, boys to make love to, see Floor, *Sexual Relations*, pp. 327-28.

44. On the coinage see Willem Floor, *The Economy of Safavid Persia* (Wiesbaden, 2000), chapter 3.

motives they say: "The young boy is like a bruised Urmiyeh grape inside a box." Now in common parlance it has become a proverb to refer to a fragrant, juicy and fresh grape.[45]

Among the other excellent fruits there are seventy different kinds, but its *peyghambar* and *melecheh* pears are peerless. They are so juicy that it oozes from them; its plums and apricots[46] are so tender as if they have no weight, and their kernels are as delicious as almonds. Because of its good climate, its beauties are well-known, but their scholars are not, although there are many pious people. There are even Sunnis who secretly perform the Friday prayer. They are all dervishes of the Khvajegan order, who inhabit the shrine of Qochagha Sultan. They say that the stellar constellation of its foundation is situated in Virgo, in the house of Mercury. Therefore, each ear of its plants produce a "hundred grains" and its flowers are like the shop of a druggist and refresh the noses of the onlookers.

It is a major town in the land of Azerbaijan. By being in the hands of the Persians it has become a mediocre one. On its west is Shahrezur; on its north is Salmas and the town of Tasuj; to the east is the city of Tabriz; and to the south is the city of Ardabil. Since Urmiyeh is in the midst of these four, it is called "town-in-the-middle" by the historians of Iran. If a young man goes on horseback he will go to the city of [Van] and Erevan in four stages. But this humble author in order to see the world did it in five to six hours.[47]

DESCRIPTION OF LAKE URMIYEH. Some call it the Sea of Urmiyeh, the Domboli Sea, the Debil (sic; Ardabil) and Tabriz Sea. It is a lake known by the names of the cities around it. Similarly, Lake Van is called Lake Vastan, Erjeysh Sea and ʿAdeljavaz Sea. But there is a long distance between Tabriz and Lake Urmiyeh. Since Urmiyeh is closer, it is called Lake Urmiyeh. It is a brackish lake. There are several hundred fishing boats.[48] These boats transport traveling merchants. On the east is the city of Tabriz; on the west there is the castle of Domboli and the city of Urmiyeh; and to the south is the city of Ardabil, which is very far away.[49] Its circumference is bigger than Lake Van. If a man walks normally he can go around Lake Van in eight days, whereas this one is done in twelve days. Its depth is seventy fathoms.[50] The historians of Iran and the historian Mighdisi[51] write that when the Holy Prophet was born in the holy city of Mecca, the Arch of Khosrow

---

45. It is interesting to note that Mostawfi, *Nozhat al-Qolub*, p. 98 has a similar expression used in Tabriz. "The Tabrizians have a phrase when they see a fortunate and wealthy man in uncouth clothes: "He is like fresh grapes in a ripped fruit basket."

تبارزه اگر صاحب حسنی را با لباس ناسزا یابند گویند: "انگور خلوقی بی چه در، درّ سوه اندرین" یعنی انگور مرغوب در سبد دریده.

46. We read *zardisi* instead of *zendesi* as Kahravan has it.

47. It is impossible to travel from Urmiyeh to Van in six hours. Therefore, Evliya Chelebi must have meant days rather than hours.

48. In "The Travels of a Merchant," in Lord Stanley ed. *Travels to Tana and Persia* (London, 1873), part 2, p. 171 it is reported, "There are also a good many fish, which are caught in a lake, a day's journey distant from the city, which is salt like those of Vastan and Van." This source is the only one to suggest that there was fish in Lake Urmiyeh whereas all other sources explicitly state that there is not any fish in it.

49. Ardabil is situated to the northeast of Urmiyeh.

50. As one fathom is about 1.8 meters this results in 126 meters. However, in reality its deepest point is about 16 meters.

51. Evliya often cites the Armenian historian Mighdisi about whom, and about whose work, nothing is known, see Robert Dankoff, "An Armenian Source for the *Seyahatname*," Wiener Zeitschrift für die Kunde des Morgenlandes 76 (1986), pp. 73–79.

and the dome of Aya Sofiya were destroyed, and that same night the city which was in the place of this lake, which was called Panjom, sank to the bottom of the earth and this lake appeared in its place. God knows best.

From all sides forty large and small rivers flow into this lake and their names are:

The Seylan [Savalan] River which waters Ardabil and comes to the lake.

THE RIVER KEHRAN comes from the castle of Nehrevan.

JEVLAN SPRING, which irrigates Urmiyeh.

THE RIVER DAVDAN comes from the Hakkari region and, passing the Pinyanish (region) and Berduq castle, flows into this lake near Urmiyeh.

Since the other names were not known, they are not given here.

{This humble author} says that of whatever I am not certain, I do not write about it. I follow the maxim: "Do what is required."

Inside this lake there are twelve large inhabited islands. One is called:

JAZIREH-YE KABUTAR {i.e., Pigeon Island}. Its circumferences is ten *mil*s (= ca. 20 km). It is a prosperous large island. It has a castle built on a steep rock with guards, armorers and slender royal cannons. The soldiers earn their livelihood by fishing. It is a strong castle. Another island is called:

THE ISLAND OF HARSEK. It has a beautiful castle on a high hill. There are guards, gunners and a sufficient number of military supplies. Since these islands are easily accessible to the governor of Tabriz, it is under his administration.[52] The soldiers are all fishermen.

CONCERNING STRANGE AND ODD THINGS. In these two islands every night fishermen catch fish without nets, fishing line, or tranquilizer.[53] They catch them as follows. There are small silvery fish in this lake, which the fishermen catch, and put wicks in its oil. At night they light these wicks in lamps and go around in the lake. The fish themselves come to the surface of the water, being attracted by the light, and gather around the boats and the fishermen catch them. It is interesting that if they make another kind of light and go onto that lake for ten days they do not catch fish.

THE TOMBS OF SAINTS AND SHEIKHS IN URMIYEH. Light of knowledge, lamp of creation, candle of the world, lamp of sanctuary, pillar of the spiritual world, mine of celestial wisdom, doubtless truth, invisible dweller of seclusion,

THE BLESSED SHEIKH QOCHAGHA SULTAN. His family goes back to the Caliph Abu Bakr. He is one of the great sheikhs of the Khvajegan order.[54] While he was living in Diyarbekr, the conqueror of Baghdad, Sultan {Murad}, martyred the Sheikh of Urmiyeh, whose ancestor was this

---

52. There are 102 islands in Lake Urmiyeh. However, there is no island called Kabutar or Hersek. Perhaps Goyun (sheep) and Eshshek (donkey) were meant. Javadi, *Peyramun*, p. 31. The *Farhang-e Joghrafiya-ye Shahrestanha-ye Keshvar (Shahrestân-e Orumiyeh)* (Tehran 1379/2000).

53. *Marg-e mahi* (q.v. Dehkhoda) is a plant (*Anamirta coculus* – Coq du Levant) whose seeds are thrown into the water to sedate fish.

54. Khvajegan is the former name of the Naqshbandiyeh order.

Qochagha Sultan. The late dear one in the year [-], when the Persians retook Urmiyeh, moved to Diyarbekr, where eventually in the year 1038 [1628-29] he was martyred by Murad Ghazi at the instigation of unbelievers. How he was martyred has been written in our travels in Diyarbekr.[55] The ancestor of the beloved martyr, Qochagha Sultan, is buried in the city of Urmiyeh. His tomb is now a sacred shrine. It is surrounded by gardens and it houses more than three hundred dervishes. Its houses, gardens and orchards are prosperous. The Persians believe in him, and travelers benefit from his bounty.

MANIFESTATION OF HIS SPIRITUALITY. When Qochagha Sultan died in the year [-] he was buried in this tomb. One of his dervishes was very wealthy, and in the year [-] one of the khans of Shah Kur Khodabandeh, Genchel Tuqmaq Khan, became envious of the aforesaid dervish, and when he tortured the man to get his wealth the dervish said: "My Khan, for the sake of the late Qochagha set me free." The unbeliever Khan replied: "What do I care for your Qochagha Sultan," and he killed the dervish and took all his wealth.

Many years later the noble body of the deceased was found to be shining as crystal, white and pure like cotton. Tuqmaq Khan said: "Hey, hey by asceticism and magic he might have put himself in this shape. Put him immediately in a kilim and bring him to the moat next to the castle." Those cruel men brought the body of Qochagha Sultan to that place and brought several hundred camel and cartloads of wood and made a fire like Nirmud did, into which they threw the beloved body.[56] When it was thrown into the fire seven times these words were heard: "O God, O God, I am the second Abraham." After seven hours the fire died down, and it was found that by the power of God from the ashes of that body a saint had been created. People who saw this cried and wept and went to Tuqmaq Khan and cursed him.

Then a group of dervishes collected the ashes that had formed into a saint, and together with thousands of prayers they buried it in his tomb. Therefore, in the *Manaqeb-e Ovliya-ye Kazeruni* (Manifestations of the Saints of Kazerun),[57] there is a special two-genuflection prayer, which refers to this incident.

Thereafter, even before the fire died out in the place where the blessed body of the sheikh was burnt, rose gardens and flowerbeds came into being. Up to now it is a place of pilgrimage, to the south of Urmiyeh Castle, near the polo field. It is so covered with flowers and plants that if a man on horseback passes he cannot be seen. It grows by itself. There are no traces of buildings. The people believe "that this rose garden is the place where the ashes of the blessed Qochagha Sultan have fallen." Truly in other places there are not such flowery places.

THE RESULT OF THE MIRACLES OF QOCHAGHA SULTAN. When Kur Sultan Khodabandeh heard of what happened to the body of Qochagha Sultan at the hands of Genchel Tuqmaq Khan, he left Qazvin and came to Urmiyeh. He destroyed some parts of the gardens of Qochagha and plundered the fruits of its orchards.

---

55. See van Bruinessen et al., *Diyarbekr*, p. 185.

56. This refers to the legend that Nimrod threw Abraham into a fire, who, however, emerged unscathed. Koran 21: 68-69.

57. This may refer to a manuscript about Sheikh Abu Eshaq Kazeruni, the founder of the Morshediyeh order (tenth century).

Kel Tuqmaq Khan said to the Shah: "Sire, we should destroy and annihilate the convents of the Sunnis."

Kur Khodabandeh replied: "My dear Tuqmaq Khan, how did you found this Qochagha, and how did you burn him? If you love red Morteza ʿAli and the twelve Imams, explain it well to me." The Khan said: "O Sire, the Sunnis of the city have started openly to perform Friday prayers. In front of their dead they say: *Vahdahu la sharika lahu* (there is no God but God).[58] Finally, this servant killed several Sunnis and soldiers. I burnt their Qochagha in the fire. My king, I do not know what magic this is. After so many years, this old Qochagha, when I opened his tomb, was white as cotton wool and every part of his corpse was fresh. Disregarding this fact I burnt him in the fire, but everyone heard his shout: "*Ya Hay, yah hay*' (O God, O God)."

Then Kur Khodabandeh said: "Bravo Tuqmaq Khan. They call you Sunni, while you are their bitter enemy. May my bread be lawful to you!" He then put a golden hat (*taj*) on his head and dressed him in a beautiful colored dress. (The Shah said): "Who are the soldiers that you sent to burn Qochagha?" (Tuqmaq replied): "Sire, these are five of them, who put Qochagha into the fire." The Shah Kur Khodabandeh again said: "We will reward them for what they did."

Then they went to the place where they burnt Qochagha's blessed body. Tuqmaq Khan, his children, those who ate his bread and those who were known to have burnt Qochagha, all seven hundred of them, were brought with their hands bound behind them into (the Shah's) presence, and he said: "You faithless Tuqmaq Khan, you are worthy to be burnt. The late Qochagha Sultan, lover of the (Holy) Family, was a great saint, who passed away from this world to the next many years ago. Without having seen him and known him, why did you have so much enmity towards him? In spite of seeing him fresh out of the grave, you burnt Qochagha in the fire just as the Jews burnt the prophet Georgius.[59] I came today to revenge him." He immediately ordered a fire to be prepared, in spite of the fact that he was worthy of the flame of God's wrath. As the saying goes: "Whoever knocks on the door eventually it will open." (*man daqqa duqqa*) I will burn these Jews, so that not only in Iran but in the whole world the story will be told." He then prepared a huge fire, and in front of Tuqmaq Khan he first burned all his children, and then he threw six hundred of his soldiers and the deceitful mufti and the judges who gave a legal opinion (*fatva*) into the fire.

In short, there are now in Iran many old people who remember the burning, the blessed Qochagha and of the seven hundred cursers who were burnt by Kur Khodabandeh, son of Shah Tahmasp.[60]

Later Kur Khodabandeh Shah repaired Qochagha Sultan's shrine in an indescribable way. It was near the guesthouse where this humble author was lodged. One of the Khvajegan dervishes took me around and showed me everything. Now it is a convent in a paradise-like garden.

---

58. Thus he implied that Shiʿites did not utter these words on such an occasion.

59. A prophet named Georgius is unknown to us. Evliya probably meant St. George (Mar Gurguis), who is believed to be buried in Mosul, where there is a St. George monastery. However, according to legend St. George was killed by the Romans.

60. Since Kur Mohammad Khodabandeh Shah or Oljeytu reigned from 1304 to 1316, this is clearly an embellishment to lend credence to this otherwise incredible story. Evliya links Shah Mohammad Khodabandeh (r. 1577-82) with his earlier namesake underlining the unreliability of this story and of Evliya as a reporter.

I heard of the praise of the beloved saint and bestowed a prayer on his soul. May God bless his tomb.

THE PLACE OF PILGRIMAGE OF BUZEVLI SULTAN. He is a saint of the Naqshbandi dervishes.

THE PLACE OF PILGRIMAGE OF SALEH EFENDI. He was of the Vahidi order[61] and he was chief *khalifeh* of Sheikh Safi, the great ancestor of the king of Iran, who is buried in Ardabil. The ceremony of Sheikh Safi, which was called "the candle extinguishing ceremony," was forbidden by Saleh Efendi after the blessed Sheikh Safi's death. May God bless his tomb.

(**AS TO THE MEANING OF THE EXTINGUISHING OF CANDLES**). In the year [...] the blessed Sheikh Safi came to the city of Ardabil as highest pillar of the Sufis. One day he achieved divine ecstasy and invited several thousand Moslems to the divine unity. Those who had been invited to the ceremony came with their wives, and all women came dressed with their burka, face and head veil and gloves over their hands, and in one corner many women became engaged in the divine unity ceremony. After dusk fell, in that dark night, {Sheikh Safi brought forth a lighted candle} and said: "Come my daughters, get into the divine unity ceremony along with my lamb-like sons." For seven hours men and women together prayed and invoked God and Sheikh Safi extinguished the candle and said: "Peace be upon all prophets and the messengers" and touched his face with his hands and said: "Each one of you embrace the person next to you and go to that person's house." In this confusion, due to the blessings of Sheikh Safi, every person found his own wife and daughter and went to his house.

Truly, in that confusion of the multitude and in the darkness, each person finding his own family is a miracle. In the life time of the blessed Sheikh Safi, he conducted several such 'candle extinguishing' ceremonies, and again the finding of one's family was repeated.

After him, several of his vice-regents performed the ceremony of 'the extinguishing of candles,' but they were unable to bring about that each man finds his own family. It was criticized that Persians took part in 'the candle extinguishing (ceremony).' Thereafter, this blessed Sheikh Saleh, who is now buried in Urmiyeh, forbade the ceremony of 'the extinguishing of candles.' Now it is practiced among the Persians, but only God knows.[62]

In the year 1056 [1646] I went from Erzerum to Persia and in the year 1060 [1650] again I went from Baghdad to the Persian city of Hamadan and Dargazin. In 1057 [1647] I went from the Crimea to Daghestan and from there I went to the Persian Iron Gate (Darband), Shirvan, Shamakhi, Gilan and Baku. From Urmiyeh, I visited Khoy, Marand, Tasuj, Qumlah and Tabriz, and in all these places I never saw the so-called candle extinguishing ceremony and the people who participate in it. But, the people of this world are evil, slanderous, perfidious and abusive.

---

61. We do not know of the existence of such an order.

62. On the candle extinguishing ceremony see note 292 supra. This alleged miracle by Sheikh Safi is not mentioned among his miracles in his biography. Ebn Bazzaz Ardabili, *Safvat al-Safa* ed. Gholam Reza Tabataba'i-Majd (Tabriz, 1373/1994).

In the province of Sivas, in the *sanjaq*s of Keskin, Bozok and Sunkur[63] there are 'candle extinguishing ceremonies,' in which everybody embraces his neighbor. I really do not know whether it is true.

After the conquest of Baghdad, this humble author traveled in those parts, and our master, the governor of Sivas I was engaged in several services in Keskin and Bozok, but I did not see anything like that. But again, the perfidious people of the provinces of Rumelia and Silistre,[64] in the districts of Deliorman and Karasu, and the province of Dobruca[65] say that there are husbands and wives who are lovers of the shah (Shahsevan), 'candle extinguishers' and wear the Safavid Sufi hat. God knows that I have gone fifty times to those parts and served in them, but I have not seen such unlawful activity. But there are men who do not pray and who deceive women. But in Syria there is a quarter for pimps. They collect 'the Persian fee' from people. In the mountains of the Druzes and Timani of Syria, there are those who are inconstant in faith and have manners that go many times beyond those of the Qizilbash, and we have described them in our travels in Damascus and Syrian Tripoli in volume [3] in detail.

THE PLACE OF PILGRIMAGE OF DAVDAN SULTAN. He is a Sheikh in the Komeyli order, and through him many miracles have been seen.[66]

THE PLACE OF PILGRIMAGE OF IMAM BOGHABAY. He was the prayer Imam of Uzun Hasan. Since he owned forty thousand buffaloes, he is called Boghabay. Every year in the month of Dhu`l-Hijjah, one night before the first night of the month, which they call the night of moon sighting, this Sheikh disappeared from the city of Urmiyeh. Three months later he returned with the hajjis to the city of Tabriz. According to this account, he would go in one night from Tabriz to `Arafat and, after performing the hajj, he would come back. Now his tomb is the place of pilgrimage for the people of faith. May God have mercy on all of them.

AN ACCOUNT OF THE STAGES, CASTLES AND LARGE CITIES SEEN WHEN WE WENT WITH THE LETTERS FROM THE KHAN TO THE DOMBULI KHAN IN ORDER TO OBTAIN THE RELEASE OF OUR FRIEND MORTEZA PASHA

First, the Khan of Urmiyeh gave us three hundred of his soldiers to accompany us. With one hundred men of `Ali Agha, the *agha* of the Morteza Pasha and with my fifty men, in total four hundred and fifty, we left Urmiyeh towards the south. While traveling along Lake Urmiyeh with Mt. Asvene on our right hand, we passed several very prosperous villages and after four hours reached

---

63. Keskin is a town and district of Kirikkale province in Central Anatolia. Bozok is the old name of Yozgat (since 1927), which is located in Central Anatolia

64. Rumelia refers to the region of the southern Balkans, of which Silistre is a part; it is a region in Bulgaria in which the districts are situated.

65. Dobruzha is a region shared between Romania and Bulgaria situated between the lower Danube and the Black Sea; the southern part is Bulgarian, which is meant here.

66. Komeyl b. Ziyad Nakha'i was one of the Companions of `Ali, and was killed by Hajjaj b. Yusof. Some Sufi orders consider him their founder Saint. The famous Komeyl prayer is attributed to him. There does not seem to have existed a Komeyli Sufi order, however.

the town of Jevlan. Its inhabitants are Sunnis. From there we again went for six hours towards the south and reached the castle of Domdomi.

DESCRIPTION OF THE CASTLE OF DOMDOMI. Its first founder was Shah Yazdegerd. It seems that the reason for its name is that this stone castle is situated on the coast of Lake Urmiyeh, and the waves battering the caves there make the sound of "boom boom" and "domdom" and therefore they call it Domdom Rock. According to another account, the prophet Solomon imprisoned a demon called Domdom in this place, and as his voice is heard they call it Domdom. Now this voice can [still] be heard, provided that you are not far away from the roaring of the sea. The castellan of the castle came out to welcome us, and we pitched our tents under the castle in a beautiful garden. This beautiful strong castle is situated in the province of Urmiyeh on the coast of Lake Urmiyeh, and its circumference is twenty thousand paces. On the northern side it has an iron gate and does not have a moat, but it is very inaccessible. On one side there are no heights overlooking it, and it is impossible to conquer it from any side.

It has six hundred houses and a mosque called Mir Quli Khan. It does not have other buildings. It has a chief of the royal slaves, a chief of the ushers, three hundred royal slaves, royal cannons and an adequate arsenal. But sometimes the sea recedes and the castle is on land. But the fortification of the suburb is in good order. It is a quandrangular, huge castle that was built by Shah Tahmasp. It seems indeed to be a recent construction. Inside the castle there are about seven hundred well-constructed houses covered with mud without gardens and orchards. It has a moat around it, and its circumference is six thousand paces, which surrounds the west side of the rock of the inner castle on which it is built.

There are thirteen mosques. First, the Shah Tahmasp mosque and the Shah ʿAbbas I mosque are very well made. The Cheghal-oghlu Senan Pasha mosque is a beautiful building and is built in the ancient style.

In the bathhouse of Kalb ʿAli Khan there is one basin. The whole bathhouse is covered with Chinese-style tiles and is well lit. The vaulted bazaar is also called Kalb ʿAli Khan. There is one caravanserai for merchants. Most of the houses are one-storied, and there is no drapers' hall or madraseh. Its water comes mostly from the summer quarters of Ushnuyeh. It has a better climate than Urmiyeh, and in its orchards they grow very excellent jujube, oleaster and mulberry. The lake is on the east side of the city, and the gardens are on the west side.

PLACES OF PILGRIMAGES OF THE CASTLE OF DOMDOM. These are [the tombs of] Sheikh ʿArab Jabbari, Mullah Dehqani, Sheikh ʿAli Tirmidhi, Sheikh ʿAli Naji and the revealer of spiritual truths, Mullah Naser Shirvani.

Traveling south from here through gardenlike villages for seven hours we reached Ushnuyeh.

DESCRIPTION OF THE TOWN OF USHNUYEH.[67] A daughter of Harun al-Rashid to improve her health came from Iraq to the summer quarters of Ushnuyeh and built this town. Later the Mongols destroyed it, and thereafter Uzun Hasan Shah made it prosperous. It is one of the towns of Azerbaijan under the administration of the governor of Domboli. It is a separate khanate with two thousand soldiers, but its castle is in ruins. Out of fear for the Kurds of Shahrezur, Harir and Ardalan they dug ditches around it. It is a prosperous and well-kept town with gates inside barricaded streets.[68] Its circumference is nine thousand paces, and its houses are not well-built. It is situated to the western and southern side of Urmiyeh. The aforementioned Mt. Ushnuyeh is situated between the towns of Urmiyeh and Ushnuyeh and borders on Urmiyeh and Donboli. Going fast from Ushnuyeh towards the north one may reach Urmiyeh in two days, but Domdomi is in the opposite direction.

This town consists of six thousand low-built nice houses, and most of them have orchards and gardens. Most of these houses have brick walls. Its roofs are thatched with chalk and felt; they are well-made roofs. Its climate is milder than that of Urmiyeh. Because of the good climate the people of Ushnuyeh sleep on the roof from New Year (*Nowruz-e Khvarezmshahi*) until autumn. But from the roof they cannot see each other's womenfolk; they are all Sunnis. Young men do not shave their beards nor do old men. Like the people of Heshdek {in Muscovy} they have long and thick beards for which they pay a special royal tax. The people of Ushnuyeh are really Sunnis. They read the *khutbah* during the Friday prayer in the name of the Shah, and they perform the Friday prayer individually. Its people are all merchants, and they love strangers and pilgrims.

In total it has twenty quarters and ten mosques. Among them are the Safi Khan, the ʿAlamshah, the Kepayasan, and the Baʿdumah mosques; the others are not known.

There is a chief of ushers, a chief of the guards, a qazi and a mufti. They have beautiful bathhouses, caravanserais, and well decorated coffeehouses and shops. But there is no drapers' hall. There are gardens and orchards; its fruits include an abundance of several kinds of apples, juicy plums, tasty grapes and delicious pears. It is a well-endowed town. We left the town of Ushnuyeh and going east towards Urmiyeh in seven hours reached:

THE STAGE OF THE VILLAGE OF QOCHAGHA BABA. Since it was built by Qochagha Sultan, who is buried in the city of Urmiyeh, it is called the village of Qochagha Baba. It is situated in the land of Donboli, and it is a prosperous village with gardens and large mosques. Here many of the ancestors of the Sheikh of Urmiyeh are buried. In six hours we arrived at Domboli.

DESCRIPTION OF THE CASTLE OF DOMBOLI.[69] Its founder is Anushirvan. After him Ghayath al-Din Kepani repaired it. The original name of the castle was Telvan. In the time of the

---

67. Ushnuyeh is situated at 11 km south of Urmiyeh. Razmara, *Farhang*, vol. 4, p. 24. For a description of the town in the nineteenth century see Maximilan Bittner, "Der Kurdengau Uschnuje und die Stadt Urumije. Reiseschilderungen eines Persers, im Originaltexte herausgegeben, übersetzt und erläutert," in *Sitzungsberichte der kaiserlichen Akademie der Wissenschaften* vol. CXXXIII (Vienna, 1896), part 3, pp. 1-97; see also H.C. Rawlinson, "Notes on a Journey from Tabriz to Takhti-Soleiman," *Journal of the Royal Geographical Society* vol. 10 (1840), pp. 15-26.

68. The translation of this sentence is tentative. The original has: *Kushebendlerde tedribler vazʿ olunup*. We think that it *kushebend* should be *kucheband*.

69. The castle of Domboli is not attested in Persian sources. The Domboli tribe was of Kurdish origin, but had become Turkicized and had been granted a district near Salmas and Khoy, which latter town they also held since the 16th century. See ʿAli Al-e Dawud and Pierre Oberling, "Donboli," *Encyclopedia*

caliph Harun al-Rashid, the Donbuli Turkmen settled in the plain and improved the town. It is a separate khanate in the khanate of Urmiyeh. The Khan came to welcome us with a great cavalcade. We embraced on horseback and entered the town, while cannons were fired from the castle. They made merry. The Khan took the *agha* of Morteza Pasha to his own palace and lodged this humble author in the house of the clerk. Since it was the time of holding the Khan's assembly, I gave the letters of Malek Ahmad Pasha Efendi to him. He kissed them and the *agha* of Morteza Pasha gave the letters of Morteza Pasha, a well-caparisoned horse and other gifts. The Khan accepted these with much joy. After reading the letters and understanding their contents he said:

> O apple of my eyes. We did not know that Morteza Pasha is a friend of ours. The gist of the matter is that our neighbor in the border area of Persia, the Khan of Tiflis, has sent post-haste a letter to the beys of Georgia saying that one of the Achiq bash beys of Georgia, who was a hostage in those parts for the Caesar of the World as well as of the king of Iran, has fled to Baghdad. If he reaches your land, put him in chains. Perhaps you can look for him on the Ottoman side.

He said this and added that this news came to me from the Khan of Tiflis. Then he said:

> Let's go to Baghdad. The Khan of Baghdad, Qara Morteza Khan, is a friend of mine. He favors me. I will get many goods from my friend for you. Because you have come from the Khan of Van, Malek Pasha, I would release Husam Mirzayi from prison, but now a letter has come from the Khan of Urmiyeh. This is an order for me, so that you have to get a writ from our chief Khan, who is the Khan of Tabriz. If the king would ask, I will have a document to show why I have set him free.

This humble author said:

> God be your protection and guard. You give this man to us and send a guard with us. We have letters and gifts for the Khan of Tabriz. When we reach Tabriz, upon my eyes, I will get that document to you.

The Khan immediately said: "O jailor, there are Georgians in the cave, bring them." When he said this the jailor left and from seven levels from the bottom of the earth they brought forth seventeen men. None of them looked like human beings; they had become very strange, as if they were Tamim al-Dari.[70]

These wretched people when they saw us, put their faces down, and since they had not been able to wash themselves and do proper ablutions, they prostrated in prayer thanking God five times. The *agha* of Morteza Pasha immediately gave them clothes and sent them to the bathhouse. God be praised, when they came back they will look like human beings. Since the business was concluded we went to the see the town.

Iranica.

70. He was one of the prophet's companions who died in 9 AH (630) and known for his asceticism and emaciated appearance.

The Domboli Sultan who was a Turkmen from Marʿash in the Ottoman lands and among our friends was an easy-going scoundrel. We went to orchards and meadows and enjoyed ourselves.

There were about fifty doe-eyed, sweet-voiced, beautiful slaves. When you saw them you would loose your wits. Apart from these youths, he has two thousand choice armed Domboli Turkmen soldiers, who look like lions. The town has a qazi, a mufti, a chief of the royal slaves, a chief of the ushers, a mayor and six hundred soldiers guarding the castle.

DESCRIPTION OF THE LAYOUT OF THE CASTLE OF DOMBOLI. It is situated at the southern side of Lake Urmiyeh at a great distance in a vast plain. It is pentagonal in form, and it is made of large white stones. Since it is in a flat place, it has a deep moat. Its circumference is seven thousand paces. It has forty strong towers and three gates. On the western side there is Harir Gate, which faces the Harir Mountains of Kurdistan. Towards the north is the Urmiyeh Gate, and in the south there is the Ardabil Gate. Inside the town there are one thousand well-built houses made of mud. They have an upper and lower storey.

Altogether they have seven mosques. In the time of Sultan Sulayman, Eskander Pasha, the vizier of Van, defeated the Khan of Dombuli and killed him, and he is buried in the Hajji Khan mosque. The one I have seen are the Shams Khan mosque, the Baqabay mosque, the Shah Jahan mosque and others. There are no madrasehs and convents.

It has about seventy small shops, and every *Nowruz* there is a lively bazaar for forty days. The Gilan and Domboli bazaars are famous in Persia. Apart from this bazaar, outside the town of Donbuli there are some three thousand useful and small shops, which are situated under the trees of the promenade. It is a big bazaar. Travelers stay here. We could not see the inside of the castle. The guards stopped us and said: "Our great king had forbidden it." But that night they illuminated the castle in such a way that I cannot describe it.

All the people of the town are Alajeh Qizilbash. They wear motley-colored (*alajeh*) turbans, striped chintz on their body, green dresses and shoes of green Morocco leather. All the uncouth Qizilbash are ruffians.

Most of the people wear the best fabrics that are made in the town such as chintz, and use various table cloths and curtains that have been stitched with marvelous variegated patterns. They have very beautiful covered bazaars and coffeehouses.

Although it is the land of the Qizilbash, I neither saw any tavern nor a drunkard, because they regard drunkenness as very bad. Other things are permissible.

They have caravanserais and bathhouses, and inside the town they have water wells, but there is no running water. They have many gardens and orchards, and its climate is good. Being faraway from the Lake, one side of it is a sandy plain. Most of the people in the summer go to the Harir and Ushnuyeh Mountains to their summer quarters.

THE PLACES OF PILGRIMAGE IN DOMBOLI CASTLE. We visited the gardens near Shuri Baba and not far from them are the tombs of Sheybeden[71] and Jeghalı Sultan, who by God's command had something like writing on his forehead when he was born; that is why he is called Jeghalı Baba.[72]

---

71. Jevdet read Shibeh Dedeh, which makes more sense as the term Dede denotes a Sufi saint.
72. *Cegha* means "plume, sign", thus *jeghalı* means "somebody with a sign."

These are the places that we went for pilgrimage. Then after receiving gifts from the Khan and participating in a feast, we went towards the west over the main road:

Concerning the stages that we traveled towards the city of Urmiyeh. First, the *agha* of Morteza Pasha, ʿAli Agha, and the friend of Morteza Pasha, the Georgian Tomris Beg, and this humble author and ten people of the Khan left the town of Domboli and went towards Tabriz. After five hours we reached:

The stage of the village of Sevendik Khan. It is a village with one thousand houses belonging to an old Khan, who had been dismissed from Dargazin. Again from here passing through prosperous and well-developed villages after six hours we reached Yar ʿAli.

Description of the town of ʿAli Yar. It is an endowment of the shrine of blessed ʿAli and every year its net revenue goes to Mashad-e Imam ʿAli (i.e., Najaf). It is situated at the foot of a high mountain and it is like a paradisiacal garden. It has a total of one thousand houses. Streams come down from the high mountain, and provide water to the town and people. The master craftsman who has built this town has built it like a chessboard; all streets are straight. Therefore, all the roads are straight. Both sides of each road are adorned with weeping willows and tall plane trees. Its large mosques, caravanserais, bathhouses and bazaars are becoming more prosperous every day.

The place of pilgrimage of Ghazi Ramazan Pasha. He was a valiant vizier and was killed in the battle of Dombuli. He is buried here. Then we went towards the west and reached:

The stage of Mirza Khan. It is the personal fief of the Khan of Urmiyeh. It has five hundred houses and it is an Armenian village. It has one church and many gardens. From there after six hours:

Another stage to the city of Urmiyeh. We reached our host and feasted with our Khan, and we had many parties and received numerous gifts. That day, the people who had gone to Van arrived. Letters also arrived indicating that twenty thousand sheep had gone to the Pasha and that our sheep as well as our other items had been given to the quartermaster. This was joyous news.

We received permission from the Khan and made ready to go to the province of Tabriz. The Khan called this humble author alone and said:

> My life, you are my brother and dear to my soul. Please, when you go to the Khan of Tabriz and when you are sitting knee-to-knee with him, remind me to the Khan in every conversation.

He said this and from his breast pocket brought out three hundred gold coins, two hundred *qorush* and one watch, and furthermore he gave one Georgian coat, one Qarachuboq horse with a Persian style saddle and two fast post horses.

He said: "Rest a while, so that I write letters to the Khan of Tabriz and other Khans who are on your way." The letters were written and given to this humble author. By God's wisdom, at that moment all the soldiers, royal slaves and raw flesh eaters started to become very upset and disturbed. The Khan's face became very pale, and he said: "O men, what is this disturbance?"

They said: "O Khan, from the high court the master of ceremonies has come post-haste." At that moment the Khan lost his mind and told me:

"My child, Evliya, I am going to the next world. Don't forget me in your prayers." I tried to console him said:

"O my Khan, I would give my life and my head for you. Let us see what is happening." At that moment from the outside of the Khan's audience hall an impressive man appeared, who was dressed in a sable coat with a bejeweled (Safavid) Sufi hat and with a studded dagger in his belt. Seeing him, all those present rose and bowed to him.

{CONCERNING A TERRIFYING SIGHT.} This master of ceremonies who came took one side of a golden and bejeweled chain in his right hand and going to the gate of the audience hall said:

> O people of Urmiyeh. O people of Iran, Turkestan and Azerbaijan khanate. Know and be aware that a royal edict has come from the king of kings 'Abbas II. Don't move. All of you are under royal arrest.

After this all the people of the divan said: "We are at the king of Iran's order," and they prostrated themselves.

The master of ceremonies put one end of the golden chain on the neck of that wretched Khan, who was lying on his face and closed it with a strong lock, while the other end was still on his own neck. In this way these two in the corner of the *divan-khaneh* were sitting knee-by-knee. At that time this humble author got up and went to the master of ceremonies and with supplication said:

"Master, you are welcome."

He got up and took my hand and made me sit next to him. I said: "Master, what is the meaning of this?" The Agha said: "Whatever has come has come from your Caesar's vizier of Van, because your Malek Ahmad Pasha sent letters to the shah with a master of ceremonies saying:

> This Khan acted against the peace; he has taken forty thousand sheep from the Pinyanish and has killed many people and has destroyed their land. Either these sheep are going to be returned to their owners under the auspices of the king of Iran, or we attack the province of Urmiyeh, and this will be a contravention of the peace by my king. When such letters came from the vizier of Van our great king sent me to put this Khan in chains.

This was the answer of the master of ceremonies.

This humble author said:

> My dear, may I be your sacrifice, my good Agha. It has been about forty days that I have received forty thousand sheep and returned them to the Pinyanish people and established the peace. I have documents indicating that I have sent forty thousand sheep to the vizier of Van. This has been recorded in the religious court. It should be looked into again. I wrote letters to those who were going into the presence of the great shah to make it known to him that the sheep had been collected. Also, I had made this known to the Khan of Tabriz, so that he would make it known to the king in a pleasant manner. I said to this effect I have written letters."

The Agha said: "Yes, when I received the order of the king and traveled from Isfahan the 'Half of the World' in two stages from Isfahan along with the courier of this Khan, your letters were being taken to the Shah. I had departed before that time."

I said: "My Agha. I pledge my head for the sake of this poor and innocent Khan. I would go to the Shah and make known that I have received the sheep."

The master of ceremonies said: "Bravo, you are a good man. You are a lover of the king. If you behave in this way you are a faithful and a good Sunni." I said: "By God, I will go. I will not stay in Urmiyeh."

Then the master of ceremonies said: "O soldiers of the Khan. The Shah's order is that you should transport all the Khan's wealth and what is in his stores to the court of the Shah."

The Khan said: "This Evliya Agha has been for forty days here in the service of the Shah. This very day he wanted to go to the Khan (of Tabriz), and I gave him one purse of *qorush* and three strings of camels, three Georgian slaves, one virgin-maiden, five pieces of amber and one good sword. By God's command it has happened. Before confiscating my property please give Evliya Agha whatever I have promised him."

The king's master of ceremonies said: "By God, he deserves it." And he gave to this humble author from the divan of the Khan all the enumerated things. When they were giving these I was almost dying of joy. All these things were loaded on the camels, and I gave them to the forty men who had been assigned to me and said: "After crossing the royal pass and reaching Ottoman lands, give the camels to the Agha of Van, Sulayman Bey, and seal the other goods with my seal and hand them over to my servants."

On the other hand the master of ceremonies of the king confiscated all the property of the Khan, in accordance with religious law and sealed them. He chained forty people and tortured them.

Description of our journey from Urmiyeh to Tabriz and Shah ʿAbbas's Isfahan, which is half of the world

In the year [1065/1654-55] in the month of Dhuʾl-Hijja [September], when we left Urmiyeh, they brought the poor Khan with chains on his neck and his legs chained under his horse together with forty of his people on their horses, chains on their neck and with hands and feet in irons. On this ill-omened day when we left Urmiyeh towards the north a big dust cloud appeared in front of us, from which a Persian army appeared. They came sounding the trumpets and horns and beating the kettle-drums, while an important Khan came to the master of ceremonies and Ganj ʿAli Khan, who was in chains, and they all began weeping. The Khan said: "O Brother, it is God's will, may our gracious king live long." With great procession he entered Urmiyeh and so many cannons and muskets were fired from the earthen castle that heaven and earth trembled. This humble author asked the Persians, "Who is this Khan?" They said: "He is ʿAli Taqi Khan, the younger son of Kel Rostam Khan, who has become Khan of Urmiyeh in the place of Ganj ʿAli Khan, who is going to confiscate all his property and send it to the Shah." I said: "What is the great Shah going to do with the poor Khan?" They said: "What do you expect him to do? The Khan has been deceived by the words of ill-wishers; attacked Ottoman lands, plundered them, and killed people. Several Kurds were killed. The great king knows well what to do with him. First he will blind him

The royal meydan – Isfahan

and then have a heated bowl put on his head. The next day he will take out his intestines through his mouth and cut his heart and liver and similarly he will torture these forty men, so that he will set an example in the land of Iran."

I really pitied this poor Khan. But what is the use?

> No one can escape calamity by caution
> It will happen if it has to happen if you take a thousand cautions.

In this miserable mood we traveled that day north for seven hours and reached:

THE VILLAGE OF IMAM REZA. Previously, when Urmiyeh and Tabriz were in the hands of the Ottomans, this village was an endowment of the Ja`far Pasha mosque. When the Persians retook it, it again became the endowment of Imam Reza. It is a big village situated in a vast plain with beautiful gardens, three thousand houses, with a mayor, conductor of guests, an endowment manager, many mosques, caravanserais, bathhouses and a sufficient number of shops.

THE PLACE OF PILGRIMAGE OF IMAM REZA, may God be pleased with him. When he left Baghdad for Khorasan, he enjoyed the climate of this village and stayed here for a while and

Royal banquet

prayed. Now, because many Shahs and Khans have added many buildings it has become a big complex; it is a Bektashi convent. Describing it cannot really do it justice.

It is a big convent, which houses three hundred bare-foot, bare-headed, Zertel, Jevellaki, Kalandar, Vahidi, Yasavi, Fakhri and Bozdoghan dervishes,[73] each one of whom is a flower from a garden, and is learned and accomplished in every science; but they are not Sunnis. Furthermore, they do not have any cursers among them.

In its huge kitchen there are eighty bare-foot dervish cooks, each one of which is worthy to be a royal cook. Every day they regularly serve rice, soup, cream of wheat soup (*hariseh*) and bread free to the comers and goers. When we took this poor Khan to this shrine he vowed: "If I am released from the whirlpool of calamity, I will make a gift of a golden chandelier to this shrine." As a matter of fact there were several thousand well-worked lanterns, and each one was the gift of a Shah or a Khan. In the soup kitchen there is a kettle given by Shah Tahmasp. It is so big they get into it with a five-step ladder. On the day of 'Ashura they cook thirty cows in it and serve them to the poor. Out of his own will this humble author put his sallow face on this shrine of Imam Reza and wrote this verse on the wall:

> O my Prophet; for the sake of God
> Intercede with God for my sake.

May God bless his resting place. Again going for five hours to the north we reached:

THE STAGE OF THE VILLAGE OF SHAHSEVAN. It is a village situated in the khanate of Salmas. It has one thousand houses, gardens, orchards, a large mosque, a caravanserai, a bathhouse and some fifty shops. Its people are Shahsevans, who when fighting receive brimful cups of liquor from the hands of the Shah.[74] They are all cursers and uncouth Qizilbash, but since most of these places are farmlands, most of the people are peasants. All the running water is subterranean, and it is very cold. Traveling for three hours to the north we arrived at:

THE VILLAGE OF BICHOR. It is situated in a beautiful grassland plain in the khanate of Salmas. It is prosperous with eight hundred houses. We passed and again after five hours to the north reached:

THE VILLAGE OF YAZDANBASH. It is in the khanate of Salmas and has one thousand households of Gökdolaq Armenians. Sultan Murad IV stopped here during his Erevan expedition. It is a prosperous village. Again from here we went for five hours and reached Salmas.

DESCRIPTION OF THE CASTLE OF SALMAS, I.E., THE CITY OF DELMAS. Its first founder was Bozorjmehr.[75] It is situated in a fertile plain. Because of the abundance of yogurt from sheep and buffaloes, the sage Bozorjmehr built a town there that he called Delmast, which means 'The City of Yogurt.'

---

73. We have not been able to identify Sufi orders known as Zertel (mad), Jevallaki (wandering), Vahidi, Fakhri and Bozdoghan. For a discussion of the various dervish groups see Ahmet T. Karamustafa, *God's Unruly Friends. Dervish Groups in the Islamic Middle Period 1200-1550* (Oxford, 2006).

74. This means that they received wages from the Shah.

75. Famous minister of Khosrow I.

Tower of animal skulls in Isfahan

Later, Hulagu Khan of the Mongol people destroyed and plundered it when he went against al-Mustansir bi'llah the `Abbasid (caliph) in Baghdad. Thereafter, in the year [-] a vizier of Jahan Shah named Salmas rebuilt it, and it was called Salmas, which means 'good health' castle. When we came to this castle, the Khan hurriedly came out to welcome us and he took the master of ceremonies and the Khan of Urmiyeh to his mansion. The *Agha* of Morteza Pasha was referred to his deputy and we were lodged with his secretary. We started visiting the castle. It is situated in a vast plain. All around it are situated Urmiyeh, Tasuj, Qumlah, Qarabaghlar, Khoy, Marand, Behestan and Churs, which have lands bordering on the plain of Salmas, which is five times bigger than that of Pasin and Mush, which is a huge plain like the Qepchaq steppe. When you enter via the north gate on your right-hand side there is a square stone on which is written: "This strong castle was built in the time of Taj al-Din `Ali Shah and its builder was Khvajeh Naqdi Miqrizi."[76] Its circumference is one thousand paces, and its climate is rather cold. On the west side there is a river that comes from the Pinyanish and the Abagay Mountains. After irrigating more than a thousand gardens, it flows towards the west into Lake Urmiyeh. Because the castle is situated on a hill, the freshwater streams do not flow into it, but rather it has freshwater wells. The waters that exist around it are all subterranean and in the main road there are many wells. The Persians captured many Ottoman soldiers who were hiding in these wells. All of the water passes underground.

But the wells of the castle of Salmas are different. Inside the castle there are three hundred houses and one large mosque; there are no other buildings. Its wall is built of lime and stone and it has a deep moat. It has *pülli* trees. The Khan's mansion is inside the castle; he also has one in the suburb. The Khan has two thousand soldiers and he is under the Tabriz provincial government. There are five hundred royal slaves. It has a mufti, a mayor, a police chief, a clerk, a chief of the ushers, a chief of the merchants and a conductor of guests. Most of the inhabitants are horsemen.

The people of the villages, if they are Sunni, do not show it. The people are all merchants. Outside the suburb there is no wall, but there is a moat around it. It has three gates. The Urmiyeh Gate is towards the south, the Tasuj Gate is towards the west, and the Tabriz Gate is towards the east. The circumference of the suburb is seven thousand paces.

Altogether there are three thousand houses and three well-built large mosques. There are nine quarters. Four of them are Persian Sunni Moslems, and five of them are Armenian Gökdolaq. Its caravanserais, bathhouses, shops and coffeehouses are very nicely decorated. The public roads are very clean. Because of the pleasant climate, its male and female beloveds are extremely beautiful, and speak nicely while showing their pearl-like teeth.

Of its edibles and beverages there is one bunch of grapes, which weighs twenty *vuqiyas*[77] and which is sweet and juicy. It has forty kinds of pears. There is a multitude of plants and cereals. Its water is all underground. It is a big and prosperous province, and the people of the city of Salmas are happy. What Sultan Murad has destroyed is now being repaired. But, the place where Sultan Murad stopped has become a site where people stroll and amuse themselves.

As described above, this city of Salmas is situated in the middle of seven cities; it is an intermediary city. The city of Salmas is situated to the west of Khoy, veering to the north. Between

---

76. Mustawfi, *Nuzhat-al-Qulub*, p. 87 mentions that this vizier of Ghazan Khan, who died in 1324, had repaired the walls of the town.

77. A *vuqiya* of 400 *dirhams* weighed 1.28 kg.

them there are seven *farsakh*s, and to Tabriz it is twelve *farsakh* to the east. Salmas is situated at seventeen degrees. It was built with the the sign of Leo in the ascendant and in the house of the fiery Sun. It is strong as a lion. The hot days are because of the sun. Turning towards the north from here in three hours we came to Koja-abad.

The village of Koja-abad. It is a paradise-like, prosperous village with one thousand houses, which does not have its like either in Azerbaijan or in Iran from the point of the pleasant climate, nice buildings and abundance of produce. It has a large mosque, a caravanserai, bathhouses and royal market. Going to the north for [-] hours we reached Serav.

The stage of the village of Serav. It is not the city of Serah. That city is situated between Tabriz and Ardabil and is called Serah. This one is the village of Serav. Persians and Mongols call it Saray. The Tabriz and the Serav gardens border on each other and there are three stages between them. The district of Serav has a total of eighty prosperous fortified villages. In each one there are is a large mosque, a bathhouse and markets. We did not go from here to Tabriz but to confiscate farmlands and other properties of the Khan. With the master of ceremonies we went to Tasuj and Qumlah.

Account of the stages between Tasuj and Qumlah that we traversed with the Shah's Agha

First, we went towards the east over a well-cultivated plain for three hours, and we reached the castle of Tasuj.

Description of the castle of Tasuj. It is situated in the province of Tabriz and borders on the jurisdiction of the sultan of Marand. It is a separate sultanate with two thousand soldiers. The castle has a qazi, a mufti, a *sar-taj-e sayyedi*, a clerk, a police chief, a mayor, a chief of the ushers, a chief of the royal slaves, and six hundred soldiers, an arsenal and cannons. In former times one of the wives of King Yazdegerd, called Tasuban built it. {That is why it is called Tasuban}. After that, Timur Leng destroyed it and then Jahanshah rebuilt it.

Its castle is situated next to the river Aras.[78] It has three thousand mud houses, seven large mosques, three bathhouses, and six caravanserais and a small bazaar. There are twelve *farsakh*s to Marand; it has a good climate, gardens and orchards, male and female beloveds, and good food products and beverages. There are twelve types of grapes, *'abbasi*, *melejeh* and *peyghambar* pears that are so sweet and juicy that their like is not found in the world, and they are particular to Tasuj.

In the year 1057 [1647] when we came to Tabriz of Azerbaijan, we gave a detailed description of this town of Tasuj traveling from Erzerum, Erevan, Nakhjevan, Khoy and Behestan, which places we visited.[79] In this town of Tasuj the Khan gave a big feast, and after eating they made an inventory of the Khan of Urmiyeh's fifty shops and twenty-six gardens. The next day on New Year's day we traveled to the east through a prosperous plain passing several villages, and after six hours we reached Qumlah.

---

78. This cannot possibly be the Aras river, which is to the north of Tasuj. The river near Tasuj is called Marvrud. Dehkhoda q.v. Tasuj.

79. See page 20 supra.

DESCRIPTION OF THE CASTLE OF QUMLAH. In the year 998 [1589-90], in the time of Sultan Murad III by royal edict the great general Koja Farhad Pasha took this castle. It is situated on the slope of Mt. Velya. It is a big quadrangular beautiful castle made of stone, three thousand eighty paces in circumference. It has all the charitable institutions, and Qumlah has one hundred and fifty prosperous villages. The grapes of the Qumlah gardens and the adjacent mountains in the plains with huge caves and well-built redoubts on its slopes have been described in our visit in the year 1057 [1647] to Tabriz.[80] This humble author, after having recorded one mansion of the Khan, one farmland, seven gardens and having received a request from the Sultan of Qumlah to the Shah, went towards the east and reached:

THE VILLAGE OF SUNJAH. It is in the land of Tasuj. It is the personal fief of **VARAQAH KHANOM**, one of the shah's daughters. Then we went to the village of Mazid Khan, and then to:

THE VILLAGE OF SHEIKH SAFI. This is an endowment of the shrine of Sheikh Safi who is buried in Ardabil and is the ancestor of the Shahs. In this place, between Qumlah and Tabriz, the river Qara Su passes, which originates in the mountains of Albaq and Qarni Yareq castles, and after watering several hundred of villages it falls into Lake Urmiyeh. The river Qara Su flows between Tabriz, Qumlah and Tasuj. All other streams in Azerbaijan flow under the streets and irrigate everything. In every corner there are wells. Then we traveled towards the east and passed all the abovementioned villages, each of which was like a small town. Then at ten o'clock in the evening we stopped at:

THE VILLAGE OF SUJEH JAN,[81] which has one hundred houses, a large mosque and a bathhouse. Then going towards the east we came to:

**THE VILLAGE OF JA`FAR PASHA KHANI,** (the Khadem Ja`far Pasha of Sultan Sulayman). It is a village like a small town and is prosperous with five [hundred] houses. Then we reached:

THE VILLAGE OF BANDEMAHI. It is a village in the jurisdiction of Tabriz with one thousand houses. Then we came to:

THE SHRINE OF MOHAMMAD SHAM GHAZAN. Being a descendant of Chengiz Khan and after having converted to Islam he was the king of Azerbaijan and built on this site a *shehbet* for himself. In the Mongol language *shehbet* means 'shrine,' and mistakenly this word became Sham Ghazan. It is a building like the Galata tower in Istanbul that rises to heaven. Later Mohammad Ghazan died in the year 693 [1294] and his tomb is here. God be praised, we visited it as we had done in the year 1057. This is a blessing from God. Then we went east to:

THE VILLAGE OF HAJJI HARAMI, which I described in volume [two]. Then we came to:

THE VILLAGE OF SHEBTERI, which we had not seen before. It is a village situated in the land of Tabriz. It has one thousand houses, a large mosque and a bathhouse. Then we all went fully armed with pomp and dignity, and the deputy of the Khan of Tabriz came to welcome us with many troops. The poor Khan of Urmiyeh with his hands chained behind him was moving in the midst of the sea of men and was ashamed, and after four hours we entered Tabriz.

---

80. See page 47–48 supra.

81. There still is a village called Sujeh about 16 km n.e. of Maragheh. Razmara, *Farhang*, vol. 4, p. 279.

Description of the province of Azerbaijan, the holy ground of the Ujan Mountain, the great city and ancient emporium of the pleasant fortified town of Tabriz, the village of Parviz

The historians of Khorasan-e Turkestan[82] mention the unique qualities of the people of Tabriz and its emporium as well as its pleasant character and climate. When we arrived in that city with much pomp and show, we visited the court of the Khan of Tabriz. The master of ceremonies first kissed the hand of the Khan, then came the poor, chained Khan who fell at the feet of the Khan of Tabriz, but he did not even look at him. When this humble author arrived, the Khan rose and said: "Peace be upon you," because the custom of the ancient Persians is such that the host greets his guests. I had been informed about their custom beforehand and I said: "Upon you be peace, my noble Khan." When it was the turn of Morteza Pasha's *Agha*, the Khan welcomed him; Morteza Pasha's *Agha* returned his greeting. Now we were altogether in the court of Tabriz.

The Khan of Tabriz stealthily glanced at this humble author. He said: "Evliya Agha, are not you the Evliya Agha who in the year 1047 [1647], when I was Khan of Gilan, paid a visit to the Khans of Shirvan and Shamakhi as well as to the ruler of Daghestan?" This humble author said: "Yes, my Khan, I am but a humble beggar. Thank God, that I see your blessed face again. But God is omniscient, I had forgotten it." The Khan said: "Evliya, you are most welcome, it is a great pleasure to see you again."

When this humble servant said: "I am pleased to see my handsome Khan again in good health, joyful and secure," I declaimed this line:

> Thank God I have reached you, my straight cypress
> I am grateful my desire did not last till Judgment Day.

In this manner I showed the Khan much modesty, while I flattered him at the same time, because despite his dignity, wisdom, intelligence, nobility, sagacity, Aristotelian intellect, and prescience, he had been dismissed from his function at that time by Isfahan (he had been dismissed from his post by the grand vizier).[83]

I handed over the letters from Malek Ahmad Pasha. He received them in his hands, kissed them, put them on his head and said: "Peace be upon you," and read the letter out aloud and boldly. He said:

> My Evliya Agha, our brother, the vizier of Van has said that he will break the peace treaty with the kingdom of Iran if the forty thousand sheep that the Khan of Urmiyeh has robbed are not immediately restituted. For that reason we will make preparations accordingly. The Ottomans intend to send soldiers, who will completely pillage and plunder the kingdom of Iran.

---

82. There did not exist anything like Khorasan-e Turkestan, but it is possible that Evliya wanted to indicate that Khorasan was in the east, towards Turkestan, similarly as when he uses the term Azerbaijan-e Ujan, with which term he possibly wanted to convey the notion that it is in the West. Another, more likely, explanation is that he could not resist rhyming these words, which is a very bad and irritating habit of his.

83. In September 1655, when Evliya was in Tabriz, the governor of Tabriz, Morteza Qoli Khan Qajar had just been in office for about six months, see Nasiri, *Titles*, p. 156.

Hey, did you hear that, you blackguard, you idiot Khan of Urmiyeh. What kind of wretch are you that the Ottomans Khans make such complaints about you? Did I not send you letters every time, O foolish son-of-a whore? Did I not tell you that you are right on the border? You should have fostered good relations with the Ottomans, in which case you would have made a good name for yourself. You said I have my uncles with the Shah and became arrogant and therefore attacked the Ottoman frontier with trumpets, cannons and guns. Since you are a brave and valiant young man, you should go and fight in India and Qandahar, or like me, to the province of Gilan, where I have fought with infidel sailors from Muscovy. Look here, Evliya Agha was there during that war, and he is my righteous witness.

The humble author said:

My Khan, by the Prophet and by the soul of 'Ali, the lion of God, the son-in-law of the prophet and by the soul of the twelve Imams, pardon him! Our vizier has written in his letter that you should do your utmost to return those sheep. And, thank God I have received all forty thousand sheep and received the documents of their restitution from the entire people of the Pinyanish, and the letter indicating that forty thousand sheep were handed over to the Pasha was sent to me. Here are those letters and the legal document from the mullah of Urumiyeh.

And I handed all these letters and documents to the Khan. I had brought with me seven Pinyanish Kurds, who giving witness said: "All the sheep were restituted and our conflict has been resolved." Reading the letters and the legal documents that had come to the Khan of Urmiyeh he said: "God be praised that we have settled our difference with the Ottomans. But Evliya Agha, the fate of this foolish Khan of Urmiyeh is above all in God's hands and then the Shah's. In any case, he has to be blinded and a heated bowl has to be put on his head and his guts should be plucked out."

This humble author said: "My Khan, God forbid, God forbid; you have seen the statements. Surely, you apply Moslem law and implement the rules of Sheikh Safi. Send these letters and statements to the Shah, and he will release the poor Khan. Prior to that I will have informed my Sultan about the restitution of the sheep. As a preliminary, I have made known the return of the sheep to the Shah's master of ceremonies."

{The Khan of Tabriz said:} "Yes, it is so. I have received a positive letter from Urmiyeh." The humble author said: "My Khan, now that the sheep have already been returned, release the unfortunate one for the love of the beloved of God ['Ali], because you have the authority and are a great general." The Khan of Tabriz said: "Master of ceremonies, for the sake of Evliya Agha and the head of the Shah, unshackle the feet of that foolish Khan, but let him remain in the Shah's chains. Guard him well, and anon I will send these letters and statements to the Shah. You and I will write letters and send them to the Shah, and then we will await what will happen."

This humble author and all officials at the court of Tabriz, the master of ceremonies {and the poor Khan} kissed his hand. At that moment they removed the shackles from the feet and the yoke from the neck of the poor Khan, but he remained with golden chains and under guard.

At that time, the Khan of Tabriz sent the letters and statements, as well as my documents about the restitution of the sheep, by messenger to the Shah. The Khan and the master of ceremonies remained guests of the Khan of Tabriz. This humble author was ordered, together with the

Agha of Morteza Pasha, to lodge with the Khan's deputy. {The humble author said to the Khan of Tabriz}: "My Khan, your brother Malek Ahmad Pasha sends his regards and gives you as a present this bejeweled dagger," and I gave the bejeweled dagger to the Khan. The Khan looked at the dagger very carefully and also showed it to those present at court, who marveled at it, after which he put it into his waist-band.

Then the humble author said: "My Khan, he [also] has sent you two excellent thorough-bred horses, one of which comes from the stables of the Ottoman court and the other from Damascus." I then had the horses brought forward. When he saw the two grey thorough-breds with their jewel-incrusted saddles and their beautiful tack, Qeytamaz Khan, who was a mature men with grey hair, was speechless and said: "Our brother the Khan has done well, God will do justice to him." He inspected the horse from all sides. He stood speechless, and when he saw the other, a chestnut with a brown spot, all dossed out with a brocaded saddlebag, he said: "God's blessings and one hundred times God's blessings." They inspected the horses until noon. Finally, he mounted the horse with the saddle that was all bejeweled and rode it a few times around the inner court and did so with such pleasure, as if the world was his.

He then returned to court, and said: "My Evliya Agha. I will send this white horse to my Shah." This humble author said: "My Khan, it is your property, you have to decide yourself. My Khan, if you sent this horse to the Shah, I promise you that I will get two thorough-breds from your brother the vizier. But my Khan, I beseech you and the Shah, release this poor Khan." He said: "Good, Evliya Agha, I will think about it." Later, a large number of Khans gathered. During the banquet the humble author said: "My Khan, invite the poor chained Khan to dinner." The Khan said: "He has angered the Shah, such is the law of Iran." Grudgingly he granted my request. When the poor Khan, together with the master of ceremonies, were eating chained together, the poor Khan once again began to beg for mercy. The Khan of Tabriz said: "It will be done," and he consoled the Khan with this verse:

A lion must not be ashamed of being in chains.[84]

After dinner he sent the Khan back to prison. Together with the *Agha* of Morteza Pasha we went to our lodgings. When we were resting, there arrived five round gold-stitched pillows, five gold-stitched coverlets, three hundred *qorush*, some sets of clothes, a ball of rough amber and one black, fast Persian horse with its accouterments sent by the Khan. That night, it seemed that he indeed sent a courier to the Shah, God knows best. He sincerely from the heart asked for forgiveness of the Khan. He sent the grey horse and the bejeweled saddle, which we had taken with us from the Pasha to the Shah. During the night I wrote cordial letters to our 'Ali Agha, who was at the Shah's court, about the release of the Khan. I wrote about the many gracious promises made by the Khan, and I handed them to the courier of the Khan of Urmiyeh.

In the morning, the Khan of Tabriz invited me to his court. He said: "Evliya Agha, what kind of a person is your Khan? From which garden hails his flower? And from which garden is its nightingale?' This humble author said: "My Khan was born in Istanbul, in the town of Top-khaneh. When he was five years of age he went with his step-mother to Abkhazia. He remained

---

84. The poem is by Rumi. The full line is as follows: عار ناید شیر را از سلسله   ما نداریم از رضای حق گله, meaning: "A lion must not be ashamed of being in chains; About fate we do not have the right to complain."

in Abkhazia for fifteen years, and then he was sent as a gift to Sultan Ahmad, who took him into the imperial harem. After forty years he occupied the position of arms bearer of Sultan Murad, the conqueror of Erevan. He also was with him in Erevan, Nakhjevan, Tabriz and Qotur, and later during the campaign to Baghdad he was with him. At this time he has been a Khan for thirty years. He is now the chief Khan of Van."

The Khan said: "My Evliya, if it so, then your vizier seems to be well-informed about the situation in these parts." This humble author said: "Yes, that is correct. My Khan, he is an old experienced vizier. There is no high post that he has not occupied." He asked: "O my Evliya Agha, in this month of Ramazan he has fought much with the Khan of Bitlis. What was the reason of that?" The humble author said: "My Khan, the story is that some Persian merchants and Janissari traders were dissatisfied because they had to pay duties, and that is why the customs house of Van suffered a loss. Also because he did not heed anything of what the Pasha said, therefore he [the Pasha] attacked the Khan of Bitlis with seventy-thousand soldiers and as many ships via the lake of Van. He had taken cannons with him and marched against the Khan. On Monday, the twenty-fifth day of Ramazan 1065 [29 July 1655] he defeated the soldiers of the Khan of Bitlis, and put his sword into them in such a manner that the angels of heaven shouted 'Bravo'. Finally, the Khan of Bitlis fled, and the Khan of Van appointed his son as Khan."

The Khan said: "Koja Malek the old vizier has done the right thing. Our traders from Tabriz were also dissatisfied with that Khan, and because of his flight our merchants can travel in safety." This humble author said: "My Khan, to have friendly relations with our vizier you might send somebody as envoy to buy good horses, then there would be be peace and security on the borders." The Khan said: "By God, my Evliya Agha, truly that is the reason why I discussed this with you. Early in the morning, I will send one of my eloquent *aghas* as envoy. But let's first wait until our spies return from Van, then I will see what needs to be done."

Early the next morning, he sent with a gentleman named Asad Agha the following presents: Fifty Tavusi camels and fifty camels with rice from Erevan, fifteen Mazandarani guns, ten young slaves from Georgia, fifty panther skins, five felt spreads from Isfahan, five silk carpets from Lahejan, one hundred dishes, plates and cups, ten piebald trotters, six black, fast full-blood horses and letters for the Pasha. As intermediary, this humble author also sent twenty of my men along. The Khan gave them thirty *qorush* and a piece of Kashan velvet. All of this was escorted by one hundred men to Van.

The arrival of dreadful news from Van and Arjish {concerning a wondrous discussion between the Khan of Tabriz and this humble author}

The next day the Khan called me to his side and said: "My dear brother Evliya Agha." This humble author said: "Yes, my Khan." The Khan said: "Do you know that my spy has news from Van and has returned. Do you wish to know what it is about?" This humble author said: "My Khan, whatever has happened has happened." The Khan said: "Call that miserable courier." The Gökdolaq spy came and said: "My Khan, the Khan of the Ottoman Empire had pitched his tent on the Gök Meydan in Van and now has gathered his soldiers around him and has pitched his tents and pavilions in the meadow. Moreover, I have seen that in front of the multi-colored parasol large caliber cannons and balls have been arrayed. They are making preparations for a major expedition.

O my Khan, the town of Van was like a cauldron, and I was like a soup ladle. I swear by God the Creator[85] and by the pure spirit of Red Morteza 'Ali that I have done my best. I gathered information, but I was unable to learn whereto they will march."

When he had finished his report, Qeytamaz Khan[86] said to me: "Evliya Agha, what kind of reconciliation is this that you as envoy come to settle matters and moreover ask for an envoy? We exchange envoys to bring about peace. But your Khan of Khans has gathered his soldiers and apparently intends to attack Iran. I am astonished."

This humble author replied: "My Khan, the spy is correct, but he has been unable to learn where the expedition was going." The Khan was bewildered and believed that the expedition was aimed at him. But I said, "My Khan, God knows and 'Ali knows that the Porte wants the expedition to go against the Khan of Bitlis, because the fugitive Khan has not yet been arrested. Now, my Khan, I am in Tabriz. If it is not like what I am saying all my words would become a lie."

The Khan said: "But my Evliya Agha; the clothes and food of our spies are paid for by us and the Shah. Each one of them is experienced, and they even have traveled to Arabia, India, the Uzbegs and the Tatars. In other times they have been able to bring news. How is it possible that now, in the age of your Khan, they are unable to report news? That surprises me."

This humble author said: "My Khan, as the saying goes: 'The meaning of the poem is inside the poet' and thus nobody knows his intention but the Pasha himself. Other nasty and sly men do not know his mind. Since the decision is with the Pasha himself, your spy has not been able to get any news. The Ottomans always think about everything and therefore they have no need for a spy. {Malek Ahmad Pasha} maintains peaceful and faithful relations with all {Persian} Khans and tribal chiefs, above all with those in the Urmiyeh area and your Tabriz region. His expedition is only aimed at the Khan of Bitlis. One day, you will learn that in Lake Van they have placed guns in vessels and that they are going for an expedition against Bitlis."

The spy immediately said: "By God, my Khan, it is as Evliya Agha says; in the harbor of Van twenty vessels were ready. They say that the expedition is probably towards that direction. But until now nobody knows where it will go."

After the spy had spoken, the Khan said: "You unfortunate spy, putting ships at those piers is a deception and make believe. The Ottomans are always up to something, they say.[87] The Ottoman Emperor has thousands of tricks. The Ottomans are like swift-moving and enemy-huning Tartars. One day you will see that while he is pretending to go to the Khan of Bitlis and to the Hakkaris and the Pinyanish, that he will plunder us in Urmiyeh, Salmas, Khoy, Marand, Qumlah and Tabriz. And just like the Tartars, he will attack in the night. Now, the preparation for a bad day should be done on a good day. They say that the work of a spy results in the neglectful guard losing his head. What think you my Evliya Agha? Are these discussions and consultations not useful?"

---

85. The original is in Persian: "Ized-e Yazdan va Parvardegar."

86. The governor of Tabriz in 1655 was Morteza Qoli Khan Qajar, see Nasiri, *Titles*, p. 156.

87. The actual term used is *khvab-e khargush* (i.e., the rabbit's dream) and the text below follows up with a word play on this expression by using a saying that also involves rabbits. The verbatim translation is: "putting ships at those piers is like the dream of a rabbit and the Ottomans hunt rabbits with carts." This expression tries to convey that a certain supposition is ridiculous and far-fetched.

This humble author said: "My Khan, the Ottomans are the descendants of the Oghuz, and because they have innumerable soldiers at their disposal they have no need for tricks. On the one hand they won't pretend [to have] a rabbit's dream, while on the other hand they get ready to attack. I swear it by the servant of two holy places that they have no tricks up their sleeves. Also, the Ottomans have never broken their promise and suddenly attack their enemies. To someone who is working against the peace, they first send envoys with letters and show moderation and later will inform him with the words 'be ready.' Only then will the Ottomans attack with countless soldiers and take revenge. My Khan, the Ottomans and their vizier do not break their promise, especially our vizier, Malek Ahmad Pasha, who has concluded friendship with you. This being the case, would he look with contempt towards this side?" With these words I calmed the Khan of Tabriz.

But the poor Khan was gripped with worry, saying: "My spies did not report about these soldiers in Van, what should I report to my beloved Shah?," and he went around in despair. Then another spy arrived from Van who said: "My Khan, there is good news. The vizier of Van has defeated the Khan of Bitlis, whom he is pursuing." When the spy had related this happy and correct news, Qeytamaz Khan gave him ten gold pieces and said: "Go back to collect other information." But the spy kneeled and said: 'Here is my neck, there is your sword. Do not make my little ones, the apples of my eyes, orphans! Where is my bosom friend, the spy Khodadad? You do not ask what has happened to him, O Khan!" And the spy wept. The Khan said: "Do tell me, scoundrel." The spy said: "My Khan, they arrested me and Khodadad when we operated as spies in the army of Van. They led me and Khodadad before the tent of the vizier Malek. His name is Malek (meaning, Angel), but he himself is cruelty itself and he made us talk. I said: 'I am a foreigner' and kneeled and I read one-tenth of the Koran and recited the *Fatehah*. Malek Pasha immediately released me because I had shown respect for the *Fatehah*. When poor Khodadad begged for help, saying; 'Help, help' the vizier's executioner felled him before the vizier's eyes with a divine sword such that poor Khodadad's head rolled away while still crying. God be praised, I escaped. Yes, my Khan, even if you were to give one thousand *aqche*s, I still would not return to spy during the rule of this Khan. I have no more skills or manly courage." While saying, by God, he assured him that he'd enough. All men present could not stop laughing.

God be praised, on the twelfth day the master of ceremonies came with a command from the Shah's court. He had taken the Khan of Urmiyeh's and my legal documents, and together with the letters of the Khan of Tabriz and my letters had handed them over to the Shah. The Shah had asked 'Ali Agha about me. "Who is he? I have heard once about him, when he was known as Evliya Agha. He came from Baghdad to the Khan of Hamadan. I also have heard once about him from the Khan of Ganjeh. Now I see his letter. Would it not be possible that this man is a child of the kingdom of Iran?" 'Ali Agha replied: "My Shah, he is originally from Kutahiyeh. He is the Imam and bosom friend of our Lord, the vizier Malek, and on his mother's side he is related to our Pasha. He is a favorite of Sultan Murad and knows the words of God (i.e. the Koran) by heart." Thus, 'Ali Agha sang my praises to the Shah.

The Shah said: "He has been given the forty thousand sheep from that wretched Khan of Urmiyeh and still Evliya Agha pleads to pardon the Khan's crime." 'Ali Agha immediately made use of this opportunity and said: "My Shah, I beg you once more," and then the royal orders were written immediately and were sent by courier to the court of Tabriz and it was read.

{The written orders of the Shah were as follows:}

First, in the name of God; second, in the name of Mohammad for whose sake (the world was created)}.[88] First, I erased the name of the ill-famed Khan of Urmiyeh from existence and said to bring him in chains into my presence. If I would burn him in fire he deserved it. At the request of Ottoman notables the book of his crime has been closed. Return all his possessions and properties to him, but take his horsetail standard, his banner, his flag, his kettle-drum, his horn and trumpet to my treasury and dismiss him from his duties for eternity and ban him from the city. Give him one thousand lashes and then let him go.

All the learned men present at court thanked him. They took the poor Khan of Urmiyeh to the field of punishment and gave him exactly one thousand lashes and then set him free.

The Khan said: "I thank God that they have not blinded me or defaced my face." Then he gave this humble author seven diamonds, one pearl rosary and one thousand gold pieces. He said: "I will give you even more things." Immediately competent surgeons and physicians came and cupped the wounds caused by the lashes on the Khan's body and caught the blood in vials. Then they applied bitumen of Judea and almond oil, and it was as if they had given him new life. On that day I took leave from the poor Khan. They exiled him and departed for Urmiyeh; I remained in Tabriz. Together with Qeytamaz Khan we made merry, and we were in the company of nobles and acquaintances.

Concerning the beautiful city of Tabriz

Previously, while going from Erzerum to Nakhjevan in the year 1057 [1647], we visited forty cities and the city of Tabriz. We stayed there for several days in the Khan's palace, and we described in great detail the beautiful city of Tabriz in the second volume of our travel book. You may look at it.[89] Therefore, we do not describe it here and leave it at that, because there is no point in describing everything several times.

Description of the castles, big cities, mountains and large rivers and all buildings during our visit in the month of Dhi'l-Hijjeh in the year 1065 [September 1655] going from Tabriz in Azerbaijan through Isfahan and Hamadan, the provinces of Shahrezur and Mosul until Baghdad

To meet travel expenses the Khan of Tabriz gave the humble author a purse full of *qorush* as well as one robe, two fully equipped Qarachuboq horses, two post horses, one beautiful Georgian slave and seventy letters for all the Sultans and Khans who were on our way. To make my burden less, this humble author sent fifty men of the people who were with me back to Van with the gifts from the Khan. 'Ali Agha, the *agha* of Morteza Pasha, our friend, was left with fifty people, and

---

88. The text has "Law laka" the initial words of a famous Tradition, according to which God told Mohammad that: "Law la ka lama Khalaqna'l-Aflaka" – "Were it not for him (O beloved Muhammad), We would not have created the worlds" (or heavens).

89. See pp. 23 ff supra.

View of Hamadan

the Khan of Tabriz gave him one purse of *qorush* and one postal horse, may God be pleased with that *agha*. He was a light-hearted, tolerant, sincere friend and companion and was very eager to travel. Deciding to travel the length and width of Persia without hesitatation saying, "In the name of God," we took our leave from the Khan of Tabriz, and after five *farsakh*s going east we reached:

THE STAGE OF THE DISTRICT OF MEHRANRUD.[90] It is a town-like village with a large mosque, caravanserai and bathhouse. In this district there are sixty villages that are prosperous. Again, going towards the east we reached:

THE DISTRICT OF KEND-E RUD,[91] which is a town-like village and then we went to:

THE VILLAGE OF DIZCHOKAN, then we went to:

THE STAGE OF THE VILLAGE OF SA`IDABAD.**[92] Because it has been built by a vizier of Shah Tahmasp, it is called Sa`idabad. When Sultan Sulayman was going to Baghdad he destroyed it, but now it is a large place with two thousand houses, a large mosque, a caravanserai, a bathhouse and royal bazaar. The abovementioned villages that we traveled through are big town-like villages. In this land of Persia the Shahs and Khans have enough treasures. All this wealth is because of the subjects in the prosperous villages. On the right-hand side of Sa`idabad, towards the north, Qumlah castle is at quite a distance. Then we passed the village of **SERAVRUD, and then to the village of **DOST** and then to:

THE STAGE OF THE VILLAGE JEVLANDURUQ. It is a prosperous village in the jurisdiction of Tabriz with one thousand houses, a large mosque and a caravanserai. Passing from Jevlanduruq towards the south we traveled through a place called:

THE VILLAGE OF ALAQ BULAQ, with one thousand problems and difficulties.

THE STAGE OF THE VILLAGE OF SARJAM KHANI. It is situated in the plain of Sarjam in the province of Maragheh and has one thousand houses, a large mosque and a caravanserai. It is a beautiful village, and its gardens and orchards are innumerable.

CONCERNING THE WAR OF THE GREAT GENERAL EBRAHIM PASHA

This plain was full of hills made of human skeletons. I asked the old *yasavol-aghasi* who accompanied us: "Whose bones are these?" He replied: "O my son, in the year 940 [1533-34], when Sultan Sulayman was staying in the Ujan summer quarters of Tabriz, he sent Ebrahim Pasha with eighty thousand soldiers to plunder and destroy the land of Persia and pillage the regions of Ardabil, Maragheh, Qahran, Qom and Kashan. The Shah learning about this Ottoman move, sent Khalaf al-Din Khan with seventy thousand soldiers as the commander-in-chief. Those two armies halted on the plain of Sarjam, when with the help of God, one of the Aq-qoyunlu *begzadeh*s, Murad Beg, came from Khorasan with three thousand young men to help the Ottomans oppose the Qizilbash. By God's wisdom, when Murad Beg was on duty in the watchtower he captured a chief

---

90. Name of a district southeast of Tabriz; it was also called Ujan.
91. Konderud near Tabriz. Razmara, *Farhang*, vol. 4, p. 428. Now called Kunderey.
92. For details see Razmara, *Farhang*, vol. 4, p. 270.

of the guards of the Persian army and brought him to Ebrahim Pasha in chains. The wise Ebrahim Pasha made the prisoner talk and learned of the coming of the Shah. Then he opened the *divan* of Khvajeh Hafez of Shiraz and took an augury and this couplet came.

> Last night from Asaf the vizier a messenger of good news came
> That from Solomon's court the news of misery of captivity came.[93]

The courage and valor of that general swelled with enthusiasm, and from the camp of Sultan Sulayman came the news that he was coming to the help of the army. Mozaffar Khan, the Khan of Gilan, Mirza Khan, from the line of Timur, and the Khan of Nakhjevan soon came from Tabriz at the order of Sultan Sulayman with seventeen thousand troops to his assistance, while the general was getting his army ready for battle. Ebrahim Khan did not give any time to the Persians and attacked them with the battle cry 'Allah, allah,' in the plain of Sarjam and fought them for seven and a half hours. On both sides forty thousand men fell and the Ottoman army was victorious and enriched itself with huge amounts of plunder. Putting forty thousand heads on spears, they threw them at the feet of Sultan Sulayman in the summer quarters of Ujan near Tabriz. Sultan Sulayman bestowed many robes of honor and high positions.

After that the Ottomans did not remain idle, and they went up to Isfahan, Hamadan and Dargazin and several other cities as far as the gates of Baghdad. They conquered several provinces and plundered them and took people prisoner. Later in this plain of Sarjam we gathered and heaped together the skeletons of the killed Persians in seven places. At that time I was a young boy of thirteen. I remember this battle well," he said.[94] From here going to the south we passed the village of **ALQABIDLES** and the village of **LAKDERAH**, which are small towns, and then we came to Sultaniyeh.

Description of the Dhu'l-Qadriyeh city, i.e., the Castle of Sultaniyeh

In 920 [1514], in the time of Selim I, Mohammad Shah Beg, son of Shahrokh Beg Dhu'l-Qadr, who had come to help the erring Shah of Persia, was defeated at Chaldiran and out of fear for Selim did not go to Mar`ash. He went to Shah Esma`il, who bestowed this province upon him as a gift. He built this castle and called it Sultaniyeh. It is a small, beautiful and useful stone castle built on a steep hill at the border of the khanate of Nahravan.[95] It has a gate looking towards the east. There are many narrow houses inside the castle, and still its Sultans are of those wretched Dhu'l-Qadrs. In the lower suburb there are one thousand houses. It has large mosques and a bazaar, but they are in a ruinous state. Then we went to the south, and we came to the village of `Alamdar, which is also called Ustashagerd. It has one thousand houses and all the buildings are well-kept. We left, and reached:

---

93. In the divan of Hafez instead of `osrat-e esarat (meaning, the misery of captivity), the words `eshrat-e esharat (meaning, permission of merrymaking) are given. *Sharh-e Ghazalha-ye Hafez* edited by Hoseyn `Ali Heravi (Tehran, 1381/2002), vol. 2, ghazal 168, p. 717. He wrote this poem after it had become known that Shah Shoja`, the new ruler of Shiraz, had revoked the ban on wine-houses in the city.

94. Since this battle took place in 1533 he cannot have been present.

95. Nahravan is a village near Zanjan. Razmara, vol. 2, p. 309.

Mosque of Uljaytu – Soltaniyeh

The village of Semadehon.[96] It is a village with two thousand houses, a large mosque, a caravanserai and a bathhouse. These villages are very close to the city of Qazvin, and the mountain pass of the town of Qarehqan.[97] From there, after five hours towards the south we reached Kajabad.

The village of Kajabad. It is a small town. After that we crossed a hard stony desert with much difficulty in the district of Rudekan and came to Qarehqan.

Description of the castle of Qarehqan. In this plain the troops of Hulagu Khan killed seventy thousand `Abbasid soldiers, and since their blood stood like a lake it was called the Qarehqan (i.e., black blood) plain. Then one of the sons of Timur built a castle there and it was called the castle of Qarehqan. Cheghal-zadeh Senan Pasha destroyed it and after remaining for a while it was again rebuilt. It is a small building made of stone, but since its suburb was built by Qara Khan of Shah Esma`il, the Persians call it Qara Khan instead of Qarehqan. It is situated in the region of Kahravan; it is an independent sultanate with one thousand soldiers, a large mosque, a caravanserai, a bathhouse and a royal bazaar. It has a steep mountain pass, and its like is nowhere else to be found; the blood of whoever passes through it will run cold. Outside the city there is a

---

96. Jevdet read Siyah Dahan, which is a village 26 km southwest of Qazvin.
97. This is Garegan or Karekan, a village in the district of Arak.

View of the town of Soltaniyeh

bathhouse that doesn't have its like in Iran. Perhaps there is a similar one in the town of Bursa. It is extremely beneficial to one's health. Again going from here to the south we came to Maragheh.

Description of the castle of the city of Maragheh. Marvan, son of Mohammad al-Himar,[98] was its founder and it is a separate sultanate in the region of Tabriz. Its description has been given earlier in our travels to Tabriz. From here we moved fast towards the south and in two stages reached the province of Shahrezur and the castle of Kirkuk. We stayed one day in Maragheh, and in the morning we went south and reached:

The village of Turnachayiri. It is a pasture land in the district of Kahravan with one thousand houses, whose inhabitants are Gökdolaq Armenians. Then we went south and passed: **the village of Setgiz** and then came to:

The village of Manmah. They are well-kept and prosperous villages with a large mosque, a bathhouse and a bazaar. We proceeded from here to Kahravan.

Description of the castle of Kahravan. While going from Tabriz to Ardabil, we described in full detail the history of this castle that was built by Safi Khan, one of the Afshar khans, out of fear of Sultan Sulayman, and which Koja Farhad Pasha's troops later took. Later, the vizier of Sultan Sulayman, Khadem Ja`far Pasha, conquered this castle while destroying the pomp and glory of Meymandi Khan, killing him and taking the castle of Kahravan.[99]

We went to the south and reached:

---

98. He is the 14th Ommayad caliph.

99. See page 53 supra.

The town of Miyaneh

THE VILLAGE OF SHAHBANDAR.[100] It is situated on the slopes of a high mountain. It has a large mosque, a caravanserai, a bathhouse and a bazaar. Then we reached:

THE DISTRICT OF BAYAT. It is part of Ardabil. From there we went towards the south and arrived at Ardabil.

DESCRIPTION OF THE BIG AND ANCIENT CITY, ABODE OF THE ERRING PEOPLE, I.E., THE OLD FORT OF KHARZAVIL[101]

It is situated near the slopes of Mt. Ardalan. It is a large city looking towards the east. Its remains can be seen. Although it was destroyed by Hulagu Khan and then in 793 [1391] by Timur Khan and later in 941 [1534-35] by Sultan Sulayman on his way to Baghdad, and in 1040 {on the twenty-seventh of the month of Safar [5 October 1630]} by the valiant vizier of Murad IV, now it has been rebuilt again. This castle in the region of Ardabil is under a *darugheh*. It is one of the Armenian cities of Azerbaijan. There are about seventy or eighty thousand wealthy Armenians there. Since it had beautiful buildings and mostly very wealthy inhabitants most of the kings have plundered it. Its first founder was Manuchehr, and Anushirvan the Just made many additions. There is a big Christian convent as if it is the Dome of the Rock in the blessed city of Jerusalem. Inside the church there are more than five hundred monks. But inside the city there are a number of faithless Qizilbash who call themselves Moslems. It has large mosques, a caravanserai, a bathhouse and a royal bazaar. But there are countless churches. Every year, the shah collects fifty-thousand gold [pieces] from the city as taxes. There are innumerable gardens and orchards. There are beautiful Armenian boys and girls with gazelle- and narcissus-like eyes. It is a big city, but there are many infidels. It has seven thousand houses with orchards and gardens, and all of them are well cultivated. All the buildings are made of bricks and lime. All the chimneys of the houses are tall like cypress trees. According to Ibn Khallikan, it is situated at the eighteenth degree. Towards the south, after three stages, we reached:

THE TOWN OF MASULEH, where there are iron mines.[102] Then to Tarom. DESCRIPTION OF THE TOWN OF TAROM OF KHALKHAL.[103] It is under the jurisdiction of Serav. It has one thousand houses, gardens, a large mosque, a caravanserai, a bathhouse, a bazaar and a suburb. Its climate is rather cool and therefore few vegetables and flowers grow here. We crossed the river Kanduz and went towards the south to Serah.

DESCRIPTION OF THE SOURCE OF LUSH VEGETATION, I.E., THE OLD CITY OF SE-RAH. In the Mongol language they call it Seraf. In the Kurdish language they call it Serav (source

---

100. This may be the village of Shahbandlu, 42 km from Qezel Deh on the road to Khoy.

101. Kharzavil is a dependency of Kuhdom, and its governorship was sometimes held together with that of Tarom, see Nasiri, *Titles*, pp. 219, 295. From the description it is clear that Evliya had not visited this town.

102. For a description of Masulah as well as a contemporary drawing of the town see Samuel Gottlieb Gmelin, *Travels through Northern Persia 1770-1774* translated and annotated by Willem Floor (Washington DC, 2007), pp. 216-19. For the mining of its iron see also Floor, *Traditional Crafts*, pp. 17, 187, 193, 261.

103. Tarom was a separate governorship, and so was that of Khalkhal, in the sixteenth century. Nasiri, *Titles*, pp. 219, 295.

of water), but the original word is Serah. All its inhabitants, both small and large, invoking "O Qahhar" (the Victorious One, i.e., God), sigh and lament that it is called Serah.[104] The stellar constellation during its foundation was Cancer in the house of Mars. This is why in this ill-omened town the Ottoman army has been defeated. At one time, Sultan Murad III's vizier Cheghal-zadeh Senan Pasha who was the commanding general did not pay heed to the Tradition of the Prophet: "Taking counsel is good," and gave several of his ministerial posts to base people. Among them he had given the governorship of Van to Tekelu Pasha and Sivas to Raziyeh Qadin-zadeh. In this way he conferred all of Anatolia to the latter. In this situation he campaigned against the Shah of Persia. It so happened that the Shah himself was watching from the top of the mountain. In the afternoon he advanced stealthily from the mountain and began attacking the Ottoman army. For a while cannons and guns were fired, and ultimately the two armies clashed, and there was a huge battle where blood flowed profusely. At the end the breeze of victory went to the side of Shah and the Ottomans were defeated, but saved themselves by fleeing to Azerbaijan. Meanwhile, Tekelu Pasha, Qarehqash Pasha and Qajar Mohammad Pasha escaped from the Persian army and took refuge with the army of Islam.

The Janissaries, the *sepahis* and the other emirs of Kurdistan rode together until they reached the camp the next morning. All the fighters came to the pasha and said: "Let us consult." The pasha' servants said: 'The Pasha is resting." In the morning the entire army of Islam was divided into factions. All the Ottoman arms, equipment and treasury as well as the cannons had been left on the battle field as well as the martyred soldiers, and Cheghal-oghlu had fled.

At this time, Jan Pulad-zadeh Hoseyn Pasha with twelve thousand soldiers and the governor of Bitlis, Ziya al-Din Khan, with eleven thousand soldiers found Cheghal-oghlu Senan Pasha defeated and fleeing. These two fresh armies belonging to Jan Pulad Pasha and Ziya al-Din Khan took up position in the redoubts in the mountains. The Persian army followed the defeated army, coming wave after wave and group after group. When the Persians came in between the two armies that were in the redoubts, they were ambushed. {Jan Pulad's} army crying "Allah, Allah" attacked the Qizilbash in such a way that twenty thousand choice Qizilbash had their heads cut off. They fled and the pursuing army followed and killed them and reached the place where the army of Islam had been defeated. The army of the Shah seeing this grievous situation fled taking with them the treasures seized from the Ottoman army the previous day. The valiant vizier Jan Pulad Hoseyn Pasha collected the armors, cannons, tents, and pavilions and twenty [thousand] Qizilbash heads and three thousand Qizilbash alive. Along with the Khan of Bitlis, Ziya al-Din Khan entered Van with great pomp and procession, and Cheghal-oghlu bursting with envy said: "Why have you interfered with my battle and behaved in such manner and he unjustly killed Jan Pulad Hoseyn Pasha and had that warrior of Islam join the other martyrs." Later on he told the High Porte that he was the cause of the army's defeat.

After that, Jan Pulad-zadeh's clan rebelled in Aleppo. In short, in this plain of Serav, such a defeat occurred that the Ottomans had never suffered before. Now in the plain of Serav there are hills of the bones of the Sunnis.

THE SECOND DEFEAT IN THE PLAINS OF SERAV. It is known that in the year 1027 (1618) in the time of Sultan ʿOthman, the viziers Delavar Pasha and Khalil Pasha became the commanders

---

104. It was called Sarav (Sarah, Sarat, or Sarab) according to Mustawfi, *Nuzhat al-Qulub*, p. 87. Now it is known as Sarab. Khamachi, *Farhang*, pp. 347-54.

of the Persia campaign and were staying in Tabriz. While Persia was inclined to peace, the Khan of the Tatars with forty thousand soldiers attacked Ardabil, being beguiled by the pride and misguided counsel of Othman Pasha. On the other hand, the finance director of the army, the far-seeing and prudent Baqi Pasha did not consent to this campaign and said: "You should not do it, never, never." But as the saying goes: "Man proposes, but God disposes." In Ardabil, Qarchaghay Khan learning of the coming of the Ottomans, marched with eighty thousand soldiers to the Kahravan Mountains and the Serav roads and readied his army in an ambush. The Ottoman army, along with the fast-moving Tatars, marched to Ardabil in such haste that they completed a four days' journey in one day, and they themselves were worn out and their horses tired. At that time the Qizilbash army attacked them shouting: "Shah, Shah," and put them to the sword. In spite of the fact that the whole army was worn out and weakened, they fought for three hours and eventually the Qizilbash were left masters of the field; the Khan of the Tatars and some of the leaders of army, (such as) Beyeqli Hasan Pasha, Arsalan Pasha, and the governor of Diyarbekr, Mostafa Pasha, and several (other) governors drank from the cup of martyrdom and forgot the world. Qareh Pasha, Elmaji Mohammad Pasha and Mostafa Pasha of Rishvan and several hundred emirs became prisoners and twenty-six thousand men were martyred in this ill-omened plain. Now their bones can be seen in heaps. This was a major misfortune. Even now, when we visited the city of Serav and were passing in front of the coffeehouses we heard the evil Qizilbash reciting the account of Cheghal-oghlu's defeat in the Bayati mode.[105]

> May you have no resting place, O Chegal-oghlu
> May you find no hope, O Cheghal-oghlu.

They sing it as a four-liner.

DESCRIPTION OF THE TOWN OF SERAV. In the blessed land of Azerbaijan of Ujan it is situated in the land of Armenia. It is a mid-sized town situated in a pastureland. When Farhad Pasha was going to Baghdad he destroyed it. Passing through the hands of many kings, this is a wretched town, which in total has four thousand houses made of brick walls covered with mud. It has large mosques, caravanserais, bathhouses and bazaars. This town is situated to the east of Mt. Seylan [sic; Sabalan],[106] and to the west are mountains at a distance of five *farsakh*s. All its water comes from the river Serah, which issues from Mt. Seylan and flows into Lake Urmiyeh. Although it has much cereal, there is no fruit. Its inhabitants are white-skinned.

THE PLACES OF PILGRIMAGE OF THE MARTYRED OTTOMAN VIZIERS BEYEQLI HASAN PASHA, ARSALAN PASHA, MOSTAFA PASHA AND SUJAH PASHA

They all have tombstones with dates and inscriptions on their blessed resting places. From Serav to Ardabil is a long distance. Going to the south after two stages we reached Kharzabil.

---

105. *Maqam* is the system of melodic modes and Bayati is the oldest and most popular form of melody singing it in this mode. For more information see [http://en.wikipedia.org/wiki/Arabic_Maqam].

106. For the district of Sabalan and its mountain see Khamachi, *Farhang*, p. 341-48.

Description of the town of Manjil-e Kharzabil.[107] It is also in the land of Ardabil, situated on the slopes of a high mountain with three thousand houses, and its olives are everywhere. It has a large mosque, a caravanserai, a bathhouse and prosperous bazaar. From Manjil you can reach Qazvin in three stages. Then we went to the south.

Description of the great district of the old capital of Iran, the glorious province, i.e., the castle of Ardabil

Although it is in the province of Azerbaijan,[108] Baghdad is closer. Tabriz is situated to the north[109] of Ardabil at six stages distance. The first founder of Ardabil was one of the kings of Ermen, Ardebil son of Ardemini. After the hijra of the Prophet, in the time of caliphate of the blessed ʿOmar, Sariyat al-Jabal conquered Nehavand, and the misguided Armenians built Ardabil out of fear of ʿOmar. It passed through the hands of many kings. The great ancestor of the kings of Iran, the blessed Sheikh Safi is buried in this city. All this has been described in detail when we came in the year 1057 [1647] to the city accompanied by the Khan of Tabriz, so look at the [second] volume of our travelogue.[110] We came to this place with the Khan of the Afshar tribe, Abuʾ-l Fath Khan, and we talked and feasted in the gardens. In the time of the caliphate of Sultan Othman,[111] while in the plains of Serav, Dilavar Pasha and Khalil Pasha were being defeated together with the army of Islam. Tekelu Pasha, Beyeqli Vizier Hasan Pasha, Arsalan Pasha, Mostafa Pasha, the governor of Diyarbekr and son-in-law of the Sheikh al-Eslam, and several other governors were martyred. According to the good advice by the great general Defterdar Baqi Pasha, the scattered army of Islam was gathered and attacked this city of Ardabil. Burun Qasem came from the Shah and brought one thousand camels with treasures and precious fabrics and said: "Ardabil is a pillar of the cities of Iran and the resting place of Shahs. We are asking you not to destroy this city and level it to the ground." His request was accepted and the gifts that he came with were divided by the great general among his Moslem soldiers. He came before Ardabil and pitched his tents. Seeing this joyous event, the inhabitants decorated the entire city and he took to the Porte whatever gold, silver, studded lanterns, other valuable objects and silk carpets were in the tomb of the ancestor of the Shahs, the blessed Sheikh Safi, as well as in the tombs of the other Shahs. To that place Ebrahim Qoli Khan came as envoy from the Shah during the reign of Sultan Ahmad, and every year, in accordance with the peace concluded by Nasuh Pasha, he brought two hundred loads of silk and one hundred loads of excellent goat hair to make peace. For three days and nights, the city of Ardabil was illuminated, and people made merry and the Ottoman and Persian troops together amused and enjoyed themselves in the city. Since it was not too long ago I still remember this peace of Ardabil. This peace treaty is kept in the shrine of Sheikh Safi in the handwriting of Defterdar Baqi Pasha, and I have seen it. As an expression of his pleasure with this peace, the Shah sent one thousand camels loaded with goods and one thousand other loads with clothing

---

107. Harzabil is situated above Manjil, which is situated on the road between Qazvin and Rasht and the first town in Gilan.

108. Evliya has here Azerbaijan of Ermen, referring to the alleged first builder of Ardabil.

109. Ardabil and Tabriz are situated at about the same latitude, hence north should be west.

110. See p. 54–58 supra.

111. The Ottomans laid claim to the Caliphate. Therefore, this sentence does not refer to the third caliph, but rather to Sultan Othman II (r. 1618-1622).

and food as gift to be distributed among the army of Islam along with an envoy, whose name was Mirza Hoseyn, with letters to the Ottoman court. Following this, the general (Defterdar Pasha) went to the Porte. Now the people of Ardabil [still] talk about this all the time.

Then we took our leave from the notables of Ardabil and of Sheikh Vajed, the custodian of the shrine of Sheikh Safi as well as of the Khan of Ardabil, and with a string of camels loaded with provisions that were given to us, we went towards the south to Mt. Seylan [Sabalan] which forms a barrier. There is a mine of Seylan [Sabalan] stone (Ceylon garnet), which is like a ruby of Badakhshan. Because it does not pay the expense of extraction it has been left idle since the time of Shah ʿAbbas I. These pure streams that issue from Mt. Seylan [Sabalan] water the city of Ardabil, and the rest of it flows into Lake Urmiyeh. I have already described this in the year 1057 [1647].

Crossing Mt. Seylan [Sabalan], going towards the south and passing through the slopes of Mt. ʿEmadiyeh we reached:

THE IRON MINES OF THE TOWN OF MUSULEH (MASULEH). It is a separate Sultanate in the land of Ardabil with one thousand soldiers. The town is situated on the slopes of the mountains and has two thousand houses and paradise-like gardens, and it is a prosperous settlement without a castle. But the water of the iron mines is not very delicious and delectable. It has large mosques, caravanserais, bathhouses and royal bazaars. All the gates and windows are made of iron. Outside the town there are seven places where iron is mined, and such iron is so good that it cannot even be found in Ganjeh and Nakhjevan.

THE WONDERS OF MASULEH. Outside the prosperous settlement there is a high and steep rock, the bottom of it is very narrow. In order not to be destroyed in the event of an earthquake, the people of this town, who are all ironsmiths, have made chains as thick as a man's forearm and secured this rock to the mountain. In this way they have safeguarded their life and property. This is a sight worth seeing. [We departed from here and came to the castle of Sahand.]

DESCRIPTION OF THE CITY OF AVAND, I.E., THE CASTLE OF SAHAND.[112] The name of its founder is Avand, son of Gayomarth. In the beginning of Islam the ʿAbbasids ruled over Iran, Turan, Hindustan, Lurestan, Multan, Khorasan, Balkh, Bokhara and Daghestan as well as Syria, Egypt and Ethiopia and the glorious banner of the ʿAbbasids was everywhere. Then Hulaga the Mongol joined forces with the Qomuq, Qeytaq, Cossacks, Bulghar and Kilmah [Kalmuk] tribes and when with his rag-tag army he invaded the lands of Persia, the vizier of Munstansir bi'llah, the ʿAbbasid caliph, called Sahand was the governor of this Avand city. Munstansir bi'llah ordered Sahand to build a strong castle here, and that is why it is called Sahand. But then Hulagu destroyed it, although it was rebuilt thereafter.

It was built under the stellar constellation of Cancer and the house of Mars and therefore it is not free from fights and battles. At Sultan Sulayman's orders, the governor of ʿEmadiyeh, Hoseyn Khan, suddenly invaded this town of Sahand in the year 962 [1555] and destroyed it in such a way that no stone was left unturned. As a result the Kurds of ʿEmadiyeh were enriched by its plunder.

---

112. Mt. Sahand, about 400 m high, is situated some 32 km south-southeast of Tabriz. No other source mentions the remains of a town at its foot.

Then they plundered Kahravan, Maragheh, Ujan, Tabriz, Qumlah, Urmiyeh, Khoy, Manand (sic; Marand), Tasuj, Salmas, Ordu Bar (sic; Ordubad) up to Nakhjavan. The governor of 'Emadiyeh destroyed the land of Azerbaijan and killed its people and sent all the plunder to Sultan Sulayman. He then returned to his own place. Later the Shah of Iran formed an army against Baghdad with the Khans and Sultans of Persia (such as) Khamis-oghlu Hamzeh Sultan, Kartabay Sultan, Memi Jan Sultan and, of the Bayat emirs, Seyfi Sultan, Jan Apardi Khan, 'Ali Sultan, Dunur Khalifeh Sultan, Meymendi Sultan, Alari Gozuboyuk Sultan and several hundred other Khans. Hoseyn Khan, the governor of 'Emadiyeh learned about the campaign against Baghdad and raised an army with the Khans of Jazireh, 'Emadiyeh, Akra, Kelerni, Hiron, Ispa'ird, Kesan, Shervi, Mukus and Hasankey. In one night he passed under Takht-e Masha and defeated the Shah's army, and Hoseyn Khan relieved Baghdad from the siege and returned victorious with several thousand camel loads of treasure to 'Emadiyeh. Later Sultan Sulayman conferred the governorship of Mosul onto him. Finally, the Shah sued for peace. Thereafter he rebuilt the town of Sahand.

Concerning the situation of the building of the town of Sahand

This town of Sahand is situated on the slopes of the 'Emadiyeh Mountains at one stage distance from the plain of Sahand. It is a garden-like paradise. Its castle is in ruins. It is an independent sultanate in the land of Ardabil with two thousand soldiers. It has a qazi, a mufti, a police chief and a mayor. It has three thousand good and well-built houses. It is a much damaged and unjustly treated city. It has many large mosques, one of them is the Pir Budaq that I know, the others I do not. It has many minarets. It has caravanserais, bathhouses, markets and bazaars. Its coffeehouses are well decorated. Its water comes from Mt. Sahand and falls into the river Seylan (sic; Sabalan) and then falls into Lake Urmiyeh.

Of it products golden wheat, barley and cotton are very good. Its grapes are produced by the Kurds of Akra ['Aqarah]. Its climate is cold.

Maragheh is situated three stages to the north of Sahand. Between the towns of Sahand, Shahrezur and 'Emadiyeh there are three stages. From here we came to Nehavand.

Description of the great town and ancient city of Nuh-e Avand, i.e., castle of Nehavand

The reason for its name and when it was built is Noah the prophet, who was the second Adam (PBUH). After the deluge, about which there is definite proof, because it is stated in the Koran: "It stayed on Mt. Judi,"[113] Noah built the city of Judi near Mosul on Mt. Judi after all his people had been saved. Then Noah traveled in these parts, and because he was delighted with the climate and nature of this place he built the city of Nehavand. It was mistakenly distorted from Nuh-avind to Nuh-avand. The Persian wits call it Nehravand. In the Mongol language they call it Sareh Sur, i.e. the castle of Sariya.[114] King Gayomarth, Anushirvan, and in the time of the caliph 'Omar, the

---

113. Koran, Hud 44.

114. As usual Evlviya Chelebi's attempts at the etymology of place names is very fanciful. For a short

general Sariya, Harun al-Rashid and king Ghayath al-Din all of them rebuilt this city. The city passed from one to the other. In the time of ʿOthman II, Khalil Pasha, and Murad IV, Khosrow Pasha, eventually Hulagu and then mighty Timur and the vizier of Sultan Sulayman, Ebrahim Pasha, and the vizier of Murad III, Chaghal-oghlu, all destroyed the city and it remains like that.

Concerning the building of the city of Nehavand. It is situated in Persian Iraq, to the south of the city of Hamadan on a high mountain. To the north on an immense and vast plain, the old capital of the kings of Iran is situated on a hill. Its castle is an impressive building. Its circumference is nine thousand paces. Although it is surrounded by a moat, it is narrow. Inside the castle there are about one thousand houses without gardens and orchards.

There are in all four large mosques, amongst which are the Caliph ʿOmar mosque, the Sariya mosque, and the Harun al-Rashid mosque; other buildings such as the caravanserais, bathhouses and the royal bazaar are in the lower city.

It has one hundred and fifty towers and bulwarks, two gates, a music band tower, seven hundred guards, one chief of the royal slaves, a chief of the ushers, a police chief, a mayor and a clerk. It is an independent khanate with three thousand choice soldiers. It had a castellan who is Georgian and is called Bureh Khan. Since he was very generous, we were his guests in the khan's mansion with our friend the *agha* of Morteza Pasha. For three days we enjoyed his company.

Description of the lower part of the fortification

Below the upper castle there is a rectangular structure that is surrounded by a moat. But it is not as strong as the castle of our time. The gate that opens to the south, called the Iraqi Gate, has a building in front of it from the time of Harun al-Rashid with a date on it. The Ardabil Gate opens to the north; the Hamadan Gate and the Sahand Gate open to the west. This big suburb has a circumference of thirteen thousand paces. Inside it has seventy mosques. The rest are small mosques. There are seven madrasehs and six Heydari, Bektashi, Qalandari, and Vahedi[115] Sufi convents, but although the Mevlevis and the Naqshbandis originated from Abu Bakr, there are no Mevlevi and Naqshbandi convents.

There are forty schools for children. They are very noble and mature. Where there is no well there is running water. Inside the town there are twenty public fountains, seventy guesthouses, and seven caravanserais for merchants. It has a royal bazaar with one thousand small shops, but there is no drapers' hall.

Because its climate is mild, its male and female beloveds are famous. The people's color is reddish and wheat-colored. Because of its high elevation it tends to be cold. Its water comes from Mt. Alvand, and it has numerous gardens and orchards full of flowers and fruits. Its apples, grapes, pomegranates and *meleche* pears are famous. Its pulses, wheat, barley, beans, cotton and other plants are famous.

Its people are mostly Kurds and Shiʿites. There are nobles and notables as well as physicians and surgeons. There are no ulama and saints, but there are many poets and authors. Among the good friends that we associated with were: Ganj Avarli, Alari ʿAli Yar, Hasan Meymandi,

---

overview see V. Minorsky, "Nihavand," *Encyclopedia of Islam II*.

115. See Karamustafa, *God's Unruly Friends*.

Khodadad Kindi, Sohrab Efendi, Shahbaz Agha, Tulungi Bay, Karetbay and Khan Jan. All the people wear coats made of chintz and multi-colored Livornian cotton cloth, which are in dark-blue or yellow colors.

All the women wear gold and silver tiaras, have veils, white pantaloons and blue footwear with green decorations.

THE NAMES OF THE WOMEN ARE LIKE THIS: Goldamidah, Goldamdam, Golandam, Golchini, Golshah, Golbuy, `Atr-e Shah, Sumehkhan, Sumeykehkhan, Huma Khan, Elenjejan, Golruh, Parimah, Peykarmah and Chekdim Shah.

THE NAMES OF THE SLAVES ARE LIKE THIS: Tirmid, Jan Polad, HayHay, VayVay, Hay Qoli, Vay Qoli, Qarchighay, Khorramkenderli, Qarehqay, Bayolan, Sandehki, Sevenduk, Gholamshad, Shadi and Azadli.

THE NAMES OF SLAVE GIRLS ARE LIKE THIS: Jekejan, Jedarli, Zanbaqa, Sonboleh, Feddeneh, Khannaseh, Sonneteh, Yamameh, Peymaneh, Kendideh, Khorrameh, Serahban, Sarvboy, Derakhshan, Shahbaz, Bay`ana and Jan-e Jahan.

In total there are seven bathhouses. The Pir Budaq Khan bathhouse, the Senan Pasha bathhouse and the Monshi Agha bathhouse are the most famous. There are one hundred and thirty bathhouses for noble families. The people quoting this are proud of it, and they are telling the truth.

The city was built under the stellar constellation of Scales and the house of Venus. Therefore the people are of a gentle nature. Around the city there are one hundred villages, and each village is like a town with large mosques, caravanserais, bathhouses, markets and bazaars.

CONCERNING THE EXEMPLARY NATURE OF THIS CITY. The province of Nehavand has one hundred and fifty villages, each one of which is like a city with large mosques, caravanserais, bathhouses and royal bazaars.

ANOTHER WONDROUS SIGHT. Outside the city of Nehavand, in meadows and tulip fields, on a quadrangular marble stone, the craftsmen of old have carved a vessel in the form of a wine cup, which is incredibly wonderful. In front of it one time a stream started flowing for forty days and it watered the gardens of the city and mosques and after forty days it dried up. Now that cup-like stone is still there, but the magic of that running water has disappeared.

YET ANOTHER WONDROUS SIGHT. The river Nehavand issues forth from Mt. Alvand. After watering the fields of the city of Nehavand it flows down. In the North, after watering several hundreds of villages it goes into the Lake Urmiyeh. In Nehavand near this river a kind of red-colored oily clay (which is similar to that of the island of Limni in the Mediterranean) exists. If it is diluted with water and a suffering man or woman drinks it and says: "In the name of God," all types of afflictions will go away. But the Persians deny its usefulness since this is caused by the miracles of the blessed `Omar. Now the Sunnis take it from the city and get cured.

ONCE AGAIN ANOTHER WONDROUS SIGHT. [Here follow three other allegedly interesting sights concerning an old sculpture of a fish that attracts thousand of fish, and people fish and eat them; the next one is about the skull of an Ifrit from Nehavand which wards off calamities; and the third one is about the sacrifice of a number of animals at a source by the peasants, after which it flows for forty days and they irrigate their lands with it].

Account of the first conquest of the castle of Nehavand in the time of lord of the believers ʿOmar b. Khattab, may God be pleased with him, by general Sariyat al-Jabal

When the prophet went from this world to the paradise of the next world, the caliphate was transferred to blessed Abu Bakr and the people split up in groups and were divided. Since the caliphate in the year 23 after the hijra [644] came to blessed ʿOmar, the Kharejites started to revolt in Persian Iraq, Basra, Kufa and Nehavand. Finally, the blessed ʿOmar, may God be pleased with him, sent the blessed Sariya with an army of eighty thousand choice Arab soldiers. After crossing many stages they arrived at Nehavand, where they fought with the Persian Kharejite armies for seven hours. Eventually the Persians were victorious and the army of Islam lost heart. By God's wisdom it was on a Friday. The blessed ʿOmar was on the pulpit of Madina and said: "I order my rebellious soul to obey God's will." While reading the *khutbah*, he saw with his inner eye that Sariya was being defeated, and he left the pulpit shouting three times: "O Sariya run to the mountains." The whole congregation remained in wonder and the blessed ʿOmar resumed his *khutbah*. Some of the congregation said: "Blessed ʿOmar made a mistake in the *khutbah* by addressing the general Sariyah when he was at a five months' distance." Another one said: "His mind was somewhere else and he made a mistake in the *khutbah*." Many others said similar things, but the Companions who were far-sighted and knowing said: "There is wisdom here." They referred to what the blessed ʿOmar said at that moment ("O Sariya, to the mountain").[116] Blessed ʿOmar in truth at the moment of the *khutbah* prayed twice and said: "God be praised," and then came down from the pulpit with joy and began the Friday prayer.

At the other end, at the foot of the castle of Nehavand, the army of Islam all heard the shout by the blessed ʿOmar ("O Sariya, to the mountain"), and all of them after having put the mountain of Nehavand at their back began fighting again with arrows, swivel guns, and slings. While shouting "Allah, Allah," they attacked the army of the renegades and Kharejites and by God's will the Qizilbash[117] were put to flight. In the year 26 [646-47], in this manner, the castle of Nehavand was conquered by the Moslems for the first time.

Later the news of this great victory together with the plunder and the keys of the castle came to the blessed ʿOmar and all the people of Mecca and Madina rejoiced and understood that the shout by ʿOmar ("O Sariya, to the mountain") was the reason for the victory. All those who had been his critics now loved the blessed ʿOmar and realized what kind of caliph he was.

Sheikh Sari became the governor of Nehavand and of all of Persian Iraq and of Ujan-Azerbaijan. Blessed Sari then conquered Qazvin, Hamadan, Dargazin, Qom, Kashan, Rey, Sahand and Kahravan. Later, in the time of the caliphate of ʿOmar, Sheikh Sari along with ʿAmr b. ʿAs were in the Egyptian campaign. Outside Fustat, Amir Juheyni and Zonnun-e Misri, Mansur-e

---

116. See Dehkhoda q.v. Sariya, who lists the various sources that relate the same tale. However, although this battle actually took place, the tale told here does not seem to be based in fact, see V. Minorsky, "Nihavand," *Encyclopedia of Islam II*.

117. At that time neither the Kharejites nor the Qizilbash existed.

Ansari and Sheikh Sari were martyred at the same time, and Sheikh Sari was buried in the upper castle of Misr-e Jadid in the cellar room of the Tavashi Sulayman Pasha mosque. Now it is the place of pilgrimage for devout people. But of the people who were fighting with the blessed Sari in the battle of Nehavand, there were seven chosen companions who were martyred, and several of them were transmitters of Traditions. Now their inscribed tombs are objects of veneration. God willing we will write about this.

In short, from the adversities of this world this city of Nehavand has passed through many hands, and in the year 940 [1533-34] in the reign of Sultan Sulayman it was conquered by Koja Farhad Pasha and then again it went back to the Persians.

Later, in the year 959 [1552] in the reign of Sultan Murad III, Cheghal-oghlu Senan Pasha came with a huge army from Baghdad and in seven hours of fighting conquered this castle. He fortified it according to his wishes and gave its governorship to his deputy Sukhteh Mohammad Pasha and he took care of the arms and equipment and put seven batallions of slave soldiers altogether twenty thousand guards in there.[118]

Thereafter, in the year 1031 [1622] the Persians retook it. Then in the year 1039 [1629-30] we know that Khosrow Pasha, the valiant vizier of Bagh-e Jenani, attacked Hamadan and Dargazin, plundered them and destroyed Nehavand. Since then this has become a very beautiful city. God's will is upon his servants forever.

Going towards the south we arrived at:

The village of Sayyedler. It is in the district of Nehavand, and all its people are Sunnis sayyeds. Then we went towards the south via Cheghal-oghlu and we reached:

**The village of Hazrat-e Sa`d-e Vaqqas.**[119] It is situated in the district of Nehavand. It has one thousand houses; it is a beautiful village like a town with large mosques, caravanserais and royal bazaar. In the battle of Nehavand, Sa`d-e Vaqqas was wounded by an enemy arrow, and he stayed in this village until he was cured. He said: "May it prosper," and prayed. Now the 'Place of Sa`d-e Vaqqas' is a site of pilgrimage. There are a number of Sunni convent dwellers, but we have heard that some of the saints are buried in several other places (to wit:) First, in the Baqi cemetery of Madina,[120] inside the Green Gate of the castle of Iskanderiyeh in Egypt, in Jisr-e Ya`qub near Damascus[121] as well as in Jubb-e Yusof (Joseph's Well),[122] which are among the main shrines that we visited. May God bless his resting place. We visited his shrine in Persia, and passing from there we arrived at Kangavar.

Description of the city of the Jevr, i.e., the castle of Kangavar. Its founder is Anushirvan. In the Georgian and Mongol languages it is called the castle of Hor Kinkevr. It is

---

118. The *kapukulu* were slave soldiers formed by Murad I into his own personal army. The Janissary corps was its most famous branch.

119. Now called Gusheh-ye Sa`d-e Vaqqas; its geographical coordinates are 34° 16' 60" North, 48° 14' 27".

120. This is the first and oldest Moslem cemetery of Madina, see A.J. Wensinck and A.S. Bazmee Ansari, "Baqi al-Kharqad," *Encyclopedia of Islam II*.

121. Probably Jisr Banat Ya`qub, on the Jordan River, which now is situated in Israel.

122. For more information on this site see [http://en.wikipedia.org/wiki/Jubb_Yussef_(Joseph's_Well)].

situated in the district of Nehavand[123] and is under a *darugheh*, but its circumference is not known to me. It is a pentagonal stone castle on a hill, which has a suburb with one thousand houses, a large mosque, a caravanserai, a bathhouse, a bazaar and gardens. Most of the people are Shahrezur Kurds and Shi`ites. From here to Nehavand is one hour distance. This castle was conquered in 995 [1587] by Cheghal-oghlu, then the Persians retook it and now is in their hands.

On the slopes of Mt. Bisotun after passing over the royal bridge and going towards the south we reached Sorkh Bid.

Description of the province of Sipid, i.e., the castle of Sorkhbid.

Its founder is one of the boon companions of Harun al-Rashid, whose name was Qizil Oghlan. In Persian it is called the castle of Sorkhbid, which means 'Red willow castle,' but the Turkmen Afshar tribes call it the castle of Qizil Oghlan (Red boy). It is situated in the district of Nehavand on a high hill covered with willows. It is a nice rectangular but small castle. It has a gate opening to the North and Nehavand. I did not enter it, but in the garden situated in the lower part I became the guest of the Sultan, who was a very old Persian, who is said to be one hundred and forty years old! It has one thousand soldiers, a qazi, a mayor and twelve officials, for the love of the Twelve Imams, who govern in accordance with the rules and regulations of the Shahs of Iran and Turan. The lower suburb has no gardens and orchards, but has running water, three thousand houses and is a town filled with red willows, especially red willow groves. This is considered part of Persian Iraq, but it is adjacent to Shahrezur (in Arabian Iraq). This town has all the necessary buildings.

This castle was conquered by {Cheghal-zadeh} in the year 995 [1586], and he made it into a *sanjaq* called Sorkhbid and gave it to `Ali Bey of `Aqrah. Thereafter, the Persians martyred `Ali Bey when taking the castle, and his tomb can be seen in the public road.

We left this castle and in the company of our good friends, we wandered, going to the north, then to the south, then to the west, then to the east, and then again to the south, while observing the many thousands of wonders of God. Then, turning again towards the east we reached the castle of Bisotun.

Description of Golgun (Rose-colored) Castle, i.e., the castle of Bisotun.

This castle was again rebuilt in the year 999 [1591] by the vizier of Sultan Murad, the great general Cheghal-oghlu Senan Pasha. When he was campaigning between Baghdad, Hamadan, Dargazin and Nehavand and between Tabriz, he built it on the slopes of Mt. Bisotun on a high hill with cut stones to make these places secure. There is no castle like it in these parts. Some base-minded people say that the Ottomans cannot build such a castle, may their face be blackened! Now this castle of Bisotun is a place worthy of seeing and an impressive one, for all of its walls and buildings are made of rose-colored stones. Its circumference is three thousand paces and having been built on a high hill there is no moat. Towards the north it has a gate, and I have not seen the like of such an iron gate in all of Persia. Inside the castle it has one hundred and fifty houses and a good mansion belonging to the Sultan of Bisotun, the Murad III mosque, and its storehouses and it has a well which is very deep.[124]

---

123. For the very early history of Kangavar, its name and its ancient monuments, which does not include this castle, see Wolfram Kleiss, "Kangavar," *Encyclopedia Iranica*; see further Mas`ud Golzari, *Kermanshahan – Kurdestan shamel-e banaha va athar-e tarikhi-ye Asadabad, Kangavar-Sahneh* (Tehran, 1357/1978), vol. 1, pp. 111-201.

124. There is no archeological evidence for the presence of an Ottoman for at Bisotun, see Heinz

Its Sultan has one thousand soldiers and castle guards as well as twelve officials. In the castle the cannons left by Cheghal-zadeh still can be seen.

Since it has been recently built, the Persians call it New Castle. From the castle of Sorkhbid it is one stage to the castle of Bisotun. The lower suburb is situated on the slopes of Mt. Bisotun; it does not have a wall. Its people consist of three thousand households of troublesome Kurds, who are Shi`ites, Rafazis and beggars. It has all sorts of buildings, and its public roads and bazaars are very clean. Because of being situated on the slopes of Mt. Bisotun, more than three hundred streams flow into the town. It has plenty of pulses and plants, but it does not have many fruits. In the mountains there is plenty of wood, which is good for winter.

DESCRIPTION OF MT. BISOTUN. God almighty has created one hundred forty-eight mountains on the face of the earth and all the commentators of the verse: "To him are the keys of heaven and earth,"[125] explain the word "*maqalid*" as "key" and "mountain." All the old sages have identified those hundred and forty-eight mountains, and one of them is Mt. Bisotun. But it is not as high as Mts. Elburz, Samur, Sobhan and Arjish (Ararat). But being an outstanding mountain there is nothing like it. For example, the people of Sodom and Gomorrah have made carvings on it. If several thousand soldiers with their animals would be placed there, there won't be lack of room. Under it there are several ponds and old courtyards and different kinds of bird's nests. When you cry "Hu" under this mountain it echoes like a thunder in the mountains and one becomes frightened.

{Inside the cave it is almost} like a plain, and above it there is this huge mountain as a shade. You would say that this impressive mountain stands without pillars and that is why it is called Mt. Bisotun, (i.e. without pillars). Some people say that "Farhad[126] has carved it," but they are mistaken. The mountains that Farhad has carved are the Amalekite Mountains situated near the castle of Amasiya, and the water channels that he has carved still can be seen there. But this Bisotun cannot have been carved by human beings.

According to the limited intelligence of this humble author, to show His power God almighty, at the time of Noah's deluge, carved out the foot of the rock with the sea waves and smashing water and by bringing the violent waves of the sea to the plains of Hamadan. Whoever looks at it is filled with wonder.[127] In this world there is nothing like Mt. Bisotun. On the top of the mountain there are very large wonderful summer quarters with much vegetation and running water, in which there are several thousand colorful fish. The remains of the old buildings and palaces of the old caliphs of Baghdad can be seen there. Kurds, Afshar Turkmen and Yaka Turkmen make their summer quarters here and in winter with several thousand people they travel six months and

---

Luschey, "Bisotun," *Encyclopedia Iranica*.

125. Koran (al-Yusuf).

126. "Farhad is romantic figure in Persian legend and literature, best known from the poetry of Nezami Ganjavi as a rival with the Sasanian king Khosrow II Parviz (r. 591-628) for the love of the beautiful Armenian princess Shirin. Khosrow, unable to dissuade Farhad from abandoning his love for Shirin, charges him with the task of cutting a road through the rocks of Bisotun, agreeing to give up, as a reward, his own claim to Shirin." Heshmat Moayyad, "Farhad," *Encyclopedia Iranica*.

127. For a discussion of the name, inscriptions and role of Bisotun see Rüdiger Schmitt and Heinz Luschey, "Bisotun," *Encyclopedia Iranica*.

spend the winter in the plains of Domdomi, Domboli, Sahand, Urmiyeh and Salmas. This is a description of a pillarless mountain or *bisotun*. It is said about Bisotun:

> The world has a heart hard as steel
> It remembers many Leylas and Majnuns
> Every tulip that grows on Mt. Bisotun
> Every flower is imbued with Farhad's scent.

بسی لیلی و مجنون یاد دارد   فلک شیدا دلی پولاد دارد
به هر گل بویی ز فرهاد دارد   ز کوه بیستون هر گل بروید

Leaving this place towards the south and passing through a well-cultivated plain and many villages we came after [-] hours to Hamadan.

Description of the royal capital, the creation of Jamshid, son of Shaddad the faithless, i.e., the peerless city of Hamadan

According to all the historians of Arabia, Persia and Hindustan, especially the author of the *Tarikh-e Yanvan-e Yunan*,[128] Jamshid son of Shaddad is the first founder of the city. He found a big treasure on Mt. Bisotun and with that he built the city of Hamadan. It is situated in the land of Persian Iraq. In the history of Mighdisi, the Armenian it is called Mardjuvaz.[129] In the Mongol language it is called Kalchak, and in Greek it is called Daranya, because the throne of Darius was in this Hamadan. The Kurds call it Hemavdan, which means the city of waters, and in Persian it is called Hamadan. The circumference of its castle is four thousand paces and it is six-cornered. It has seventy towers and each of its stones is like the dome of a bathhouse and like a Mahmudi elephant's trunk. It has a moat around it, but it is not very deep. Although its walls are not so high they are very thick. It has four gates, called the Qom, Bisotun, Dargazin and Baghdad gates. In the castle there are about two thousand small rooms. It has a bathhouse, a caravanserai, a large mosque and shops. It has sufficient arms, big cannons and about one thousand soldiers. The province has five hundred prosperous villages, which are [each] like a town.

Concerning the officials. It is a separate khanate situated at the border of Iraq. Its Khan is called Jan Apay Khan who had three thousand choice, well-armed royal slaves, raw flesh eaters, retainers, soldiers and irregulars. He also has three thousand courageous mounted soldiers. The

---

128. We have not been able to identify this chronicle.

129. For the early history of Hamadan see Stuart C. Brown, "Ecbatana," *Encyclopedia Iranica*, which does not have these details. For the history of Hamadan after the Islamic conquest of Iran see Parviz Adhka'i, "Hamadan," *Encyclopedia Iranica* and Bert Fragner, *Geschichte der Stadt Hamadan und ihrer Umgebung in der ersten sechs Jahrhunderten nach der Hijra* (Vienna, 1972). For a short description of Hamadan in 1664 see Jean Thevenot, *The Travels of M. de Thevenot* 3 vols. in one (London, 1686), vol. 2, p. 72.

officials are: a mullah for the Shafe'is, a *khvajeh-ye anam*,[130] a *sayyed al-sadat*,[131] a chief of the royal slaves, a chief of the ushers, a mayor, a clerk, a police chief and a chief of the merchants. In short, each retainer and soldier is well-armed.

CONCERNING THE MADRASEHS. There are in total nine schools and institutions for learning, each of which has been built by the Shah's ancestors. Now, the scholars having spent their fixed stipends all the rooms are vacant, although each one of them has a porter.

DESCRIPTION OF THE SCHOOL FOR BOYS. There are forty schools for young boys; among them Khorramabad, Jahan Shah, Ganj-e Yar and Humevaran schools are famous. These schools are full of smart loveable boys.

CONCERNING SUFI CONVENTS. There are eleven Sufi convents. Among the gardens of the city the convents of Ganj-e Yar, Imam Taqi, 'Arab-e Jabbari, and the Shahrokh convent next to the Baghdad Gate are famous; all of them are Bektashi dervishes.

CONCERNING THE RUNNING SPRINGS. It has one hundred and fifty springs. If I describe each one of them I cannot write my Travel account. The spring of Farhad Pasha and 'Ali Esen are the only Ottomans works that are well wrought. Its water comes from Mt. Alvand.

CONCERNING THE PUBLIC FOUNTAINS. Inside the city there are many public fountains for thirsty people in the markets and bazaars. But when we asked about them their number was not known. The water comes from Mt. Alvand and is very clear and in summer it is ice-cold.

CONCERNING THE NUMBER OF THE MANSIONS OF THE NOTABLES. Altogether there are eight thousand upper and lower brick buildings. But the mansions of Khodaverdi Khan, Hamzeh Sultan, Pir Budaq Sultan and 'Alamshah Khan are the most famous. All of them are covered with clean earth.

CONCERNING THE HOSTELS FOR TRAVELERS. In three places they have beautiful guest-houses made of bricks. The best well-worked among them are the caravanserai of Fardad Pasha and the hostel of Alvand Khan. In this city there are no buildings with lead.

CONCERNING THE BUILDINGS OF MERCHANTS. There are eleven renovated caravanserais and in them merchants from India, Sind, Rum, Arabia and Persia stay. Each one is like a castle with fortifications, and the gates are made of Nakhjevan steel.

CONCERNING THE BAZAAR AND THE DRAPERS' HALL. Its royal bazaar has two thousand small shops, and they are very clean, prosperous and well-decorated. However, they are not like the shops made of brick, which exist in Aleppo, Damascus and Bursa. The main roads are covered with wood.

CONCERNING THE BATHHOUSES. It has seven bathhouses.

---

130. This term occurs a few times, also as *khvajeh-ye Islam*, the meaning of which is unclear. Given the context and the literal meaning, i.e., 'leader of the people,' we think it is perhaps a synonym for *pish-namaz* or the prayer leader.

131. This term probably is a synonym for the *naqib* or the chief of the sayyeds, i.e., the descendants of the prophet Mohammad.

Concerning the private bathhouses of the notables. The leading notables of Hamadan boast that "there are in total two hundred mansions with bathhouses," and they praise God. In fact, I went to a bathhouse in the Khan Avenue, which was beautiful and well-lit and reminded me of the bathhouse in Bitlis.

Concerning the nobles and notables. The notables and aristocrats that we encountered were: Heba-oghlu, Qessar-oghlu, Ganj ʿAli, Mehman Qoli, Pir Yar and Shah Bodaq, and they are well-versed in the Persian language.

Concerning experienced physicians. There are few physicians. But among those are the experienced Jan Qoli of Shiraz, Yar ʿAli Badakshani, Khvajeh Nukkal Tirmidhi, Khoy'i Hasan Meymandi and Chanarut Hamadani. They have offices and are masters.

Concerning surgeons and phlebotomists. In this city there is no surgeon, because they are an ignorant people in this branch of learning. When one of my slaves fell from his horse and got wounded slightly we could not find a surgeon. We found somebody who was itinerant and had come from Duhukli near ʿEmadiyeh.

Concerning Sufi saints and Sheikhs. There was only one from Rum (Anatolia), but they called him a Sunni and they did not care for him. But Sufi Sheikhs such as Mullah Berzenji, Mullah Herami and Sheikh Sorkhbidi are eremites and secluded from the world and people.

Authors and poets. There is no end to authors and poets in Hamadan. Although it is the land of Persia, the poets excel in eloquence and knowledge of Arabic. They even said this poem in Arabic about Hamadan:

> It is a city about whose quality and reputation I say
> That is the worst of cities because there is no good in it;
> In unseemly behavior its youths are like its sheikhs,
> And in wisdom its sheikhs are like its youths.

بلد اكلو بفضله
لكنه اقبح البلدان صبيانه
فى القبح مثل شيوخيهى
وشيوخه فى العقلى وا لصبيانى

Description of mens' clothes. The men wear multi-colored *qalamkar* chintz, wrap multi-colored turbans around their heads and, proud Safavid Sufi headdresses, their trousers have shoes sewn onto them, and (they wear) a green dress, a multi-colored vest and green, cyan-blue or orange-colored footwear.

The various clothes of women. The women wear golden and silver felt hats, silken skull-caps, put silk veils over their face, wear white (Livornian and Bahrampuri) cottons, fine cotton pantaloons and wrap themselves in fine cotton (*metqali baz*) covers, and in this way they frequent the city.

Names of beardless boys. Most of them are called Qareh Khan, Qareh Jan, Qarehqul Khan, Qareh Pireh, Seyf al-Din, Shams al-Din, Esmadin, Khorramay, Sunqurqay, Shahlavand Qay, Ganjeh Bay and Alvand Aq.

Female names. Most women are called Marjaneh Khanom, Hangoleh Khanom, Shadbad Khanom, Marhaba Khanom, Sevenduk Khanom, Gol Ban Khanom, Enzeleh, Tanzileh, Golchehreh, Malekruh, Jandelan and Shahban.

Names of slaves. Most of them are Georgian slaves and their names are such as: Quli, Yashar, Kendibal, Shah-bandeh, Khodabandeh, Gelgit, Charapar, Alatli, Parviz, Bahrehman Yar `Ali, Qutlu, Qalandar and Siyami.

Names of slaves girls. Georgian slave girls and wretched Russian ones are brought from Gilan. They have names such as: Shelefeh, Halajeh, Galehjeh, Haneseh, Sevdayeh, Mahriyeh, Tabandeh, Golchin, Mahchin, Kuneseh and Emateh.

Languages of the people of Hamadan. They speak Yaka Turkmen: *Harada idin, pes men neylerem, men dildigim idermen, heze telisemen.*[132] Their oaths are: *Guzelche Shah bashiychun va kirmizi Murtaza Ali hakkiychun ve Duvazda Imamlar ervahiychun.*[133] They also know the Kurdish and Armenian languages.

The color of the faces of youths. Most of the people are swarthy and tawny, tall and strong. They are Shi`ite, Rafezi, Mu`tazelite, Moshabbehi and Hurufi of religion. There are Sunnis among them who practice in secret.

Male and female beloveds. The male and female beauties are swarthy of color and sweet of disposition. The women are desirable. But their male beauties are less desirable and common place, because the people of Hamadan mostly are desirous of women, for the women are not slanderers and gossipers, and they are passionate lovers.

Concerning its good climate. The city of Hamadan's climate tends to be cold. But in summer and fall, because of its location, it is very healthy, and all of its people, male and female, old and young, and all of its cattle and quadrupeds are stout and fleshy.

Concerning its running streams. All the city's springs have running water and are coming from the western side of the high Mt. Alvand and are distributed among the houses. According to the city's inhabitants, there are nine thousand and sixty wells. The reason for that is that when there is a siege they take refuge with all their property and family in these subterranean places and fight and battle against the people that have come against them.

The climes of the city. According to the saying of Mullah Ahun, this city of Hamadan is situated in the middle of the eighteenth clime. They also celebrate the Eve of Yalda.

---

132. Where were you, what would I do, this is what I heard, do not make haste.

133. By the head of the beloved Shah, and by the right of Red Morteza `Ali and the soul of the Twelve Imams.

THE AUSPICIOUS CONSTELLATION UNDER WHICH IT WAS BUILT. This city of Hamadan was built under the constellation of Aries and the house of fiery Mars. Therefore, each forty to fifty years there is a rebellion and in the fashion of Mars there is much bloodshed in war.

THE CHURCHES. There are seven churches of the infidel Armenians, among them the church of Behtak Deyri, built by Anushirvan, is very well done. There are no Greeks (Rum), Franks and Copts, but there are many Jews. The Jews of Hamadan are well-known. But, as the saying goes:

On the day of resurrection the Rafazis will serve as a donkey to the Jews.

رافضی روز قیامت خر بود زیر یهود

EXEMPLARY PROSPERITY. When he rebuilt the city of Hamadan, the wretched Jamshid placed pillars where the sun rose, and put talismans on them, but in many places his writings have been trodden by animals.

PULSES AND CROPS. There are ten different types of wheat that are very shining and large-grained and inside they are full-bodied. Its beans, rice, broad beans and other pulses are plentiful. It has plenty of herbs and vegetables.

IN THE PRAISE OF EDIBLE THINGS. Three Sheikh Safi *man* of bread are sold for one *qazbeygi*. One *qazbeygi* is two *derhams*, which is one *mangir*. One *man* is equal to two hundred and sixty *derhams* and three *man* of bread cost one *qazbeygi*, while two *oqqeh* of bread costs one *mangir*.[134] But its bread is somewhat dark.

CONCERNING ITS FRUITS. There are many gardens, and they have many types of apples, *meshmeshi* plums, Bokhara plums and Gilani pears, which are famous. Its grapes are a bit bitter; they have pomegranates, lemons, oranges and figs, but they are not very good.

THE KINDS OF BEVERAGES. The sherbet made from the manna of Mt. Alvand is honey-like. The snowflake, cilantro-mint chutney sherbet, poppy-seed sherbet and pomegranate sherbets are famous, but there are no almonds. Its fermented rice beer (*boza*) is plentiful.

PUBLIC KITCHENS. There are three buildings in the city where they give wheat boiled with milk (*keshkek*), cream wheat soup, and *khosk pilau* to all comers. Among the most well known public kitchens are the Jahan Shah and the Shah Khodabandeh.

THE GARDENS. Altogether it has forty-six thousands gardens. To the west is Mt. Bisotun where there are trellised gardens. People from other cities have gardens in Hamadan. Whenever you enter any garden you are bewildered. All trees and the mansions are geometrically planned.

---

134. This seems to refer to the small canonical *batman* that weighed 833 gram. Hinz, *Islamische Masse*, p. 21. *Mangir* is a copper coin of small value like the *qazbeygi*.

General aspects of the beautiful city of Hamadan

The city of Hamadan is situated in Persian Iraq. It is considered a mountainous city, i.e. it is one of the cities situated in the eastern part of the Kurdistan mountains, and the ancient city [of Qom] is situated to the east of this city of Hamadan. Between them there are five stages, and each stage is twenty-four thousand paces. The cities of Qasr-e Losus, Qazvin and Hamadan are so close to one another that they are like the legs of the tripod plate for bread-making (*saj*). Their territories are adjacent to each other, but there are no other cities in between. Outside the city are the summer quarters of Mt. Alvand, which are famous among Arabs and Persians. The Kurdish and Turkmen tribes spend the summer there with their several hundred thousand animals. There is even a Kurdish poem:

> Our Alvand, our Beautiful One
> > Our reward and our boon companion,
> Give one cup with that wine to the
> > Child of our Mt. Alvand.

الوند ما لوند ما
باداش یار غار ما
یک جام بده این باده را
فرزند کوهٔ الوند ما

In this area and near Mt. Alvand and the hills around it, there are huge caves that extend into the surroundings of Hamadan and every time a rebel attacks Hamadan all of the inhabitants take refuge in that cave. From here to the plain of the district of Zalim ʿAli is one stage and it is very prosperous. Poem:

> Sahand, Savalan and Mt. Alvand
> > All three complain to God
> {Who says: Sahand and Savalan do not boast
> > For Mt. Alvand has a thousand springs.}

سهند ساوالان کوه الوند
هر سه شکوه کنند پیش خداوند
سهند ساولان تو لاف مزن
هزاران چشمه دارد کوه الوند

The conquest of the old city of Hamadan. Twenty-eight years after the hijra [648-49] in the time of the caliphate of the blessed ʿOmar, the companions of the blessed Sariyat al-Jabal wrested this castle of Hamadan by the sword from the hands of the Kharejites.

It was again conquered in the year 244 [858-59] by Harun al-Rashid. In short, it was saved from many troubles and struggles. Eventually in the year 940 [1533-34] in the time of Sultan Sulayman, Koja Ebrahim Pasha conquered it and granted quarter sending the keys to Sultan Sulayman. The province of Hamadan became an Ottoman governorship-general.

The Shah of Persia retook it in 995 [1587] in the time of Sultan Murad III, when Cheghaloghlu Senan Pasha, one of his viziers, came from Baghdad to Hamadan with an innumerable army. Shah ʿAbbas I received news about his coming and at that time the governor of Kurdistan, Shahverdi Khan, was still in the service of the Shah and had received a Safavid Sufi hat (*taj*) from him. The erring Shah appeased Shahverdi Khan and elevated him to the rank of vizier. He put on his head a royal feather and on his waist a bejeweled sword. Sending Qorkhmas Khan with some brave Sultans to his aid with forty thousand soldiers, he made him commander of the army and set him against the army of Islam. Near the city of Hamadan along the high mountains these evil troops were silently lying in ambush, and the army of Islam under Hamadan pitched their tents and rested. Some who were going to graze their horses were captured. Senan Pasha armed himself and sent several *bey*s and *beylerbeyi*s to four sides to guard and skirmish. He assigned somebody called ʿAli Faqi, a courageous Pasha, as skirmisher. At the same time, the Persians fell upon these two brave men and both of them were martyred. On the other side, the army of Islam shouted "Allah, Allah" while attacking the Qizilbash, who were waiting in ambush, and they came out from their holes shouting "Shah, Shah". On the plains of Hamadan the two armies clashed in such a way that for seven hours a river of blood was flowing. It seems that from the side of Nehavand soldiers came with green banners, who joined with the Ottoman army.

One of the soldiers said: "My Sultan! What kind of army are you that you do not have any swords and your horses don't have any armor."[135] One of them said: "We are the souls that have been martyred in the blessed battle of Nehavand." The army of Islam like hungry wolves once again attacked the Kurdish and Qizilbash army, and at that hour they killed forty thousand Qizilbash horsemen and brought Qorkhmas Khan, the wretched general of the Qizilbash, in chains to the general. But the royal vizier, Shahverdi Khan, fled to Kahravan. The remainder of the army fled to the high mountains.

God be praised that this happened on the Day of the Feast of Sacrifice and instead of sacrificial blood (of sheep) Qizilbash blood was shed. The general having become victorious, the inhabitants of Hamadan peacefully submitted the keys of the castle to Cheghal-oghlu Senan Pasha while saying: "O chosen of the Ottomans, mercy, mercy!" .

Later, in the year 1032 [1623], in the time of the caliphate of Sultan Mostafa, the king of Persia conquered and took possession of Hamadan, Dargazin, Qom, and Kashan. In the beginning of this inauspicious year he conquered Baghdad. Because in the year 1033 [1624] Sultan Murad IV acceded to the throne, in 1035 [1625] he sent the great general Hafez Ahmad Pasha as commander of the Baghdad campaign. He besieged Baghdad for seven months, and when the Shah of Persia came to the help of Baghdad, Hafez Ahmad Pasha remained between Baghdad and the Shah of Persia. Since no provisions were left, the army of Islam became unified and of one mind and attacked the Shah's army. But neither the Shah nor the Ottomans could win a definite victory. Finally they went to the trenches, while from inside Baghdad they shouted: "The Qizilbash came to conquer the trenches!"

The Ottomans fought the Shah and the castle of Baghdad and were weakened being short of provisions and arms as well as because of the hot weather; in this way they continued the siege of Baghdad for nine months. They suffered thousands of difficulties and miseries. In the end the Shah showed inclination to peace, and from both sides envoys were sent. The entire Ottoman

---

135. The word used is '*suhayl*', which normally means the star Canopus, but which does not make sense here. We therefore have guessed that it perhaps means here, given the context, 'armor.'

army withdrew to Diyarbekr. Hafez Ahmad Pasha, being disappointed and having failed and being without victory, returned and fell from favor.

The second time, in the year 1036 [1626-27], Khalil Pasha became grand vizier. Dishlen Hoseyn Pasha became general over Abaza Pasha. Abaza Pasha killed Dishlen Hoseyn Pasha with his tribe. After him, Khosrow Pasha, in the year 1038 [16268-29], became general over Abaza. From Abaza he conquered Erzerum and he took Akhiskha and Qars from the Persians, telling the Khans of Hamadan, Dargazin, Nehavand and Baghdad, "Let us be ready." He brought Abaza Pasha in chains to Sultan Murad. Sultan Murad set Abaza Pasha free and gave him the border province of Bosnia.

Later in the year 1039 [1629-30] the grand vizier Khosrow Pasha became general for the Baghdad campaign, and after passing many stages he reached Diyarbekr. From there after twenty stages he reached Mosul. When he saw the Euphrates, which was like a sea, he said: "With such a numerous army of Islam one cannot leave them idle." From below the castle of Mosul he ordered them to go to every side, and with much plunder he came the second day to Hamadan. He pillaged and destroyed poor Hamadan and its environs. He destroyed and plundered the peerless houses, gardens, orchards and several thousand of its paradise-like gardens with their beautiful Khorasan-like mansions, ponds and fountains in such a way that they became the resting places of crows. The Qizilbash who were besieged in the castle asked for quarter, saying: "O chosen one of the Ottomans," and submitted the keys of the castle to Khosrow Pasha in the year 1039 [1629-30]. Getting several hundred loads of plunder, he returned to the castle of ʿEmadiyeh and appointed the brother of the governor of ʿEmadiyeh, Zeynal Beg, as governor of Hamadan. Then he turned to Baghdad, which we will explain in its proper place, God willing. {But since that destruction it has become so prosperous as if it is half of the world.}

DESCRIPTION OF THE PLACES OF PILGRIMAGE OF HAMADAN. From the time of the conquest by the blessed Sariya in the time of the caliphate of blessed Omar there have been more than two thousand tombs of Emigrants, Companions, and the Arbab-e Soffeh,[136] buried there; now their tombstones are known. They are the blessed Jaʿfar Ansari, Khalil b. Hesan Shaʿer, Naser al-Din b. Ayub Suhyani and Shehab b. Dhu'l-Nun al-Misri. Of Persian scholars, authors and writers there are several hundred thousand buried there. I do not know which ones to mention. In the year 995 [1587], near the river the tombs could be seen of those who were martyred in the battle of Cheghal-oghlu (such as): ʿAli Faqi Pasha, Deli Dizman Bey, and Seyami Pasha. Leaving here we traveled towards the south and we reached after seven hours:

THE STAGE OF THE VILLAGE OF AVEH.[137] It is a village in the district of Dargazin with three thousand houses, markets, and many large mosques, caravanserais and bathhouses. It is town-like village under a *darugheh*. Most of the inhabitants are weavers and gardeners. There are many crops and fruits. Going towards the south we passed many prosperous places in two days and came to Kermanshah.

---

136. A group of poor Moslems, who were given permission by the Prophet Mohammad to live in a corner of the Madína mosque. The *Ahl-e Soffeh*, as they also are referred to, had given up worldly desires and devoted their lives to the better understanding of God's will.

137. Aveh usually is mentioned in one breath with Saveh, and thus cannot possibly be in this phase of the itinerary.

DESCRIPTION OF THE CASTLE OF KERMANSHAH. It was built in 915 [1509-10] by Shah Esma'il and therefore it was called Kermanshah.[138] It is situated in the district of Hamadan in a vast plain. It is a beautiful brick building. It is pentagonal, has two gates, one thousand soldiers, and it is a separate sultanate. At present it is under the shah's vizier, Sheikh 'Ali Khan Luri, whose representative is its Sultan. Originally this city was on the border of Lurestan; it is a big city. All its buildings, gardens and orchards are well-made. Going from here towards the east for nine hours we came to:

THE STAGE OF THE MOUNTAIN PASS OF DARGAZIN. May God aid us, because it is a narrow pass, dark, with steep precipices, and the mountains tower over it. On the rocks there were eagles, hawks, hunting owls, goshawks and vultures. In these rocks there are old and huge caves similar to the caves of Van castle.

In 1039 [1629-30], when the great general Khosrow Pasha was passing by, several thousand of the evil and head-shaved Qizilbash troops had taken refuge in those caves and several thousand of good Moslem fighters for the faith were killed. In that pass of Dargazin all the martyrs are buried in one line on the side of the kings of Persia so that it will be an admonishment to the Ottomans. From there after [-] hours we reached Dargazin.

DESCRIPTION OF THE CASTLE OF DARGAZIN.[139] Its first founder was Yazdegerd. It was called Dargazin because Shah Yazdegerd built a big gate of Nakhjevani steel to protect the land of Iraq from the invasion by the Arab, Kurdish and Mongol people and every night they closed that pass. Later, he built this castle and called it Dar-e Guzin (the chosen gate), hence the name. Now mistakenly they pronounce "from (*dar-e*) *guzin*" as *dargazin*. It is a pentagonal, strong castle situated on a low hill in Persian Iraq to the east of the pass of Dargazin in the plains of Hamadan. Its every stone is as big as the kettle-drums of Isfahan or of Baghdad. But this castle is smaller than that of Hamadan and its circumference is five hundred paces and altogether has forty towers, three gates, which are the Hamadan, Baghdad and Mosul gates. It is surrounded by a moat, and there are large mosques inside the castle. The caravanserais, bathhouses and bazaars are on the outside. I do not know how many houses there are inside.

CONCERNING THE GOVERNORS OF DARGAZIN. It was a sultanate in the time of Shah Tahmasp. Thereafter, Shah Safi, who gave Baghdad to Sultan Murad in the year 1048 [1638-39] in gratitude because cities like Hamadan, Dargazin, Ardabil and Qazvin remained in his hands, made the district of this castle of Dargazin into a khanate.[140] Shah Safi gave the governorship of Dargazin to the younger brother of Khalaf Khan, who had been released from Baghdad through Sultan Murad's amnesty. He was an old wretched Qizilbash and would say: "By God, by red Morteza 'Ali, I am a Sunni."[141] He has three thousand soldiers and one thousand guards in the castle, a chief of the royal slaves, a mayor, a police chief, a clerk, a chief of the ushers, a chief of the guards, a qazi, a *khvajeh-ye Islam* and the overseer of the sayyeds. The castle has middle-sized artillery and an adequately stocked arsenal.

---

138. Kermanshah was centuries older, see A.K.S. Lambton, "Kirmanshah," *Encyclopedia of Islam II*.

139. For a brief history of Dargazin see Parviz Adhka'i, "Darjazin," *Encyclopedia Iranica*.

140. It was already a seat of a khan in 1572, see Nasiri, *Titles*, p. 176.

141. Starting as early as 1572 the Safavids had appointed Uzbeg Sunni princes as governor of Dargazin. It is likely that Khalaf Khan was also an Uzbeg. Nasiri, *Titles*, p. 176.

The town of Dargazin

LAYOUT OF THE OUTER SUBURB. It is surrounded by a deep moat and it is a big suburb. Its mayor, Qirchighah Agha, said: "It has seven thousand houses, seven large mosques, five madrasehs, ten elementary schools, seven caravanserais, four bathhouses, seven thousand gardens and orchards and six hundred royal shops." Its royal bazaar is well embellished; its coffeehouses and barbershops are greatly loved.

The male and female beloveds because of its pleasant clime are fragrant like the musk of Khotan. Dargazin is a beautiful town with gardens, and embellished mansions with fountains and streams.

The city's land is vast and productive and is a place where everything is cheap and a man does not want for pulses and wheat. Since most of the people are peasants, they farm for a livelihood. One *kileh* (of seed) yields eighty *kileh* (of produce).[142] It is a prosperous town and all of its people are happy, the various products are plentiful and charities abound; it is a big city. But in former times it was a small village. After Shah Yazdegerd built it in the year 740, a lower fortification was added. It was built under the stellar constellation of Virgo in the house of earthy Mercury. Therefore, from this pure earth one grain produces one hundred. It is situated in the nineteenth clime.

They also celebrate the Eve of Yalda.[143] Most of its people value the art of (using) the astrolabe and mathematics; there are men like Aristotle, but they are all Shi`ites. In the gardens and orchards of this town we spent ten pleasurable days. Every moment was like the breath of Jesus, and every gathering was like that of Hoseyn Beyqara. When I say that we enjoyed ourselves and had fun you should not understand it in a different way. Since it is the land of the evil Qizilbash let our friends not conclude differently than what we meant.

God almighty knows all the secrets; up to now this sinner has wandered among Arabs and Persians and for seven years, with special letters of recommendation, I have traveled to kings with five or ten servants in Europe. I swear by God almighty that neither in the presence of the king nor in the presence of these Persian Khans have I drunk one drop of arak or wine. God be praised, that from my childhood God has made this my fate that I should travel and go around the world and enjoy it. May the infinite God grant good health.

In the year 1066 [1655-56], on the tenth of Moharram, the day of `Ashura, when we were in the town of Dargazin, the public criers announced that the Khan of Dargazin had banned 'festivities', and the people gathered for the food of `Ashura.

CONCERNING THE `ASHURA CELEBRATION AND THE RECITATION OF THE 'DEATH OF HOSEYN'. On the twelfth[144] of the said month the Khan of Dargazin pitched several hundred tents and canopies for women as well as gilt pavilions outside the town, and the notables of the town came and stayed in them. That plain, with the multi-colored tents, looked like a field of tulips. The town cooks rolled up their sleeves and for several days cooked well-scented and spiced foods and *`ashuras*. The Khan with much pomp and show, came and took his place in

---

142. The *kileh* varied in weight (8.3 to 51.3 kg) with its location and as it is not known which *kileh* Chelebi refers to we refer the reader to Hinz, *Islamische Masse*, pp. 41-42.

143. The Festival of the Eve of the Winter Solstice, the longest night of the year.

144. `Ashurah is celebrated on the tenth as the name indicates. Jevdet, vol. 4, p. 355 has the day as the eleventh, demonstrating how indifferent the Sunni author and his copyists were to Shi`ite religious sensibilities.

a special pavilion, while the trumpets and horns were blowing, and all the notables of Dargazin gathered there; (they are) all Shi`ites, Rafazis, vilifiers (*sebbab*), cursers of the three caliphs, beggars (*tulungi*), dervishes, *qalandar*s, heretics, and Kharejites, and sat row by row, knee-to-knee and listened to the recitation of the '*Death of Hoseyn*.' Then they brought a pulpit inlaid with mother-of-pearl with five steps.

From behind the pavilion an ill-famed sheikh emerged in an inauspicious manner; he had a special Persian hat,[145] long ears, lips like the lips of a camel; his feet were wrapped with puttees, his eyes were done with kohl, his beard and moustache were properly shaved, and he looked very detestable and ugly-faced, and all young and old rose and greeted him. The sheikh greeted them in his turn and sat down on the pulpit and recited the *Fatihah* and then he prayed for the Shah and the people present. He then started reciting one of the disagreeable works of the poet Fozuli of Baghdad, called the Death of Hoseyn (Maqtal-e Hoseyn), which is full of errors and nonsense. When he came to the event of Kufa and the martyrs of the plain of Karbala, such tumult rose up from the multitude of Persian soldiers as if the day of resurrection had arrived. All shouted in unison: "O our friend, O Shah Hoseyn, O warriors of Badr and Honeyn, friends of the grandfather of Hasan and Hoseyn,"[146] and they wept and stood up. They were in such an ecstasy as if they were epileptics.

At this time, seven or eight hundred barbers with razors went around. The barbers had a lighted candle in their hands and stood ready with a cotton wick. At that moment all those present shouted:

> Who bares his head, who bares his chest?
> Who will receive the wound, who will suffer?

کیمی سر برهنه، کیمی سینه چاک
کیمی زخمه گشا، کیمی دردناک

Shouting, "Ya `Ali, Ya Hoseyn," they became excited and their eyes turned into cups of blood and they got ready.

The Khan said: "O my Evliya Agha, get up and see what a sight this is." This humble author sat down and was ready for the spectacle. When the sheikh, who was sitting on the pulpit, came to (the event of) 'The death of Hoseyn', a curtain opened behind him and a man with a green turban representing Imam Hoseyn appeared and everyone saw that blood was running from his face and neck. His blessed head was severed and by artificial means his blood was running profusely, and in this manner Hoseyn together with his children and companions and the martyrs of Karbala appeared on the scene. Everyone was shouting his love for the house of the prophet and saying: "Ah Hoseyn, Shah Hoseyn," and the barbers, like "the noble butcher,"[147] with their razors made

---

145. The *zurzuvile*; may be Evliya Chelebi meant the *zurqiyeh*, something like a skull-cap (q.v. Dehkhoda).

146. The battles of Badr and Honeyn are two of the decisive battles in the career of the prophet Mohammad.

147. The so-called *qassab-e javanmard* or the noble butcher refers to a butcher, who after he met with `Ali, but did not recognize him, took out his own eyes with his knife to atone for this terrible mistake, but `Ali took pity on him and restored his eyes and sight.

many cuts in their chests and arms for the love of Hoseyn and blood ran abundantly. Some master barbers shouting for the love of Hoseyn put a wick on the cuts on the heads of several thousand people. To give their blood, several thousand people had their teeth drawn for the sake of the tooth of the Prophet, which was lost in the battle of Uhud.

As a result, that day of 'Ashura, the region of Dargazin was stained with the blood of human beings and became a tulip-like field. The hearts of all those who loved and adored [Hoseyn] dearly throbbed with grief, and from their arms and chests rose-colored blood was running. After this spectacle all the friends made a great prayer while shedding their blood and were outside themselves and bewildered. After the recitation of the belief in the oneness of God they brought tablecloths and several thousand plates with well-scented dishes of *ashura*, good viands, and saffroned pelow, and *beryani* and all of God's creatures ate. They prayed for the martyrs of the plains of Karbala. In this plain that day *ashura* and other types of good food were consumed in several thousand places, and we returned in the afternoon to the city of Dargazin. This was an outing worth seeing.

FURTHER DESCRIPTION OF THE TOWN OF DARGAZIN. First the melons of the town are sweeter, more delicious and juicy than those Diyarbekr, Begbazari and Buhtan and are very long and big.

THE HISTORY OF THE CONQUEST OF DARGAZIN. In the year 28 after the prophet's hijra [648-49], in the time of the caliphate of the blessed 'Omar, the blessed Sariyat al-Jabal conquered it. Later, in the year 941 [1534-35] in the time of Sultan Sulayman, Rostam Pasha conquered it. Thereafter, in the year 955 [1548-49], Cheghal-oghlu Senan Pasha, Murad III's famous general, conquered it. Then, as is well-known, Khosrow Shir Pasha, one of Sultan Murad IV's viziers, when he conquered Hamadan in the year 1039 [1629-30], laid siege to Dargazin and pitched his tent below its castle and stayed there for ten days. From the four corners of the plain of Dargazin, from its prosperous villages and from the caves of its mountains, he took several thousand mules and camel-loads of goods and captured many virgins and women and brought them to his camp. From the cellars and caves of the suburb of the town he took brocade, *shib* (coarse kind of gauze or canvas), gold-embroidered stuffs, brocades and costly wrought silken stuffs and distributed them among the fighters for the faith. He set on fire the villages in the plains and mountains, and so much damage was inflicted upon the Qizilbash that it cannot be described. When the evil Qizilbash saw it they said: "O Ottoman fighters for the faith, mercy, mercy," and they surrendered. Thus, in the year 1039 [1629-30], God be praised, Dargazin fell into Ottoman hands, and the great general appointed Sohrab Khan with seven thousand soldiers of Islam to guard it and he himself went to paradise-like Baghdad. From there we went towards the east.

DESCRIPTION OF THE CASTLE OF PILEVAR. Its founder was the Mongol governor of Shahrezur by the name of Pilevar Khan. Located on a high hill, it is a rectangular, small castle, but standing alone, it is very inaccessible. I do not know its circumference. It is situated in the district of Dargazin and is under a *darugheh*. It has four hundred soldiers and a sufficient arsenal with cannons. It has a gate opening to the east. This high castle is situated to the north of Baghdad on the road of Jam-Jamal castle. In the lower part there is a suburb with one thousand houses, a large mosque and a bathhouse. From here we went towards the east and reached Dinavar.

Description of the castle of Dinavar. This castle is situated on a hill in the land of [Persian] Iraq within the jurisdiction of Dargazin,[148] and it is an almond-shaped, stony and beautiful building. Below it there is a town with five hundred houses, a large mosque, a bathhouse and a bazaar. It is under a *kalantar*. In the year 994 [1586] the vizier of Murad III, Cheghal-zadeh Senan Pasha, conquered it at the same time as the abovementioned castle of Pilevar. We went to the south and reached Jam-Janab.

Description of the region of Mt. Bab, (the castle of Jam-Janab). The founder was one of the ancient kings, Parviz Jam-Janab. That is why it is thus named; it is a beautiful and well-wrought castle. It has geometrical designs and patterns and artistic displays, and it is well worked with carvings. It is a hexagonal building situated on a hill, designed in the shape of Solomon's seal. It is a beautiful castle with a circumference of three thousand paces. Inside there are three hundred houses with three hundred guards (*tulungi*), and it has one gate looking towards Baghdad. It is a separate khanate. It has two thousand soldiers and twelve officials. It has one hundred and eighty villages. Below the castle there is a prosperous town with gardens and orchards, streams, a large mosque, a caravanserai, a bathhouse and about one thousand mud houses. It has a prosperous bazaar. From there going towards the east we came to Dast-Pol.

Description of the castle of Dast-pol. I do not know its founder, but in the Mongol language *daspol* means 'a lame man.' Situated in Persian Iraq in the midst of a promenade and a forest on the banks of river Janab, surrounded by gardens, it is a circular shaped castle. It has a moat, a gate and soldiers, but its houses are narrow. In the khanate of Jam-Janab it is under a *kalantar*. Below the castle there are one thousand houses, a bathhouse, a large mosque and a bazaar; it is a well-developed suburb. The Dast-pol castle was conquered in the year 994 when Chaghal-oghlu took the castle of Jam-Janab. From here we went east and reached Qasr-e Shirin.

Description of the auspicious abode, (the ruins of the building of Qasr-e Shirin). The first founder was the Persian king Parviz of the line of Anushirvan. Later, Shirin, Harun al-Rashid's daughter, built a palace here, and that is why it is called Qasr-e Shirin. Otherwise its name in the old histories is mentioned as Qasr-e Parviz. It is situated in Persian Iraq, close to Baghdad in the southern plains. Qasr-e Shirin is an isolated and ruined palace and is now a palace of crows. In the time of Harun al-Rashid this city was so prosperous that its gardens and orchards were extended for as much as one stage. Now its remains can be seen. It was destroyed by mighty Timur. This city with Hamadan and Hulvan are like the legs of the tripod of the cooking plate (*saj*). To the east of Qasr-e Shirin Qazvin is the closest, but it itself is a strange place. Now it is in ruins. In the past it was a strong castle with a circumference of twelve thousand paces. Now its remains can be seen. Each stone is like the dome of a bathhouse and is built with iron bars, lime and mortar of Khorasan and it has gates in twenty places. The reason why it is in ruins is because it is the resting place of the Arab tribes of Keysin, the Bani Meval and other Arabs as well as other tribes. It has become a wasteland for crows. Its climate is very bad, and each time the Samum blows, people perish. Therefore it is not so prosperous. One of my slaves died because of poisonous winds.

---

148. Dinavar is located near Kermanshah, while Dargazin is near Hamadan, ergo Evliya's statement is wrong. In fact, the early Arab conquerors used to refer to Kermanshah and Dinavar together as Mah al-Kufa. A.K.S. Lambton, "Kirmanshah," *Encyclopedia of Islam II*. For a short history of Dinavar see L. Lockhart, "Dinawar," *Encyclopedia of Islam II*.

In this place we heard of the cleaning of the irrigation channels of the Tigris River by Morteza Pasha, governor of Baghdad.

WE WENT FROM QASR-E SHIRIN WHILE HUNTING AND TRAVELING TOWARDS THE EAST, AND I WILL DESCRIBE THE PLACES THAT WE SAW

First, towards the east we passed Doquz Ulam on horseback, a river with clear water, which issues froth from Mt. Alvand-e Demavandi and from Mt. Jam-Janab and merges with the Diyala River and then flows into the Shatt al-Arab. Then we went to the east and reached Hulvan.

DESCRIPTION OF THE CITY OF HULVAN OF IRAQ. Its founder is Sultan Sulayman, one of the Ottoman kings. Later on Timur destroyed it.[149] Now it borders on Baghdad and it is a prosperous royal fief. Then going towards the east we came to Qazvin.

DESCRIPTION OF THE ANCIENT CITY OF QAZVIN.[150] The learned early historians of Rum and the insightful authors of the past, such as *Tarikh-e Khalliqan*,[151] the *Tarikh-e 'Avan-e 'Onvan, Tarikh-e Khitat*[152] and the *Taqvim al-Buldan*,[153] have mentioned the names of this city. First, there is a Tradition of the Prophet, which is mentioned in the *Divan-e Imam Yafi'i*. He quotes Jaber b. 'Abdollah Ansari, who says:

"The prophet said: 'Love Qazvin, because it is one of the highest gates of Paradise.'"

قال رسول صلى الله و سلم اعز قزوين من اعلى ابواب الجنه

Therefore, in the beginning its name was Qazvin, but the Persian wits call it Qazbin. The wits of Fars call it Ghazvin, the Persian common soldiers (*tulungis*) call it Qazmin, the Arab scholars call it Ghazmin, and the people of Khorasan call it Kand-e Qazmin. In the Indian language it is called Kazemin, because Imam Muza Kazem for a long time stayed there. In the Mongol language it is called Qazmun. In short, since it is an ancient city, it is mentioned in different languages in different forms.

CONCERNING ITS BUILDERS. According to Persian historians, its first founder after the deluge was Noah (PBUH). In the place where it was built, Nuh avand (Nehavand), his son Yafeth built it and called it Yafith in the Arabic language.

Later, Nebuchadnezzar came forth from this place to revenge the blood of the prophet Yahya (PBUH), campaigned against the Israelites and destroyed all the cities of Syria–the Bani Kan'an, the city of Sefat, the cities of Tabaristan and Zaghzaghi, the city of Asqelon, the land

---

149. This means that Sulayman Khan could not be the founder of Hulvan as he reigned from 1512 and Timur died in 1405.

150. For its history see A.K.S. Lambton, "Qazwin," *Encyclopedia of Islam II*; Parviz Varjavand, *Simay-e Tarikh va Farhang-e Qazvin* 3 vols. (Tehran, 1377/1998).

151. Chelebi refers to Abu 'Abbas Ahmad Ibn Khalliqan's *Wafayat al-A'yan wa anba' abna al-zaman*.

152. These two texts are unknown to us.

153. This work is by Abu'l-Fida Isma'il b. 'Ali (1273-1331)

of Palestine, the city of Hasan and the holy land. He killed several hundred thousand Jews. He found the prophet Daniel in the city of Sefat, captured him and put him in chains and returned to Qazvin with such countless plunder that only God almighty knows its amount, and he called it the "Place of the Prophet Yafeth" and made it very prosperous. He built it in such a way that the cities of Hamadan, Dargazin and Hulvan became a quarter of Qazvin.

Then Nebuchadnezzar said: "God be praised, that I have taken revenge for the prophet Yahya on the Jews." He then set free the prophet Daniel and built him a large temple and made him a judge. The people of Qazvin believe that the prophet Daniel is buried outside Qazvin and that his shrine is there. The cities of Qazvin and Hamadan are the "Place of the Prophets and the holy lands." It is not improbable. This humble author knows a building built by the Abbasids, which I believe to be the shrine of Daniel in the vicinity of the city of Adana inside the castle of Tartus. People go for pilgrimage there.

After that Nebuchadnezzar with seven thousand camel loads of precious goods came out of Qazvin and wandered around the world, and he was one of those who ruled over the world. Similarly another two who did the same were Alexander the Great and Solomon.

Later, Nebuchadnezzar returned hale and sound to Qazvin and died there. Some people say that he became a Moslem. Inside Qazvin he rests in the temple of Daniel.

Thereafter, when Hulagu was attacking the Abbasids in the city of Baghdad, he destroyed the city of Qazvin. Then Ardashir Babakan, the king of Iraq, rebuilt it.

Later, mighty Timur destroyed it in the year 791 [1389] and conquered Baghdad. Then Shah 'Emad al-Din of Shiraz rebuilt it in such a way that the splendor and glory of Nebuchadnezzar was forgotten, and it became the capital of the kings of Iraq of Isfahan (Persian Iraq).

Eventually, Sultan Sulayman, when he conquered Baghdad, said: "We conquered Iraq" {which comes to the year 941 [1534-35]}. Thinking about their future weal, the people of Qazvin kissed Sulayman's stirrup and gave the keys of Qazvin castle to him. It was freed and it became a governorship-general.

In 992 [1584] the Persians retook it and later in the time of Murad III, Cheghal-zadeh Senan Pasha conquered it again.

In 1032 [1623] the Persians retook it and it was in their hands until 1039 [1629-30], when in the time of Sultan Murad IV, the valiant Khosrow Pasha conquered Hamadan, Dargazin, Hillah and Bagh-e Jenan. The people of Qazvin sent him gifts and submitted to him. He put the Pasha of Adana over Qazvin and returned to Baghdad. By God's will the conquest of Baghdad was not possible. In the castle of Tokad he fell ill. Hafez Ahmad Pasha in accordance with the royal writ killed Khosrow Pasha and returned to Rum.

Later, in the year 1048 [1638-39], Sultan Murad IV captured Baghdad from the Persians and, not caring for Hamadan, Dargazin and Qazvin, returned to Constantinople having saved the holy shrine of the Imam [Hanafi]. In the year 1048 Murad IV died, and since then this city of Qazvin has been in the hands of the Persians. It has become very prosperous, and it is as beautiful as Damascus and a wonderful city.

DESCRIPTION OF THE BUILDINGS OF THE CITY OF QAZVIN. The city of Qazvin is situated in Persian Iraq and borders on the region of Baghdad, and it is an important khanate. At this time its khan was the servant of Shah Safi, Cheghali ʿAli Khan. He was a khan from Hormuz, eloquent and outstanding, who wanted to be near Baghdad, and he had seven thousand soldiers. According to the law of Iran he has twelve officials, who rule as well. He has three hundred forty-five large villages under him, each one of them is almost like a town. It has a mullah, a mufti and an overseer of the sayyeds.

THE MOSQUES OF THE CITY OF QAZVIN. Large and small mosques number about two hundred

> This poem is appropriate in this place:
>> If face hair grows, the beautiful eyebrows are still there,
>> If a mosque is destroyed, the prayer niche can still be there.

According to this poem, although the mosques and its prayer niches stand, no people attend.

First, inside the bazaar there is the old Baytamur mosque. The inner-courtyard has one qanat-fed[154] well with running water, and if there are people they use it to make their ablutions; it is an old place of worship.

The Shahestan mosque was built by al-Muqtadir bi'llah, one of the Abbasid caliphs.

The Saveh Khan mosque has no minarets and it is a brightly-lit. Its *mehrab* and pulpit are beautifully carved.

The Duhuk mosque. It is built by the founder of the castle of Duhuk, who was Sheikh Duhuk, a member of the ʿAbbasi [Kurdish] clan. In this spiritually uplifting mosque there is an otherwordly atmosphere that you cannot find elsewhere. It creates an awe among the pilgrims; it is a Sunni mosque, but the Shiʿites frequent it as well.

Then there is the very big Tirmedi mosque.

The Salekan mosque is very high.

You have to visit the Deylami mosque, which has a very spiritual atmosphere, and its founder was the author of the *Tafsir-e Deylami*. It is said that he wrote his book here.

Among the wondrous and spectacular sights of the important buildings is the Moshabek mosque. It is very large. It is close to the old wall of Qazvin and it is impressive. Neither in Turkey [Rum] nor Iran have I seen such a finely worked building. It has several thousand different beautiful geometrical designs. Inside this mosque there is a screened enclosure for the former kings. When you see it you will be astonished and bewildered and you cannot describe it. The founder of this beautiful mosque is Amir-e Humaʾ Yas, the servant of the fourth rebuilder of Qazvin, Shah ʿEmad al-Din. According to Persian historians, one camel load of gold was spent for the construction of this mosque. In spite of being such a beautiful mosque, people do not frequent it. The big dome over the *mehrab* rises to heaven. All the domes in every land are made in the form of a cup, but this dome is like the earth globe. Inside it there are so many works beautifully inlaid with mother-of-pearl and precious stones that the viewer is astounded. This humble author has

---

154. The text has *qana*, which does not mean anything within this context and therefore we think that reading *qanat* (subterranean channel) makes sense here.

traveled so extensively and observed everything carefully, but I have never seen anything so beautiful and wonderful like the dome of the Qezelelma mosque inside Estergon castle[155] and the dome of the mosque of Qazvin. This poem might be appropriate:

> We saw all the mosques of the world
> But we did not see anything like this.

There are several other mosques in the city of Qazvin, but the most outstanding among them is this mosque that man cannot really describe.

DESCRIPTION OF THE BUILDINGS OF THE CASTLE OF QAZVIN. Situated in a vast and fertile plain without any barrier it is a quadrangular well-built building made of carved stones. First it was built by Ardashir Babakan, and later it was repaired by Shah Ghayath al-Din. On the door of the above-described mosque the names of the founders as well as the years are mentioned. In front of this door there is a large cemetery, which contains several thousand graves of scholars of old. The Baghdad Gate is one of the gates.

There are [-] gates. The Mushabbak Gate is opposite a big cemetery, in which innumerable ulama are buried. Then the Baghdad Gate, and then comes …

The circumference of this ancient castle is twenty [thousand?] paces, and inside the castle there are [-] houses.

THE HOUSES OF LEARNING. There are several madrasehs, but there are no institutions that teach Koranic studies or exegesis.

THE WELLS AND SPRINGS. It has many delightful springs, but they mostly draw water by means of water wheels operated by horses and oxen.

PUBLIC FOUNTAINS. There are many public fountains. First, the Yasavol Aqa, Quli Khan, Va'ez, and Khvajeh Hosam fountains, which are famous and well-made. There are well-built public fountains in the bazaar.

STREAMS. In the city of Qazvin there are no streams, but inside the city near the bazaar close to the Baytamur Khan mosque, a stream flows which is said to be a miracle by the prophet Daniel. Its water is as delicious as that of the Kowthar well in paradise, but its [output] is not sufficient for the people.

THE ROYAL BAZAAR. According to the mayor, there are two thousand and sixty royal shops. Some are manufacturies, and the drapers' hall, the coffeehouses and barbershops are very clean and nicely decorated; it is a nice bazaar.

WELLS IN HOUSES. Since this city of Qazvin does not have running streams, according Mullah Jar, there are seventeen thousand houses with gardens and orchards with wells, each one of them with good water, like the water of life. The entire city is irrigated by these wells.

---

155. Esztergom, 50 km n.w. of Budapest.

Learned physicians and surgeons. This city of Qazvin is distinguished among all other cities. Accomplished master physicians and surgeons have come here from every city, but in his profession Ganj `Ali is really outstanding, and the surgeon Lavand is without peer.

Saints and Sufi sheikhs. Most of them are living inside the city and are Shafe`i Kurds and Deylamites. There are Arabs and Persians in abundance, but since it is close to Baghdad, they are mostly Shafe`is. Khoja Sadeq and `Ali Baqer are Sufi leaders.

Authors and poets. When this humble author was in the city there were twenty poets who had divans. The famous ones are: Homa'i-ye Kashani, Benjahi, Yari, Farhi, Kashani, Saba'i, Va`ezi and Khita'i.

The brothers and friends that we met. All of them are well-behaved, easy-going, tolerant, serene, decent and well-disposed people, and in the few days that we mixed with them they became very friendly with us. They are: Yar `Ali, Jan `Ali, Qorban Shah, Reza Qay and Yazdankar.

Some examples of people of ecstasy. Among its people there are *abdals* and *melamatis* who are men of ecstasy.[156] Among them are Sunjeli Dedeh and Mardan Dedeh, who performed a number of miracles.

Clothes of men and women. Men wear a multi-colored headband and a white turban, multi-colored chintz and colored twilled cottons (*boghasi*). Women are covered with the veil, face-mask or half-mask, which are white, and they wear multi-colored high boots.

Female and male names. Most of the people are called: `Ali Beshnu, Qoli Sunjeh, Mirza Juli, Heydar Qoli and Hormuz Aqa.

Ladies have names such as: Semer Khanom, Aslan Khanom, Yarimeh, Qandimeh, Hoveyda, Mahiye and Homa Khanom.

Names of servants and slave girls. The names of the slaves are: Faraj Gholam, Sarand Gholam, Alvand Gholam and Budaq Gholam. Most of the slave girls are from Georgia and they have names such as: Zobeyda, Damsaz, Charehsaz, Mahpare, `Eshvahbaz and Shahnaz.

Persian speaking people. Most of the people are eloquent and talk wittily to each other in the Persian language. But they know Arabic so well as if they are Imru'l-Qays or Mullah Jami, and most of them are scholars.

The color of the faces of old and young. Since its climate is moderate most people are white, strong of body, sometimes swarthy, with average height. Some are very wealthy.

Praising the lovely boys. The boys of the city of Qazvin in Persian Iraq and Kashghar are praised for their beauty, their gait and their Khotanese doe-like eyes and beautiful faces.

Its temperate climate. The weather is very mild. The north wind and the breeze when it blows in the morning gives one new life. Those who are sleeping on the roofs enjoy it.

---

156. See Karamustafa, *God's Unruly Friends*, pp. 19-20, 30-31.

Description of the astronomical situation of the city. According to Khoja Naqdi and the science of astrolabes, Qazvin is in the middle of the twelfth clime.

The constellation under which it was built. Its first builder was Yafeth son of Noah (PBUH), according to the sayings of Jewish priests. He built it under the stellar constellation of Taurus and the house of Venus.[157] People are joyous and happy, and there are many cypress trees.

Description of its wheat. There are seven types of wheat, its like may be found in Hawran in Syria. It has an abudance of oily barley, cow-peas, beans and mung beans for horses, mules, camels, cows and donkeys.

Description of its foods. There is pebble-bread white as cotton and *lavash* bread, Hamadani biscuits, thick soup, Turaj[158] pastry with fillings, *Mastaba* soup, noodle soup,[159] flat wheat-barley bread, ʿashura, and millet broth, and their like is nowhere to be found.

The fruits of the city. There are forty kinds of pears, but the *Beybini* pear is musky by God's will; its juicy grapes, tasty plums, almonds, hybrid peaches, melons and water melons are well-known.

Description of the beverages. In this city of Qazvin most of its water is from rain. Many of the good people of the past have built *qanat*s, which are sufficient for the drinking water needs of the city.

Concerning the blessing of food kitchens. Formerly, there were seven hundred charitable institutions. The city having passed from king to king all of them except seven have been destroyed. Among them, the Salekan and the Jahan-sud charitable institutions are left.

Places of recreation. Although everywhere in the city it is pleasant, there are seventy special places of recreation and repose, each of which is like paradise. The most famous ones are: Hazar Bagh, Chahar Bagh-e Shahan, Quyagh Bagh-e Shahan, Khiyaban and Mendimah.

Description of the gardens. According to Khvajeh Bali, there are seventeen thousand gardens, orchards, flowers and vegetable gardens. There is a shortage of water; therefore sometimes they are watered by rainwater or water that is produced by subterranean canals.

Concerning language and expressions of the people. People speak Kurdish, Yaka Turkman, Persian, Arabic and Pahlavi. The irregular troops speak Qeytaqi and a dialect of the Mongol language. God willing we will explain this in its place.

Strange sights of the city. For several thousand years there was a Jewish cemetery in this city, but no building remains standing there. For example, if they want to bury a Jew they cannot put one stone on another. Those stones go to the bottom of the earth, and therefore no trace of that construction remains. It is a dreadful place.

---

157. It was built when the Sign of Gemini was in the ascendant, according to Mustawfi, *Nuzhat*, p. 62.
158. Turaj sometimes means Turan or Turkey or Turkish, which perhaps is meant here.
159. *Lahishbasi*, i.e., *lakhsha*.

Another strange thing. In the city of Qazvin, if a horse or another animal feels a deadly pain in its stomach and is near death, it is taken around the cemetery several times and by God's will that pain will be cured; this has been tested several times.

Another strange thing is that there is an old well in a garden and the governors take somebody who is suspected of a crime or a murder and chain him there. If the man is really guilty, a bad smell and a black smoke rises up from the well and kills him. If there is no smoke he is set free.

Another strange thing. Near the temple of the prophet Daniel in a garden is a water well. The governors put somebody who has committed a theft next to the well, and if he is guilty then a voice is heard from the well saying: "This is he." They then kill him. If he is innocent, no voice is heard and they set him free. Therefore, in the city of Qazvin there are no thieves or murderers. But there are many nimble-handed knaves. In this city of Qazvin there are several hundreds of strange and wondrous things, which are talisman-like remains. Several of them were destroyed when the holy prophet was born, and their magic became ineffective. Now several of them, as we mentioned, are still working.

General description of Qazvin. This city is close to Deylam. Baghdad is towards the south. Isfahan is at ten stages from Qazvin. On the main road the important cities are Saveh and Qom. Formerly Qazvin was the capital. Now, when a king accedes to the throne, he will not be considered an independent king until he comes to this city of Qazvin and sits on the throne. From there he goes to the city of Ardabil, pays respect to all his ancestors and girds the royal sword; this is the law of Iran.

Places of pilgrimage of the city of Qazvin. First, the temple of the prophet Daniel is close to a paradise-like garden; it is his shrine. Although it has not been embellished with domes, his blessed tomb is covered with a huge stone that in this world such a multi-colored, wonderful stone has not been seen. On top of it writings are carved in Hebrew and Greek. It seems that a talisman had been inscribed there.

The shrine of Khameyth b. Yafeth b. Nuh (pbuh) is interesting. The Armenians of that place pay special attention to it. Among the tombs of kings, the shrine of Shah Ghayat al-Din, the founder of Qazvin, and the shrine of Amir Zahed Khama'i bash are in a wonderful mosque with latticework. The shrine of Jandemah Khanom, the daughter of Harun al-Rashid, is buried under a beautiful dome. The shrine of Afkand Shah b. Farrokhzad; when he was the governor of Baghdad he died here.

The shrine of Qarageh-ye Kubra. In front of the latticed gate of the castle of Qazvin there is a cemetery, and there are so many grave stones that in one year you cannot finish reading the dates on them. In this valley of silence there are several thousands saints, great sheikhs and several thousands of writers, authors, commentators of the Koran and transmitters of Traditions, and you cannot possibly give a description of them all. There is a place called Kan-e Sahba. Here, three thousand ascetics are buried. They are those whose prayers will be answered. Therefore, day and night this place is bright with light as if it were daylight.

Nearby is a cemetery called **Place of Pilgrimage of the Martyrs**. Every Friday night several hundred ascetics gather and engage in prayer from the early night till morning. Several thousand people see the bright light; it is a blessed shrine. May God sanctify their graves and may he take them all to Paradise.[160]

After visiting the city and having received the Khan's gifts, we went north and after six *farsakh*s arrived at the town of Alamut.

Description of the town of Alamut, the castle of Mut. It is under a *kalantar* in the jurisdiction of Qazvin. It is a grand castle with an unimpeded view and is rectangular in form. Its founder was Sultan Mut, and therefore it is called Alamut.[161] I do not know its circumference, but it is small with a moat. It has three hundred royal slaves and sufficient arms and cannons.

The layout of the suburb. In the year 246 [860] the castle was built by Hasan b. Zeyd al-Bamer. It surrounds the castle. It is pentagonal in form. It is made of bricks, mortar, lead and earth very much like the earthen castle of Urmiyeh near Tabriz. Its circumference is six thousand Meccan cubits, which makes eleven thousand paces. There are a few deep moats. It has two gates. One side is to the south towards Qazvin and the other to the east towards the town of Deylam. Inside the castle there are a total of six thousand houses, large mosques, bathhouses and a sufficient number of royal bazaars. In its district it has fifty-seven prosperous villages and some of them have well-built castles. Since I did not go and observe them myself, I did not want to write about them, but it is a prosperous district. In spite of the fact that it has an abundance of wheat, its bread is somewhat darkish. Its fruits are boundless. From there we traveled to the east and arrived at the town of Deylam.

Description of the great ancient town, the Abode of Scholars, the castle of Deylam. Situated in Persian Iraq in the district of Qazvin, it is now a sultanate with one thousand soldiers. Its Sultan is Pir Yar Sultan. Its founder is the Abbasid al-Mustaqfi bi'llah, who, being a cruel caliph, exiled his son to this town and imprisoned him. That is why he built this castle, and because of the location they call it Deylam. Now it is called Deylam-e Iraq, meaning the Iraqi prison.[162] This Deylam is in Persian Iraq, but Deylam in Arabian Iraq is the castle of Kerek near Jerusalem. The prison of Rum is the castle of Rhodes, in Persia (such a prison) is Qahqaheh castle, in the Crimea it is Menkup, in Poland it is Kamaniche, in Buda it is Usturghun, and in Germany it is Pojon. The aforementioned castles are like hell's pits. But this one in Persian Deylam is the worst. Its circumference is similar to that of Sorkhbid. Situated on a low hill on the slopes of Mt. Deylam it is a spectacular castle and prison. Its lower suburb has barely two thousand houses, but they are very old buildings. Because its people are mostly scholars, they obeyed every king who came there. The town has been preserved from destruction and has remained as it was originally built. It has beautiful old houses. It has a large mosque, a caravanserai, a bathhouse and a royal bazaar.

---

160. None of these places of pilgrimages nor the fanciful stories told by Elviya are confirmed by other sources.

161. "According to legend, an eagle indicated the site to a Daylamite ruler; hence the name, from *aloh* (eagle) and *amu(kh)t* (taught)." Bernard Hourcade, "Alamut," *Encyclopedia Iranica*.

162. *Deylam* in Persian, among other things, means misfortune.

Since its climate is good, the young boys are noble and mature. Its people are Shafe'is and studious like Aristotle. The *Tafsir-e Deylami* is thus called because its author comes from this town. It has many gardens, orchards and fruits. Its wheat is very productive, big and red; hence its bread is very tasty like that of Hamadan. The best wheat comes from the region of Rudbar, where the castle of Alamut is situated.

THE DESCRIPTION OF THE ANCIENT CITY, I.E., QASR-E LOSUS OF PARVIZ.

It was a thriving large city in the time of Shah Parviz. Since several kings invaded and robbed it from each other, it is called the castle of Losus, which means the castle of robbers. Originally, its name was Parvizabad. Before it was destroyed by Timur Khan, the description of the castle by the historians of Persia was as follows: "This palace was built like a big castle with twelve stories, and since the tomb of the blessed 'Ali, may God be pleased with him, can be seen from a distance of five stages, it was built as a beautiful place and at all levels has twelve thousand windows." At present, the remains of the buildings can be seen.

It is a sultanate within the province of Qazvin. It has one thousand soldiers. In its territory the Keys and Meval Arab tribes are living, and that is why it is not very prosperous. The castle is also not prosperous. There is a well-lit mosque inside the castle, and from the point of construction and lighting it is like the Ommayad mosque in Damascus. It has no congregation and is left isolated among the Shi'ites. The town is close to the castle of Asadabad. It is close to Hamadan and Qazvin. In the plains up to the river Diyala, cotton and cereals are plentiful and the people are Shi'ites and faithless. Most of the people are robbers and warriors and (even) one of their old men can face ten people. They are brave and thievish. Because they are under the influence of Losus castle, most of them are highway-men, and like the Circassians they fleece you without you noticing it. They are such incredible thieves.

PLACES OF PILGRIMAGE OF QASR-E LOSUS.

First of all, Sheikh Shoja' of Qazvin, Shah Mansur-e Ba'zravi and the blessed 'Ali Tirmidhi have their shrines there. Then we went to the south and reached Asadabad.

DESCRIPTION OF THE CASTLE OF ASADABAD.[163]

Situated in Persian Iraq in the province of Hamadan, it is a sultanate with one thousand soldiers. You go from Hamadan to (Arabian) Iraq in two stages. Since it was built by king Asad al-Din Kermani it is called Asadabad. The castle is situated in a valley; it is rectangular in form and well built.

DESCRIPTION OF THE GOOD TOWN AND THE CASTLE OF BAGH-E JENAN.

It is situated in Persian Iraq between Mosul and Hamadan on a steep hill in an inaccessible forested area. It is a high castle, which rises to heaven.

Its founder is the caliph al-Ma'mun, but at the threshold of the castle's gate it is written: "King of kings Shah Esma'il." It was conquered in 941 [1534-35] by the vizier of Sultan Sulayman, Rostam Pasha. It was conquered by the Persians in 1032 [1623], and in 993 [1585] in the time of Sultan Murad III, Cheghal-zadeh Senan Pasha conquered it.

Later on after it was retaken by the Persians in the year 1039 [1629-30]. The vizier of Sultan Murad IV, Khosrow Pasha came with a huge army and took the castles of Dargazin, Jam-Janab and Pilevar and laid siege to this castle. He realized that laying siege was a difficult undertaking

---

163. Situated at some 120 km from Kermanshah, the last stage on the road to Hamadan.

and there he abandoned the idea and ordered his army to plunder and pillage whatever was in the plains of Bagh-e Jenan up to the castle of Chik ʿAli, which encompassed some eight hundred villages, and then they pillaged and tortured its inhabitants. When the people of the aforementioned castle saw the fighters for the faith with so much booty coming to Bagh-e Janan, the evil Qizilbash asked the army of Islam for quarter and gave the keys to Khosrow Shir. The governor of Palu, ʿAli Bey, was appointed as its castellan. The valiant vizier went from there to Baghdad and he returned without conquering it. This castle went into the hands of the Persians and it has remained like that until now.

Thereafter, the conqueror of Baghdad Sultan Murad IV took Baghdad in person, but not caring for Hamadan, Dargazin and this Bagh-e Jenan, he returned to the High Porte and died by the order of God in 1048 [1638-39]. The castle of Bagh-e Jenan stayed in the hands of the Persians and gradually became prosperous. It is an independent khanate, and its khan has three thousand soldiers, a mullah, a *khvajeh-ye Islam*, a chief of sayyeds, and because of the twelve Imams it has twelve officials.

We went from here to the south to:

YASAVOL VILLAGE. It is a village with five hundred houses. Again going towards to the south in the plains of the castle of Chik Ahmad we arrived at:

THE VILLAGE OF BADANLIJEH. It was originally under Shahrezur, but now under the administration of Mehraban castle. It is a big village with eight hundred houses, gardens and orchards, a large mosque, a caravanserai, a bathhouse and a royal bazaar. Again we went towards the south and came to Mehraban.

DESCRIPTION OF THE ROYAL THRONE, I.E. OF THE CASTLE OF MEHRABAN. It is situated in Persian Iraq and its first builder is Shah Parviz. Later, in 873 [1468-69] the king of Azerbaijan, Uzun Hasan Shah Bayandor rebuilt it, when he was ruler of Baghdad. Thereafter, in 941 [1534-35] it fell into the hands of Sultan Sulayman. Then, in the year 995 [1587], the vizier of Sultan Murad IV, Khosrow Pasha, conquered it and what is known to us we will relate in brief.

CONCERNING THE CONQUEST OF THE CASTLE OF MEHRABAN AND THE DEFEAT OF ZEYNAL KHAN. When the great general Khosrow Shir laid siege to Hamadan, Dargazin, Bagh-e Jenan and Hillah, and some (other) well-known castles in the land of Persia, he did not spare them. He conquered seventeen strong castles without fighting, and while he rebuilt Chik Ahmad castle and Hillah castle he pillaged the upper castle of Mehraban. He sent the Albanian Deli Yusof Pasha of Rumelia province, the Pasha of Aleppo, Chekes Mohammad Pasha and the *Janissary aghasi* with forty batallions of slave troops, the *sepahis* of four districts and an adequate number of cannons, armorers, eighty royal cannons and forty thousand soldiers. The soldiers arrived below the castle and pitched their tents. The heretical Shah sent Zeynal Khan with fifty thousand soldiers to oppose them and pitched his multi-colored pavilion there.

The far-sighted general (Khosrow Shir) sent news to great general Khosrow Pasha and asked for help. The great general immediately sent ten thousand select and brave soldiers to assist him, saying: "This is it, I do not have more." Zeynal Khan faced the army of Islam with a multitude of his faithless soldiers. Truly, the first attack of the wretched Qizilbash was tremendous. They easily overcame the army of Islam and the Qizilbash penetrated from one side and got their hands on hundreds of tents. Khalil Pasha and Hoseyn Pasha seeing this terrible situation said: "Whatever will happen will happen; how are we going to face Khosrow Pasha?" Saying this all the fighters of the faith drew their swords and attacked while shouting "Allah, Allah" and taunted the evil Qizilbash crying "Hu, Hu," not giving them time to blink and gave battle.

From the other side the fighters of the faith from Rumelia province took the Kostanice loading poles[164] from the cannons and attacked. To save themselves, the Qizilbash, being [now] between the armies, attacked Khalil Pasha, who counter attacked. The Qizilbash could not withstand the army of Islam that attacked from five sides and were defeated. Then they rushed to the Shah bridge, situated over the river Mehraban, and the Ottoman army pursued and killed them. While crossing the bridge many of them perished in the river.

In this great battle the army of Islam acquired much plunder, so that even a [simple] soldier received one camel load of booty. One of them, while wandering about, said: "What can I do with so much plunder?"

Thereafter, the victorious fighters of the faith who had not been wounded came to the camp and were honored and given rewards in accordance with their deeds, and with joy and happiness the great general advanced on the castle of Mehraban. Coming from the castle of Chik Ahmad towards the east in two stages, he laid siege to the castle of Mehraban, and the soldiers started digging trenches, wasting no time. In 1039 [1629-30] he conquered the castle of Mehraban and put the Pasha of Mar`ash, Sulayman Pasha, there as its castellan. After that he returned as commanding general to Baghdad.

By the will of God he was unable to take Baghdad, so he returned dejectedly to the castle of Mosul where he made a big castle and then repaired the castle of Shahrezur. He spent the winter in Tuqat and then was martyred and went to the other world. On the other side, the wretched Qizilbash thanking God made it an occasion for an illumination and festivity. Eventually in 1048 [1638-39] Sultan Murad himself conquered Baghdad, but he did not bother about the castle of Mehraban. When he reached his capital, he passed from this world of pride to the world of happiness. In this way, the city of Mehraban remained with the Persians.

CONCERNING THE GOVERNMENT OF MEHRABAN. Now it is in the hands of the Shah. It is an independent khanate in Iraq, which has four thousand soldiers under a high-ranking khan. In the time I was there the name of its khan was Tolabar Khan. He was from the land of Kahravan and was valiant and courageous. The city of Mehraban has a mullah, a *khvajeh-ye Islam*, and a chief of sayyeds as well as a mayor, a clerk, a police chief, a chief of the ushers, a chief of the royal slaves, and a chief of the merchants–in total twelve administrative officials. It forms the border with the province of Baghdad.

DESCRIPTION OF THE ANCIENT TOWN OF SENNEH. It was built in 616 (1219) by one of the rulers of Kurdistan, Amir Ghayath al-Din. Then it passed from king to king. It is in the land of Baghdad, to the east, situated in a vast plain. It is surrounded by a mud wall and is a sultanate, now in the hands of the Persians. Since its castle borders on Baghdad, Mosul and Shahrezur, it is prosperous. Inside there about three hundred narrow houses, one mosque and three wheat storage places, but other buildings are situated in the suburb.

THE SUBURB OF SENNEH. It is surrounded by a mud wall and its circumference is sixteen thousand paces. It has a well-built moat and two gates. The Baghdad Gate faces the south and the

---

164. These poles or ramrods presumably were from Kostanice in Montenegro.

Mosul Gate faces north. Inside the wall there are six thousand houses, and the best built among them are the houses of the sultan and the mullah. It has twelve officials, caravanserais, bathhouses and a sufficient number of shops. Since its surroundings are wasteland there are few gardens. The city's environs are all moats. Since it was built in former times with mortar it became ruined due to the passage of time. Later in 1039 [1629-30] the vizier of Sultan Murad IV, Khosrow Pasha, when he became the general of the Baghdad campaign, approached the town of Senneh. The shaven-headed Qizilbash troops who had taken refuge in the castle were unable to oppose the huge and valiant army and took all valuables from the castle, leaving their arsenal, and fled to Iran.

Khosrow Pasha with a huge army arrived below the castle and pitched his tents. While looking at the castle he noticed that for the conquest of Baghdad it is an important castle to the east of that city, as it is a suitable place of refuge. At any rate, it was a useful place to assist Baghdad, but had very badly fallen into disrepair. Therefore, he gathered able masons from everywhere and ordered his numerous troops to dig a huge moat. In one month, with bricks and mortar they built a fine, strong castle and a beautiful city that you cannot describe.

He equipped it completely with an arsenal and other necessaries, equipped it and appointed Khalil Pasha, Dhu'l-Feqar Pasha and several other emirs as its defenders. He himself went to lay siege to Baghdad but failed to conquer it by God's will. While returning, the Shah of Persia realized that if the castles of Senneh and of Chik Ahmad remained in Ottoman hands Baghdad would not be safe. Therefore, he came with the army of Iraq against the castles of Senneh and Chik Ahmad, and the people who were besieged inside left their arsenal and arms and fled without a fight. As soon as they reached the castle of Mosul they gave the news to Khosrow Pasha, who called all the emirs and officers and told them:

> You cursed ones! I spent so much for God's sake on the arsenal and I made Senneh castle so strong that it would withstand a siege for one month, but you could not keep up a fight for three days. By God's grace I would have come to your assistance in two days. Why did you not fight and leave Senneh castle with so many supplies to the enemy?

He then ordered the heads of one hundred and fifty of them to be cut.

From that time onwards the castle of Senneh has remained in the hands of the Persians. In 1047 [1637-38] when Beyram Pasha became the commanding general of the Baghdad campaign and was going there, Kuchek Ahmad Pasha, the vizier of Syria, formed the vanguard of the army with forty thousand select soldiers from the province of Syria. Coming below Senneh castle, Kuchek Ahmad Pasha faced eleven khans with seventy thousand Iranian soldiers and they started fighting. By God's wisdom, Ahmad Pasha was sick in his litter, but he fought bravely, and the army of Islam was left leaderless, while the Redheads attacked them from the south. After fighting for some time the army of Islam was put to flight, many were killed and a few were saved. Now in the castle of Senneh the bones of the Ottomans martyrs are gathered in three heaps, and the bones of the Qizilbash are gathered in one place. In this way the castle of Senneh remains in the hands of the Persians and has become prosperous since then.

ADDITIONAL REMARKS ON THE CASTLE OF SENNEH. Since we have mentioned the pilgrimage to the shrines of all saints and prophets of this old city when we went to Baghdad, they are not described here.

Description of the city of Qom. Historians have described this truly alluring castle of Qom, but according to the Armenian historian Mighdisi, after the deluge the blessed Noah, (PBUH), came with his ship to Mt. Judi[165] at Mosul. After he had traveled everywhere he came to this city of Qom, enjoyed its climate and stayed for a long time in this sandy place and built a village there.

[Follows a long story about the conquest of Qom by the Jinns and how the prophet dealt with them, which we have not translated].

Another city of Qamar al-Qom. In his travels in the Crimea this humble author saw a lake, which the Greek historians call Qamer al-Qom situated near Aq Kerman. In 889 [1484], Sultan Bayazid conquered the castle of Sin and incorporated it into the Dar al-Islam, but the sea situated to the east of Aq Kerman is now in the hands of Jinns. If a man enters there it will be at his peril. One time the Cossacks of Aq Kerman plundered the area of Qamar al-Qom and they went into the sea with one hundred and fifty ships, and no person returned alive and one hundred and fifty ships came back empty. Since this happened not so long ago there are many people who have seen them.

In Qamar al-Qom small bows and arrows, vessels, and pots and pans that are small as nutshells were seen that are goods belonging to the Jinns. If you want to burn them they do not burn; if you want to sink them they do not sink. These are very wondrous things. God willing we will explain it in its proper place.

But this place was dominated by the Arab tribes of Meval and the Bani Qeys, who were Jinns, and they do not allow anything to be built there. After Anushirvan, in 254 (868), it was rebuilt on the order of the caliph Ma'mun. Then Shah Ghayath al-Din (and later) Ya'qub Shah, son of Timur Khan rebuilt it. Lately, Sultan Sulayman and Sultan Murad III conquered it. But again it went to the Persians. In the time of Sultan Sulayman in {953 [1546]}, Alqas Mirza, son of Shah Esma'il, destroyed it.

The reason for the destruction of the city of Qom. The older brother of Alqas Mirza was Shah Tahmasp of Iran. He gave the younger brother Alqas the governorship of Shirvan and Shamakhi, but Alqas was aiming for the throne. Eventually Alqas Mirza was not sure of his safety on account of Shah Tahmasp. He went from the Qipchaq steppe to the Crimea, and from there by ship he came to the Ottoman court and kissed the throne of Sultan Sulayman and was housed in a big palace. Later on from the Turkmen lands, Kurdistan and other places, brave soldiers were given to Alqas Mirza and with eighty thousand soldiers he went to Baghdad and from there to Hamadan, Dargazin, Mehraban, Bagh-e Jenan, Jam-janab, Shariban, Qom, Kashan, and Isfahan, half of the world. In eight months he destroyed all of Iran, Turan and Azerbaijan. Then with Croesus-like treasures he returned to the winter quarters of Aleppo and kissed the throne of Sultan Sulayman and gave many presents. From that time on this city has not recovered from the blows it received.

The wells of the houses. It has one thousand six hundred wells. Outside of it, towards Baghdad, is a desert and does not have running streams. All the buildings are watered by water mills.

---

165. According to the Koran 11:44 (al-Hud) the resting place of the Ark of Noah. The mountain has been traditionally identified with a hill near the town of Jazirat b. Omar in Mosul province.

THE SAINTS AND SHEIKHS. There are very many of them, but most have come from other cities and Kurds of Surandan who came to study; among them are people of the Shafe`i school. The people of the city are all Shi`ites and when they get up, stand or sit down, they say: "Ya Ali."

THE CONSTELLATION UNDER WHICH IT WAS BUILT. According to Ptolemy, the city is situated in the nineteenth latitude. It was built under the constellation of Sagittarius in the house of Saturn. Its weather is very hot.

THE PULSES AND EDIBLES. Its wheat and barley do not suffice because it is a sandy place and mostly comes from Kashan and Hillah. But other products are very good, especially its sweatmeats of Basra and *zolbia*[166] of Qonya, which are fresher, tastier and more fragrant than the halvah.

ITS FRUITS. In its beautiful gardens hazelnuts and pistachios are in plenty.

AS TO ITS BEVERAGES. Shiraz and Hormuz sugary sherbet, jullabi, *koknar, mothallath*[167] are very sweet and tasty.

THE NUMBER OF GARDENS. It has about one thousand gardens and orchards, and promenades and for many years it has been beautified with pavilions and kiosks. The garden of Sarjam is one of the most famous.

ADDITIONAL DESCRIPTION OF THE PLEASANT CITY OF QAMAR AL-QOM OF IRAQ. This city of Qom is on the east side of Hamadan five stages from it. In old times it was a strong castle with a big wall. It is close to the castle of thieves (Qasr al-Losus).

THE PLACES OF PILGRIMAGE OF THE SAINTS OF THE CITY OF QOM. There are six hundred chosen one, buried there, May God bless them all, and the Abbasid caliphs have made domes over their tombs. (From Qom) we went to Kashan.

DESCRIPTION OF THE CITY OF KASHAN. The historian Mighdisi traveled these parts and beautifully described them. The first founder is Manuchehr. Because of having been ruined by an earthquake it was left for a few years and became the place for scorpions and mice. Later, because of its very good climate, it was considered improper to let it remain in ruins in the land of (Persian) Iraq. Therefore, in the year 243 [857-58] the wife of the Lord of the Believers, Harun al-Rashid, Zobeyda Khanom, spent a treasure worthy of Croesus and rebuilt this place and made it so prosperous as if it were city of Lorestan. Many master magicians have put forty different types of talismans there. Their signs can still be seen.

Later it passed from the hands of one king to another. Sometimes it was destroyed, sometimes it was rebuilt. Eventually, the Mongols attacked the caliph Mustansir bi'llah and captured Baghdad. At that time, in Kashan, a vizier named Aqa Bay was governor and made it so prosperous as if it were Damascus of Syria. The last Mongol king being Shah Inchul[168] came from Baghdad to Kashan and it became the capital of the Injuyids and very prosperous. Among the Mongols the kings are called *inchu*. In total, there were three Mongol Injuyid kings.

---

166. A very sweet confectionary traditionally prepared during Ramazan, the month of fasting.

167. Syrup or wine reduced to one third by boiling.

168. He was Sheikh Abu Eshaq Inju, who was put to death in 1357.

All three of them ruled in this Kashan, and the third one was killed here. Now, their tombs are outside Kashan under one high dome. Inside they are buried in the shrine of the Mongol Injuyids. But the Mongols call this city in their own language Kishvan. The Kurds call it Keshan; in the Indian language they call it Kezhdoman (land of the scorpions), while in Arabic it is called Kaseban (workers). In the Chaghatay language they call it Keshan, and in Pars language Kashan or Qashan, because "Q" and "K" are close in pronunciation. But some people call it Qashiyan and Qasiyan, but its true name is Kashan. The old name of the city is Qilman.

Later, because she completed its construction in 452 weeks, Zobeyda Khanom, the wife of Harun al-Rashid, gave it the name of Qashan, which according to the *abjad* calculation comes to 452 hijri; therefore it is called Kashan.

Then, in 791 [1389], when Timur Khan was the ruler of Iraq, and in accordance with his cruel custom destroyed every city and town in every land, he spared Kashan and gave it to his son Ya`qub Shah, who made it his capital. Later, at the order of Sultan Sulayman, Alqas Mirza, the son of Shah Esma`il, came with an army and destroyed Kashan as well as Hamadan. Since that time, it is becoming prosperous again. Here we attempt to describe it in a manner just like the saying goes: "A drop from the sea, a particle from the sun."

DESCRIPTION OF THE CASTLE OF QIN OF KASHAN.[169] The founder of the castle of Qin (Fin) was Manuchehr. It is full view of the city of Kashan, on a plain. South of it is Mt. Qin, which is very high.[170] On its slopes, for a distance of two *farsakh*s, are beautiful meadows full of gardens and orchards. It is built with special clay and is rectangular. It is a beautiful castle as if it were the castle of Maghus[171] in the island of Cyprus. Its circumference is three thousand seven hundred paces. The walls of the castle are included. But on the outside, the edges of the moat are covered with vegetation. It is a very deep moat. Its bottom is very clean. To prevent the top of the walls being ruined by rain and sun they are covered with Khorasani mortar made of brick, dust and lime, and it is a pearl-like castle. From the bottom, the walls measure eighty cubits and their width is twenty (cubits). On its top, horsemen can play polo.

DESCRIPTION OF THE SUBURB. The number of houses is somewhat smaller than in Qom.

THE RUNNING STREAMS. In this Kashan all its water comes from Mt. Qin, which merges with the river of Dunyasir and waters all the gardens and orchards of the city.[172]

THE CLIMES AND WIDTH OF THE CITY. According to Ptolemy, the city of Kashan is situated at the nineteenth degree latitude.

---

169. The complex of buildings referred to here are called Fin not Qin. For the history of Kashan see J. Calmard, "Kashan," *Encyclopedia of Islam II*; `Abdol-Rahim Kalantari Zarrabi, *Tarikh-e Kashan* ed. Iraj Afshar (Tehran, 1342/1963).

170. Mt. Qin or Fin does not exist. Evliya probably referring to Fin gardens here assumed that the neighboring mountain was also called Fin. For a list of the mountains near Kashan see Zarrabi, *Tarikh*, pp. 39-69 and index (q.v. *kuh*).

171. Maghusa is the Turkish name for the town of Famagusta in Cyprus.

172. The river Dunyasir is not mentioned in the list of rivers recorded by Zarrabi, *Tarikh*, pp. 60-69 and index (q.v. *rudkhaneh*).

THE HOROSCOPE OF ITS BUILDING. According to Mullah Kulga Shah, it was built in the sign of Cancer in the house of Mars, and that is the reason why in this city there are very many scorpions and centipedes and the people are so valiant and warlike.

PRAISEWORTHY CRAFTS. The people are craftsmen and shopkeepers. The arms and weapons that are produced in Kashan cannot be found anywhere else. Truly, in this way the people of the city have shown their craftsmanship.[173]

IN PRAISE OF ITS FRUIT. All of its fruits are good, and the *nehar* plums are big like duck eggs, the *melejeh* and *'abbasi* pears are the best of Iraq and the *qamari* and apricot are very juicy and delicious as if they were like those of Hama in Syria.[174]

ADDITIONAL DESCRIPTION. Since there are many scorpions, some call it the city of scorpions. The scorpion is like a crab in the Mediterranean. When it raises its tail and goes hunting insects, which are in the soil, it jumps like a lizard. It stings the mule in its hoof and a camel in its heel and kills them instantly.

In accordance with God's wisdom, when the wife of Harun al-Rashid built this city, she employed a soothsayer, who created a talisman and buried it in a convent called Navan. On that talisman was written, in accordance with the science of geomancy, "I am a traveler; I am a traveler." Now, if a Kashani inhabitant or a traveler from outside comes to the city and says three times "I am a traveler," by the grace of God nothing happens to him. It is true that these harmful insects do not cause your body much harm. Even our travel friend, Baba 'Abdi of Khorasan, has suffered from the fleas of Balekesri in Anatolia and has written a poem mentioning the scorpions of Kashan.

> Flea (*Bergus*) poems:
> What kind of flea? Not a flea, but a deceiving devil
> What flea? It has no mercy, it takes your soul
> The fleas attack people as one horde
> If you chain a demon there he cannot stand it
> In truth, if they had seen fleas like these
> The people of Kashan would say: give me scorpions any time!
> If in the city of Balekesri God does not help 'Abdi
> The fleas make a martyr out of him.

DESCRIPTION OF THE PLACES OF PILGRIMAGE OF THE PAST KINGS. The blessed 'Omar, may God be pleased with him, after having liberated Basra from the hands of the Kharejites, came with his Helpers (*Ansar*), including the blessed Khaled b. Valid, to Kashan and gave battle and a number of them were martyred here. In the end, the conquest of Kashan was achieved by Asvad b. Miqdad. For several years it remained in the hands of the Companions, who made Kashan prosperous, and some of their children are buried in a place called Qaraqeh-ye 'Arab.[175] Their shrines have domes and everyone goes there.

---

173. Kashan was famous for its copper work, not for the production of arms, see Floor, *The Economy of Safavid Persia*, pp. 318-22.

174. These fruits are not mentioned in the long list of fruits produced by Zarrabi, *Tarikh*.

175. This place is not mentioned by Zarrabi, *Tarikh*.

We visited and looked at this city properly, and going to the east passing through prosperous villages we came to:

THE STAGE OF THE VILLAGE ZULYEZAN.[176] It has two thousand houses, gardens and orchards, and it is a beautiful suburb. Again we went to the east and reached the town of Jarbanqan.

DESCRIPTION OF THE TOWN OF JARBANQAN.[177] In the year 6 of the hijra [727-28] it was built by the brother of Hatam Ta'i the Arab, whose name was Emir Jerban Qan, and therefore it is called Jarbanqan. The Mongols call it Qan, because in Chinese and Mongolian it means governor. It is situated in (Persian) Iraq under the rule of the Shah of Persia. In the province of Kashan it is a separate sultanate, with one thousand soldiers. Although its walls are in ruins, the city is prosperous. It is entirely surrounded by an earthen moat. It has fourteen gates. They are: the Mehraban, Isfahan, Kashan, Saveh, Demavand, Baghdad, Deylam, Dartang, and Alamut gates and (five) others. Inside there is big prosperous city with seven thousand well-built houses.

In total it has seventy mosques. There are well-built and embellished large mosques, caravanserais, bathhouses, markets and bazaars. All of its people are Shi`ites. The wits and the mystic scholars are numerous. All of them are witty, know Persian and are divinely inspired poets. Especially, their young boys are very noble and mature.

IN THEIR SCHOOLS THE PERSIAN ALPHABET IS TAUGHT AS FOLLOWS: First,

> Elif, be ile ela eblü ale ülüli ele üub
> Be, be ile bela beblü bela bel bülü ve li bül büb
> Te, te ile tela tetül ve telatül tülüli tetül tüt
> The, the ile thela thethül va thela thel theli thel thüth
> Jim, jim ile jela jejil va jela jel cülüli jül jüj
> Ha, ha ile hala hajel va hala hah huhuli hah, etc.

There are twenty-nine letters and they are pronounced in this way:

> Alef, zeber zīr pish-e u
> Be zeber be zīr pish-e bu
> Te zeber te zīr tī pish-e tī
> The zeber the zīr thi pish-e thu
> Jim zerb je zīr-e jī pish-e ju
> Ha zeber ha zīr hī pish-e hu, etc.

The people of Jarbanqan know several kinds of strange and wonderful sciences and philosophies, but in the end they are hopeless Shi`ites. All of them wear chintz, gold embroidered robes, double-lined caftans, a Safavid Sufi hat (*taj-e ravaj*), green pants and also green silken velvet footwear. Most of its inhabitants are readers of musicology books, so that each one in the various

---

176. May be named after the mythical pre-Islamic hero Sayf b. Dhu'l-Yazan.

177. This is the name the Arab geographers used for the city of Golpeygan. Evliya's account of its history, as usual, is fanciful and entirely invented. For its history see Firuz, Eshraqi, *Golpeygan dar a'ineh-ye tarikh* (Isfahan, 1383/2004). According to Jevdet, vol. 4, p. 378 it is the birthplace of the poet Qa'ani. However, he is not listed among the many poets of Golpeygan discussed in Eshraqi, *Golpaygan*, pp. 421-687.

places where there is dancing and singing plays a dulcimer wonderfully in twelve *maqam*s, forty-eight arrangements and twenty-four rhythmic patterns. Whoever listens to them would say that this is eternal life. Most of their quatrains and their songs are written in the Khorasani style, and most of their poems and compositions are recited in this way. Here are some appropriate examples:

A Saba *maqam*, in the rhythmic pattern of Owfar,[178] and in Qaracheqa arrangement.

> The gardens of Tabriz are beautiful, my darling
> > Its mountain and orchards are beautiful, my darling
> Yesterday I heard my rival has died
> > This is good news, o darling.

تبریزک باغی گوزل ای جانم
باغچه سی، داغی گوزل ای جانم
دون ایشتیدم که رقیبیم اولمش
بوخبر دخی گوزل ای جانم

The other one is in the Iraqi mode, in the *Sema'i* rhythmic patterns and the style of Larestan.

> Neither good gardens or good music
> Nor at the side of our plantation
> We all wonder why the
> All-knowing peasant has left us
> Dargazin has left us
> Shahreban has left us[179]

نه هوای باغ و نه ساز نه کنار کشت ما را   همه حیرتم به دهقان همدان بهشت ما را
در گزین بهشت ما را، شهربان بهشت ما را
دیر، دیر تن ، تن، تانا درنی   تللره تللره تانی تانی ، تانی تانی

In this way they go around the fields and play music and sing.

---

178. Owfar is one of the twenty-four rhythmic patterns (*osul*) with five beats (*zarb*), two bass and three sharp.

179. This apparently is a corrupted form of a poem by Dhowqi Ardestani, a Safavid poet who died in 1054/1644 in Isfahan, see Dehkhoda q.v. Dhowqi. His original poem is as follows:

نه هوای باغ ساز و نه کنار کشت ما را | تو بهر کجا که باشی بود آن بهشت ما را | نه طراوتی نه برگی نه ثمر نه سایه دارم | همه حیرتم که دهقان بچه کارکشت ما را

Neither garden's air nor that of the field agrees with us / Because wherever you are it is paradise for us / Neither freshness nor a leaf, a fruit or shadow I possess / I wonder, for what reason has the peasant sown us.

In Persian there is a word play which cannot be translated. The key-word used is *hamadan*, which can be read as the name of the city of Hamadan, but also as *hamehdan*, meaning 'all-knowing.'

{According to Persian historians, because the watermelon of this city is so juicy and plentiful, they call it the city of Hendevaneh (the city of the watermelon) and other fruits are extremely plentiful.}

THE PLACES OF PILGRIMAGE OF THE CITY OF JARBANQAN. Qom is at one stage distance. On this route outside the city is a cemetery, and as the hemistich goes,

> If the dead would speak, they'd say how many Daras and Jams would be lying here.[180]

Many kings and rulers are buried here. There are many places of pilgrimage like the shrine of Khedhr, the Panj Hoseyn shrine, the Men of the Unseen shrine, the Omana Maqami shrine and the Nobles shrine.[181] The abovementioned shrines are in forty places and all the Persians believe in them, and on Friday nights they are the place of pilgrimage. May God have mercy on all of them. We went from here to the east and came to Saveh.

DESCRIPTION OF THE ANCIENT CITY OF SAVEH. According to the historians, the city was built by Noah after the deluge. [Now follows a fantastical and uninteresting story about Noah and Saveh, which we have not translated.] After it was built they called it Savi – *qa'di* and *qa'd* in Hebrew means city. Even Coptic historians used worlds like qa`da-ye Iskander, qa`d-e Misr, qa`d-e Fustat, qa`d-e Hasan, qa`d-e Filastin, and qa`d-e Dimishq-e Sham. After the deluge, this city of Savi became so prosperous that its width and length could be traversed on foot in three days.

Later, six hundred years before the prophet Jesus was born, Nebuchadnezzar marched from Kurdistan, wanting to revenge the killing of the prophet John, and came to Saveh and killed more than two hundred thousand Jews and destroyed the city.

Later, Shah Yazdegerd rebuilt it, and the name was shortened to Saveh. Now it is situated in the province of Kashan and is a separate sultanate. It has one thousand choice soldiers and a mullah, a *khvajeh*, an overseer of the sayyeds and twelve officials, but there is no castle. Since old times its walls were made of earth and because it was at the very end of border, it has fallen into ruins over time. But outside the city there are altogether five hundred very nice houses covered with earth.

In short, all its endowments and buildings are like those of Qom. After Hamadan, its climate and the people's health are better than of all other cities. There are quite a number of Sunnis. They do not curse the four chosen ones; furthermore, they also have the king's order to exile forever those who curse them. If we describe the city properly it will become a very large book. But among its beauties two things are praiseworthy.

First, most of the people of this city are soldiers, and they do not want for anything. Secondly, their administrative and fiscal laws are truly good. Every night all the shops are left open and everyone sleeps at home without fear. The guardsmen and the watchmen keep watch until dawn. The city is so well administrated that nobody steals foodstuffs or beverages from the shops or gardens. Also, eggs, cooked chicken, soup, pilau, wheat-mutton stew *(hariseh)*, and soup are sold by the weight of `Ali. *Kelek* [sic: possibly *keyl*], *shinik* [measure of cereals equaling one-quarter bushel], *gülbe* and *peymaneh* are not used at all here. People keep their promises. There is so much abundance that one *kez* of excellent wheat is half an *'abbasi,* and one *batman* of white

---

180. This line probably is by Omar Khayyam.

181. None of these buildings are mentioned in Eshqaqi, *Golpeygan*.

bread, one Tiflis *qazbeygi*. One skin (*sheq*) of amber-like butter is three *qazbeygi*s. All of its people are scholars and learned men. In business affairs their calculations are very accurate, saying that it is in accordance with the law of Sheikh Safi, and they charge the rates fixed by the Shah.

The town of Saveh

Concerning the city's prices and weights. *Kez* is 748,800 *derham*s. *Sheq* is 62,400 *derham*. *Qafez* is 12 *sa'*. *Makul* is 1,560 *derham*s. *Sa'* is 1,040 *derham*s. *Mudd* is 520 (*derham*s). *Man* is 260 *derham*s. *Ratl* is 130 *derham*s. *Istad* is 600 *derham*. One *derham* is 33 *arpa* in weight. *Mithqal* is 100 *arpa*. *Qirat* is 5 *arpa* by weight. [Length.] *Farsakh* is 12,000 paces. *Mil* is 100 paces. *Addem* is four paces and one moderate pace (*ayak-e miyan*), which is exactly twenty *arpa* in length. One tailor's *zira'* (cubit) is three lengths of a hand (*qaresh*). One *qaresh* is 20 *arpa*. A cloth measure (*chuqa*) is five *qaresh* and two fingers in width. The mason's *arshin* is equal to a tailor's cubit plus one-third extra. The Meccan cubit came into being when the holy Ka'ba was being repaired and is equal to one and half tailor's cubit. Apart from these weights and measures, the people of Saveh are so good in matters of calculation and measurement, as if they are Feyzollah Hindi.

Description of the tombs of the martyrs of the city of Saveh. South of the city of Saveh is the big village of Heydar Qan. It has one hundred houses, a large mosque and a caravanserai. We went south and reached the village of Sultan Durugh. It is the personal fief of the Khan of Kashan; it has one thousand houses and is prosperous. Again going south we reached Rey.

DESCRIPTION OF THE FAMOUS CITY OF REY.[182] According to the historians of Persia, the first founder of the city was Gayomarth Shah, one of the ancient kings of Iran and Turan. Because of the passage of time, it suffered many rebellions and wars and fell into ruin. Shah Hushang rebuilt it. It became so prosperous that, compared to it, ancient Baghdad was a village. As is the custom of the world, it passed through the hands of many kings and now it is part the land of Persian Iraq. It is situated on the left side of Mt. Demavand, inside a beautiful meadow land, like the city of Bursa in a hilly country. It has many gardens, and it is a delightful and prosperous city.

This city from the east to the west is two *farsakh*s, (twenty-four thousand paces). Like Tyre and Magnesia, it is situated lengthwise with its width only half a *farsakh*. To its west at two stages distance is Mt. Aqra`, which is on the border of Kurdistan. The city of Saveh is on the east side of Rey and [they say] at three stages distance, but we traveled it slowly in two stages.

CONCERNING THE GOVERNORS OF THE CITY OF REY. Its Khan has seven thousand soldiers. The city has a mullah, a *khvajeh-ye anam*, an overseer of the sayyeds, a mace-bearer and a conductor of guests. These officials really practice justice as if they were Anushirvan.

IN PRAISE OF THE BUILDINGS AND HOUSES OF THE CITY OF REY. It is unlike other cities because it does not have a well-built castle, but it is very prosperous. It has nine thousand and eight hundred street gates, which are houses with gardens and orchards. Behind each gate there are at least ten or fifteen houses. All buildings are constructed with bricks, and the roofs are covered with earth. All around the walls a moat has been dug, which is very deep, and it protects the city from rebels and robbers. It has eight gates, but all of them are made of wood.

The roads of the city are very narrow, because they are afraid of Arab and Kurdish rebels. They have made them such that when the enemy tries to conquer it, it will be difficult for the enemy troops to gather in the narrow streets, and when they are passing through, the householders will attack them with arrows, muskets, stones and slings from the roof of every house, from the windows and from the balconies. Every house of the city, like the houses of the island of Chios and those of Aleppo, is like a castle.

RUNNING STREAMS. Inside the city there are in total one hundred and ten streams, from which travelers and their animals drink. But the wealthy people of the city drink well water.

FOUNTAINS IN THE NAME OF THE MARTYRS OF KARBALA. Inside and outside the city there are seventy public fountains for the thirsty. Each one of them has been erected in memory of the martyrs of Karbala. Among them, the Shah public fountain is the most outstanding.

SPRINGS AND RIVERS. To the west side of the city, coming from Mt. Demavand, two small rivers water the gardens, houses and buildings. Later it merges with another river.

WELLS OF THE HOUSES. Its running water coming from Mt. Demavand, passes through iron mines and is not good. Because of this, inside the city there are nine thousand very good wells.

---

182. For the history of Rey see V. Minorsky – C.E. Bosworth, "al-Rayy," *Encyclopedia of Islam II*; Hoseyn Karimiyan, *Rey-e bastan* (Tehran, 1354/1975). Evliya cannot have visited this city as described, because it had been destroyed by the Mongols in 1220. He may have meant to refer to nearby Tehran, which sometimes was also called Rey.

THE CLIMATE OF THE CITY OF REY is not as good as that of the other cities and it is very hot. In summer and winter [sic] all people spread their beds on the roofs and sleep there to keep cool. The nights are very cool. When they dig outside the city in several places they come across very expensive cornelians like those of Badakhshan rubies and garnets. The farms and orchards of the city are watered by the water that comes from Mt. Demavand.

DESCRIPTION OF MT. DEMAVAND AND ITS SUMMER QUARTERS. This is a very high mountain, and in the old times it had seven strong walls and the castle of Demavand was known to everybody. In 995 [1586] the vizier of Sultan Murad III, Cheghal-zadeh Senan Pasha, conquered the castle of Demavand in seven days and destroyed it. He collected five hundred thousand sheep. Now, in these summer quarters there are grazing one million quadrupeds and cattle. To the east of them are the summer quarters of the Afshar, Kahrani, Domboli and Domdomi Turkmen and the Khan of Rey receives a portion of their taxes, to which end the Khan has been appointed by the Persian Shah. To the south of Mt. Demavand and to the west are the summer quarters of the Arabs, Turkmen, and Zebari Kurds,[183] and their summer-quarter fees go to the governor of ʿEmadi-yeh as well as to ʿAqra Bey. It is a very fertile mountain, and there are many iron mines. From this point of view its water is no good. In the north there is Mt. ʿAqrah.

DESCRIPTION OF MT. ʿAQRAH. Its real name is Mt. Aqraʿ. It is situated to the north-west of the city of Rey at a distance of three stages; it is bare, without trees. It is a bald [*aqraʿ*] mountain situated between the *beyliq* of Aqraʿ in Kurdistan and Persia.[184] First, when we went to ʿEmadiyeh we stayed there. But Mullah Karni said that there is a gold mine in this mountain, but being in Kurdish lands the cost of its extraction would be more than the yield of pure gold. But this was wrong. When this humble author was traveling in Rey from Mt. Aqraʿ, seven mule loads of gold ore were brought. The Khan processed it with sulphur then put it into a hot fire, and the result was a soft pure gold. He then sent the mules with the gold to the Shah. If they dig the foundation of a building in Rey they will find ten or fifteen pieces of precious rubies and cornelians.

STRANGE THINGS. Every year, either outside or inside this city, one or two treasures are found. Therefore, a number of people have abandoned their work, and day and night, like Farhad, they dig looking for treasure and in this way waste their time. Another bad thing about this is that several hundred people, thinking that they will find treasure, take spades and destroy this prosperous city and make it like the ruins of ancient Egypt.

DESCRIPTION OF THE PLACES OF PILGRIMAGE OF THE CITY OF REY. In the time of the caliphate of the blessed ʿOmar, several of the chosen Companions and Helpers (*ansar*) lived in the city of Rey. Eventually, they left for the other world and were buried here. Now, the tombs of the chosen Companions constitute an important place of pilgrimage to the south of the city.

THE SHRINE OF SHAHROKH QAY is under a high dome.

THE SHRINE OF SALMAN-E KUFI. He is the spiritual leader of the water carriers and the blessed ʿAli girdled him. He died at the age of thirty. He is buried outside the city under a dome.

---

183. Zebari Kurds live in the northernmost part of Iraqi Kurdistan. See Mark Sykes, *Dar-ul-Islam* (London, 1904), pp. 221-28.

184. Aqrah, Akre or Akra is situated in Ninewa governate (Iraq). For a description of the town and its mountain see Sykes, *Dar-ul-Islam*, pp. 173f.

After seeing the city of Rey we went to the west, south of Mt. Demavand and reached:

The village of Shir ʿAli. It is under a chief (*kalantar*) and part of Rey. We passed from there passing through lovely gardens and a promenade-like plain and drank from many springs and reached the castle of Demavand.

Description of the castle of Demavand. In the past, the Abbasid caliphs built one castle here. But since the building was made of bricks, it fell apart due to the passage of time. Later, in the year 995 [1586], the vizier of Sultan Murad III, Cheghal-zadeh Senan Pasha, the commanding general, came to the region of Baghdad and with a huge army turned towards the beautiful city of [Tabriz] in Azerbaijan via Jam-Jamal. He passed through Rey, Qom, Kashan, Dargazin, Hamadan, Mehraban, Bagh-e Jenan, Shahr-e Losus, Qazvin, Jam-Janab, the castle of Shahraban and arrivied at Tabriz. He destroyed and plundered many of these cities and castles and gave them no quarter. This was because he was defeated at the the castle of Serav, so he took his revenge on the Persians; he campaigned from Baghdad and passing many castles and stages he came to Mt. Demavand. However, he realized that there was no castle that would provide security on the road from Baghdad to Hamadan and Tabriz.

In the end, he consulted his troops, and they agreed to construct a strong castle on Mt. Demavand. He himself with the troops conquered about sixty castles in those parts until he reached the city of Tabriz. He destroyed all the towns, villages and cities and leveled them, because he wanted to erase the evil Qizilbash from the pages of existence. From these places that were plundered such an amount of booty was gathered that only God knows its extent. All the fighters of the true faith received so much booty that it was a million fold of what they had lost in the past when they were defeated at Serav, and thus they took revenge on the Persians a hundred thousand times over. This has now become a legend in Persia. Then general Cheghal-zadeh turned to Baghdad, conquered many strong castles, and when he reached the castle of Demavand it was not yet completed. With his victorious army he did his best and finished it in 995 [1587], and he put three thousand men there with seventy cannons and several thousands different armaments. Then he returned to Baghdad.

The layout of the peerless castle of Demavand. It is situated on the slopes of Mt. Demavand on a high hill. It is a large, elevated castle, built with mortar and lead. There is no moat and it has two gates. One is called the Rey and the other the Baghdad Gate. Inside the castle there are now three hundred houses, the mosque of Sultan Murad III, a caravanserai, a bathhouse and sufficient number of shops. Its circumference is two thousand paces. It is under the Persian government and forms a separate sultanate. It has one thousand choice soldiers. Its climate, gardens and orchards are an adornment. It has beautiful gardens with bowers, but all of its inhabitant are Shiʿites.

In praise of Mt. Demavand. This mountain is high like Bisotun and Alvand mountains. Several thousand animals graze in its pastures and become fat. In these mountains, Arabs, Persians and Turkmen nomads make their summer quarters and pay their rights to the Khan of Rey and the governor of Baghdad.

Again we went into the plain of Demavand and passed prosperous villages and cities, and in five hours we reached:

SHAH KÖRPÜSÜ. This bridge is called in Persian *pol-e shahi* [i.e. the royal bridge]. It is a famous bridge with nine arches and each one reminds you of the Arch of Khosrow. From the side of Demavand, towards the side of Mt. Bisotun, large rivers passes under this huge bridge. We passed from this impressive bridge to the slopes of Mt. Bisotun into the plains of the castle of Sorkhbid. We traveled for four days and reached the castle of Kermanshah.

THE STAGE OF THE CASTLE OF KERMANSHAH. This castle has been built by Shah Esma`il, and that is why it is called Kermanshah; we have previously described it. From this place we visited Nehavand, Qom and Kashan, and then we returned to Kermanshah, because we were expected there. Kermanshah is three stages from Hamadan, on the road to Baghdad. But this humble author's traveled all over the place to see all these place and from Kermanshah went south for three hours and reached:

THE STAGE OF THE VILLAGE OF FAJAR KHAN. It is a beautiful village with one thousand houses, a large mosque, a caravanserai and a bathhouse. Then I went south for seven hours and came to:

THE STAGE OF VILLAGE OF SOHRAB. It is a prosperous village in the land of Kermanshah with five hundred houses and a large mosque. We went to the south and after five hours came to:

THE STAGE OF THE VILLAGE OF SARKHALEH.[185] It is a prosperous village with three hundred houses and a paradise-like garden. Going to to the south for eight hours we reached:

THE STAGE OF THE TOWN OF TAQ-E GIRAY.[186] Hulagu Khan created it in ancient times when was the master of Baghdad. The son of Hulagu, called Giray Khan, enjoyed hunting in this area and built a town, which they called Taq-e Giray Khan. Now it is not very prosperous, but remains of arches can still be seen. The general of Sultan Murad IV, Khosrow Pasha, when he destroyed Hamadan and Dargazin en route to Baghdad, came to Taq-e Giray via a road known as Yeni Imam and destroyed this arch. Since that time the arches are in ruins. It borders on the castle of Dartang and the village of Taq-e Giray, which has one thousand houses, a large mosque, a caravanserai, a bathhouse, a royal bazaar and a stream. We left and after two hours to the south and reached:

THE DARTANG PASS. God forbid, it is such a dreadful and dangerous pass that many merchants with merchandise who cross it with mules and camels fall and lose their goods. People pass through this narrow pass on foot with difficulty, and therefore it is called the narrow pass. In the Pars language *dar* means gate and *tang* means narrow. At this place Anushirvan the Just built an iron gate, which was called *dartang*. On two sides are high mountains, where the hawk and eagle make nests.

Returning to the High Porte after the conquest of Baghdad with the grand vizier, Qara Mostafa Pasha, and the governor of Diyarbekr, Malek Ahmad Pasha, Sultan Murad IV passed through here and with the agreement of the Shah of Persia made the border here. Now at the

---

185. Now called Sar-qal`eh or Sarkaleh.

186. Taq-e Gireh in the pass of the same name, situated between Zohab and Kermanshah. Gireh is said to be the name of one of the officers of Khosrow. However, see H.C. Rawlinson, "Notes on a March from Zohab," *Journal of the Royal Geographical Society* vol. 9 (1839), p. 34 who wrote that the name means the arch holding the road.".

entrance of the Dartang pass is written in bold script on a marble pillar that it is the border. From its inside towards the south begins the Ottoman territory of Baghdad, and outside it is the Persian side. At the entrance of this pass and at the royal pass there are deep storage spaces and caves as tall as camels. When the Persians wanted to lay siege to Baghdad, they stored their supplies there and then went to Baghdad. May God protect it. We crossed the Dartang pass safely in five hours and arrived at the castle Dartang.

DESCRIPTION OF STONE MOUNTAIN, THE CASTLE OF DARTANG. Anushirvan the Just built this castle to protect the land of Iraq against the Mongols, Uzbegs, Indians and Tatars. He built it at the entrance of this narrow pass. Now, in accordance with Sultan Sulayman's law, it is the capital of a *sanjaq* in the region of Baghdad, with one hundred soldiers. It is an imperial fief with an income of 320,000 *aqcheh*s, but in its *liva* there are no *alay-beg*, *cheri-bashi*, or *ze'amat* and *timar* title holders. Because, according to the edict of Sultan Sulayman, this region is part of Iraq, which does not have *timar*s and *ze'amat*s. The surrounding area is allocated as a personal fief of the emirs; twenty purses annually are allotted to the *bey*, and five purses to the qazi. The castellan of the castle has three hundred soldiers, a market inspector, a customs official and a chief of the merchants. We went to the south and after five hours we came to the castle of Darna.

DESCRIPTION OF THE CASTLE OF DARNA. It is built by Yazdegerd after the hijra. In the past it was a large town, but it was destroyed by Timur. In spite of being prosperous, in the year 1039 [1629-30], in the time Sultan Murad IV, Khosrow Shir destroyed it. Now, under the Ottomans it has again become a rather prosperous place. In accordance with Sultan Sulayman's law, it is a capital of a *sanjaq* in the administrative district of Baghdad. The personal fief of the *bey* amounts to 406,932 *aqcheh*s. It does not have an *alay-beg*, a *cheri-bashi*, *timar*s or *ze'amat*s. Since in the land of Iraq it borders on the district of Karane, they call it Darna-ye Karane. It has a qazi, a castellan, a garrison, a market inspector, a chief of the merchants and a customs official. We went to the south and after six hours came to:

THE STAGE OF THE KHANEQAH-E KABIR. It is in the district of Darna. In the past, there was a huge hostel for travelers and merchants that was built by Shah Esma'il. It is still prosperous. Then the Persians rebuilt about one thousand houses in this place and it has numerous large mosques, caravanserais, bathhouses and a sufficient number of useful shops. We went to the south and after 6 hours reached:

THE STAGE OF KHANEQAH-E SAGHIR. It is in a delightful place and has a big caravanserai. Its builder is unknown. In the district of Darna and on the main road there is also a small caravanserai. There is a village on either side with five hundred houses, a large mosque, a caravanserai, a bathhouse and gardens and orchards. Going for eight hours we came to Haruniyeh.

DESCRIPTION OF THE TOWN OF HARUNIYEH. In the year 244 [858-59] it was built by Harun al-Rashid, and that is why it is called Haruniyeh.

DESCRIPTION OF THE TOWN OF ZANGABAD. In ancient times it was built in the time of the caliph Harun al-Rashid by his treasurer called Zangi and hence the name. Now in the land of Baghdad it is a separate *sanjaq* on the Persian side. It has one thousand choice soldiers. According to the law of Sultan Sulayman its *bey* receives 270,000 *aqches*, which normally is equal to eighteen purses. Because it is situated in Iraq, it has *timar*s, *ze'amat*s, a *cheri-bashi*, an *alay-begi* and a judgeship of one hundred and fifty *aqche*s and seventy villages, these are assigned as fiefs for the garrison of Baghdad. One of the distinguished aghas of the Pasha, with his two hundred retainers has been assigned forty loads of *aqcheh*s and ...

From there we went south and after five hours came to the village of Qizil Rabat.

DESCRIPTION OF THE FIEF TOWN OF QIZIL RABAT. It is situated in the province of Baghdad and is part of the district of Zangabad and nine loads of *aqche*s have been assigned as fief for the garrison of Baghdad. The Pasha has appointed an *agha* to collect fifteen loads of *aqche*s as wages for the soldiers.

Going to the south we came to Baqubah.

DESCRIPTION OF THE FIEF TOWN OF BAQUBAH. It is in the land of Baghdad in the Persian part of Baghdad and has been assigned as fief to the garrison. The pasha has farmed it out to one of the distinguished *agha*s for seventy purses, who collects one hundred purses; it is a wonderful fief.

Going to the south we came to Bayat.

DESCRIPTION OF THE TOWN OF THE DISTRICT OF BAYAT. In accordance with Sultan Sulayman's law it is a separate *sanjaq*. The Bey's personal fief is two hundred thousand *aqceh*s. Because it does not have any *timar*s and *ze'amat*s in its land, there are no *alaybegi* and *cheri-bashi*. It has a judgeship of one hundred and fifty *aqceh*s. These villages are all farmed out. One of the Pasha's *agha*s gets it for seven hundred, *aqceh*s and with his one hundred and fifty retainers he collects the revenues.

Then we went south.

DESCRIPTION OF THE BIG TOWN OF DEBALA SANJAQ.[187] It is situated in Iraq in the Persian part and in accordance with the law of Sultan Sulayman is the capital of a separate *sanjaq*. The *mir-liva* has got 260,000 *aqceh*s. There are *timar*s and *ze'amat*s as well as *alaybegi* and *cheri-bashi* and a judgeship of one hundred fifty *aqceh*s. It has eighty-six prosperous villages.

DESCRIPTION OF THE TOWN OF KEREND. It is in Iraq on the Persian side, and according to the law of Sultan Sulayman it is a separate *sanjaq*. The Bey's personal fief is 239,600 *aqceh*s. It is a judgeship and the district has been assigned to the garrison of Baghdad.

DESCRIPTION OF THE TOWN OF THE SANJAQ OF KARANIYEH. It is in the province of Baghdad, and in accordance with the law of Sultan Sulayman it is the seat of a separate *sanjaq*. The imperial fief of the Bey is two hundred thousand *aqceh*s and the judgeship has one hundred and fifty *aqceh*s. The revenues of the villages are collected by one of the Pasha's *agha*s.

DESCRIPTION OF THE TOWN OF THE SANJAQ OF GILAN. It is in the Persian side of Iraq. It is the seat of an independent *sanjaq*. The personal imperial fief of its *mir-liva* amounts to two hundred thousand *aqceh*s, and with one hundred and fifty *aqceh*s for the judgeship. In the olden times it was a village called *Jilan*. Since it was the birthplace of Sheikh 'Abdol-Qader, they

---

187. This must be a writing error for Diyala.

call it Sheikh `Abdol Qader Jilani.[188] But it is not Jilani, because Jilan[189] is situated in Persia, in the north, close to the provinces of Shirvan and Shamakhi, near the Caspian Sea, and close to castle of Darband, where it is a big port. But this Jilan is a separate *sanjaq* in the land of Baghdad.

DESCRIPTION OF THE TOWN OF THE SANJAQ OF AL-E SAH. Its founder is Al-e Salehi-yan. According to the law of Sultan Sulayman, it is a separate *sanjaq* with a personal fief of two hundred thousand *aqcheh*s for its Bey, and one hundred and fifty *aqcheh*s for the judgeship. In the time of the Bayandors it was an important district, but now it has fallen from prosperity. Most villages are assigned for the wages of the garrison of Baghdad. One of the pasha's *agha*s has farmed it for ten loads of *aqche*s.

A Peasant Plowing

DESCRIPTION OF THE TOWN OF THE SANJAQ OF QARADAGH. It is in Iraq and it is governed in the manner of a *yurdluk* and *ojaqliq* like Basra. The land does not have *timar*s and *ze'amat*s at all. The personal fief of the *bey* amounts to 804,387 *aqcheh*s.

DESCRIPTION OF THE TOWN OF THE SANJAQ OF JANGULEH. It is a *sanjaq* in the Persian side of Iraq. The *bey*'s imperial fief is two hundred thousand *aqcheh*s. The abovementioned district towns of Darna and Dartang have been noted while discussing Baghdad's *sanjaq*s. We returned to the stage of Haruniyeh; then we went to south passing through Baqubah, prosperous villages and hostels. After seven hours we reached Shahriban.

---

188. `Abdol-Qader Jilani is the founder of the Qaderi order. See D. Lawrence, "`Abd al-Qader Jilani," *Encyclopedia Iranica*.

189. Meaning the Caspian province of Gilan. For this Gilan in Iraq see H.C. Rawlinson, "Notes on a March from Zohab," *Journal of the Royal Geographic Society* vol. 9 (1839), pp. 42-44.

DESCRIPTION OF THE ANCIENT CITY OF SHAHRIBAN. According to the historians, its first founder is the daughter of Anushirvan the Just, Shahbanu, and it was called Shahr-e Banu. Because of the passage of time this has been shortened to Shahriban. Truly, it is like a garden of paradise just like Mada'in and Kufa in Iraq, and like the capitals of the Arabs and Persians. It is situated two stages east of Baghdad on the far side bank of the river Diyala in a region with beautiful gardens and palm groves. It is a beautiful town, which all the kings of the past desired.

Then we went to the south on the Persian side of the Diyala river and passing the canals, which come from that river, we rode through several hundred prosperous villages and after twelve hours came to Behruz.

We left on the second of Rabi` al-Avval of the year 1066 [30 December 1655], the auspicious day of the birth of the Prophet and we arrived in Baghdad.

[Traveling from Baghdad to the south Evliya arrived in Basra]

DESCRIPTION OF THE ANCIENT LAND OF ABADAN, ON THE COAST OF HORMUZ AND OMAN, I.E., THE MAKRAN-E HAZRA, THE CASTLE OF BASRA

According to all historians, the descent of the pure Adam at the beginning of the world was on the island of Sarandib (Ceylon). From there by the will of God, pure Adam came to the land of Hormuz, and he prayed to the land and the sea and the city of Hormuz was built and the peerless pearl came into being in the sea of Hormuz. Then he came to the land of Basra and settled there and he prayed and Basra was built. Then he came to the land of Abadan, and because of his prayer it was built. Then he came to the land of Oman, and it was built. Then he came to Mt. Mekran and it was built. Then he went to the land Lahsa, then to the land of Yemen, then to the land of Aden, then to Mecca, where on Mt. Arafat he met and recognized Eve, and that is why it is called Mt. Arafat.[190] Later on with six prophets, the prophet Adam built the city of Kufa. Then the sons of the prophet Seth[191] built the city of Basra. After the Flood the prophet Noah rebuilt it. Then his descendants built Yemen. Then in the time of the caliphate of the blessed `Omar, may God be pleased with him, in the year [-], he wrenched it from hands of the Kharejites and appointed the blessed Sari al-Jabal[192] as governor. In three years with pure earth he built a castle, and several thousand Companions emigrated from Mecca, Medina, Yemen and Aden, and they rebuilt it in such a way that in the just age of the caliph `Omar there was no better city than this in the land of Islam. There were a total of seven large and small mosques. Now their remains can be seen. There are six hundred madrasehs, one thousand caravanserais and bathhouses, seven hundred drapery shops, two hundred public kitchens, and seventy-six thousand houses.

Then, in the time of the Abbasids, Basra was surrounded by the river Shatt, the river Euphrates, the river [-], and the river [-], and it had twelve thousand canals, and ships sailed on them.

---

190. The origin of the name `Arafat is unknown. It has been suggested, among many other fanciful etymologies that after their expulsion from paradise the first couple found each other at this location and recognized each other (ta `rafa) and hence the name. A.J. Wensinck and H.A.R. Gibb, "`Arafat," *Encyclopedia of Islam II*.

191. Seth was the third son of Adam and Eve.

192. In the text normally written as Sariyat al-Jabal.

The wife of Harun al-Rashid, Zobeyda Khanom, dug a canal from the Shatt and channeled it to the land of Yemen, which is now called the town of Yelemlem, the place where the pilgrims of Yemen put on their ritual pilgrimage robe [*ehram*]. From Basra to the town of Yelemlem[193] they come by ship, and after putting on their ritual clothing they go to the Ka'ba. From the time of the Abbasids Basra was very prosperous. Thereafter, it was passed from king to king, and sometimes it prospered and sometimes it was destroyed.

Then, in 945 [1538-39], Kaqaqis b. Emir Rashid, whose family for generations had struck coins and read the *khutbah* in their name, submitted to Sultan Sulayman. Finally, he sent his son Mani' Khan and his vizier Mir Mohammad with gifts and the keys of Basra to Sultan Sulayman and the governorship of Basra was given to Emir Rashid, while coins were struck and the *khutbah* read in the name of Sultan Sulayman.[194]

Later, in 1048 [1639-40], Afrasiyab 'Ali Pasha obeyed Sultan Murad IV, who granted the province of Basra to him forever. But now, the governor of Basra is Hoseyn Pasha, son of Afrasiyab Pasha, who in the form of an *ojaqleq* obeys and is subject to the Ottomans, and he holds the rank of vizier and governor. The deputy of Morteza Pasha [...] and [?] Aqa, with our friend Hoseyn Pasha, came to welcome us with ten thousand soldiers in a grand procession when we arrived. When we were entering the castle of Basra [...], the cannons of joy were fired and we reached Hoseyn Pasha. After kissing his hand, Morteza Pasha's gifts were presented but were treated as being of no importance, while we were treated very respectfully and graciously, as if he were giving a party for Malek Ahmad Pasha, the Khan of Bitlis. After the party, he gave Morteza Pasha's deputy one gold-embroidered robe and the humble author one robe and one saddled horse. Morteza Pasha's deputy was hosted by the deputy of Hoseyn Pasha, and this humble author was hosted by the the pasha's secretary (*divan effendi*) and the retainers were sent as guests to the sons of 'Abdol-Salam. Later, this humble author received one purse of Mohammadi *qorush* and a robe and Morteza Pasha's deputy two purses and a robe of honor. And each time we talked with the Pasha and his companions, we learned about the situation in Basra and, therefore, will try to describe it as much as possible.

CONCERNING THE GOVERNORS OF THE PROVINCE OF BASRA. It is a major governorship. The pasha's personal fief, in accordance with the law of Sulayman, is 681,057 *aqchehs*, which is one *aqche* more than that of the governor-general of Mosul. But there are no *ze'amats* and *timars* in its province, and there are no *alay-begi* and *cheri-bashi* either. Because the taxes of seven hundred villages are farmed out, according to the law, the famous historian 'Eyn-e 'Ali Efendi,[195] is the *defterdar* of Basra, Lahsa and Baghdad. But it has a deputy of the *chavosh*,[196] *defter emini*,[197]

---

193. Yelemlem is a valley near Mecca.

194. For the history of Basra prior to 1500 see S.H. Longrigg, *Four Centuries of Modern 'Iraq* (Oxford, 1925). For its history in the sixteenth and seventeenth century see Floor, *The Persian Gulf. A Political and Economic History of Five Port Cities 1500-1730*, chapter 3 and 8. Needless to say that Evliya's early history of Basra is sheer fantasy.

195. Probably the author of the *Kanunmama-i Al-i Othman* (Ankara, 1962) written in 1602 and/or *Kavavin-i Al-i Othman der hulasa-i mezamin-i defter-i divan* (Istanbul, 1979).

196. The *chavosh* corps was initially used as messengers, but in Evlya's time they were employed as guards, attendants and ushers at court. Gibb-Bowen, vol. 1, p. 87.

197. The Commissionair of the Register of fief documents. Gibb-Bowen, *Islamic*, vol. 1, p. 124.

cavoshlar emini, chavoshlar katebi[198] and the *timar defterdar*.[199] Now, H.E. Hoseyn Pasha of the Afrasiyabs holds the government of Basra. According to the law, every three months gifts should go to the governor of Baghdad, and every year once to the grand vizier and the Sultan.

Every year, the Pasha of Basha collects one thousand purses. Five hundred purses are collected from customs duties, because every year, two hundred ships from India, Europe, Yemen, Aden and Ethiopia come here. Its pasha, with three thousand troops, rules over Lahsa, Yemen, Oman, Makran, Mecca, and as far as the Ane and the Seleme deserts. His territory abuts that of Baghdad. Gordelan castle is situated right at the Shatt al-Arab, which is three stages from the castle of Dowraq and the castle of Hoveyzeh. Because of this, the governor of Basra had enjoining land between the aforementioned Shatt and Persian castles. Towards the south it borders on the province of Hormuz in Persia. This is such a great province that he owned [-] castles. In his province seventy royal kettledrums, Afrasiyab trumpets and Ottoman drums are beaten. There are *sanjaq-beg*s and two hundred Arab tribal chiefs without drum and chief sheikhs.[200]

THEIR *SANJAQS* ARE AS FOLLOWS: First, the *liva*s of Qorna, Iskanderiyeh, built by the great Alexander, and ʿAmarah, situated on the banks of the Shatt on the Persian side. The *liva* of Abadan is on the Basra side. The *liva* of Zakiya; where the shrine of the prophet Uzayr is situated on the banks of the Shatt, and further down than Basra is the *liva* of the castle of Muhannavi,[201] which is very close to Basra. Further away is the *liva* of Qaban, which is a large port, and opposite from Basra's Shatt Ashri[202] is the *liva* of Bogurdelen,[203] which has a strong castle. Since it is on the border with Persia it has sufficient troops and arms. In this place the river Karun merges with the river Shatt, and in the land of Persia it issues from the mountains of the city of Hoveyza and has very good water. The farmed out towns of the southern and northern *liva*s and the *liva* of the town of Aqqara and the farmed out town of Mansuriya, and also next to the Shatt the farmed out town of Jaʿfariya, are situated on the banks of the river Shatt and they are prosperous settlements. The *liva* of the castle of Arjaʿ and the farmed customs duties yield annually five hundred purses. Six *farsakh* below Basra the farmed town of Ubulle and the farmed (area of) Jerjeh and the big *liva* of Basra, is a *sanjaq* almost as big as a province. Its chief castle is Tuzla. The others will be mentioned in their appropriate place. The town of Vehma and the town of Imam Mohammad Hanafi and the town of Mina and the town of Ubulle and the *liva* of Qatif (...).[204]

The *sanjaq*s and farmed lands mentioned above all are situated near the Shatt and on the banks of the Euphrates and along canals. There are castles, caravanserais, large and small mosques, and bazaars and they are prosperous towns. God willing, I will mention the other *liva*s and the well-built towns in their own places. The Pasha of Basra is the overlord of all these places mentioned and another official, according to the religious law, is a qazi with three *aqcheh*s.

---

198. Respectively the Commissioner and Secretary who jointly controlled the chavosh corps. Gibb-Bowen, vol. 1, p. 119.

199. He was in charge of the records for the fiefs or *timar*s. Gibb-Bowen, *Islamic*, vol. 1, pp. 150-51.

200. For the Pasha of Basra's revenues and the extent of his realm see Floor, *Persian Gulf*, chapter 7.

201. This is called Manawi.

202. This is the al-ʿAshar creek.

203. This is (Borj) Gordolan or Gardalan situated on the the bank of the Euphrates opposite Manawi.

204. On the administrative organization of Basra see Floor, *Persian Gulf*, pp. 479-80.

In total, [-] villages yield annually ten thousand *qorush*. The *sheikh al-Islam* is the religious judge. The muftis of three Schools are under the authority of a Hanafi *sheikh al-Islam*. There is also an overseer of the sayyeds, a chief of merchants, a castellan and seven hundred men in the castle, eight hundred right wing and eight hundred left wing soldiers, as well as gunners, armorers, and others, in total three thousand soldiers.

CONCERNING THE SHAPE OF THE CASTLE OF BASRA. Situated in the land of Mecca, on the banks of the great river Shatt al-Arab, it is a big and ancient castle in quadrangular form made of mortar, bricks, lime and pure soil. It was wrested by the great blessed ʿOmar himself, may God be pleased with him, from the hands of the heretics and Kharejites. It was destroyed and rebuilt again. Even in popular parlance, "After the destruction of Basra," has become a proverb.[205] Now in looking at the castle of Basra, there are holes in many places. But one side is absolutely safe from the enemy, because on all sides it is surrounded by the dams and canals of the Shatt al-Arab, and the entire plain is cultivated with rice. When an enemy comes they open the dams and they flood the Basra plain, which becomes a sea, drowning men, horses and even Mahmudi elephants. If the enemy comes from the side of Baghdad then the castle of Qorna is an obstacle. If an enemy comes from the side of the Sea of Hormuz, the castles of Muhannavi and Gordelan are obstacles.

Since Basra is situated in a very secure place they are not very careful in maintaining its castle. It is bigger than the castle of Mosul and smaller than that of Baghdad. The circumference of the castle of Basra is [-] paces and its moat is not deep. Some parts of it have been filled with earth. But the walls are very thick and high. It has several hundred well-built towers and bastions. There are not very many big caliber cannons and arsenals. The best of them are in the castle of Qorna, because it is the main defense and bastion of Basra.

There is a moat on three sides of Basra. But on the side of the Shatt it does not have a moat or bridge, because in this place the Shatt al-Arab is like a sea with a width of three *mil*. The Shatt is so wide that you cannot [see] the difference between men and women (on the other side). The castle of Basra on the side of the Shatt is very well built. Basra has a total of [-] wooden gates. These gates are strong and have well-built towers. On the Baghdad side there is the Mishraq Gate, which becomes the field of the javelin game during the two Festivals [of Ramazan and the Hajj]; the youths play on swings and merry-go-rounds in the field, which is near this gate. The Varosh Jisri (Suburb bridge) Gate, on the side of [-], and the Qorna Gate on the side of [-], and the Rabat Gate faces the Baghdad side. The Muhannavi Gate faces the ʿAshri creek at Gordelan. The Bahir Gate faces the eastern side, and the Hasan-e Basri Gate faces south.

CONCERNING THE BUILDINGS OF THE CASTLE OF BASRA. Inside Basra, according to the chief of merchant's calculation, the total of well-built two-storey houses amounts to ten thousand except for the houses of the poor. Most of the walls are made of bricks and lime, and the columns are covered with mud and they look miserably. The houses of the poor are made of reed, wicker and palm tree branches. For the pashas there are well-built houses. Altogether there are ten thousand two hundred houses, mansions and well-lit bathhouses and beautiful houses close to the Mishraq Gate, situated near the customs house and the palace of the Pasha. The houses that we saw were the house of deputy, the house of the sons of ʿAbdol-Salam, the mansion of Hoseyn Jamal and that of Hajji Khalil.

---

205. Meaning "after death the doctor' or 'after the horses have bolted closing the barn door.'

Altogether several quarters are enumerated. One quarter is called ʿAshshar Straight and has a wooden bridge. There are good and useful houses of the people, whose water is provided by the ebb and flow of the Shatt (al-Arab), and the quarters of Mishraq, Pasha, Hindi, and Black Arabs are all close to the Mishraq Gate. And there are so many [-] mosques of the caliphs. First, among all the ancient Arabs' places of worship is the large mosque built by the blessed ʿOmar, may God be pleased with him. Behind the Pasha's palace there is the Ayas Pasha mosque, which is frequented by many people and which is well-lit and very well-built. The ʿAbdol-Salam mosque is also well-built as well as that of Sheikh Habibollah and of Rostam Pasha. In front of the gate of the Pasha's palace there is the Hoseyn Pasha mosque, and in it Qara-Mostafa is buried. Inside the bazaar there are the much frequented Hoseyn Pasha, the Mishraq, the Guvzelar and the Seymer mosques.

All the large mosques are well-built with minarets and are well-lit, but among them the large mosque of blessed ʿOmar is the highest and oldest place of worship. None of these large mosques are built with lead. The surface of all their domes is covered with lime, because the lead melts due to the heat.

Apart from these there are small mosques.

In total there are [-] madrasehs. There are [-] elementary schools.

There are [-] dervish convents. At the beginning of the bridge over the ʿAshshar channel is the convent of Sheikh Mostafa Uryani.

There are [-] beautiful public fountains.

There are [-] convents

There are a total of one thousand draper shops. First, in front of the Pasha's palace is the wheat market, the Mishraq, the Seymer, the Seyf, the shoemakers' and the flax bazaar, which are well furnished. In the middle of the city is the herbalists' bazaar, which is a big and a long covered bazaar, the rice bazaar and the textiles bazaar.

There are [-] houses of the washers of the dead. At the beginning of the ʿAshshar channel's bridge is the Seyf bathhouse and the Mishraq bathhouse, the Shoemakers' bathhouse and on the other side of the bridge of Ribat, i.e., on the side of ʿAshshar, the Balad Sayas bathhouse, the Seymer bathhouse, the Ayas Pasha bathhouse and the Charsu bathhouse. All of these bathhouses are covered with tar and bitumen.

DESCRIPTION OF THE NOTABLES AND THE ELITE. The deputy of the *chavoshes*, Sarhan Beg, has become the *amir al-hajj* of Basra several times.[206] The offices of the pearl merchants, such as One-eyed Hajji Mohammad, Deli Beg, the *Agha* of the *Mohtaseb*, and the noble Sayyeds have caught fire several times, but by the grace of God were not burnt.

CONCERNING THE ULAMA AND THE SEMINARISTS.

CONCERNING THE SURGEONS AND PHLEBOTOMISTS

CONCERNING THE LEARNED SUFI SHEIKHS.

CONCERNING AUTHORS AND POETS.

---
206. Leader of the annual caravan of pilgrims going to Mecca.

Concerning the great holy dervishes

Concerning the color of young and old.

Concerning the dress of men and women.

Concerning the face of the beloveds.

Concerning the names of men.

Concerning the names of women.

Concerning the names of servants.

Concerning the names of female slaves.

Concerning of the language of the people of the city.

Concerning the impressive view of Abadan.

Description of the very hot climate.

Concerning the saying of the astronomers of the city.

Concerning the fortune of the buildings.

The nameless convent of Magi. There are [-] houses of idol worshippers and seventy-two erring sects of which there are very many in this city. Especially, the Hindi fire-worshippers, the sect of Banyans and the group of the Magians, and all of them are numerous. There are a very great number of Gabrs, Christians, Jews, and Europeans, Arabs and Persians.[207]

Description of famous crafts. Most people pierce pearls. On one street they do nothing but pierce various perfect pearls, and like the pearl bazaar there are heaps of pearls everywhere.

About the work and profession of men. Most people go to India, China and beyond and bring jewels and musk of Khotan, aloe wood, ambergris, several thousand good-smelling items of perfumes and other merchandise, and in this particular bazaar one's nose is overwhelmed by the scents and smells.

Concerning the charitable institutions.

In the praise of the harvested pulses.

Description of the tasty sweetmeats. It is a bounty being a nourishment for the spirit. There is a delicious salty food that cannot be found in the seven climes except in Basra. The master confectioners of the city are famous for making two hundred types of halva.

Description of the fruits.

Mention of the various kinds of beverages.

---

207. This is pure fiction and a great exaggeration; see Floor, *Persian Gulf*, pp. 497-500.

Concerning paradisiacal places of recreation.

Concerning the number of palm groves and gardens.
In total there are one thousand and sixty gardens and orchards, where every kind of plants, herbs, flowers and blossom abound. One flower is called *razaqi* (Arabian yasmine), which is white, and God knows its scent revives your soul.

The view of the rivers and streams
The city of Basra and the castle Dar al-Nasrat are situated on the banks of the sea-like Shatt al-Arab, and the river Shatt and Euphrates are branched off from it and water the land of Basra. There are twelve thousand channels which have been dug and maintained by the Sasanians, Kayanids, the Ommayads and Abbasids and several hundred kings in the land of Basra, and in each channel, creeks, and inlets ships are sailing. Several thousand of them have been filled by the passage of time, and now only six hundred of them are left. The Shatt and the Euphrates rise and water the land of Basra and in each channel ships are sailing, but the biggest one is the Shatt al-Arab, which is in front of Basra and looks like a sea. Below Basra in the Sea of Hormuz it joins with the all-encompassing Ocean.

On the Oman Sea galleons, grabs, carracks, galleys, fly-boats and [other] different types of ships go to the port of Jeddah, Abbysinia, Yemen, Aden, Lahsa and India. By God's will the ebb and flow of the Shatt al-Arab (the river Shatt) swells and overflows the land for two stages until the castle of Qorna.

When the Shatt recedes, several Indian ships in front of Basra and also lower at the castle of Muhannawi (Manawi) are stranded at the foot of it on the sand. Later on, when the Shatt al-Arab rises, all the ships rise up from the sand and float on the Shatt. By God's will the situation before Basra is sometimes ebb and sometimes flow. Inside the city of Basra there is a channel that flows from the Shatt. It is called in the language of the common people:

Nahr ʿAshshar.
It flows between Basra and the Ribat and over it there is a wooden bridge. By issuing forth from this Shatt, its ebb and flow is a spectacle of the marvels of God. The other one is near the south of Basra and is called:

Nahr-e Muhannavi (Manawi).
It separates form the Shatt and again joins the Shatt. Another river is:

Nahr-e ʿAntar,
which separates from the Shatt and again falls into the Shatt.

The River Karun
is situated on the Persian side of Basra and at the foot of the castle of Bogurdelen it comes from the mountains of Hoveyzeh in the land of the Persians and falls into the Shatt.

The ships that sail in these rivers and inside Basra in the ʿAshshar channel are called *maʿshuq,* and they are very wonderfully built boats. The boats called *merdileh* are steered with a special kind of pole, and the *jelbeh* boats that are made and woven of reed that has come from Yemen are called *markab.* They call the Indian boats *grab,* and the galleons can take five thousand people.[208] All these boats lie in front of Maqam ʿAli in the Shatt and wait for the tide for three months and then go to India. But in the castle of Qorna island:

---

208. This number is, of course, much too high and shows that Evliya was not very critical in assessing the information that he received.

THE RIVER ZEKKE separates from the Shatt and inside the island of Qorna waters the villages and castle of Fethiya, and then it falls back again into the Shatt, and:

THE RIVER MAK`AL separates from the Shatt near Banu Nahr after watering the land of Basra. Near the ruins of the city of Mina, it falls into **THE RIVER UBULLEH**. When these two river merge they call it the **RIVER SAFRAYDENK**.

In the time of the blessed caliph Omar when Basra was conquered, Malek Mak`al b. Beshsharah in order to develop the lands around Basra separated the Safray river before it entered into the Tigris at six *farsakh*s further down than the outlet of the Mak`al. It passed Basra near the mouth of the town of Ubulleh at the west side of the river Ubbuleh. Then near Basra it merged with the river Mak`al at the place of the castle of Muhannawi. Further down from there, where the Shatt ebbs and flows, this river Safray-e Mak`al merges with the Shatt River. In this land of Iraq and the land of Basra they say: "This river Mak`al and the river Ubulleh make half a circle," and also: "The river Shatt is similar to seven stars of the (astronomical) wheel."[209] According to the ancient sages and the authors of the *Geography*[210] and *Minor*,[211] at almost one *farsakh* near the river Ubulleh it separates from the Shatt and flows among the ruins and wilderness and falls into the Shatt al-Arab.

Between **THE RIVER ABU'L-KHATIB** and the river Yahud there are two *farsakh*s of land and they join with the Shatt, while between Abu'l-Khatib and the river Emir there is one *farsakh* of land and they fall into the Shatt above Basra.

The Sandal-e Akbar River, issuing forth from the Shatt, irrigates the environs of Basra. When you go from here to the provinces of Lahsa, Oman, Kij-Makran and Jazayer they call the Sheikh of the nomad Arab tribes Sheikh Barravi.

CONCLUDING DESCRIPTION OF THE WONDERFUL CITY OF BASRA. First of all, in the city of Basra there are several thousand wondrous sights and many believers of false religions. Among them are people of strange behavior who are fire worshippers. When one of them dies they give the Pasha several thousand *qorush* and they burn that cursed one in public in the castle of Muhannavi. And if the wife is devoted enough to her husband she is burnt along with him.[212]

THE GUR GROUP. These are an accursed tribe. They do not eat food from the hands of Moslems and do not socialize with them.

THE BANYANS. They dress in white turbans and white garb. They do not take food from anyone. When they eat God's bounty, they go and do their ablution in water.

---

209. Up until the 1700's, astrologers used in their Zodiac chart wheel the seven heavenly bodies that were known since ancient times and could be seen traversing the sky with the naked eye, to wit: the Sun, the Moon, Mars, Mercury, Jupiter, Venus, and Saturn.

210. Probably reference is made to the Arabic translation of Ptolemy's *Geographia*, by Georgios Amirutzes and his son, commissioned by Sultan Mohammad II.

211. This probably is the *Atlas minor* by Gerhard Mercator (1512-1594) of which Katib Chelebi (1609-1657) made a translation for his *Jahan-numa*.

212. The term fire worshipper seems to indicate Zoroastrians, a common mistake made by Moslems, but as is clear from Evliya's description they are Hindus.

The Water Worshippers. Every morning they go to the banks of the Shatt and say: "We have seen God and we have found life through water," and they adore and prostrate before water.

The Mughan (Magi). They are David' people. Most of their ill-auspicious life is spent in fasting according to David's rule.

Sun Worshippers. When the world-illuminating sun appears in the east and goes down in the west they worship it.

Cow worshippers. They call them Guran. In the city of Basra inside a paradisiacal garden in a stable there is a yellow cow. They give it sweet syrups, rice, barley and different kinds of wheat and it has become like the buffalo of Van and has ten servants. These servants save the dung of this cow and with their finger rub it on the foreheads of those who come there to worship. With this appearance they walk openly in the bazaar. It is a strange sight.

Concerning the places of pilgrimage of the Saints and Sufis in the city of Basra

First of all, inside and outside the city of Basra in the desert there are several thousand Saints and Sufis buried. Departing from Basra to the south from the Mishraq Gate for three full hours we traveled in the desert hunting gazelle and fighting with lions; we returned unharmed.

The place of pilgrimage Hasan of Basra, may God bless his dear resting place. He is the leader of the Sufis and all the Sufi orders. They call him the Pillar of the Order. He is divinely blessed. He died at the age of one hundred seventy and is buried under a beautiful dome.

The place of pilgrimage of the mosque of the blessed Talha. It is a large mosque at the roadside. But it is in ruins. From here at one hour's distance the wilderness starts. The blessed Talha, may God's grace be upon him, is the chosen of the chosen companions, who is one of the ten receivers of good news. That is to say, the holy prophet has said to ten people you are "people of paradise" and gave them glad tidings. The first of them was the blessed Talha b. Obeyollah, the second the blessed Zobeyr b. `Avvam, the blessed `Abdo'l-Rahman `Awf, the blessed Sa`d b. Abi Vaqqas, the blessed Sa`id b. Zeyd b. `Omar, the blessed `Obeyd b. Jarrah, the blessed Abu Bakr al-Sidiq b. Qohafa, the blessed `Omar al-Faruq b. al-Khattab, the blessed `Othman Dhu'l-Nureyn b. `Affan and the blessed `Ali al-Razi b. Abi Taleb, may God's blessing be on all of them.

These ten people are called the ten receivers of good news, because the holy prophet gave them glad tidings. This blessed Talha is one of them. His shrine is venerated by the higher and the lower classes. Again in the land of Basra is:

The place of pilgrimage of the blessed Asaf-e Barkhiya. He learned the art of ironsmith from the blessed prophet David. The prophet David fought with King Goliath in Aleppo near the Merjidabik plain,[213] and David killed Goliath with his sling and became the king in his place as well as a prophet, and for this the following Surah is evidence thereof. David killed

---

213. In this plain Selim I defeated the Mamluk Sultan al-Qansuh in 1516.

Goliath, and God gave the kingdom to him,[214] which came down from God to his prophet. In this great battle the ironsmith Asaf fought valiantly against the army of Goliath and displayed his swordsmanship in such a way that the blessed David gave Asaf-e Barkhiya his blessing and the castle of Van, which was in the possession of Goliath. Later, the prophet David died and Asaf-e Barkhiya became the vizier of Solomon, and for a while he raised the throne (of Solomon) to heaven, and that is why the Greeks and the author of the *Tarikh-e Migdisi,* the Armenian, call him a prophet. But there is no doubt that he was the sage-vizier of Solomon, and his shrine is a big place.[215]

THE PLACE OF PILGRIMAGE OF ANAS B. MALEK. He died at the age of one hundred and three in the time of the Ummayad caliph Valid b. ʿAbdol-Malek in the year 91 [709-10] and left a hundred and twenty children. Some of them were killed by the tyrant Hajjaj b. Yusof. The blessed Anas has quoted two hundred and ten Traditions.

CONCERNING THE PASSAGE FROM THE CITY OF BASRA TO THE REGION OF ABADAN, TO THE PROVINCE OF JAZAYER HARIDAT AND THE SEA OF HORMUZ; GOING TO THE PROVINCE OF HORMUZ AND THE TOWN OF HOVEYZEH IN THE LAND OF THE PERSIANS

First, the governor of Basra, Hoseyn Pasha, ordered one hundred select fully armed soldiers to accompany us. We went from Basra towards the south to the banks of the Shatt and we travelled for one hour.

DESCRIPTION OF THE SULTANI CASTLE, THE OLD CITY OF MUHANNAVI. It was built in 241 [855-56] by Zobeyda Sultan, the wife of Harun al-Rashid. They call it Sultani Castle, but its proper appellation, according to some historians, is Muhannavi, because in the time of the caliphate some ladies were staying here who had dyed their nails with henna, hence the name of Muhannavi castle. It is a common mistake to call it the Muhannavi Castle. The castle of Basra is a beautiful quadrangular castle made of bricks and mud. Its circumference is six thousand sixty paces, and it is fully equipped with an arsenal and has many cannons. Because in this place on account of the ebb and flow of the Shatt the Indian ships, the Portuguese galleons and Dunkirk carracks remain in front of it and its small pier, i.e., the customs-house and the ships pay customs duties; it is a beautiful port. There resides the castle governor with seven hundred troops and there are watchmen for the ships. Altogether it has two thousand mud houses which are well-built.

It has a large mosque, caravanserais, and sufficient number of shops. But there is no guest-house, but it has many gardens, orchards, rose-gardens and palm groves. For the people of Basra the castle of Muhannavi (Manawi) is a place of recreation. Since it is at one hour's distance, the people of Basra come there by land and by water, on foot and by boat, and [return the same way] to Basra. It is said that the original reason for building this castle is that "the ships should not be able to escape without paying customs." Now, because of the ebb and flow, all the ships stay under the cannons of the castle and if they do not pay the customs they would be destroyed by cannons. If we explain all that has happened to this castle in the land of Basra, as in the case of

---

214. Koran 2: 251 (al-Baqara).
215. A. J. Wensick, "Asaf b. Barakhya," *Encyclopedia of Islam II.*

several similar castles, a description of each one would be a book by itself. But I should describe each one briefly.

Because long-windedness will create much boredom for the listener. This castle of Muhannavi...

DESCRIPTION OF THE CASTLE OF QAPAN.[216] It was built by Mekran Shah, one of the kings of Abadan, in the year 213 [828-29]. It is called Qapan Castle because it is situated at the Strait of Hormuz, and since it collects customs duties from ships, it is thus called Qapan Castle, which means weigh-bridge. This big, pentagonal castle in the land of Basra is situated on the banks of the island of the river Shatt near the Strait of Hormuz and is one well-prepared castle. Because once its people gave this castle into the hands of Portuguese heathens, those unbelievers completely razed the castle to the ground, and later on Malek Mansur in the length of the foundation built one castle with mud, but it was very strong and well-built. Its circumference is nine thousand paces and it has two bridges; one opens towards the east on the shore of the Sea of Hormuz. The other opens towards the west to the land of Ubulleh. Altogether it has three thousand small and useful huts. The people do not wear woolen dress because of the heat but put on a cotton dress, whereas the poor only wear a loincloth, so oppressive is the heat. But by the wisdom of God the people are very healthy. In the evening the weather becomes so pleasant that it is as if your soul revives. Every night a breeze frequently blows from the sea.

It has many large mosques, caravanserais and one bathhouse, but they are not in a need of a bathhouse, because all of the people there are covered with sweat as if they are standing in a bathhouse. It has two hundred shops built of wood and odds and ends. It has a *sanjaq-bey* appointed by the pasha of Basra. Its judge and castellan are *mir-e liva,* and apart from them there are no other officials. Altogether it has three thousand ill-equipped Arab troops. After three stages comes Ubulleh.

DESCRIPTION OF THE CITY TOWN OF UBULLEH.[217] According to ancient historians, when the blessed Eskandar Dhu-l-Qarneyn came to this land, he was accompanied by the blessed prophet Khizr and he built this city. It was called Dar-e Ebulhe, i.e., the city of Oghuz. But now in the people's language they added a "u" before the *alef* and the rest of the word was shortened ; the 'a' added was called Ubulleh. In ancient times it was an important city. Its remains can be seen. Now it is a town with one thousand houses with many large mosques, caravanserais, bathhouses and small bazaars; it is a town in the *liva* of Qapan and its administration is farmed out. The river Mak`al and the river Safra merge with the river Shatt near this place, and everywhere there are palm groves.

We went to the south and in five days we reached the Haridat Jazayer. In seven days we visited a number of small castles that were similar to each other and built of mud. First,

---

216. This is Qubban or Gubban, at the head of the Qanaqeh branch of the Khor Musa. At this time it was the chief settlement of the Banu Ka`b and not a major port. See Willem Floor, "The rise and fall of the Banu Ka`b. A borderer state in southern Khuzestan," *IRAN* XLIV (2006), pp.277-315.

217. Ubulleh is the name of the port of old Basra on the Shatt al-Arab, which by the tenth century was a place of some importance, but it no longer existed in Evliya's time.

THE CASTLE OF SAHHAR. It is far from the province of Oman and the Jazayer, but close to the city of Oman and it is not very prosperous. But again it has a large mosque, caravanserai, a bathhouse, a madrasa, and buildings. We traveled here for three hours towards the south.

DESCRIPTION OF THE ISLANDS OF THE REGION OF OMAN AND THE GREAT CITY OF UBBADAN. According to ancient historians, this city is known to have been built by the prophet Noah. {Later it was rebuilt by Oman b. Na`san. He was from the blessed Abraham's family. The sea in front of this city is called the Sea of Oman, as it is adjacent to the city. As between Persia and Muscovy there is the Caspian Sea, which is also called the Sea of Gilan, because Gilan is situated on its coast. But this Sea of Oman merges with the all-encompassing Ocean. In the Holy Koran in a surah it is mentioned that "it comes from distant and deep places."[218] The commentators believe that this refers to the Sea of Oman. The prophets may peace be upon him, has said: "Whoever fears for his nourishment let him go to Oman."[219]

At the coast of the Sea of Oman and the Sea of Fars there is no ancient and large city like Umman, and it is situated at the beginning of the second clime.} In the past it was such a big city that it could not be described by tongue and pen, but now it is very prosperous. In the province of Basra, under the administration of a *sanjaq-begi*, at the place where the Shatt al-Arab merges with the Sea of Hormuz and the all-encompassing Ocean is the city of Ubbadan.[220] It is a beautiful city with seven thousand small and practical houses, forty large mosques, caravanserais, bathhouses, madrasas, maktabs, Sufi convents and bazaars. The reason for it being called Ubbadan is that in the time of Jesus they were all Christians. When six hundred years before the coming of the Holy Prophet when Jesus prophesized the coming of the Last of the Prophets Mohammad Mostafa they were converted to Islam, six hundred years before his advent. They all became upright and devout Moslems.

Later on in Baghdad, the Arch of Khosrow was ruined and the fire in the fire temple of Nimrud in Urfa went out in the night when the Holy prophet was born, and the people of Ubbadan renewed their faith. This is why they are called Ubbadan (the faithful). When at the age of forty the blessed Mohammad was honored with prophet hood, these people went to him and renewed their [faith in] Islam and the prophet said: "O devout and faithful people of Ubbadan! God almighty has opened a gate from heaven so that day and night the bounty and blessing would come down to you, your animals and your land will be safe from seventy heavenly and earthly disasters," and he gave this good news to the people of Ubbadan.

Truly it has a very lively people and it is very good city, whose dates (have gone all over the world. The city of Merre is close to the city of Umman, but it is not very prosperous. There is no wheat. Their food, bread, drinks and beer are all prepared from rice, and their animals are all camels. There are many cows and their language has become Persianized and they speak such a dialect that you only can understand them through an interpreter.) This city of Umman is below the city of Basra and on the coast of the Sea of Umman. Ships from India, Sind and China stay at the port, which has a pier of one *farsakh*.

---

218. Koran 22: 27 (al-Hajj).

219. May be a variant of the Tradition quoted in the *Sahih* of Muslim, Book 31, Number 6175 [http://www.usc.edu/cgi-bin/msasearch].

220. On Abadan see L. P. Elwell-Sutton, X. de Planhol, "Abadan," *Encyclopedia Iranica*.

We visited and saw this land of Umman, the Haridat Islands, the city of Muhriyeh[221] and [-], and in agreement with our friends we desired to go to the lands of the Persians with cordial letters from the governor of Basra, Hoseyn Afrasiyabzadeh.

Description of the travels from the islands in the province of Basra to the land of the Persians and the stages that we passed and the villages and castles that we saw

First, from the ports of the Haridat islands is **Bandar-e Mekranabad**, which is the name of a port and a big city. Situated on the border of Basra and Lahsa and at the place where the Sea of Hormuz and the Ocean merge, under the government of Basra, Mekranabad is one thriving port. Its governor is appointed by the governor of Basra with seven thousand soldiers and seventy ships and is a city with eight thousand houses and seventy mosques, caravanserais, bathhouses, soup kitchens, small mosques, madrasehs, elementary schools, Sufi convents and bazaars, but all its houses are constructed with mud and are very well-built. It has innumerable palm groves. We stayed one night in this city and in the early morning and with all our friends embarked on seven ships, and trusting in God we made a good crossing in one day over the Sea of Hormuz.

Description of the royal province of Hormuz at the border of the lands of the Persian high king, the lord of Iran, Turan and Qandahar (Bandar-e Tajdar)

First, on the coast of Hormuz.

Description of Bandar-e (…) Abad. It is a separate khanate within the governorship of Azerbaijan in the Shah's Iran. Seven thousand armed soldiers guard this port, because it borders on the realm of the evil and warlike Portuguese. In 925 [1519] in the time of Shah Esma'il, when the Portuguese attacked this port, twenty thousand Persians were captured and Shah Esma'il built a strong fort, which is like the famous Qahqaheh fort. Inside the fort there are nearly two thousand square houses and several large mosques, caravanserais, bathhouses, Sufi convents, elementary schools, madrasehs, soup kitchens and a royal bazaar, but as it is on the coast and its climate is very hot, one really cooks there. There is much rice, sugar cane, lemon, oranges, pomegranates, olives, figs and Cypress trees. Its youths are not attractive. Most of its inhabitants are Arabs who believe in predestination and therefore are worse than heretics. Its governor is called Khan Qoli Khan, of Georgian descent, who is drunk most of the time. But he is a pleasant and easy-going good companion.

Going to the east for seven hours we passed urban settlements.

Description of the great district, i.e., the prosperous city of Hoveyzeh. After traveling south for five hours we reached:

---

221. Even from the scant information provided by Evliya it is clear that he never visited Oman and very likely never even traversed the Persian Gulf.

THE STAGE OF MEHMANDAR VILLAGE. It is under the administration of Dowraq with one thousand houses, a large mosque, a caravanserai and a bazaar; it is a prosperous village. Its inhabitants are Shi'ite Arabs. Again we went to the south and with horses we crossed with difficulty the river Karun, which comes from Persia. After seven hours we reached the stage of the village of Senjuvan. It is under the administration of the Khan of Dowraq, and it has one caravanserai with palm groves, a large mosqu and bazaars; it is a large village. All its people are sayyeds, but they are truly Qizilbash.

DESCRIPTION OF THE DISTRICT OF THE KHAN OF DOWRAQ, I.E., THE PROSPEROUS CITY OF DOWRAQ

In the year [-] in the time of Kur Khodabandeh Shah, a famous Khan called Dowraq came to the province of Hormuz and took it from the hands of the Portuguese and conquered it. In the aforementioned year, because of the conquest of this blessed land and having made it prosperous, it is called and pronounced as Dowraq. It is an independent khanate with three thousand soldiers and twelve administrative officials. The city is situated in vast spacious pastureland near the river Karun and has six thousand houses, a large mosque, a caravanserai, bathhouse and a bazaar; it is a good town. Both Persian and Arab male and female youths are very pleasant, well-spoken, with gazelle-eyes and bright-faced.

In this place the land of Persia comes to an end, and we set foot in the land of Basra. Because to the east of the Shatt, in the land of the Persians, Basra has a castle called Bogurdelen. In peace time, in the land of Persia, Bogurdelen was built. Again from there we went to the southwest, and we traveled for nine hours on the banks of the river Karun.

DESCRIPTION OF THE CASTLE BOGURDELEN ("the castle that sticks in the side").[222] In the year [-], in spite of the enemy, this castle was built in the land of Persia to be a gadfly in the side of the Persians, and it was called Boghurdelen. It is built lengthwise on the banks of the Shatt, quadrangular, and very strong. Its circumference is three thousand paces, and it has a moat. It has a gate at the bank of the Shatt facing south. On the side of the wilderness there is the Dowraq Gate. Inside the castle stays the *sanjaq-beygi*, who is the governor and has about one thousand soldiers. Being on the border in the land of Persia, this castle has a castellan and eight hundred castle guards. It [further] has an administrator of customs. The merchants who come from the land of Persia and Hormuz pay customs duties on their goods. From Bogurdelen which has royal canons they can target the Persian and European ships. Inside the castle there are six hundred small and practical huts, a large mosque and houses, a wash house for the dead and several shops, but there is no soup kitchen. But the rose gardens and palm groves are many.

Then we embarked on the ships, and on the other side we reached the Arab city of **BASRA**. God be praised that we arrived safely. To Hoseyn Pasha, the governor of Basra and our master, as well as to Morteza Pasha and our friend, we gave our presents from the ships of the city of Hoveyzeh (...): Gujarati cotton fabrics and apples and pears from Dowraq, and again we spent several days in pleasant companionship in the city of Basra.

By the will of God, at this time an envoy arrived at Basra from Shah Abbas II, a famous khan called Yar 'Ali Khan.[223] In spite of being an enemy, there was a big gathering on the sea of

---

222. This is (Borj) Gordolan or Gardalan, see above.

223. This embassy is not mentioned in Persian sources.

galleys, boats and ferryboats called *ma 'shuqa*. When they were bringing the khan to Basra, a salvo of several hundred cannon shots and several thousand musket shots was given from the castle of Basra, and the sea of people moved like the waves. The people of Basra welcomed the envoy with one big procession of Moslems that cannot be described or written about.

Later the envoy respectfully came into the presence of Hoseyn Pasha; he kissed the ground and gave the great king's letter to the Pasha. After it was read and its contents became known to Hoseyn Pasha, he then one by one took note of the presents from the Shah and accepted them and gave them to the treasurer.

A SIGN OF GOD'S GREATNESS. The envoy brought a cage in which there was a black ant, with a narrow waist moving inside the cage as much as its strength allowed, but it was as big as a hound. They even had fastened it with a golden chain to the cage. This was a great sign of the work of God.

OUR JOURNEY FROM THE ABODE OF VICTORY, I.E., THE CASTLE OF BASRA TO BAGHDAD. First, from Basra, we went north with Morteza Pasha's deputy and our friend with five hundred well-armed soldiers to Baghdad on the banks of the Shatt.

GLOSSARY

`abbasis:	see coinage.
`ashura:	sweet pudding eaten at the occasion of the `Ashura festival commemorating the martyrdom of Imam Hoseyn.
ab-e shileh:	cilantro-mint sherbet.
alay-bey:	the second highest ranking officer of the *sipahis* and other local feudal levies.
aqcha:	a small Ottoman silver coin.
bazzazestan:	see bedestan.
bedestan:	originally meaning the drapers' bazaar, is a covered and central part of the bazaar that can be closed and where all shops with precious goods were kept. Elsewhere in Iran it was also known as *Qeysariyeh*.
beylerbeyi:	governor-general of a large province.
bistis:	see coinage.
chavosh:	officials attached to the law courts of grand vizier.
cheri-bashi:	second highest ranking officer of the *sepahis* and other local feudal levies, after the *alaybeg*.
coinage:	The Safavid monetary system was based on the system where one *tuman* = 200 *shahis* = 10,000 *dinars*. With the coining of the `abbasi of 200 dinars in 1587, a reform of the monetary system took place. Henceforth, the following main monetary face values existed: `abbasi (200 dinars); *mahmudi* (half `abbasi or 100 *dinars*); *shahi* (1/4 `abbasi or 50 *dinars*); and *bisti* (1/10 of an `abbasi or 20 *dinars*) which were all silver coins. Finally, there was the copper *qazbeygi* (1/40 of an `abbasi or 5 *dinars*) with its fractional values.
darugheh:	chief of police.
dara'i:	a figured or non-figured fabric woven from simple silk, or a mixture of silk and cotton.
defterdar:	director of finance.
dizchokan aghasi:	chief of the royal slaves (Iran).
dizdar:	castellan.
draper's hall:	see *bedestan*.
farsakh:	the length of measure of 6 km, but, depending on the nature of the terrain, the length an animal can travel in one hour.
ishik-aghasi:	mace-bearer.
kalantar:	chief of a village or district; mayor of a town.
kapukulu:	Ottoman slave soldiers.

khanlar-khan:	see *beyler-beyi*.
khutbah:	Friday sermon.
khvajeh anam:	a leader of people, probably a prayer leader or *pish-namaz*.
khvajeh-ye Islam:	see *khvajeh anam*.
koknar:	a drink prepared from a mixture of opiates, hydrocarbons, protein, resin, oil, and pigments.
liva:	a sub-district of a district or sanjaq.
mehmandar:	conductor of guests.
mir-liva:	chief of a *liva* or sub-district.
mir-miran:	see *beyler-beyi*.
naqib:	see *sayyed al-sadat*.
oda:	battalion.
ojaqliq:	see *yurdluq*.
qazbeygis:	see coinage.
qazi:	a religious judge.
qorush:	an Ottoman silver coin, aka piaster, equal to 40 para.
quruji-bashi:	chief of the guards.
sanjaq-bey:	a governor of a district or sanjaq.
sayyed al-sadat:	chief of the *sayyeds*: chief of the descendants of the prophet Mohammad.
sharif al-shorafa:	see *sayyed al-sadat*.
sheikh al-Islam:	religious judge, but higher in rank than the qazi.
taj:	Safavid Sufi order hat.
timar:	military fief yielding a revenue up to 19,999 *aqches*.
tuman:	see coinage.
yasavol-aghasi:	chief of court ushers.
yurdluq:	an autonomous district, held by hereditary title.
ze`amat:	a military fief yielding from 20,000 up to 99,999 *aqches*.

SELECT BIBLIOGRAPHY

`Abdollah, Abu Bakr. *Tarikh-e `Othman Pasha. (Sharh-e yuresh-e `othmani beh Qafqaz va Azerbayjan va tasarrof-e Tabriz) 993-996 qamari*. Edited by Yunes Zirak and translated into Persian by Nasrollah Salehi. Tehran, 1387/2008.

Allen, W.E.D. *A History of the Georgian People*. London: Kegan-Paul, 1932.

Bakikhanov, Aqa Qoli. *The Heavenly Rose-Garden: A History of Shirvan and Daghestan.* translated and annotated by Willem Floor and Hasan Javadi. Washington DC: Mage, 2008.

Batmanglij, Najmieh. *New Food of Life: Ancient Persian and Modern Iranian Cooking and Ceremonies*. Washington DC: Mage, 1993.

Bidlisi, Sharaf Khan. *Cherefnama ou Histoire des Kourdes*, publiée par V. Veliaminof-Zernof, 2 vols. St. Petersburg 1860-62.

Bulut, Christiane. *Evliya Chelebis Reise von Bitlis nach Van*. Wiesbaden: Harrassowitz, 1997.

Cevdet, Ahmet. *Evliya Chelebi Sehayatnamesi*. 10 vols. Istanbul: Ikdaam matbaasi, 1314/1896-97. (in Arabic script)

Chardin, Jean. *Voyages*, L. Langlès ed. 10 volumes, Paris, 1811.

Dankoff, Robert. *Evliya Chelebi in Bitlis*. Leiden: Brill, 1990.

———. *The intimate life of an Ottoman statesman: Melek Ahmed Pasha (1588-1662) as portrayed in Evliya Chelebi's Book of travels (Seyahat-name)* Albany: State University of New York Press, 1991.

———. *Evliya Chelebi glossary. Unusual, Dialectical and Foreign Words in the Seyahat-name*. Harvard, 1991, translated into Turkish by Semih Tezcan, *Evliya Chelebi Seyahatnamesi Okuma Sözlü ü* Istanbul, 2004.

Eshraqi, Firuz. *Golpeygan dar a'ineh-ye tarikh*. Isfahan, 1383/2004.

Ferdowsi, Abolqasem. *Shahnameh: The Persian book of Kings* translated by Dick Davis. New York: Viking, 2006.

Floor, Willem. *A Fiscal History of Iran in the Safavid and Qajar periods, 1500-1925*. New York: Bibliotheca Persica, 1998.

———. *The Persian Textile Industry, Its Products and Their Use 1500-1925*. Paris: Harmattan: 1999.

———. *The Economy of Safavid Persia*. Wiesbaden: Reichert, 1999.

———. "The Secular Judicial System in Safavid Persia," *Studia Iranica* 29/2000, pp. 9-60.

———. "The khalifeh al-kholafa of the Safavid sufi order," *ZDMG* 153/2003, pp. 51-86.

———. *Traditional Crafts in Qajar Iran*. Costa Mesa: Mazda, 2003.

———. *Safavid Government Institutions*. Costa Mesa: Mazda, 2003.

———. "Kalantar," *Encyclopedia Iranica*.

———. *A Social History of Sexual Relations in Iran*. Washington DC: Mage, 2008.

———. "Who were the Shamkhal and the Usmi," *ZDMG* 160/2010 (forthcoming).

Floor, Willem and Faghfoory, Mohammad H. *Dastur al-Moluk. A Safavid State Manual*. Costa Mesa: Mazda, 2007.

Gibb, H.A.R. and Bowen, Harold. *Islamic Society and the West* 2 vols. Oxford: OUP, 1963.

Gmelin, Samuel Gottlieb. *Travels through Northern Persia 1770-1774* translated and annotated by Willem Floor. Washington DC: Mage, 2007.

Hinz, Walther. *Islamische Masse und Gewichte*. Leiden: Brill, 1970.

Karamustafa, Ahmet T. *God's Unruly Friends. Dervish Groups in the Islamic Middle Period 1200-1550*. Oxford, 2006.

Kahraman, Seyit Ali et al. *Evliya Chelebi Sehayatnamesi*. 10 vols. Ankara, 1996-2007. (in Latin script)

KeyKhosrovi, Faruq. *Kurd dar tarikh-e hamsayegan: siyahatnameh-ye Evliya Chelebi,* Urumiyeh, 1364/1985

Khamachi, Behruz. *Farhang-e Joghrafiya-ye Adharbayjan-e Sharqi*. Tehran, 1370/1991.

Khayyampur, `Abdol-Rasul. *Farhang-e Sokhanvaran*. Tabriz, 1340/1961.

Laleh, Ayub Niknam and Dhowqi, Fariborz. *Tabriz dar Godhar-e Tarikh* (Tabriz, 1374/1995).

Riyahi, Mohammad Amin. *Tarikh-e Khoy*. Tehran, 1372/1993.

Shafi` Javadi, *Peyramun-e Tabriz* (Tabriz, 1350/1971); Sayyed Aqa `Ownollahi, *Tarikh-e Pannsad Saleh-ye Tabriz* translated by Parviz Zagh Shahamrasi (Tehran, 1387/2008);

Marvarid, Yunes. *Maragheh 'Afrazehrud' az nazar-e owza`-ye tabi`i, ejtema`i, eqtesadi, tarikhi*. Tehran, 1360/1981.

Morier, James. *A Second Journey through Persia, Armenia, and Asia Minor ... between the years 1810 and 1816*. London: Longman, Hurst, Rees, Orme, and Brown.

Müller, Gerhard Friedrich. *Sammlung russischer Geschichte*. 9 vols. St. Petersburg: Kayserl. Akad. d. Wissenschaften, 1732-64

Mustawfi, Hamd-allah. *The geographical part of the Nuzhat al-Qulub*. Translated by G. le Strange. Leiden/London: Brill-Luzac, 1919.

Nasiri, Mirza Naqi. *Titles and Emoluments in Safavid Iran* translated and annotated by Willem Floor. Washington DC: Mage, 2008.

Razmara, Hoseyn `Ali. *Farhang-e Joghrafiya-ye Iran*. 10 vols. Tehran: Setad-e Artesh, 1328-32/1949-53.

Savory, R. M. *History of Shah `Abbas the Great,* 2 vol. Boulder, 1978,

Standfield-Johnson, Rosemary. "The Tabarra'iyan and the Early Safavids," *Iranian Studies* 37/1 (2004), pp. 47-71.

Van Bruinessen, Martin and van Boeschoten, Hendrik. *Evliya Chelebi in Diayarbekr* (Leiden, 1988)

Von Hammer-Purgstall, J. *Narrative of Travels in Europe, Asia, and Africa, in the seventeenth century, by Evliya Efendi* 2 vols. in 3 (London 1834-50).

Woods, John E. *The Aqquyunlu. Clan, Federation, Empire* (Minneapolis, 1976)

The Cambridge History of Iran. 7 vols. Peter Jackson and Laurence Lockhart eds. Vol. 6. Cambridge: Cambridge UP, 1986.

Zarrabi, `Abdol-Rahim. *Tarikh-e Kashan*. ed. Iraj Afshar. Tehran, 1342/1963.

INDEX

Ayn

'abbasi 11, 19, 44, 49, 59, 80, 173, 229, 232
'Abbas I xv
'Abbasi Hakkari (Kurds) 130
'Abbas II xvi, 140
'abbasis 10, 18, 42, 59, 62, 68, 81, 85, 106, 127, 148, 154
'Abbasis 131
'Abdo'l-Rahman 'Awf 249
'Abdol-Salam 242, 244
'Abdol-Salam mosque 245
'Ad 133
'Adeljavaz Sea 155
'Ajam xv
'Ajlak Sariyat al-Jabal 47
'Alamdar 184
'Alamshah Khan Saray 201
'Alamshah mosque 162
'Ala'ul-Din Marqadi 20
'Ali Agha 73, 129, 142, 147, 149, 160, 165, 180
'Ali al-Razi b. Abi Taleb 249
'Ali Aqa 118
'Ali Baqer 218
'Ali Baqi 136
'Ali Bey 145, 148, 198, 223
'Ali Bey of 'Aqrah 198
'Ali Faqi 206
'Ali Faqi Pasha 207
'Ali Handi 20
'Ali Khan mosque 153
'Ali Quch Dedeh 81
'Ali Subashi 104
'Ali Sultan Bayat 193
'Ali Tirmidhi 222
'Ali weight 154
'Ali Yar Pasha 139
'Allameh Taftazani 20
'Amr b. 'As 196
'Ani 126
'Aqra Bey 235
'Arab Jabbari 161
'Ashri creek 244
'Ashshar channel 245, 247
'Ashshar Straight 245
'Ashura xix, 38, 60, 170, 210, 212
'ashura (pudding) 38, 60, 212
'Atikah 96
'azab-aghasi 116, 119
'Emadiyeh 192, 193, 202, 207, 235
'Eyn 'Ali 47, 59
'Eyn-e 'Ali Efendi 242
'Eyntab 109
'Obeyd b. Jarrah 249
'Omar xii, 20, 22, 47, 54, 93, 122, 191, 193, 195, 196, 205, 212, 229, 235, 241, 244, 245
'Omar al-Faruq b. al-Khattab 249
'Omar Efendi mosque 122
'Omar Gulsheni xii
'Omar mosque 245
'Othman Dhu'l-Nureyn b. 'Affan 249
'ud 6

A

Abadan 241, 243, 246, 250, 251
Abagay 19, 132
Abagay Mountains 19, 172
Abaza Pasha 207
Abazas 77, 107
Abbysinia 247
abdals 218
ab-e shileh 6
abjad 228
Abkhazia 177
Abraham 15, 157, 252
Abu Bakr al-Sidiq b. Qohafa 249
Abu'l Fath Khan Afshar 191
Abu'l-Fath Mohammad Khan 47
Abu'l-Hasan al-Kharaqani 120, 122
Abu'l-Khatib river 248
Acharis 99, 115
Acharpenk 110
Achiq bash 72, 77, 107, 108, 112, 163
Adam 193, 241
Adana 111, 215
Aden 241, 243, 247
Adhami 30
adharshast 8
Afkand Shah b. Farrokhzad 220
Afrasiyab 12, 21, 47, 83, 118, 243
Afrasiyab 'Ali Pasha 242
Afshar Baba 76
Afshar hunting dogs 39

Afshar Khan mosque 89
Afshar language 32
Afsharli xxii, 63
Afsharli Sultan 140
Ahmad Bey xxi, 10
Ahmad Pasha xii, xvii, 2, 13, 27, 225
Ahmad Pasha mosque 13
Ajara 110
Ajisu xxi, 47
Akharis 114
Akhilk alak 112
Akhiskha 5, 65, 93, 105, 106, 108, 109, 110, 111, 112, 113, 114, 115, 120, 124, 207
Akra 193
Al 113
Alaja-atli Hasan Agha 3, 6
Alajalar 2
Alajeh Qizilbash 164
Alamut xxvi, 2, 221, 222
Alamut Gate 230
Alaq Bulaq xxv, 183
Alari Gozuboyuk Sultan Bayat 193
Alatar steppe 95
alay-bey 49
alay-chavush 49
Albaq xxiv, 136, 174
Aleppo 29, 67, 73, 109, 120, 134, 143, 149, 150, 153, 189, 201, 223, 226, 234, 249
Al-e Sah 240
Al-e Salehiyan 240
Alexander the Two-Horned 89, 91, 99, 106
Alinjak Van 17
Allahverdi Khan Saray 29
al-Ma`mun 222
almond oil 181
aloe wood 81, 246
Alqabidles 184
Alqalandis 39
Alqas Mirza xv, 24, 79, 226, 228
Alti Aghaj 82
Altun 113

Alvand Aqa 30, 64
Amasiya xv, 199
ambergris 34, 59, 81, 85, 145, 147, 246
amir al-hajj 245
Amir Ghayath al-Din 224
Amir Guneh Khan 65, 73
Amir Guneh Yusof Pasha 67
Amir Gunehzadeh 67
Amir Juheyni 196
Amir Khan 72
amir-miran 49
Amir Qiz (Khiz) quarter 29
Amir Yusof bathhouse 123
Amir Yusof Pasha mosque 122
Amir Zahed Khama'i bash 220
Ane desert 243
ansar 235
Ansar Khalifeh Sharaf Khan 73
Anti-Christ 75
Anushirvan 1, 8, 93, 97, 98, 99, 106, 107, 108, 118, 124, 126, 162, 188, 193, 197, 204, 213, 226, 234, 237, 238, 241
Anvari 46
Aqa Bay 227
aqas 125
Aqil 28, 38
Aqil convent 28
Aq kerman 17
Aq Kerman 226
Aqqara 243
Aqsu xxiii, 74, 76, 78
Aramshah 58
Ararat 124, 125, 199
Aras xxi, xxii, 2, 4, 5, 10, 18, 19, 60, 61, 62, 63, 67, 71, 72, 74, 106, 112, 114, 115, 124, 125, 127, 173
Arash 68, 72
Aras River xxi, 2, 4, 5, 10, 18, 19, 60, 63, 72, 124, 125
Arbab-e Soffeh 207
Archangel Michael 15
Arch of `Ali Shah 32

Arch of Khosrow 27, 32, 80, 155, 237, 252
Ardabil xv, xxii, xxvi, 12, 24, 44, 54, 55, 56, 57, 58, 81, 155, 156, 159, 173, 174, 183, 186, 188, 190, 191, 192, 193, 208, 220
Ardabil Gate 54, 164, 194
Ardabil (son of Ardamani) 54
Ardahan xxiii, 65, 105, 110, 113, 114, 115, 120, 124
Ardalan 138, 139, 141, 188
Ardalan Kurds 142, 162
Ardanij 110, 113
Ardashir Babakan 215, 217
Ardebil son of Ardemini 191
Aristotle 14, 32, 89, 149, 210, 222
Arja` 243
Arjang 23
Arjish 178
Armenian churches 8, 46
Armenian(s) 2, 4, 7, 8, 11, 17, 46, 50, 52, 54, 71, 74, 98, 99, 106, 115, 116, 118, 126, 129, 130, 138, 140, 165, 170, 172, 186, 188, 191, 200, 203, 204, 220, 226, 250
armorers 93, 104, 111, 114, 120, 151, 156, 223, 244
army camp kitchens 45
army of Islam xv, 25, 64, 66, 86, 92, 119, 135, 139, 189, 191, 196, 206, 207, 223, 224, 225
Arpa River 124, 125
Arsalan Pasha 190, 191
arsenal 65, 83, 104, 119, 122, 130, 161, 173, 208, 212, 225, 250
Asad Agha 178
Asad al-Din Kermani 222
Asadi sword 148
Asaf al-Moluk Firuz Aqay 119
Asaf-e Barkhiya 149, 249
asbestos 8

Ashraf Khan 85
Asqelon 214
Astrakhan 83
Atike Khatun 92
augury 184
Avah 5
Ayas Pasha bathhouse 245
Ayas Pasha mosque 245
Ayyub Khan 62
Azak 57, 95
Azaq castle 90
Azerbaijan xv, xviii, 5, 11, 12, 17, 18, 19, 20, 22, 24, 25, 27, 34, 36, 39, 45, 46, 50, 52, 53, 54, 58, 60, 61, 62, 64, 66, 68, 76, 79, 81, 99, 104, 109, 124, 127, 129, 133, 136, 139, 141, 143, 151, 152, 155, 162, 166, 173, 174, 175, 181, 188, 189, 190, 191, 193, 196, 223, 226, 236, 253
Azerik quarter 28
Azghur xxiii, 104, 106, 108
Azghura 105
Azgur-e gur 106

B

Baba ʿAbdi of Khorasan 229
Baba Farrokh 46
Baba Haqqi caravanserai 29
Baba Hasan Meymandi 46
Bab al-Abvab 79, 82, 87, 89, 91, 96, 97, 109
Bab-e Berservan 23
Bab-e Sarv 23
Bab-e Sham Ghazan 23
Bab-e Tabriz 23
Bab-Manand 61
Badakhshan cornelian 55
Badeljivanli 118
Baʿdumah mosque 162
Bağdat Köşkü xiii
Bagharseq 124

Baghdad xv, xvii, 1, 14, 23, 44, 51, 53, 67, 108, 118, 135, 136, 144, 156, 159, 160, 163, 168, 172, 178, 180, 181, 183, 184, 188, 190, 191, 193, 197, 198, 199, 205, 206, 207, 208, 211, 212, 213, 214, 215, 217, 218, 220, 223, 224, 225, 226, 227, 234, 236, 237, 238, 239, 240, 241, 242, 243, 244, 252, 255
Baghdad Gate 200, 201, 217, 230
Bagh-e Janan 197
Bagh-e Jenan 67, 215, 222, 223, 226, 236
Bahador-e Shaghad b. Hoseyn Beyqara 18
Bahir Gate 244
Bahram Pasha Gate 122
Bahrampuri cottons 202
bakranis 34
Baku xxiii, 12, 64, 68, 82, 83, 84, 85, 86, 87, 93, 94, 104, 105, 159
Balad Sayas bathhouse 245
Balgami turquoise 38
Balkh 46, 192
Balkhan 83
balsam oil 126
balyamez 49
Bandar-e Mekranabad 253
Bandemahi xxv, 174
Bani Asfar 90
Bani Kanʿan 214
Bani Meval, Arab tribe 213
Bani Qeys 226
Banu Nahr 248
Banyans 246, 248
Baqabay mosque 164
Baqi cemetery 197
Baqi Pasha xvii, 2, 190
Baqubah 239, 240
barbers 38, 125, 153, 211
Bardaʿ 71
Barduz xxiii, xxiv, 118

barley 13, 33, 34, 44, 142, 154, 193, 194, 219, 249
barley-money 66
barter 97
Barut-khaneh xxi, 4
Bash-acheq 108
Basra xvii, xxvi, 54, 196, 227, 229, 240, 241, 242, 243, 244, 245, 246, 247, 248, 249, 250, 251, 252, 253, 254, 255
bathhouse money 14, 22, 117, 146
bathhouse of Darvazeh-ye Rey 33
bathhouse of the Khiyaban quarter 33
bathhouse of the Sorkhab quarter 33
bathhouse poem xx, 33
Bayandors 240
Bayat 193, 239
Bayat district 188
Bayati mode 190
Bayazid 2, 67, 108, 226
Bayazid Khan 109
Baytamur Khan mosque 217
Baytamur mosque 216
Bazaars 29, 43
Bazarkoy grapes 154
beach martens 135
beans 7, 33, 52, 154, 194, 204, 219
beards 61, 75, 162
beaver 3, 85, 87
Bedustan 40
Begbazari 212
Beg Divan 108
Begum Khan caravanserai 29
Behestan 59, 67, 172, 173
Behruz 241
Behsand 52
Behtak Deyri church 204
Bektashi 9, 81, 201
Bektashi convent 28, 48, 81, 170, 194

Benachun 52
Benjahi 218
Berduq xxiv, 133, 137, 138, 156
Berejiq 134
beryani 6, 212
Beyeqli Hasan Pasha 190
Beyeqli Vizier Hasan Pasha 191
Beyram Khan 65
Beyram Pasha 225
Bichor xxv, 170
big caliber guns 49
Bigh kerman 17
Bingöl 124
Biredus Mountains 19
Birejik 120
Birth of Prophet 38
Bisetun 198, 199, 200, 204, 236, 237
Bisetun Gate 200
bisti 44, 147
bistis 10, 22, 59, 68, 83, 85, 154
Bitilis (treasurer) 89
Bitlis xvi, xvii, xix, 67, 99, 105, 130, 132, 136, 145, 178, 179, 180, 189, 202, 242
bitumen 181, 245
bitumen of Judea 181
Bizhan 52, 118
Black Arabs quarter 245
Black Sea 76, 87, 89, 90, 91
boghasi 218
Boghol 83
Bogurdelen 243, 247, 254
Bokhara 47, 192, 204
Bombuj 120
borax 125
bow string(s) 21, 85
boza 36, 204
Bozca ada grapes 154
Bozdoghan dervish 170
Bozok 160
Bozorjmehr 170
Breach Gate 49
bread 6, 16, 34, 44, 105, 142, 145, 154, 158, 170, 204, 219, 221, 222, 232, 252

Bridge Gate 68
brocade 59, 145, 154, 212
Buhtan 212
Bulduk Khan convent 28
Bulghar 85, 192
Bulghar leather 85
Bureh Khan 194
Bursa 72, 186, 201, 234
Burun Qasem 191
butter 16, 95, 131, 232
Buzevli Sultan 159

C

Caliph `Omar 54, 194
Candle Extinguishers 74
candle extinguishing ceremony 159
caravanserais 11, 18, 19, 20, 29, 39, 40, 49, 50, 52, 54, 60, 61, 62, 63, 68, 70, 73, 80, 84, 95, 97, 98, 112, 118, 122, 138, 139, 140, 151, 153, 162, 164, 165, 168, 172, 173, 190, 192, 193, 194, 195, 197, 201, 207, 208, 210, 225, 230, 238, 241, 243, 250, 251, 252, 253
carpets 148, 178, 191
carracks 247
carts 94, 99, 141, 145, 179
Caspian Sea 10, 19, 64, 76, 83, 87, 89, 90, 91, 105, 240, 252
castellan xix, 5, 80, 104, 114, 115, 116, 118, 119, 120, 122, 125, 126, 130, 131, 161, 194, 223, 224, 238, 244, 251, 254
cemeteries 46
Ceylon 192, 241
Ceylon garnet 192
Chaghisman 113
Chaghla Gurna xxi, 5
Chaharbagh 154
Chahar Manar quarter 29
chain-mail 95
Chalderan xv, 99, 109
Chaleq-Safar Agha 125
Chaqliq 111
charitable institutions 174, 219,
246
Charkhi 89
Charsu bathhouse 245
Cheghali `Ali Khan 216
Cheghali Baba 164
Cheghali Sultan 164
Cheghal-oghlu 25
Cheghal-oghlu Senan Pasha 24, 151, 189, 197, 205, 206, 212
Cheghal-oghlu Senan Pasha mosque 161
Cheghal-zadeh Senan Pasha 139, 185, 189, 222, 235, 236
Cheghal-zadeh Yusof Pasha 65
Chekes Mohammad Pasha 223
Cheldir 65
Chengiz Khan 33, 135, 174
cheragh-e afrukhteh 140
Cheragh Khan 92
cheragh-koshan 74
chief of sayyeds 223, 224
chief of the guards 22, 25, 93, 162, 184, 208
chief of the merchants 68, 172, 201, 224, 238
chief of the raw flesh eaters 12, 25, 93
chief of the royal household troops 68
chief of the royal slaves 5, 12, 18, 20, 25, 68, 80, 93, 136, 145, 151, 161, 164, 173, 194, 201, 208, 224
chief of the sayyeds 25
chief of the ushers 25, 68, 93, 136, 152, 161, 162, 164, 172, 173, 194, 201, 208, 224
Chiftehchi `Othman Aqa 37
Chik Ahmad 223, 224, 225
Chik `Ali 223
Childir 102, 104, 105, 108, 109, 110, 111, 112, 113, 114, 115
China 44, 85, 95, 142, 246, 252
chintz 13, 22, 54, 62, 164, 195, 202, 218, 230
Chios 87, 234

Cholaq Mir ʿAziz Bey 137
Cholumerik Mountains 131
chorbi-bashis 120
Christians 7, 11, 43, 49, 52, 107, 126, 129, 246, 252
Chulanduruk xxi, 50
Churs 59, 62, 67, 172
Circassia xii, 93, 94
Circassians 77, 222
City of Women 85
City of Yoghurt 170
clay (remedy) 195
clerk 12, 18, 20, 49, 54, 68, 71, 73, 152, 163, 172, 173, 194, 201, 208, 224
clerk of the mayor 12
climate 5, 10, 11, 13, 18, 19, 20, 21, 23, 29, 32, 33, 40, 54, 55, 61, 62, 72, 80, 84, 87, 89, 95, 97, 99, 106, 108, 112, 115, 125, 126, 134, 140, 151, 155, 161, 162, 164, 168, 172, 173, 175, 188, 193, 194, 203, 213, 218, 222, 226, 227, 232, 235, 236, 246, 253
clothes 218
clothing 30, 191, 242
cock-fights 38
coffeehouses 72, 80, 153, 162, 164, 172, 190, 193, 210, 217
Companions 160, 196, 207, 235, 241
conductor of guests 22, 25, 49, 58, 60, 61, 63, 68, 76, 78, 80, 93, 145, 152, 168, 172, 234
Constantinople 27, 79, 215
convents 7, 28, 48, 50, 51, 72, 80, 153, 158, 164, 201, 245, 252, 253
Copts 204
Cossacks 84, 88, 192, 226
cotton 8, 13, 19, 33, 34, 52, 61, 71, 80, 84, 96, 97, 105, 157, 158, 193, 194, 222, 254
cotton dress 251

cow 219, 249
Cow worshippers 249
crafts 33, 229, 246
crenellated walls 151
Crimea xii, 79, 90, 93, 94, 95, 159, 221, 226
Crimean Tatars 94
crime test 220
cursing 20, 22, 145, 153, 158, 170, 211
customs official 238
Cyprus 8, 87, 151, 228

D

Dadian(s) 72, 77, 107
daftardar 49
Daftardar Baqi Pasha 191
Daftarzadeh Mohammad Pasha xii, 83
Daghestan xxiii, 73, 74, 75, 76, 82, 86, 87, 89, 91, 92, 93, 94, 95, 96, 97, 98, 109, 110, 159, 175, 192
Dal Mohammad Efendi 95
Damascus xii
Damascus Mosque 26
Damirji Hasan xxii, 68
Daniel 215, 217, 220
Danube 78, 85
Daqayeq al-Haqayeq 15
daraʾi 34, 154
Dar al-Nasrat 247
Dar al-Qorra of Sadizadeh xii
Dara Shah 83
Darband xxiii, 12, 25, 79, 82, 84, 87, 88, 91, 97, 159, 240
Darband Gate 84
Dargazin xxvi, 159, 165, 184, 196, 197, 198, 206, 207, 208, 210, 212, 213, 215, 222, 223, 226, 231, 236, 237
Dargazin Gate 200
Dari xviii, 14, 15
Darna 1, 238
Dartang xxvi, 1, 237, 238, 240

Dartang Gate 230
darugheh 49, 188, 198, 207, 212
Darugheh bathhouse 153
Darvazah-ye Saray 29
Darvazah-ye Ujan 23
darvazeh (city quarters) 29
Darvazeh-Pol 68
Darvazeh-ye Sar quarter bathhouse 33
Darvazeh-ye Sarzud 23
Darvish Mohammad Zilli xii
Dast-Pol xxvi, 213
Davdan xxiv, 131, 138, 156
Davdan Sultan 160
Davud Khan 99
Death of Hoseyn 38, 60, 210, 211
Debala 239
Dede Jan 30
Dede Khorkhut 96
Dede Shurimi 30
Dehqani xviii, 14, 22
Delavar Pasha 189
Deli Dizman Bey 207
Deli Mohammad Aqa caravanserai 112
Deliorman 160
Deli Yusof Pasha 223
Demavand Gate 230
Demirkapu 25, 79, 82, 84, 87, 89, 91, 92, 93, 95, 96
derhams 44, 154, 204, 233
Derjerut 52
Dervish Agha 112
Deylam Gate 230
Deylami mosque 216
Dhat-e ʿEmad 58
Dhuʾl-Feqar Khan 12
Dhuʾl-Feqar Pasha 225
Dideherder 40, 58
Dilavar Pasha 191
Dimashkiyeh quarter 29
Dinavar xxvi, 212, 213
Diri Baba 81, 82
Dishlen Hoseyn Pasha 207
Div ʿAli mosque 80

divan effendi 242
Divan-e Imam Yafi`i 214
divan-khaneh 166
divans 30, 218
Divriji cats 58
Diyala 214, 222, 239, 241
Diyala River 214
Diyarbekr xv, 1, 67, 109, 152, 156, 190, 191, 207, 212
Dizchokan 39, 183
dizchokan aghasi 49
dizchokan tulungi 5
dizdar xix, 5
Dniester 78
Dobruca 160
Domboli xvii, 55, 155, 162, 164, 165, 200, 235
Domboli Turkmen 164
Dombuli bazaar 164
Domdomeh 55
Domdomi 161, 162, 200, 235
donluq 45
Dost 183
Dowlat Mirza Khan 14
Dowraq 243, 254
drapers 20, 29
drapers' hall 29, 80, 161, 162, 201, 217
draper shops 245
Druzes 160
dualists 82
Dudiman 118, 119, 120
Dudiman Kejivan castle 118
Duhuk 216
Duhukli 202
Duhuk mosque 216
dulcimer 231
Dumli Sultan 116
Dumlu Dedeh 117
Dunkirk carracks 250
Dunur Khalifeh Sultan Bayat 193
Dunyasir 228
Dushkaya xxi, 5
Dusht xxi, 50
duzde beryani 34

E

Ebrahim Pasha 183, 194, 205
Ebrahim Qoli Khan 191
Edil 84
Edirne 79
Edirne Gate 79
Egri 18
Egypt 22, 27, 57, 89, 95, 123, 192, 197, 235
Ejmiatsin 7, 8
Ekmekchi `Isa Agha-oghlu caravanserai 112
elementary schools 28, 72, 80, 153, 201, 210, 245, 253
elephant-eared whale 87
Elmaji Mohammad Pasha 190
Elqabendilis 39, 50
Emir Jerban Qan 230
Enderi 82
Enzeli Mountains 154
Enzeli Sultan xxiv, 140
Erchek Bala 130
Erdel 78
Erdemit 131
Erechek 131
Erekle Bey 73
Erevan xvii, xxii, xxiv, 1, 2, 3, 4, 5, 6, 7, 10, 17, 18, 25, 59, 60, 62, 63, 64, 65, 67, 68, 71, 79, 81, 82, 83, 85, 93, 111, 112, 117, 118, 122, 124, 125, 126, 127, 135, 136, 139, 146, 149, 150, 155, 170, 173, 178
Er gerchek 131
Erjeysh Sea 155
Erzerum xii, xxiii, 2, 5, 21, 41, 55, 64, 65, 104, 109, 111, 114, 115, 116, 118, 120, 122, 124, 125, 127, 133, 151, 159, 173, 181, 207
Esfandiyar 88
Esfeh 39, 53
Esfenaj 39
Eskandar Dhu-l-Qarneyn 251
Eskander Pasha 164

Eskelib 111
Esma`il I xv, 12
Estergon 217
E`temad al-Dowleh 49
Ethiopia xiii, 192, 243
Euphrates 105, 116, 120, 207, 241, 243, 247
Europeans xiv, 14, 246
Eve 203, 210, 241
Evliya Bey 132, 133
ewers to wash hands 45
executioners 12, 45

F

Faghfur 95
Fajar Khan xxvi, 237
Fakhri dervish 170
Falaki-ye Shirazi 46
Falaki-ye Shirvani 46
falcons 39, 108
Famagusta 151
Faraj Khan bathhouse 80
Farhad 24, 37, 111, 235
Farhad Pasha mosque 13, 49, 80, 153
Farhi 218
Farrokh Bey 139
Farrokhzad Shah b. Timur Khan 62
Farsi 14, 15
Fasheh River 90
Fatehah 21
Feast of Sacrifice 206
feathers 5, 12, 14, 138, 142
ferry boats 255
Feyzollah Hindi 233
fighters for the faith 53, 67, 70, 73, 92, 103, 104, 123, 131, 208, 212, 223
Fin 228
fire worshippers 248
fishermen 132, 156
fishing boats 55, 155
Fiver Ja`faris 13
flax bazaar 245
fly-boats 247

food from the bazaar 45
The Forty (tombs) 96
foundations 80, 119
Frankish sword 141
fruits 11, 13, 18, 19, 20, 34, 50, 52, 55, 61, 115, 141, 155, 157, 162, 194, 199, 204, 207, 219, 221, 222, 227, 229, 231, 246
Fustat 196, 232
Fuzuli xx, 33, 211

G

Gabrs 246
Galata tower 48, 174
Galenus 89
galleons 87, 247
galleys 247, 255
Ganj `Ali Khan xvii, xix, 147, 167
Ganjeh xxii, 25, 64, 65, 68, 70, 71, 72, 73, 79, 83, 93, 106, 109, 112, 180, 192
gardeners 52, 207
gardens of Eram, Aspoza, Maram and Sudaq 39
gauze 13, 154, 212
Gayomarth 52, 71, 234
Genchel Tuqmaq Khan 157
Geography 248
Georgia 65, 73, 77, 85, 86, 96, 98, 99, 102, 104, 106, 107, 109, 110, 112, 114, 115, 116, 125, 163, 178, 218
Georgians 77, 98, 103, 104, 106, 107, 109, 163
Georgius, prophet 158
Ghayath al-Din al-Muqtadir bi'llah 132
Ghayath al-Din Kepani 162
Ghazi language 14, 15
Ghaziqeran 138, 139, 148
Ghazi Ramazan Pasha 165
Ghazi Sefer Pasha 114
Gilan xxii, xxiii, 17, 64, 75, 83, 84, 85, 87, 94, 96, 105, 159, 175, 176, 184, 203, 239, 252

Gilan bazaar 164
Gilan-chay 74, 75
Gilan Gate 84
glasswork 21
Gog and Magog 89
Gökdolaq 10, 17, 30, 72, 74, 83, 95, 98, 106, 115, 140, 170, 172, 178, 186
Gök Meydan 178
Göksu xxiii, 76
golden chain, manacles 166
Gole 115, 124
Gol-e Rostam Khan fountain 28
Goliath 249
Gordelan 243, 244
grabs 247
Greek 11, 54, 200, 220, 226
Green Gate of Iskanderiyeh 197
Gugumlu river 95
Gujarat cottons 146
Gujarati atlas 59
Gulun (?) Hazar Ahmadi 71
Gulusakht 106
Gumek 114
Gur 248
Guran 249
Guril 77, 107
Gurji Mohammad Pasha 66
Gurji Mostafa Pasha 95
Guvzelar mosque 245
Guzel `Ali Pasha mosque 13

H

Habbena 140
hadd punishments 46
Hafez 184
Hafez Ahmad Pasha 206, 207, 215
Hajjaj b. Yusof 160, 250
Hajj Bashir Agha xiv
Hajji Harami xxii, 60, 174
Hajji Khalil saray 244
Hajji Khan mosque 164
Hajrek 110, 113
Hakkari region 131, 156
Hakkaris 138

halva 16, 17, 246
Hama 127, 132, 229
Hamadan xxvi, 17, 44, 54, 159, 180, 181, 184, 194, 196, 197, 198, 199, 200, 202, 203, 204, 205, 206, 207, 208, 212, 213, 215, 222, 223, 226, 227, 228, 232, 236, 237
Hamadan Gate 194
Hamid xii, 104
Hamid Efendi Madrasa xii
Hamzeh 47, 74
Hamzeh Sultan Saray 201
Hanafi 42, 52, 67, 80, 105, 215, 244
Haniya 95
Hanumrud 40
Harbor Gate 84
Hardat Jazayer 251
Haridat Islands 253
Harir xxiv, 138
Harir Gate 164
Harir Kurds 162
Harir Mountains 138, 139, 140, 141, 154, 164
Harir Sultan 140
hariseh 44, 170
Harsek 156
Harun al-Rashid 152, 205
Harun al-Rashid mosque 194
Haruniyeh 238, 240
Hasan Agha 3, 14, 125
Hasan Agha Alajeh-Atli 14
Hasan Bey 64
Hasan b. Zeyd al-Bamer 221
Hasan-e Basri Gate 244
Hasani and Hoseyni horses 65
Hasani Castle 133
Hasankey 193
Hasan Meymandi school 28
Hasan of Basra 249
Hasan Pasha 104
Hasan Qal`eh xxiii, 66, 118
Hasht Behesht 27
Hashtrud 52

Hatam Ta'i 230
Hatem Tay 132
hat makers' bazaar 29
hawks 5, 39, 108, 208
Hawran 154, 219
Hazrat-e Sa`d-e Vaqqas xxvi, 197
head butler 142
Hebrew 56, 57, 220, 232
Helpers 235
Hendevaneh 231
herbalists' bazaar 245
herbs 8, 30, 105, 126, 151, 204, 247
Hersek 135
Hesan 14
Hesham `Abdol-Malek 96
Hesham b. `Abdol-Malek 109
Heshdek 83, 95, 162
Heydari convent 194
Heydar Mirza 71
Heydar Qan 233
Heydar Shah 24
Heydar Shah mosque 84
Heyhat desert 79, 95
Hezarpareh Ahmad Pasha 149
High Mosque 28, 123
Hillah 215, 223, 227
Hindi fire-worshippers 246
Hindi qaurter 245
Hindustan 86, 192, 200
Hine 138
Hinis Qal`eh 2
Hippocrates 89
Hiron 193
Hobash xxiv, 137
Homa'i-ye Kashani 218
Hormuz 97, 216, 227, 241, 243, 244, 251, 252, 253, 254
Hosam Ata 30
Hoseyn Afrasiyabzadeh 253
Hoseyn Beyqara 14, 18, 36, 62, 210
Hoseyn Jamal saray 244
Hoseyn Kadkhoda mosque 122
Hoseyn Khan 192, 193

Hoseyn Pasha 189, 207, 223, 242, 243, 250, 254, 255
Hoseyn Pasha mosque 245
Hoseyn Taftazani 20
hostel 201, 238
houses for travelers and bachelors 29
houses of the poor 244
Houses of Traditions 28
Hoveyzeh 243, 247, 250, 253, 254
Hulagu 23, 51, 52, 62, 88, 118, 172, 185, 188, 192, 194, 215, 237
Hulvan xxvi, 213, 214, 215
Hundusten 130
Hurufi(s) 11, 203
Husam Mirzayi 163
Hushang Shah 50

I

Ibn Hawqal 95
Ibn Khallikan 188
Iki Yahni 126
Ilderim Bayazid 109
Ilistre xii
Imam `Ali Reza 10
Imam Boghabay 160
Imam Hafedane 46
Imam Hosam Efendi 106
Imam Mohammad Hanafi town 243
Imam Muza Kazem 214
Imam Qoli Khan 104
Imam Reza 168
Imrani 57
Imru'l-Qays 218
India 42, 85, 123, 176, 179, 201, 243, 246, 247, 252
Injuyid 227
Ipshir Mostafa Pasha 149
Ipshir Pasha 134, 143, 150
Iraq 48, 54, 86, 129, 162, 194, 196, 198, 200, 205, 208, 213, 214, 215, 218, 221, 222, 223, 224, 225, 227, 228, 229, 230, 234, 238, 239, 240, 248
Iraqi Gate 194
iron gate(s) 52, 92, 93, 122, 129, 151, 161, 192, 198, 237
ironsmiths 192
Isfahan 17, 22, 40, 44, 61, 79, 139, 149, 167, 175, 178, 181, 184, 208, 215, 220, 226
Isfahan Gate 230
Iskanderiyeh 243
iskandil 87
Ispa`ird 193
Ispir 111
Istanbul xii, xiv, 8, 10, 13, 25, 34, 64, 65, 79, 131, 136, 150, 154, 174, 177
It-til tribe 74
Iyd 116

J

Jabal-e Sahlan 54
Jaber b. `Abdollah Ansari 214
Jabi 30
Jabris 11
Ja`far Ansari 207
Ja`faris 11, 55
Ja`fariya 243
Ja`far Pasha caravanserai 29
Ja`far Pasha Khani 174
Ja`far Pasha mosque 153, 168
Jaghal-oghlu mosque 13
Jahan Shah 29, 33, 172, 201
Jahan Shah bathhouse 33
Jahan Shah mosque 33
Jahan Shah public kitchen 204
Jam `Ali Efendi 106
Jamjaba 226
Jam-Jamal 212, 236
Jam-Janab xxvi, 213, 214, 222, 236
Jamshid son of Shaddad 200
Janab bathhouse 13
Janab river 213
Jan Apardi Khan Bayat 193

Jan Apay Khan 200
Jandemah Khanom 220
Janissaries 25
Janissary aghasi 223
Jan Pulad-zadeh Hoseyn Pasha 189
Jan Pulad-zadeh Mostafa Pasha 65
Jarbanqan 230, 232
jarchi-bashi 12
javelin-game 244
Jazayer 248, 252
Jazayer Haridat 250
Jazireh 34, 156, 193
Jazireh-e Majd ol-Dinis 34
Jazireh-ye Kabutar 156
Jeddah 247
jelbe 247
Jerjeh 243
jetty 95
Jevellaki dervish 170
Jevlan 138, 161
Jevlandoruq 39, 183
Jevlan Mountains 154
Jevlan spring 156
Jevlan Sultan 139, 143
Jewish cemetery 219
Jews 11, 43, 158, 204, 215, 232, 246
Jilan 239
Jinns 226
Jisr-e Ya`qub 197
Joseph's Well 197
Julo 137

K

Ka`ba 233, 242
Kabir Valeh 112
Kafa 79
Kagheh bazaar 154
Kaghezman xxiv, 120, 122, 124, 125, 127
Kahrani Turkmen 235
Kahravan xxii, xxv, 53, 140, 185, 186, 193, 196, 206, 224
Kahravan Mountains 190
Kahriz xxi, 20
Kajabad xxv, 185

Kajijan 46
Kakht 98, 106
Kalandar 170
kalantar xix, 6, 48, 49, 213, 221, 236
Kalantar bathhouse 153
Kalantar garden 6, 22, 39
Kalantar mosque 153
Kalb `Ali 30
Kalb `Ali Khan 21, 41
Kalb `Ali Khan bathhouse 161
Kalb `Ali Khan bazaar 161
Kalin 46
Kalmukia 85
Kamal Pasha-zadeh 15
Kan`an Pasha 66
Kanderud 53
Kan-e Sahba 220
Kangavar xxvi, 197
Kanut river 73
kapichi-bashi 25
Kaptan Husamzadeh 9
Kaqaqis b. Emir Rashid 242
Karaniyeh 239
Karasu 160
Karbala 38, 60, 149, 153, 211, 212, 234
Kardul 52
Kargha-bazar 115
Karim al-Din 118, 119
Karim al-Din Khatun 118
Karish xxi, 5, 6
Karniyareq 137
Kartabay Sultan 193
Karun 243, 247, 254
Kaschau 99
Kaseban 228
Kashan 146, 178, 183, 196, 206, 226, 227, 228, 229, 230, 232, 233, 236, 237
Kashan Gate 230
Kashani 59, 218, 229
Kashani bathing-gown 59
Kashan velvet 178
Kashghar 218
Kastamonu 104

Kaya Sultan 8
Kazan 94, 95, 114
Kehran 67, 156
Kehran river 55
Kejivan 118, 120
Kelerni 193
Kel Rostam Khan 167
Kel Tuqmaq Khan 158
Kend-e Rud 183
kent 6
Kepayasan mosque 162
kepi 87
Keremish xxii, 60
Kerim castle 103
Kerkene xxi, 19
Kerman (castle) 17
Kermanshah xxvi, 207, 208, 237
Kesan 193
keshkek 204
Kesik Gonbad xxi, 18
Keskin 160
Ketenchi Othman Pasha xii
kettle-drum (emir's paphernalia) 181
kettle-drums 21, 59, 142, 167, 208, 243
Keyseriya 65
Keysin, Arab tribe 213
Khadem Hasan Pasha 71
Khadem Ja`far Pasha 13, 25, 49, 141, 151, 174, 186
Khadem Ja`far Pasha castle 32
Khadem Ja`far Pasha mosque 13
Khalaf Khan 208
Khaled b. Valid 229
Khalil Agha mosque 112
Khalil b. Hesan Sha`er 207
Khalil Pasha 65, 189, 191, 194, 207, 223, 224, 225
Khameyth b. Yafeth b. Nuh 220
Khamis-oghlu Hamzeh Sultan 193
Khaneqah-e Saghir 238
Khani xxv, 98
khanlar-khan 49
Khan Qoli Khan 253
Khan Saray 29

Khan Serai quarter 29
Khan valley 118
Kharaj 82
Kharbe 113
Kharejites 54, 96, 196, 205, 211, 229, 241, 244
Kharman-e Shahi xxiv, xxv, 141
Khartin 104
Kharzabil 190
Kharzavil xxvi, 188
Khatla 111
Khavareji 92
Khazars 93
Khedhr shrine 232
Khezr Zendeh xxiii, 82
Khirtiz 110, 112
Khita'i 218
Khiyaban-e Shah 24
Khiyaban quarter 29
Khodaverdi Khan Saray 201
Khodray Khan 99
Khoja Farhad Pasha 18, 64, 70
Khojajan 120
Khoja Naqdi 30, 42, 150, 219
Khoja Sadeq 218
Khoja Sari Khan 87
Khorasan-e Turkestan 175
Khorasani mortar 228
Khorasani style 7, 36, 231
Khoshab xxiv, 1, 130, 131
khoshab (compote) 143
khoshneshin 141
Khosrov Shir 223
Khosrow Khan bathhouse 80
Khosrow Pasha 54, 194, 197, 207, 208, 215, 222, 223, 225, 237
Khosrow Shir 212, 223, 238
Khosrow Shir Pasha 212
Khotan 13, 62, 71, 85, 95, 210, 246
Khovarnak 151
Khoy xxii, 59, 60, 61, 62, 67, 159, 172, 173, 179, 193
khvab-e khargush 179
Khvajegan 98, 137, 155, 156, 158

khvajeh 208, 223, 224, 232
Khvajeh Ahmad Yasavi 41, 76
Khvajeh Ahmad Yasavi b. Mohammad Mehdi 41
Khvajeh Bali 219
Khvajeh Khan Lahejani 64
Khvajeh Mohammad Kajijani 46
Khvajeh Naqdi 144, 145
Khvajeh Naqdi Miqrizi 172
Khvajeh Shah fountain 28
khvajeh-ye anam 234
khvajeh ye Islam 223
khvajeh-ye Islam 201, 224
khvajeh-ye Islami 208
kilerji 3
Kilmah 192
Kimame Church 129
Kinze 114
kiosks 37, 39, 152, 227
Kirkuk 186
kissed (letter) 175
Kochagha Sultan garden 146
Koja-abad 39
Koja Baghi 68
Koja Farhad Pasha 53, 76, 174, 197
Koja Ken`an Pasha 111
koknar 36, 227
Komeyli order 160
Konya 65
Koran reading houses 28
Kostanice 224
Kotatis 108
Kovin 82
Kowthar 153, 217
Kozlu 82
Kreutel, Richard xiii
Kuba Kalmakh Khan 95
Kuban river 76
Kuchek Ahmad Pasha 66, 67, 225
Kufa 196, 211, 241
Kufic 96
kuku 6
Kunbet-oghlu mosque 111
Kundur Rud 39

Kurdistan 49, 86, 110, 132, 164, 189, 205, 206, 224, 226, 232, 234, 235
Kureh xxiii, 97
Kur Khodabandeh fountain 28
Kur River 19, 74
Kurun river 70
Kutahiyeh 180
Kutatis 108, 112
Kuyah pass 139

L

laban-e khass 154
Laghosh-oghli Ahmad Bey mosque 73
Lahejan 85, 178
Lahsa 241, 242, 243, 247, 248, 253
Lakderah 184
Lakderukh 50
Lakdirih 39
Lake Van 55, 131, 155
Lake Vastan 155
Laleh Farhad Pasha 102
Laleh Mostafa Pasha 65, 73, 79
Laleh Qara Mostafa Pasha 71, 73, 115, 119
Laleh-ye Mostafa Pasha 79
lamps with grease 84
lepache 62
Levand district 72
Levand Khan 73, 115
Livane 110
Livornian bogassins 51
Livornian cotton 195, 202
Livorno fabrics 146
long beard tax 61
Lur 73, 83
Lurestan 71, 192, 208
Luri 71, 106, 111
Lusa bathhouse 33
lynxes 133, 135

M

Ma-Chin 95

Ma`dikarb 55
Maghan 75
Maghus 228
Magian(s) 7, 43, 71, 246
Magnesia 234
mahfuz al-qalam 139
Mahmudabad xxii, 74, 75, 79
Mahmudi Beys 1
Mahmudi Deli Ebrahim Bey 145
Mahmudi Ebrahim Bey 130
Mahmudi elephants 244
Mahmudi horse 133
Mahmudis 130, 131, 132, 133
Mahmud Pasha 119
Mak`al river 248, 251
Makhchil 110, 113
Makran 241, 243, 248
Maku xvii, xxi, 1, 2, 3, 104, 135, 136, 145
Malatiyeh 109
Malazgird 1
Malek Ahmad Agha 65
Malek Ahmad Pasha xii, xvii, 1, 144, 147, 163, 166, 175, 177, 179, 180, 242
Malek Ahmad Pasha Efendi 74
Malek `Ezz al-Din Aq-Qoyunlu 118
maleki grapes 34, 36
Malek Mak`al b. Beshsharah 248
Malek Pasha xix, 8, 150, 163, 180
Mamravan 114, 115, 116
Manaqeb-e Ovliya-ye Kazeruni 157
Manawi 243, 247, 250
man daqqa duqqa 158
Manjil-e Kharzabil 191
Mankerusi elephant 130
Manmah xxii, 53, 186
manners of eating 143
Mansur-e Ansari 197
Mansuriya 243
Mantasha 104
Manuchehr 10, 188, 227, 228
maqam 231
Maqam `Ali 247
Maragheh xviii, xxii, xxv, 50, 51,
52, 183, 186, 193
Marand xxi, 19, 20, 25, 61, 67, 72, 159, 172, 173, 179, 193
Mar`ash 73, 109, 111, 119, 164, 184, 224
Mardan Aqa Jan 30
Mardan Dedeh 218
Mardin 74
Mardjuvaz 200
Marizat xxiii, 81
markab 247
market inspector 45, 238
Marula 108
Marvan b. Mohammad al-Himar 51, 186
Marwan Himar 17
ma`shuqa, ferryboats 247, 255
masseurs 13, 33, 80, 112, 153
mastaba 6
mastaba churbasi 34
master of ceremonies 21, 68, 145, 152, 166, 167, 172, 173, 175, 176, 177, 180
Masuleh xxvi, 188, 192
mayor xix, 18, 20, 22, 25, 49, 50, 52, 54, 58, 60, 61, 63, 68, 71, 76, 78, 81, 93, 97, 137, 152, 154, 168, 172, 173, 193, 194, 198, 201, 208, 210, 217, 224
Mazandarani 2, 6, 67, 73, 136, 178
Mazid Khan xxii, xxv, 22, 60, 174
Mecca xii, 55, 97, 155, 196, 241, 243, 244
Medina xii, 241
mehmandar 22, 49, 254
Mehraban 223, 224, 226, 236
Mehraban Gate 230
Mehranrud xxv, 32, 39, 53, 183
Mekranabad 253
Mekuchuvur 71
melamatis 218
melejeh 11, 19, 80, 173, 229
melons 80, 212, 219
Memijan 47
Memi Jan Sultan 193

Men of the Unseen shrine 232
Meram garden 133
mercantile courts 29
merdile 247
Merjidabik 249
Merre 252
merry-go-rounds 244
metqali baz 202
Meval (Arab tribe) 226
Mevlevis 194
Meydan bathhouse 80
Meydan Gate 68
Meydanjiq 118
Meydan quarter 80
Meykhvaran quarter 29
Meymandi Khan Afshar 53
Meymendi Sultan Bayat 193
Mighdisi 155, 200, 226
Mijingerd 118
Milani sibets 34
Milanli `Ali Pasha 119
Millili 62
millstones (quarry) 125
mina 87
Mina 243, 248
Mingrelian(s) 77, 107
Minor 120, 248
minstrels 42, 62, 154
Mir Heydar convent 28
Mir Mir quarter 29
Mir Quli Khan mosque 161
mirun-yaghi 126
Mirza `Ali Bey mosque 73
Mirza Bay 30
Mirza Khan 22, 84, 165, 184
Mirza Khan bathhouse 84
Mirza Shahan 41
Mishraq bathhouse 245
Mishraq bazaar 245
Mishraq Gate 244, 245, 249
Mishraq mosque 245
Mishraq quarter 245
Miyar Miyar quarter 32, 33
mo'ambar 6
Mo`awiya ibn Abi Sufiyan 143

Moghadh Khan 125
Moghan 73, 83
Mohammad Amin Pasha 130
Mohammad Bey 2
Mohammad Efendi xii
Mohammad Ibn Eshaq 90
Mohammad III 10, 12, 18, 70
Mohammadi qorush 242
Mohammadi tablecloth 83
Mohammadi turbans 59
Mohammad Pasha 2, 70, 73, 104
Mohammad Shah Beg 184
Mohammad Shah Ghazan 32, 48, 135, 136, 150
Mohammad Sham Ghazan 9, 23, 25, 48, 52
Moharram xiii, 38, 83, 210
Mohnad Hill 66
Molla Qotb al-Din 17
Mongol xviii, 17, 22, 48, 74, 75, 88, 135, 172, 174, 188, 192, 193, 197, 200, 208, 212, 213, 214, 219, 227, 228
Mongolia 86
Mongolian language 14
monks 7, 127, 188
monshi 49
Monshi Agha bathhouse 195
mortar of Khorasan 213
Morteza Pasha xii, 65, 133, 139, 142, 145, 146, 160, 163, 165, 172, 175, 177, 181, 194, 214, 242, 254
mosafer kondur 49
Moses 55, 57
Moshabbehi 203
Moshabek mosque 216
mosque of Baybars 27
mosque of Charmenar 27
mosque of Shah `Abbas I 28
Mostafa Bey 2
Mostafa Pasha 65, 73, 113, 129, 177, 190, 191
Mosul 158, 181, 193, 207, 208, 222, 224, 225, 226, 242, 244

motafarriqas 66
mothallath 227
Mount Bingol 78
Mount Demavend 78
Mount Kamar 78
Mount Perizat 112
Mount Sahand 51, 52
Mount Sahansamur 78
Mount Shah 72
Mount Subhan 78
Mount Valiyan 48
Moyonjak Khan 95
mozaffari 6
Mozaffar Khan 184
Mt. Aghri 124
Mt. Alvand 194, 195, 201, 203, 204, 205, 214
Mt. Aqra` 234, 235
Mt. Arafat 241
Mt. Arghin 93
Mt. Arjish 199
Mt. Asvene 160
Mt. Bisetun 199
Mt. Deylam 221
Mt. Duneb 93
Mt. Elburz 76, 98, 99
Mt. Judi 193, 226
Mt. Masir 6
Mt. Mekran 241
Mt. Oda (Oda Mountains) 106
Mt. Sahand 28, 32, 192, 193
Mt. Sahlan 23
Mt. Samur 199
Mt. Sarhadd 40
Mt. Seyhan 23
Mt. Seylan 52, 55, 190, 192
Mt. Sobhan 199
Mt. Sorkhab 32
Mt. Ujan 23, 52
Mt. Velya 174
Mt. Verek 129
Mu`awiya 92, 96
mufti 61, 80, 114, 126, 152, 158, 162, 164, 172, 173, 193, 216
Mughan (Magi) 249

Muhannavi 243, 244, 248, 250, 251
Muhriyeh 253
Mukus 193
Mullah Ahun 203
Mullah Berzenji 202
Mullah Dehqani 161
Mullah Herami 202
Mullah Jami 218
Mullah Jar 217
Mullah Kulga Shah 229
Mullah Naser Shirvani 161
Mullah Shoja` al-Din Kermani 137
Multan 192
Murad Beg 183
Murad III xv, 24, 25, 36, 48, 54, 64, 71, 73, 79, 92, 99, 104, 174, 189, 194, 212, 213, 215
Murad III mosque 198
Murad IV xii, xv, 5, 8, 10, 12, 13, 18, 33, 37, 51, 54, 60, 61, 65, 68, 79, 89, 93, 111, 135, 144, 170, 188, 194, 215, 223, 237
Musa Pasha 65
Muscat grapes 36, 154
Muscovite Cossacks 94
Muscovy 57, 83, 84, 85, 87, 94, 95, 107, 162, 176, 252
Mushabbak Gate 217
Mushkur 82, 84, 86, 89, 94
music band tower 194
musicians 14, 36, 54, 62, 154
musk 34, 59, 147, 210, 246
Muskir 84, 85, 89
Mustaqfi bi'llah 221
Mutawakkil bi'llah 23
Mutawakkil bi'llah mosque 25
Mu`tazelite 203

N

Nahr `Ashshar 247
Nahravan 184
Nahr-e `Antar 247
Nahr-e Muhannavi 247
Najaf 165

Najaf crystal 14
Najaf marble 27
najm-e Ahmadis 34
najm-e khalaf pears 34
Nakhjevan xviii, xxi, 2, 3, 4, 5, 7, 8, 9, 10, 11, 12, 14, 17, 18, 25, 60, 62, 64, 67, 73, 79, 83, 84, 119, 126, 131, 173, 178, 181, 184, 192
Nakhjevani steel 201, 208
namakdan 6
naphtha 84, 85, 94
naqib 126
Naqib al-Ashraf 114
Naqshbandis 116, 194
Naser al-Din b. Ayub Suhyani 207
Navan 229
Nazarbat 114
Nebuchadnezzar 8, 214, 215, 232
nehar plums 229
Nehavand xxvi, 44, 47, 54, 191, 193, 194, 195, 196, 197, 198, 206, 207, 214, 237
Nergok 129
Nesf Livane 110
Neshanji Pasha 65
Nikasa 5
Nil-chay 76
Nile xiii, 78
Niyazabad xxiii, 75, 97
Noah 38, 90, 193, 199, 214, 219, 226, 232, 241, 252
Nobles shrine 232
notables 14, 25, 29, 30, 33, 38, 45, 56, 60, 78, 85, 96, 115, 120, 122, 124, 125, 132, 139, 147, 148, 149, 181, 192, 194, 201, 202, 210, 245
Nu`man b. Thabit 42

O

Oczakov xii
Odurya 113
Oghuz 75, 180, 251
ojaq-bey 134
Okhchu 113
Olghar's summer quarters 114
Olti 110, 114, 115
Olti river 115
Oman 241, 243, 248, 252
Omana Maqami shrine 232
Oman Sea 247
Ommaya b. `Omar b. Ommaya 47
Orchivek 124
Ordubad 67, 193
Ordubadi 11
Ordubari 67
Orfi 30
Osama b. Sharik 47
Osha 111
osul 231
Othman Pasha 25, 190
overseer of the sayyeds 61, 68, 120, 152, 208, 216, 232, 234, 244
Owfar 231
Ozdamir-oghlu Othman Pasha 84, 92, 94, 95, 151
Ozdamir Othman Pasha 62, 79
Ozdamir Pasha 25
Ozdamir Pasha Mosque 80
Ozdamir-zadeh Othman Pasha 72, 82, 89, 93
Özü xii

P

Pahlavi xviii, 14, 52, 219
pajamas 140
Palu 223
paludeh 34
Panachum 52
Panj Hoseyn shrine 232
Parsi 14, 218
Pasha quarter 245
Pasik Agha xxiv, 133
Pasin 118, 120, 172
pastry 34, 219
peace treaty xvi, xvii, 1, 3, 135, 144, 175, 191
pearl bazaar 246
pearl merchants 245
Penk 110, 115
perfumes 246
Persian alphabet taught 230
Persian fee 160
Persianized language 252
personal fief 19, 20, 48, 50, 63, 68, 71, 89, 95, 97, 111, 113, 114, 115, 119, 120, 125, 126, 131, 165, 174, 233, 238, 239, 240, 242
Pertak 110, 114
Pertev Pasha xiv, 79
peshk-push dress 13
peyghambar pears 34, 173
Phasus River 90, 91
physicians 218
physicians (Hamadan) 202
pilaus 34
  abshileh pilau 44
  chelow pilau 6, 44
  dozen (twice-steamed) 6
  duzde pilau 44
  hariseh pilau 44
  khoshk pilau (perhaps "khoresh") 6
  Khosh pilau (perhaps "khoresh") 6
  koseh (garlic pilau) 6
  kuku pilau 44
  Kuseh pilau (perhaps "kufteh") 6
  mo'ambar (perfumed) 6
Pilevar xxvi, 212, 213, 222
Pilevar Khan 212
Pinyanish 18, 129, 134, 135, 136, 137, 138, 140, 141, 143, 144, 146, 148, 149, 150, 156, 166, 176, 179
Pinyanish Castle 133
Pinyanish Kurds 18, 137, 148, 176
Pinyanish Mahmudi tribe 138
Pinyanish Mountains 172
Pinyanish notables 129
Pir Bash Agha 30
Pir Budaq Khan 21
Pir Budaq Khan bathhouse 195
Pir Budaq Khan Saray 29

Pir Budaq mosque 193
Pir Budaq Sultan Saray 201
Pir Darkuh Sultan 81
Pirehdus Sultan xxiv, 140, 143
Piri Pasha 78
Pir Marizat Sultan xxiii, 81
Pir Merza 81
Pir Shafiq 47
Pir Yar Sultan 221
Pish-Koshk bathhouse 33
places of recreation 219, 247
poets xix, 14, 30, 46, 60, 202, 218, 230, 245
poets (of Nehavand, named) 194
pokhin 131
Pol-e bagh quarter 29
Pol-e bagh quarter bathhouse 33
pol-e shahi 237
police chief 12, 18, 20, 22, 25, 45, 49, 50, 54, 58, 61, 68, 71, 97, 137, 152, 172, 173, 193, 194, 201, 208, 224
polo 68, 142, 146, 151, 157, 228
Polo Mall 37, 38
Portuguese 250, 251, 253, 254
Portuguese galleons 250
postal horses 146
post-horses 59, 64, 165
Posthu 110, 113
price control 154
priests 7, 8, 56, 107, 127, 129, 219
private bathhouses 33, 202
prophet David 107, 249
Ptolemy 227, 228
public criers 22, 145, 210
public fountains 28, 194, 201, 217, 234, 245
public kitchen(s) 36, 95, 115, 204, 241
public punishment 45
pülli trees 172
pulses 33, 62, 105, 123, 194, 199, 204, 210, 227, 246
punishment for cheating 44
purity of coins 154

Purkan 112
Purtekrek 110
Pythagoras 89

Q

Qabur river 73
Qadaris 11
Qaderi 118, 240
Qaderis 99
Qaghaj xxii, 63
Qaghzaman 65
Qahqaheh 2, 24, 76, 90, 130, 221, 253
Qajar Mohammad Pasha 189
qal`a- aqalik 111
Qalandari convent 194
Qalmaq(s) 83, 87, 94, 95
Qaltaqji-zadeh mosque 122
qamari 229
Qamer al-Qom 226
qanats 219
Qandahar xvi, 176, 253
Qapan 251
qapuchi-bashi 49
Qapudan Deli Hoseyn Pasha 66
Qara Ardahan 114
Qarabagh xxi, 11, 18, 25, 73
Qarabaghlar 10, 172
Qarachuboq 42, 59
Qarachuboq horses 18, 22, 59, 81, 141, 146, 148, 165, 181
Qaradagh 240
Qarageh-ye Kubra 220
Qarahbali, name of a cannon 66
Qara Hisar 132
Qara Kuneq 116
Qara Laleh Mostafa Pasha 104, 112
Qaraman 78
Qara Mohammad Pasha xii
Qara Morteza Khan 163
Qara Mostafa Pasha 1, 66, 135, 149, 237, 245
Qaraqeh-ye `Arab 229
Qara Senan Pasha 72
Qara Su 174

Qara Tay'i 126
Qara Yusof 109
Qarchaghay Khan 190
Qarchigha Khan 94
Qareh Pasha 190
Qarehqan xxv, 185
Qarehqash Pasha 189
Qargabazari 124
Qars xxiv, 5, 65, 112, 115, 117, 118, 119, 120, 122, 124, 125, 126, 127, 207
qasabeh 6
Qasem Khan 2, 3, 5
Qasr-e Losus 205, 222
Qasr-e Shirin xxvi, 213, 214
Qassab-e javanmard 211
Qatif 243
Qaya Pasha 114
Qaya Sultan handkerchiefs 98
Qazan 73, 95
Qazaq 73, 83
Qazaq Khan bathhouse 80
qazbeygis 44, 96
qazi 12, 20, 49, 50, 54, 61, 62, 68, 71, 73, 75, 76, 80, 97, 99, 113, 119, 152, 162, 164, 173, 193, 198, 208, 238, 243
Qazvin xxvi, 157, 185, 191, 196, 205, 208, 213, 214, 215, 216, 217, 218, 219, 220, 221, 222, 236
Qepchaq 90, 94, 95, 172, 226
Qeytamaz Khan 147, 177, 179, 181
Qeytaq xviii, 74, 75, 93, 96, 192
Qeytas Bey 72
Qeytemaz Khan 147
Qezelelma mosque 217
Qimiq 83
Qipchaq 75, 93
Qizilbash xv
Qizildagh 23
Qizil Oghlan 198
Qiziloren 52
Qizil Rabat 239
Qiziqli tribe 140

Qizlar 113
Qobad Pasha 84
Qochagha Baba 162
Qochagha Sultan 153, 155, 156, 157, 158, 162
Qochagha Sultan mosque 153
Qom 183, 196, 205, 206, 220, 226, 227, 228, 232, 236, 237
Qom Gate 200
Qomuq 72, 74, 75, 83, 87, 94, 96, 192
Qonya 133, 227
Qorban Qoli 30, 144
Qorkhmas Khan 206
Qorna 243, 244, 247, 248
Qorna Gate 244
Qotb al-Din Mohammad Yazdi 39
Qotur xxiv, 1, 135, 136, 145, 148, 178
Qoyun Gechdi 73
Qumlah xxv, 47, 48, 67, 141, 159, 172, 173, 174, 193
Qumlah Chemeni 141
Qurayas 11
Qurqud Khan bathhouse 153
quruji-bashi 49
Qushlunja 71

R

Rabat Gate 244
Rafazis 21, 199, 204, 211
rain-producing stone 56
ra'is al-kottab 49
Rakhsh 22
Rakka 111
Ramazan Efendi 111
Ranguran 52
Rashidiyeh castle 32
raw flesh eaters 200
razaqi 247
razaqi grapes 34
Razi 30
Raziyeh Qadin-zadeh 189
rebat 130
recreation site 36, 37, 39
Red Hats xv
Redheads 65, 68
Red Morteza `Ali 42, 145, 203
Regal xxiii, 82, 89
Reval 93
Revan 1, 64
Revan Qoli Khan 64
Rey 29, 47, 196, 233, 234, 235, 236
Rey quarter 29
Reza al-Din Khan 14
Reza fountain 28
Rezvan Agha 106
Rhodes 87, 151, 221
Ribat 245, 247
rice 5, 11, 16, 36, 44, 59, 61, 63, 64, 68, 71, 78, 80, 84, 127, 142, 154, 170, 178, 204, 244, 249, 252, 253
rice bazaar 245
Rik quarter 28, 29
Rineb 84
Rishvan 190
robe of honor 14, 117, 242
rosary 2, 3, 21, 83, 181
Rostam Khan Saray 29
Rostam Pasha 13, 212, 222
Rostam Pasha mosque 245
royal pass 136, 139, 148, 149, 167, 238
Rubajiq Sultan 135
Rudekan 185
Rudeqat 40, 50
Rukal 82
Rumeli 65, 119, 223, 224
Rumelia 66, 160
Rus Hasan Pasha mosque 62
Rustam Khan the Bald 133

S

Sabadabad 46
Saba'i 218
Sa`d b. Abi Vaqqas 249
Sadd-e Islam 108
saddlers 153
Sa'ebi 30
Safar Pasha 112
saffron 6, 44, 142
Safi al-Din 58
Safi I xv
Safi Khan Afshar 186
Safi Khan mosque 162
Safra river 251
Safraydenk river 248
Sahand xxvi, 23, 51, 55, 192, 193, 196, 200
Sahand Gate 194
Sahban 14
Sahlan xxi, 20, 23, 32, 55
Sahlan juice 36
Sa`idabad xxii, 39, 46, 53, 183
Sa`id b. Zeyd b. `Omar 249
Sa`id Khoja Rashid al-Din Donboli 48
saj 205, 213
Sal`at tribes 90
sale by weight 44
Saleh Efendi 159
Salekan mosque 216
Salman-e Kufi 235
Salmas xxv, 61, 67, 137, 143, 155, 170, 172, 179, 193, 200
salt mine 125
saltpeter 4
Samson 127
Sanasun xxiv, 137
Sandal-e Akbar river 248
sanjaq-bey 49, 89
Sarab xxv, 48, 135, 139
Sarandib 241
Sara peninsula 90
Saray 83, 152, 173
Sardab quarter 29
sardar-vazir 49
Sardeh quarter 47
sareshileh 143
Sari Ahmad Pasha 70
Sari `Ali Agha 139
Sari al-Jabal 241
Sarir al-Lan 97

Sariya mosque 194
Sariyat al-Jabal 54, 191, 196, 205
Sarjam xxv, 183, 184, 227
Sarjam Khani 183
Sarkhaleh xxvi, 237
Sarraj-khaneh 28
sar-taj-e sayyedi 173
Sasin 111
Saveh 207, 216, 220, 232, 233, 234
Saveh Gate 230
Saveh Khan mosque 216
sayyed 43
sayyed al-sadat 201
Sayyedler 197
Sayyed Vahedi 30
scales 44
Scutari 65
Sea of Fars 252
Sea of Gilan 10, 252
Sea of Hormuz 247, 250, 251, 253
security 80, 85, 178, 236
Sefat 214
segah mode 42
Selehdar Pasha 65
Seleme desert 243
Selim I xv, 108, 110, 111, 112, 184
Semadehon 185
Semaghar 114
sema`i style 42
Senan Pasha bathhouse 195
Sendan 84
Senjuvan 254
Senneh 224, 225
sepahis xii, 49, 66, 189, 223
sepahsalar 49
Serachun 52
Serah xxvi, 173, 188, 189, 190
Seran 17
Serav xxv, 173, 188, 189, 190, 191, 236
Seravrud xxi, 39, 50, 183
Setgiz xxii, 52, 186
Seth 241

Sevendik Khan xxv, 165
Seyami Pasha 207
Seyf al-Din xxii, 63
Seyf al-Din Khan 63
Seyf `Ali Khan 2, 3
Seyf bathhouse 245
Seyf bazaar 245
Seyfi Agha 112
Seyfi Sultan Bayat 193
Seyf Qoli Khan 63
Seyf Qoli Khan Afshar 53
Seylan [Savalan] River 156
Seymer bathhouse 245
Seymer bazaar 245
Seymer mosque 245
Shabi 30
Shaburan 82, 88, 89
Shaburan quarter 80
shafe`i basin 10, 33, 80, 153
Shafe`is 13, 52, 55, 60, 74, 95, 97, 133, 152, 201, 218, 222
shaftalu 105
Shah Amin Mosque 27
Shahband xxii, 54
Shahbandar, village 188
Shah-bandeh caravanserai 29
Shah Bandeh Khan Saray 29
Shah bridge 224
Shahburi bathhouse 80
Shah `Emad al-Din 215, 216
Shah-e Mardan 24
Shah Esma`il fountain 28
Shah Esma`il mosque 27, 32
Shahestan mosque 216
Shah Gedighi 136
Shah Ghayath al-Din 217, 220, 226
Shah Heydar Karrar 61
Shah Hushang 234
Shah Inchul 227
Shah Jahan Madraseh 28
Shah Jahan mosque 164
Shah Kend 30
Shah Khodabandeh public kitchen 204

Shah Körpüsü 237
Shah Kur Khodabandeh 76, 157
Shah Mansur-e Ba`zravi 222
Shah Maqsud b. Sultan Hasan mosque 27
shahneh 137
Shah Parviz 222, 223
Shahraban 236
Shahrezur 1, 53, 139, 141, 155, 181, 186, 193, 198, 212, 223, 224
Shahrezur Kurds 162
Shahriban 240, 241
Shahrokh Beg Dhu'l-Qadr 184
Shahrokh Mirza 5
Shahrokh Qay 235
Shahsevan(s) 73, 84, 160, 170
Shah Tahmasp xv, 24, 53, 70, 79, 80, 141, 150, 158, 161, 170, 183, 208, 226
Shah Tahmasp I 53
Shahverdi Khan 206
Shah Ya`qub garden 36
Shahzadeh Mohammad 95
Shahzadeh mosque 79
Shakeri 30
Shamakhi xxiii, 12, 25, 64, 68, 75, 78, 79, 80, 81, 82, 85, 87, 94, 96, 97, 98, 159, 175, 226, 240
Sham Ghazan 174
Sham Ghazan Mohammad Shah 21
Shams al-Din Sobhasi 46
Shams-e Tabrizi convent 28
Shams Khan mosque 164
Shams Pasha 130
Shapuran 84
Sharab-khaneh xxii, 63
Sharafnameh 99, 106, 109
Shariban 226
Shatan 113
Shatt al-Arab xxvi, 214, 243, 244, 247, 248, 252
Shatt Ashri 243
Shavshadistan 98, 99

Shavshat 99, 110, 113
Shavsheti 72, 77, 99, 107
Shayi' 72
shayqa 87
Shebteri xxv, 174
Shehab b. Dhu'l-Nun al-Misri 207
Sheikh 'Abdol Qader Jilani 240
Sheikh Akay mosque 153
Sheikh 'Ali Khan Luri 208
Sheikh 'Ali Naji 161
sheikh al-Islam 12, 54, 120, 244
Sheikh 'Ali Tirmidhi 161
Sheikh Amir Sultan 98
Sheikh Badr al-Din Kermani 46
Sheikh Barravi 248
Sheikh Duhuk 216
Sheikh Ebrahim 32, 46, 58
Sheikh Ebrahim b. Heydar 32
Sheikh Ebrahim Efendi 117
Sheikh Ebrahim Kuvanan 46
Sheikh Ebrahim Shirvani 81
Sheikh Habibollah mosque 245
Sheikh Haqqi school 28
Sheikh Hasan Belghari 46
Sheikh Heydar 58, 61
Sheikh Malin-e Tabrizi 46
Sheikh Merza Sultan 82
Sheikh Mostafa Uryani 245
Sheikh Nasrollah b. Aq Shams al-Din 47
Sheikh Ne'mat-Dedeh 10
Sheikh Nur al-Din Bimarestani 46
Sheikh of Urmiyeh 152, 153, 156, 162
Sheikh of Urmiyeh (bathhouse) 153
Sheikh-oghlu xv
Sheikh Safi al-Din xv
Sheikh Safi (price regime) 43
Sheikh Safi (village) 174
Sheikh Saghuji 47
Sheikh Salami Reyi 47
Sheikh Sayyed Jan Memi 47
Sheikh Shoja' 46
Sheikh Shukur-khvan 46
Sheikh Sorkhbidi 202

Sheikh Susmari 20
shekasteh 8
Sheki xxii, 72, 73, 74, 98
shelesi juice 18
Shemr 38
sherbet 6, 22, 36, 154, 204, 227
Shervi 193
Shesh Derakht 82
Sheybeden 164
Sheykhani sword 133
Sheytan castle 113
shib 212
Shi'ites xv, 10, 11, 20, 21, 27, 55, 98, 137, 198, 199, 210, 211, 216, 222, 227, 230
shileh 6
Shir 'Ali 236
Shirin 37
Shirvan 12, 17, 25, 64, 68, 71, 73, 75, 76, 78, 79, 80, 82, 83, 84, 88, 89, 92, 95, 96, 104, 109, 129, 159, 175, 226, 240
Shoemakers' bathhouse 245
shoemakers' bazaar 245
sholeh 6
Shotorban quarter 29
Shotorban quarter bathhouse 33
shrines xiii, 18, 46, 197, 222, 225, 229, 232
Shun Jahan 30
Shuran 104
Shurehgel xxii, 63, 65, 67, 126
Shuri Baba 164
Shushik xvii, xix, 2, 4, 5, 118
Sidirgi xxi, 10
Silistre 160
Silistria xii
silk 8, 16, 34, 62, 71, 73, 74, 78, 85, 95, 105, 126, 138, 154, 178, 191, 202
silver mines 125
Simeon 126, 127
Simon 108
Sind 123, 201, 252
singers 7, 14, 36, 54, 62, 154

Sinjaran quarter 29, 47
Sivas 65, 104, 109, 111, 154, 160, 189
skirmisher 206
slaves xiii, 2, 5, 22, 42, 43, 59, 61, 64, 84, 85, 93, 97, 114, 125, 136, 145, 148, 161, 164, 165, 167, 172, 178, 195, 200, 202, 203, 213, 218, 221, 246
Socrates 89
Sofia xii
Sohrab xxvi, 22, 80, 195, 212, 237
Sohrab Khan 212
Solaq Farhad Pasha 104
Soleyman Bek Chayiri 130
Solomon 161, 184, 250
Sorkhab quarter 29
sorkh andam 87
Sorkhbid 198, 199, 221, 237
soup 6, 16, 34, 80, 94, 170, 204, 219, 232, 253, 254
soup-kitchen 170
springs 10, 28, 32, 60, 201, 203, 217, 236
squirrel 8, 57, 75, 85
staff bearers 25
stags 131, 133
su-bashi 49
subterranean canals 32, 48, 219
subterranean channels 18
Sufi convent 63, 81, 126, 130
Sufi hat 5, 12, 13, 30, 160, 166, 206, 230
Sufiyan xxii, 60
Sujah Pasha 190
Sujeh Jan xxv, 174
Sukhteh Mohammad Pasha 197
Sukun 5, 9
Sulayman Bey 130, 167
Sulayman Efendi Mosque 122
Sulayman-e Zaman 130
Sulaymani ointment 125
Sulayman Pasha 141, 224
Sultan Durugh 233

Sultan ʿEzz al-Din 119
Sultan Hasan bathhouse 33
Sultan Hasan mosque 29
Sultan Hasan Mosque 27, 153
Sultan Hasan school 28
Sultani Castle 250
Sultaniyeh 23, 184
Sultanjiq district 72
Sultan Karim al-Din Begum 119
Sultan Mohammad Ghazan 23, 141
Sultan Mohammad Khodabandeh 23
Sultan Mohammad Sham Ghazan Mosque 26
Sultan mosque 32
Sultan Murad III 89, 119, 197, 205, 222, 226, 235, 236
Sultan Murad III mosque 73
Sultan Murad IV 59, 132, 206, 212, 215, 222, 223, 225, 238, 242
Sultan Owhadollah Mosque 6
Sultan Yaʿqub school 28
Sunjah xxv, 174
Sunjeli Dedeh 218
Sunkur 160
Sun Worshippers 249
Suran xxiii, 106
Surandan 227
Sur-e tila-ye Ghazan 150
surgeons 30, 125, 181, 194, 202, 218, 245
Suruj 120
Sus-e Marvan 17
Susushmarvan 17
swings 244
Syria 25, 34, 48, 78, 96, 119, 154, 160, 192, 214, 219, 225, 227, 229
system of justice 43

T

Tabaniyassi Mohammad Pasha 12, 67
Tabaristan 17, 214

Tabarraʾ 11, 20
Tabarsaran 82, 96, 97
tabarzeh apricots 34
Tabriz xii, xv, xvii, xix, xxi, xxii, xxv, 2, 3, 4, 18, 19, 20, 22, 23, 25, 27, 28, 29, 32, 33, 36, 39, 40, 41, 43, 44, 46, 47, 48, 49, 50, 52, 53, 55, 58, 59, 60, 61, 62, 64, 66, 73, 79, 83, 89, 118, 131, 135, 136, 138, 139, 141, 143, 147, 149, 151, 152, 155, 156, 159, 160, 163, 165, 166, 167, 168, 172, 173, 174, 175, 176, 177, 178, 179, 180, 181, 183, 184, 186, 190, 191, 193, 198, 221, 231, 236
Tabriz Gate 49, 172
Tafsir-e Deylami 15, 216, 222
Tahkt-e Masha 193
tailors 33, 153
taj 5, 12, 30, 139, 140, 141, 142, 152, 158, 206
Taj al-Din ʿAli Shah 172
Taj al-Din Monshi bathhouse 6
taj-e ravaj 230
taj, zurzuvileli 13
Talash 126
Talha 249
Talha b. Obeyollah 249
Taman 17, 76
Tamara 108
Tamarrud 108
tambourine 42
Tamim al-Dari 163
Taq-e Giray xxvi, 237
Taq-e Kesra 27
Taqi ʿAli Khan 85, 127
Taqi Khan 2, 3, 80, 167
Taqi Khan school 28
Taqvim al-Buldan 214
Tarikh-e ʿAvan-e ʿOnvan 214
Tarikh-e Khalliqan 214
Tarikh-e Khitat 214
Tarikh-e Migdisi 250
Tarikh-e Tohfa 90

Tarikh-e Yanvan-e Yunan 200
Tarkhu 82
Tarom xxvi, 188
Tash mosque 122
Tasuban 173
Tasuj 19, 137, 143, 159, 172, 173, 174, 193
Tasuj Gate 172
Tatars 87, 95, 179, 190, 238
Tatary 85, 95
Tavashi Jaʿfar Pasha 25, 49, 53
Tavashi Sulayman Pasha 151
Tavashi Sulayman Pasha mosque 197
Tavil Mohammad Pasha-zadeh Hasan Pasha 119
Tavusi camels 85, 148, 178
Taymuraz I 94
Taysi Shah 95
teeth drawn (ʿAshura) 212
Teke 104
Tekelu Pasha 189, 191
Tekleti 126
Telvan 162
Terek 19, 94
Terek River 19
Termenis 68
Tesuy xxi, xxv, 19, 137, 173
textiles bazaar 245
Tholth 96
Throne of Alans 77
Throne of Solomon 97
Tiflis xxiii, 25, 44, 68, 77, 93, 98, 99, 103, 104, 105, 106, 108, 109, 112, 163, 232
tigers 133, 135
Tilfirak xxii, 63
Timani 160
Timur 33, 64, 109, 173, 213
Tireh 104
Tireli Fazli Pasha 139
Tirmedi mosque 216
Tise 78
Tokad 215
Tomanis 93, 109
tomb of Shams-e Tabrizi 61

Tomris Beg 165
Tomris Khan 65, 94
Topkhaneh 177
Toprak Castle 150
Tortum 115
torture 45, 154, 168
Trabson 57, 91, 109, 113
tranquilizer 156
trestled vinyards 50
tumans 14, 18, 22, 23, 42, 59, 62, 68, 83, 85, 86, 93, 96, 106, 127, 148
Tumek 104
Tuqmaq Khan 65
Tuqmaq Khan castle 68
Tuqmaq Khan mosque 89
Tuqmaq Khan palace 64
turbans 30, 75, 138, 164, 202, 248
Turkistan 110
Turkmen 30, 32, 63, 72, 74, 75, 82, 83, 84, 87, 125, 140, 141, 163, 199, 235, 236
Turla 78
Turnachayiri xxii, 52, 186
tusks 85
tusks (of walrus) 85
Tut alusi xxii, 63
Tuzla 243
Tyre 234

U

Ubbadan 252
Ubulleh 243, 248, 251
Ubulleh river 248
Uch Kilisa xxi, 7, 8, 9, 126
Uhud 212
Ujan xxii, 22, 23, 52, 67, 136, 183, 184, 190, 193, 196
Ujan Mountain 175
Ulama Pasha 78
Ulama Tekelu xv
Ulghar 124
Umman 252, 253

Umudum Sultan 116
uncouth rabble 65
Urdnik 40
Urmiyeh xvii, xxv, 36, 55, 136, 138, 139, 140, 141, 142, 143, 145, 146, 148, 149, 150, 151, 152, 153, 154, 155, 156, 157, 159, 160, 161, 162, 163, 164, 165, 166, 167, 168, 172, 173, 174, 175, 176, 177, 179, 180, 181, 190, 192, 193, 195, 200, 221
Urmiyeh Gate 172
Ushnuyeh 161, 162
Uskudar 65, 90
Ustashagerd 184
Uzayr 243
Uzbekistan 86
Uzun Hasan xv, xix, 5, 27, 62, 109, 124, 133, 160, 162, 223
Uzun Hasan Kurd mosque 89
Uzun Hasan mosque 89, 152

V

Va'ez Efendi mosque 122
Va'ezi 218
Vahedi 30
Vahedi convent 194
Vahidi 159
Vahidi dervish 170
Vahidi order 159
Vale 113
Vali Agha 3, 5
Valid b. 'Abdol-Malek 250
Vali Pasha 124
Valiyan xxi, 48
Vameq and Azra' 39
Van xii, xvii, xxiv, 1, 5, 11, 17, 18, 19, 25, 67, 79, 99, 120, 125, 129, 130, 131, 132, 133, 134, 135, 136, 137, 138, 143, 145, 146, 148, 149, 155, 163, 164, 165, 166, 167, 175, 178, 179, 180, 181, 189, 208, 249, 250
vanak 129
Vanak Verek xxiv, 129
Van Kulu Chayiri 130
Varaqah Khanom xxv, 174
Varishan 120
Varosh Jisri 244
Vasi 'Alisi Daftardar Pasha 139
Vastan 131
Vat 108
vegetables 6, 33, 44, 52, 151, 188, 204
Vehma 243
Verdichuk quarter 29
Veshleh Chayi 60
Volga 84

W

washers of the dead 245
water carriers 38, 235
water mills 226
Water Worshippers 249
wax candles 84
weavers 10, 19, 50, 51, 52, 207
weavers' bazaar 33
weekly bazaar 58, 71, 97, 137
weekly market 135
weighing 147, 154
weight 44
weight of 'Ali 232
weights and measures 45, 233
wells 19, 20, 32, 48, 151, 152, 164, 172, 174, 217, 226, 234
wheat 6, 7, 11, 13, 16, 33, 44, 52, 55, 94, 104, 151, 154, 193, 194, 204, 210, 219, 221, 222, 224, 227, 232, 245, 249, 252
whetstone 125
wine 10, 17, 18, 32, 36, 41, 42, 136, 205, 210
wooden bridge 151, 245, 247
woolen dress 251
wound-stone 125

Y

Yafeth 214, 215, 219
Yahud 248
Yaka Turkmen 87, 142, 199
Yaka Turkmen language 203, 219
Yalda 203, 210
Ya`qub Shah 37, 152, 226, 228
Yaqut Mosta`sami 27
Yar `Ali 28, 42, 58, 165
Yar `Ali fountain 28
Yar `Ali Khan 255
Yari 30, 42, 218
Yasavi 76
Yasavi dervish 170
yasavol-aghasi 49, 183
Yavari 30
Yaylachik xxi, 4
Yazdan Aqa 30
Yazdanbash xxv, 170
Yazdegerd 75, 78, 93, 105, 161, 173, 208, 210, 232, 238
Yazid 38, 143
Yazid b. `Abdol-Malek 92, 96
Yedi Kilisa 118
Yelemlem 242
Yemen 133, 154, 241, 242, 243, 247
Yemeni cornelian 38
yenecheri 49
yenecheri-aghasi 49
Yeni Imam 237
Yeyla Gate 68
Yusof Pasha 65, 95, 149

Z

Zagam 103
zagharji-bashi 66
Zaghzaghi 214
Zahir al-Din Faryabi 46
zakat 74
Zakhur xxiii, 98
Zakiya 243
Zalem Ahmad 1
Zal Pasha bathhouse 13
Zal Pashazadeh Ahmad Pasha 10
Zaminites 11

Zangabad 238, 239
Zangi river xxi, 10, 18, 64, 66, 67, 68, 73, 124, 127, 238
Zarju quarter bathhouse 33
Zarshad 120
Zarshod xxiv, 126
zaviyeh-ye Ahmad Pasha 10
Zebari Kurds 235
Zeiro 78
Zekim 103
Zekke river 248
Zennuse 19
zerdeh 143
Zertel dervish 170
Zeynab convent 28
Zeynal Beg 207
Zeyn `Ali 47
Zeynal Khan 223
Zeyn grapes 154
Ziya al-Din Khan 189
Zobeyda Khanom 227, 228, 242
Zobeyda Khatun 23, 33, 36
Zobeyda mosque 25
Zobeyda Sultan 250
Zobeyr b. `Avvam 249
Zokhorya 98
zolbia 227
Zonnun-e Misri 196
Zonuz 19
Zoroastrian 7, 43
Zulyezan 230

www.ingramcontent.com/pod-product-compliance
Lightning Source LLC
Chambersburg PA
CBHW081150290426
44108CB00018B/2501